SEVEN SEAS ENTERTAIN...

DRAGONAR ACADEMY
VOLUME 11

art by **RAN** / story by **SHIKI MIZUCHI** / character design by **KOHADA SHIMESABA**

TRANSLATION
Nan Rymer

ADAPTATION
Libby Mitchell

LETTERING AND LAYOUT
Paweł Szczęszek

COVER DESIGN
Nicky Lim

ASSISTANT EDITOR
Jenn Grunigen

PRODUCTION ASSISTANT
CK Russell

PRODUCTION MANAGER
Lissa Pattillo

EDITOR-IN-CHIEF
Adam Arnold

PUBLISHER
Jason DeAngelis

DRAGONAR ACADEMY VOL. 11
© Ran 2016, © Shiki Mizuchi 2016
First published in Japan in 2016 by KADOKAWA CORPORATION, Tokyo.
English translation rights reserved by Seven Seas Entertainment, LLC.
under the license from KADOKAWA CORPORATION, Tokyo.

Seven Seas books may be purchased in bulk for educational, business, or promotional use. For information on bulk purchases, please contact Macmillan Corporate & Premium Sales Department at 1-800-221-7945 (ext 5442) or write specialmarkets@macmillan.com.

Seven Seas and the Seven Seas logo are trademarks of Seven Seas Entertainment, LLC. All rights reserved.

ISBN: 978-1-626922-95-2

Printed in Canada

First Printing: April 2017

10 9 8 7 6 5 4 3 2 1

FOLLOW US ONLINE: *www.gomanga.com*

READING DIRECTIONS

This book reads from *right to left*, Japanese style. If this is your first time reading manga, you start reading from the top right panel on each page and take it from there. If you get lost, just follow the numbered diagram here. It may seem backwards at first, but you'll get the hang of it! Have fun!!

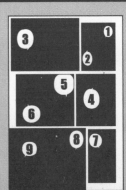

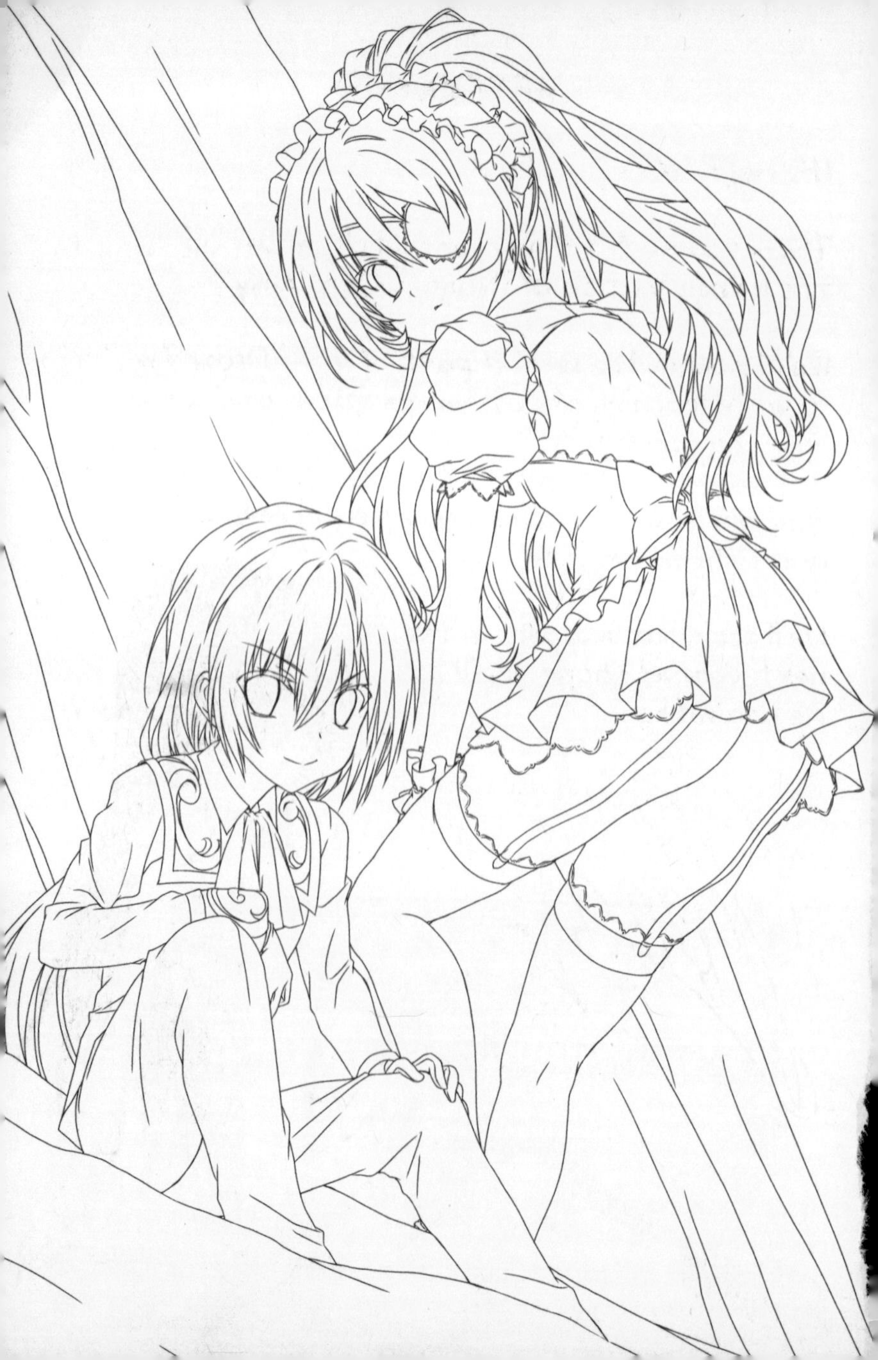

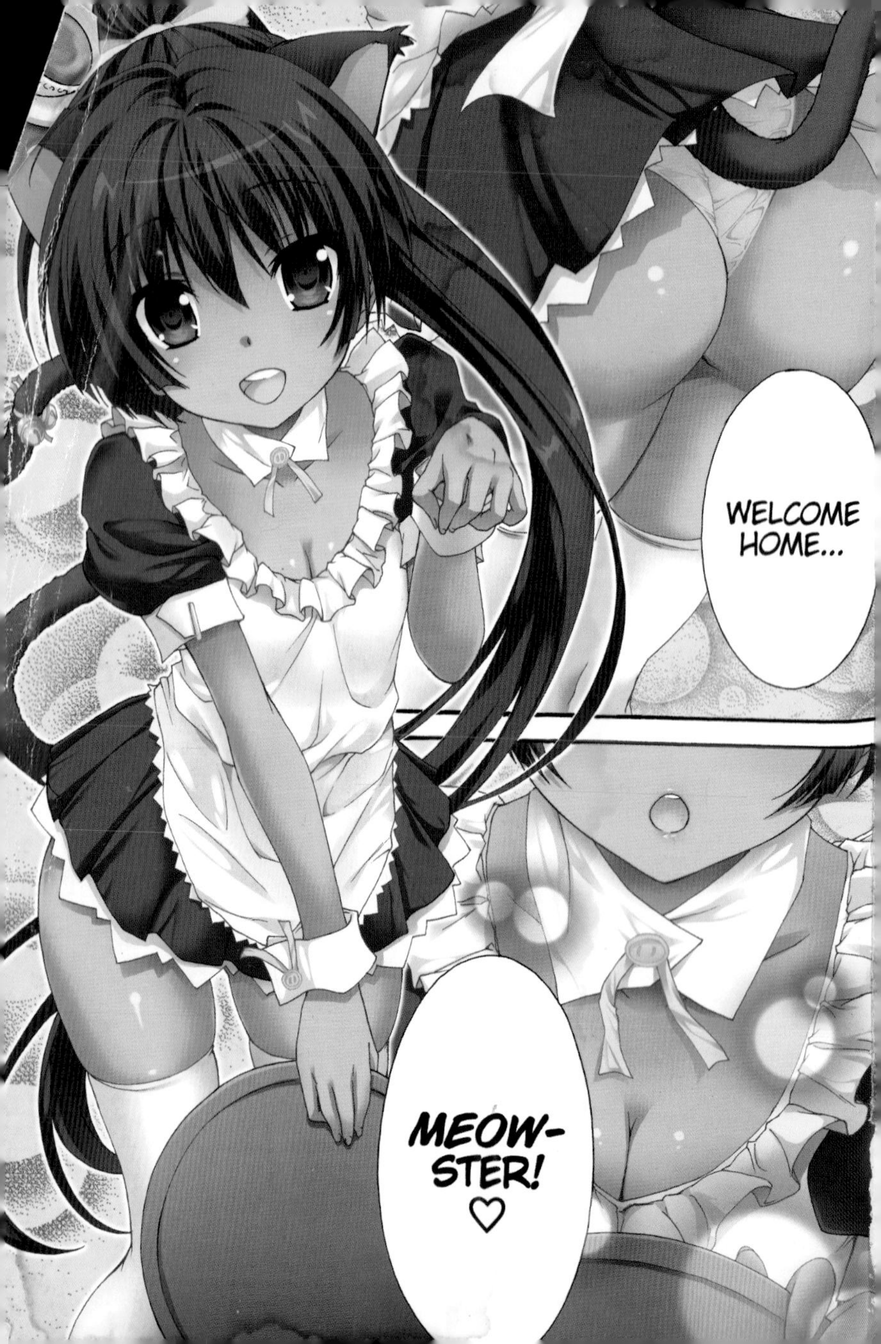
WELCOME HOME...
MEOW-STER! ♡

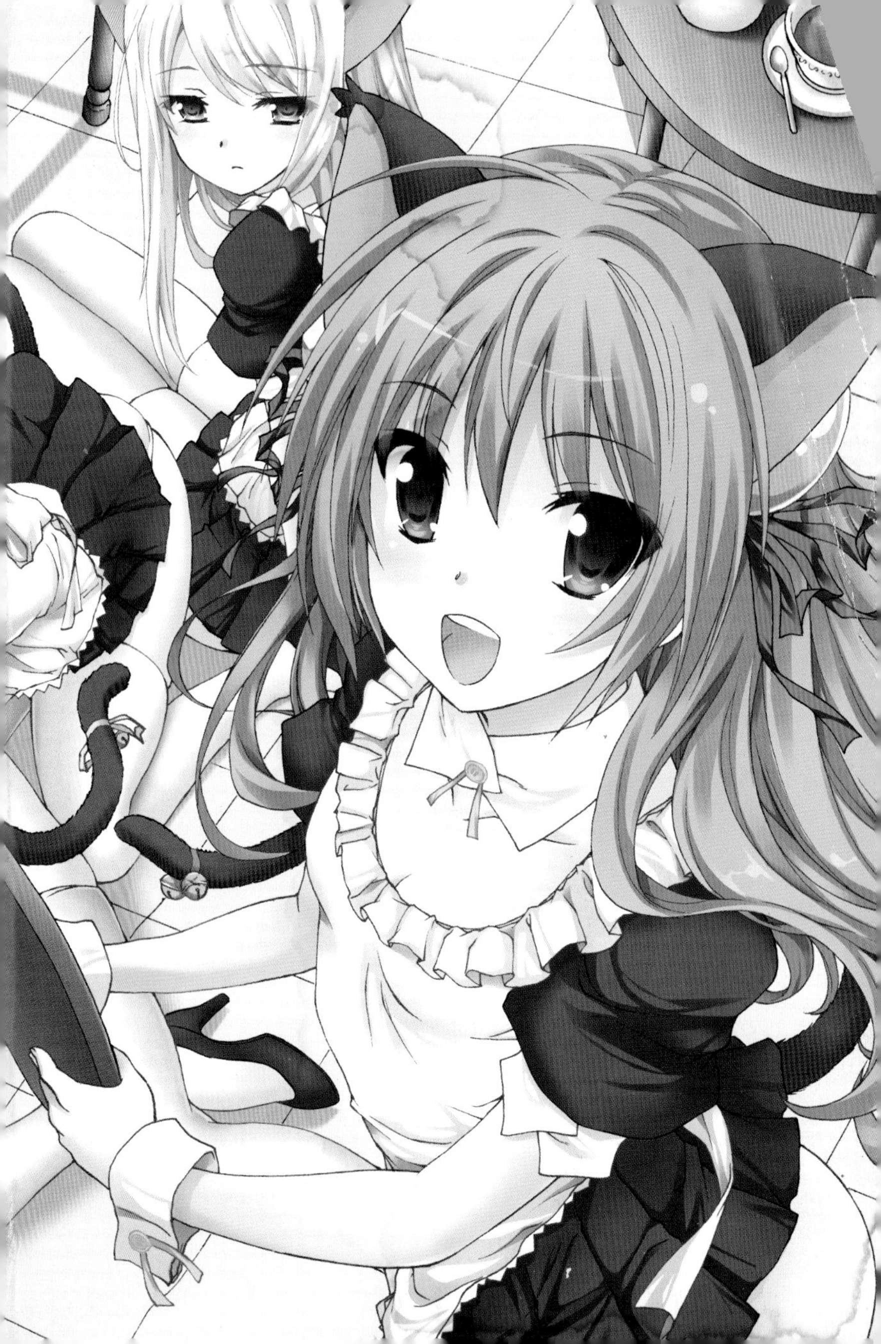

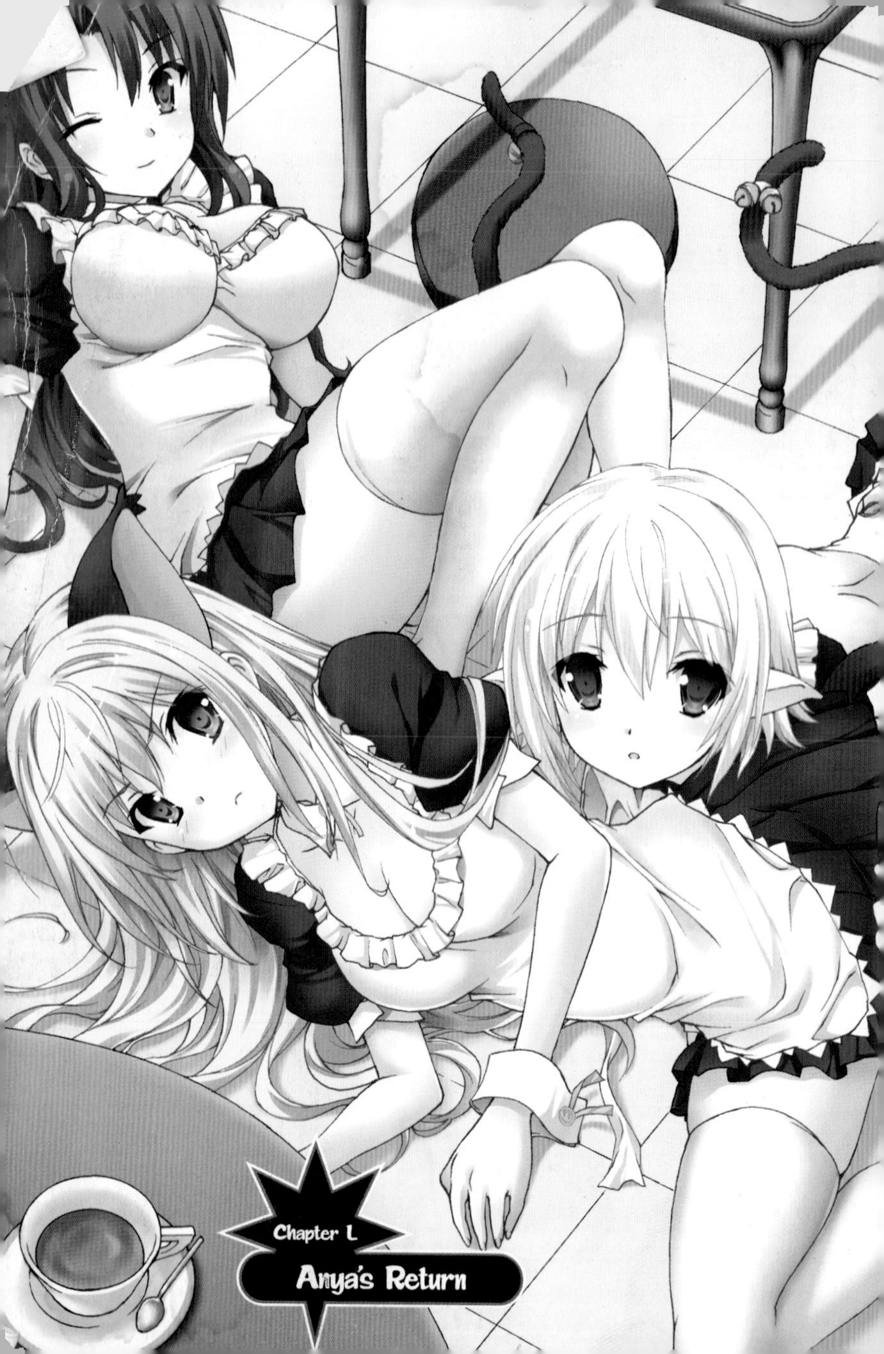
Chapter L
Anya's Return

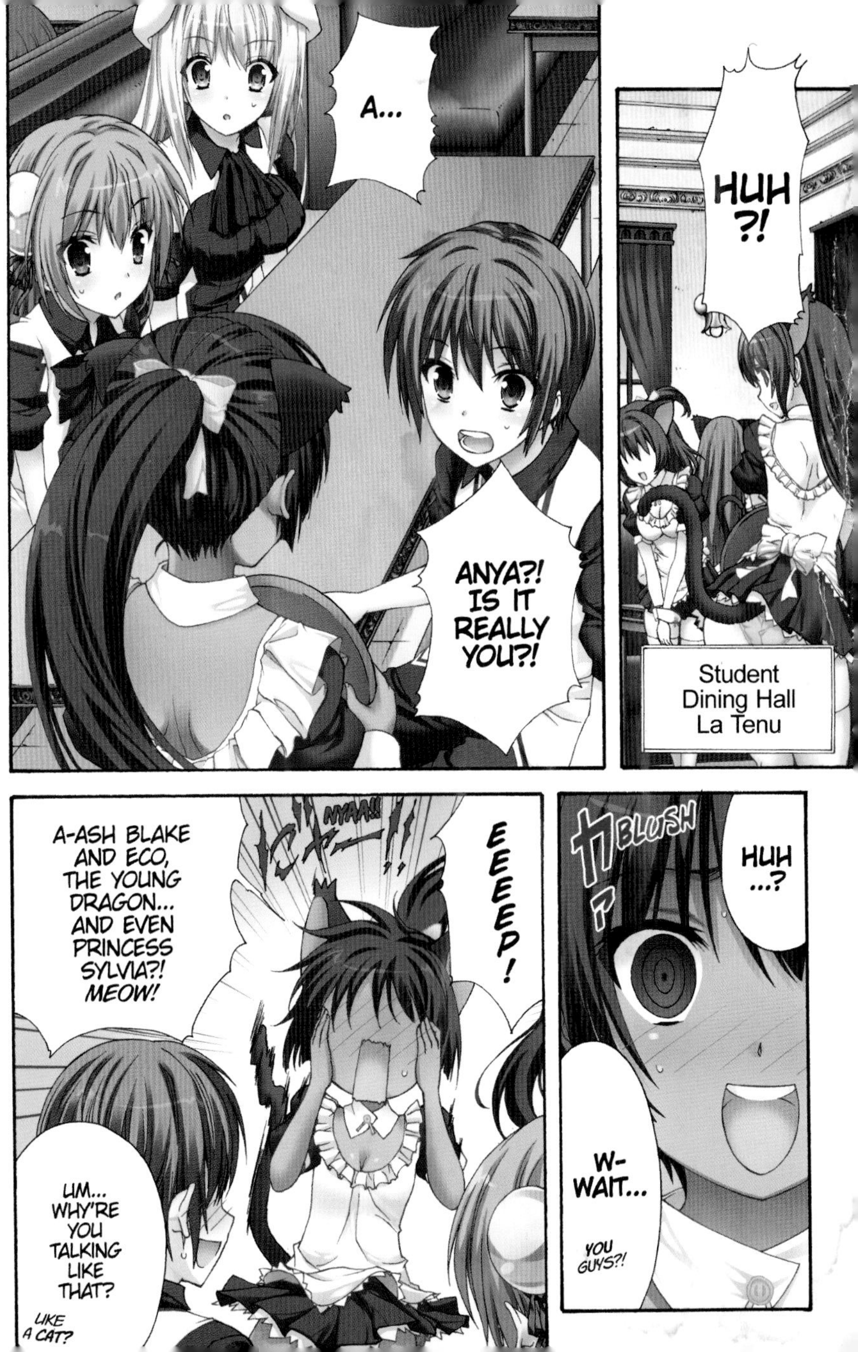
HUH ?!
Student Dining Hall La Tenu
A...
ANYA?! IS IT REALLY YOU?!
BLUSH
HUH ...?
W- WAIT...
YOU GUYS?!
EEEEP!
NYAA!!
A-ASH BLAKE AND ECO, THE YOUNG DRAGON... AND EVEN PRINCESS SYLVIA?! MEOW!
UM... WHY'RE YOU TALKING LIKE THAT?
LIKE A CAT?

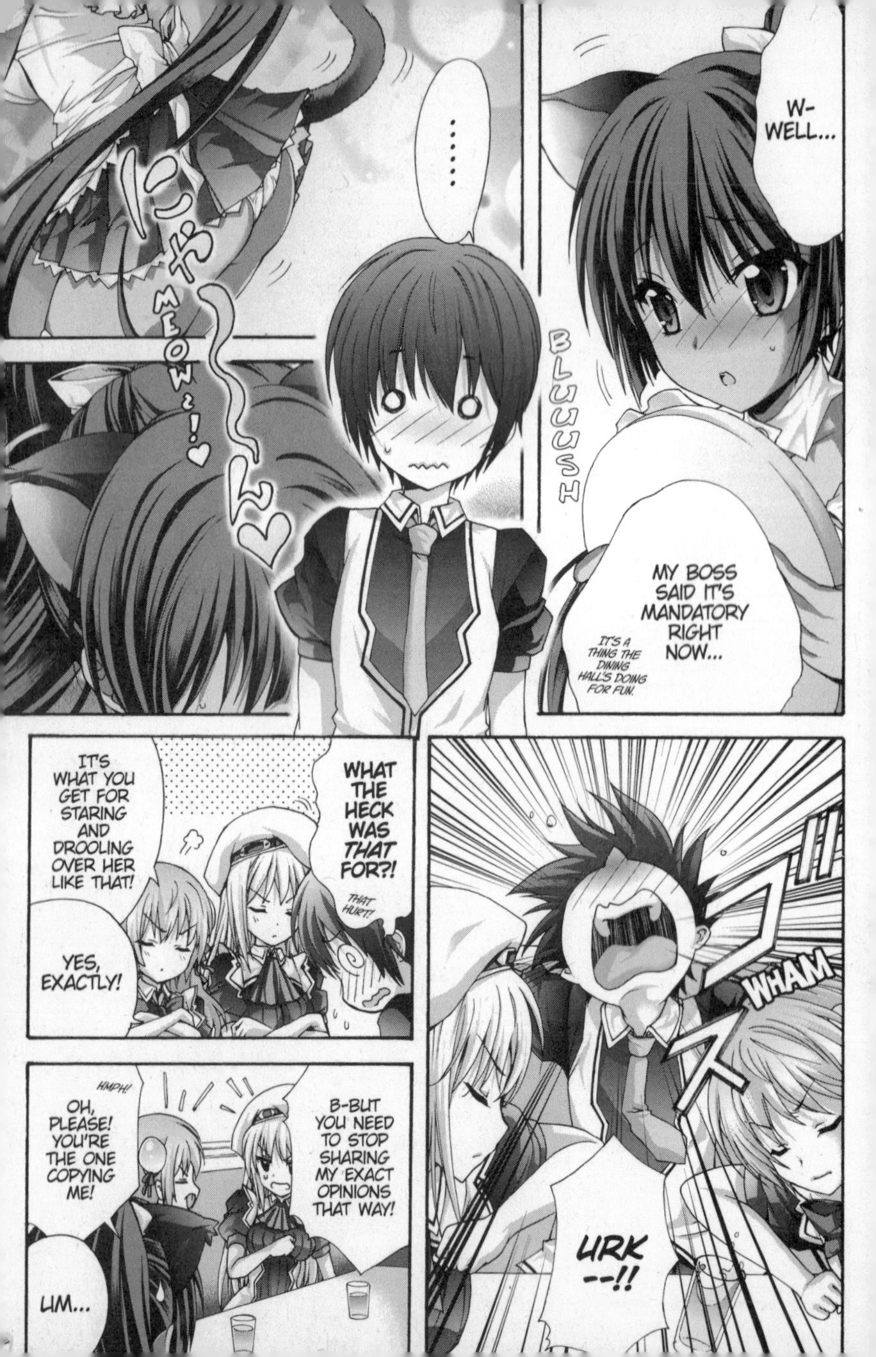
W-WELL...
BLUUUSH
MY BOSS SAID IT'S MANDATORY RIGHT NOW...
IT'S A THING THE DINING HALL'S DOING FOR FUN.
......
MEOW~!
WHAM
URK--!!
WHAT THE HECK WAS THAT FOR?!
THAT HURT?!
IT'S WHAT YOU GET FOR STARING AND DROOLING OVER HER LIKE THAT!
YES, EXACTLY!
B-BUT YOU NEED TO STOP SHARING MY EXACT OPINIONS THAT WAY!
HMPH!
OH, PLEASE! YOU'RE THE ONE COPYING ME!
UM...

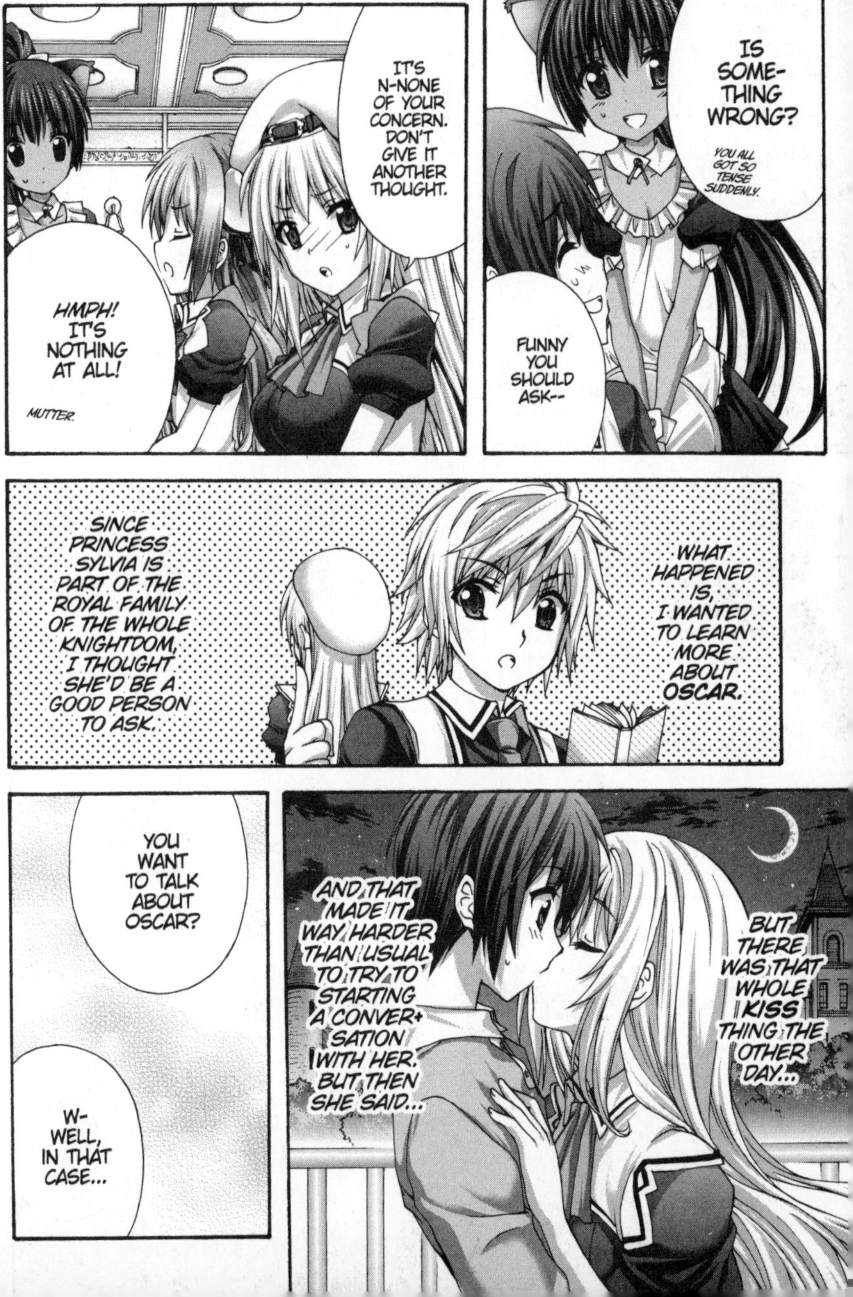
IS SOME-THING WRONG?
YOU ALL GOT SO TENSE SUDDENLY.
FUNNY YOU SHOULD ASK--
IT'S N-NONE OF YOUR CONCERN. DON'T GIVE IT ANOTHER THOUGHT.
HMPH! IT'S NOTHING AT ALL!
MUTTER.
WHAT HAPPENED IS, I WANTED TO LEARN MORE ABOUT OSCAR.
SINCE PRINCESS SYLVIA IS PART OF THE ROYAL FAMILY OF THE WHOLE KNIGHTDOM, I THOUGHT SHE'D BE A GOOD PERSON TO ASK.
BUT THERE WAS THAT WHOLE KISS THING THE OTHER DAY...
AND THAT MADE IT WAY HARDER THAN USUAL TO TRY TO STARTING A CONVER-SATION WITH HER. BUT THEN SHE SAID...
YOU WANT TO TALK ABOUT OSCAR?
W-WELL, IN THAT CASE...

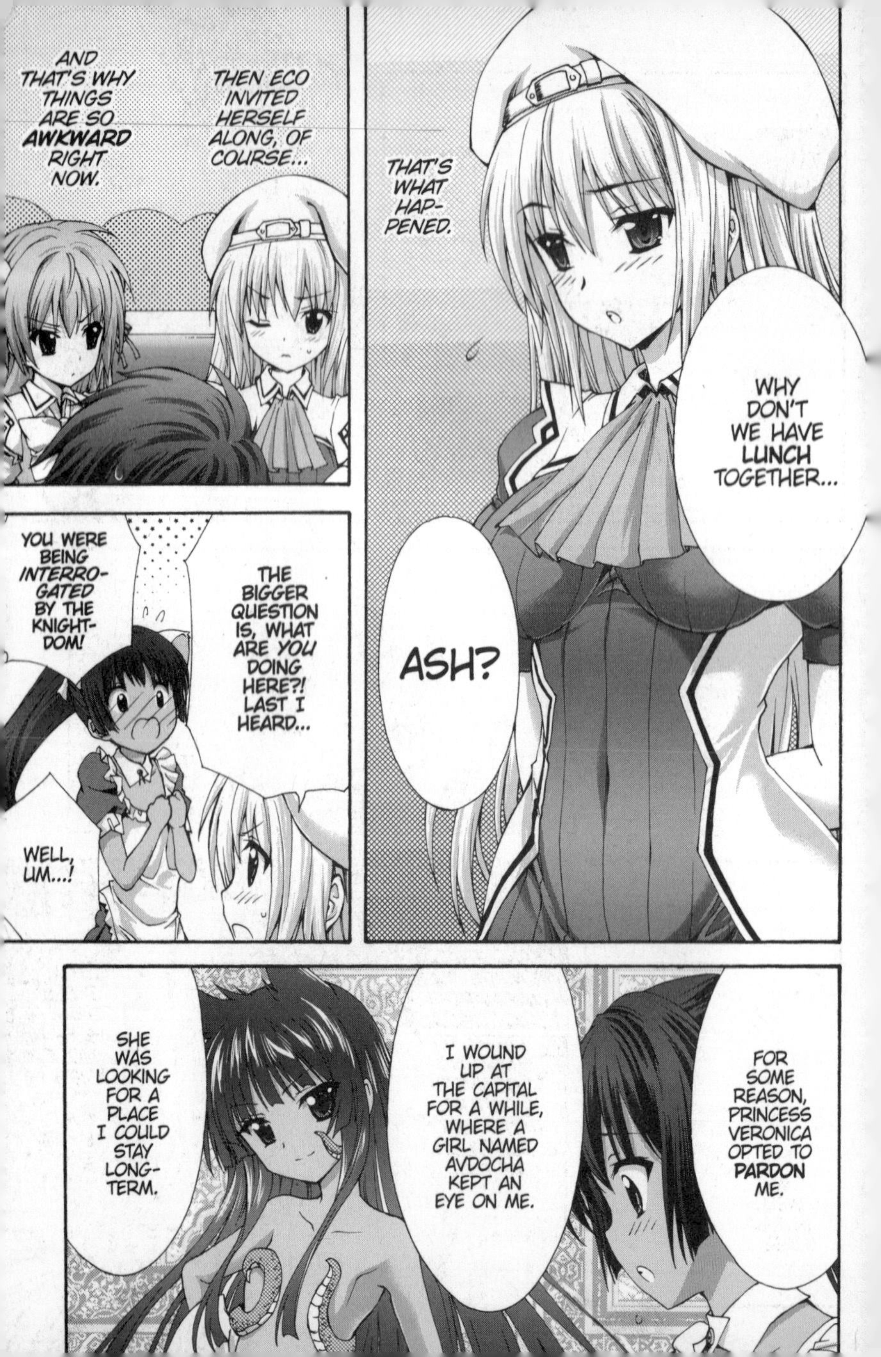

THAT'S WHAT HAP-PENED.
WHY DON'T WE HAVE LUNCH TOGETHER...
ASH?
THEN ECO INVITED HERSELF ALONG, OF COURSE...
AND THAT'S WHY THINGS ARE SO AWKWARD RIGHT NOW.
THE BIGGER QUESTION IS, WHAT ARE YOU DOING HERE?! LAST I HEARD...
YOU WERE BEING INTERRO-GATED BY THE KNIGHT-DOM!
WELL, UM...!
FOR SOME REASON, PRINCESS VERONICA OPTED TO PARDON ME.
I WOUND UP AT THE CAPITAL FOR A WHILE, WHERE A GIRL NAMED AVDOCHA KEPT AN EYE ON ME.
SHE WAS LOOKING FOR A PLACE I COULD STAY LONG-TERM.

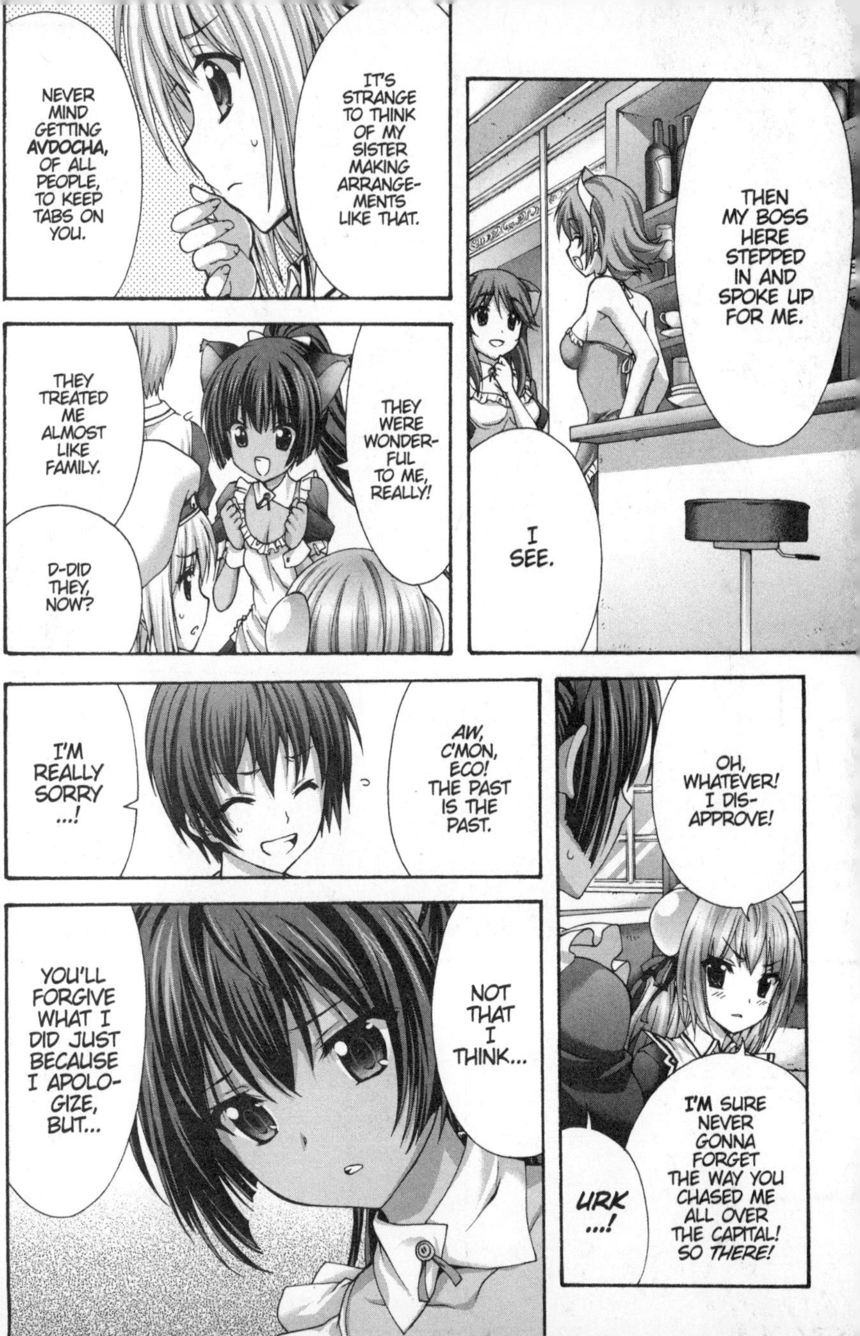
THEN MY BOSS HERE STEPPED IN AND SPOKE UP FOR ME.
I SEE.
IT'S STRANGE TO THINK OF MY SISTER MAKING ARRANGE-MENTS LIKE THAT.
NEVER MIND GETTING **AVDOCHA,** OF ALL PEOPLE, TO KEEP TABS ON YOU.
THEY WERE WONDER-FUL TO ME, REALLY!
THEY TREATED ME ALMOST LIKE FAMILY.
D-DID THEY, NOW?
OH, WHATEVER! I DIS-APPROVE!
I'M SURE NEVER GONNA FORGET THE WAY YOU CHASED ME ALL OVER THE CAPITAL! SO *THERE!*
URK ...!
AW, C'MON, ECO! THE PAST IS THE PAST.
I'M REALLY SORRY ...!
NOT THAT I THINK...
YOU'LL FORGIVE WHAT I DID JUST BECAUSE I APOLO-GIZE, BUT...

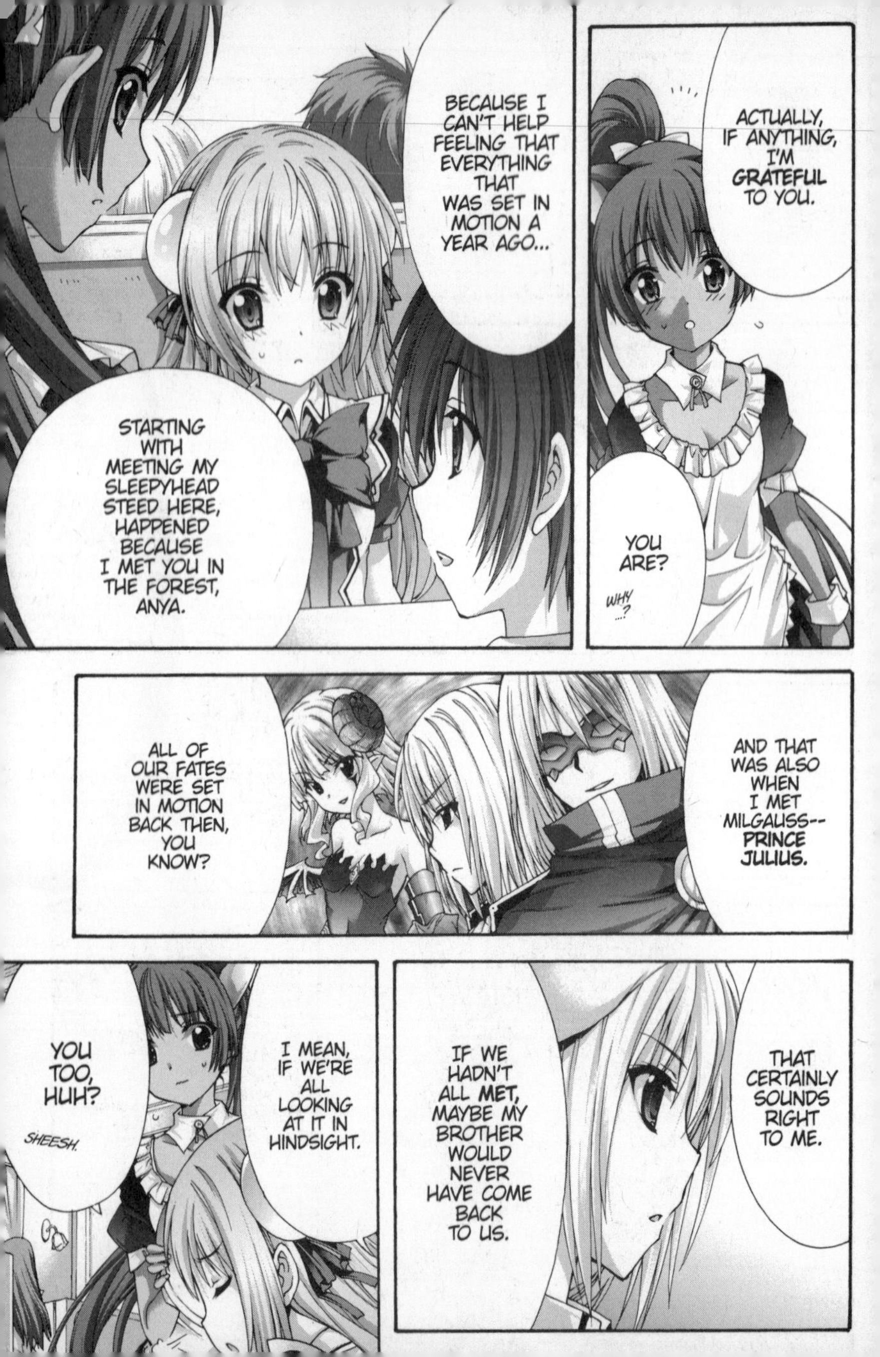
ACTUALLY, IF ANYTHING, I'M GRATEFUL TO YOU.
YOU ARE?
WHY ...?
BECAUSE I CAN'T HELP FEELING THAT EVERYTHING THAT WAS SET IN MOTION A YEAR AGO...
STARTING WITH MEETING MY SLEEPYHEAD STEED HERE, HAPPENED BECAUSE I MET YOU IN THE FOREST, ANYA.
AND THAT WAS ALSO WHEN I MET MILGAUSS--PRINCE JULIUS.
ALL OF OUR FATES WERE SET IN MOTION BACK THEN, YOU KNOW?
THAT CERTAINLY SOUNDS RIGHT TO ME.
IF WE HADN'T ALL MET, MAYBE MY BROTHER WOULD NEVER HAVE COME BACK TO US.
I MEAN, IF WE'RE ALL LOOKING AT IT IN HINDSIGHT.
YOU TOO, HUH?
SHEESH.

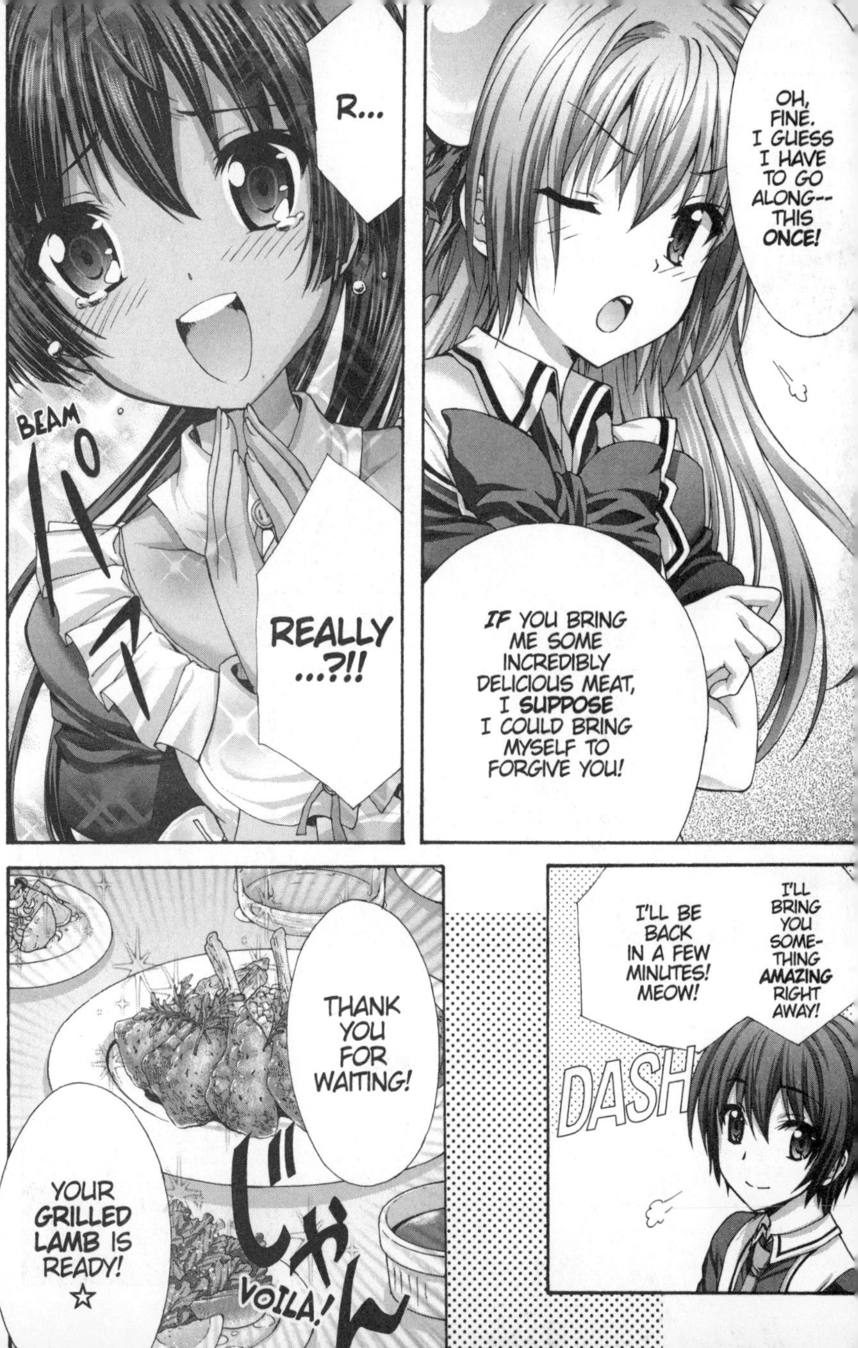
OH, FINE. I GUESS I HAVE TO GO ALONG-- THIS ONCE!
IF YOU BRING ME SOME INCREDIBLY DELICIOUS MEAT, I SUPPOSE I COULD BRING MYSELF TO FORGIVE YOU!
R...
REALLY ...?!!
BEAM
I'LL BRING YOU SOME-THING AMAZING RIGHT AWAY!
I'LL BE BACK IN A FEW MINUTES! MEOW!
DASH
THANK YOU FOR WAITING!
YOUR GRILLED LAMB IS READY! ☆
VOILA!

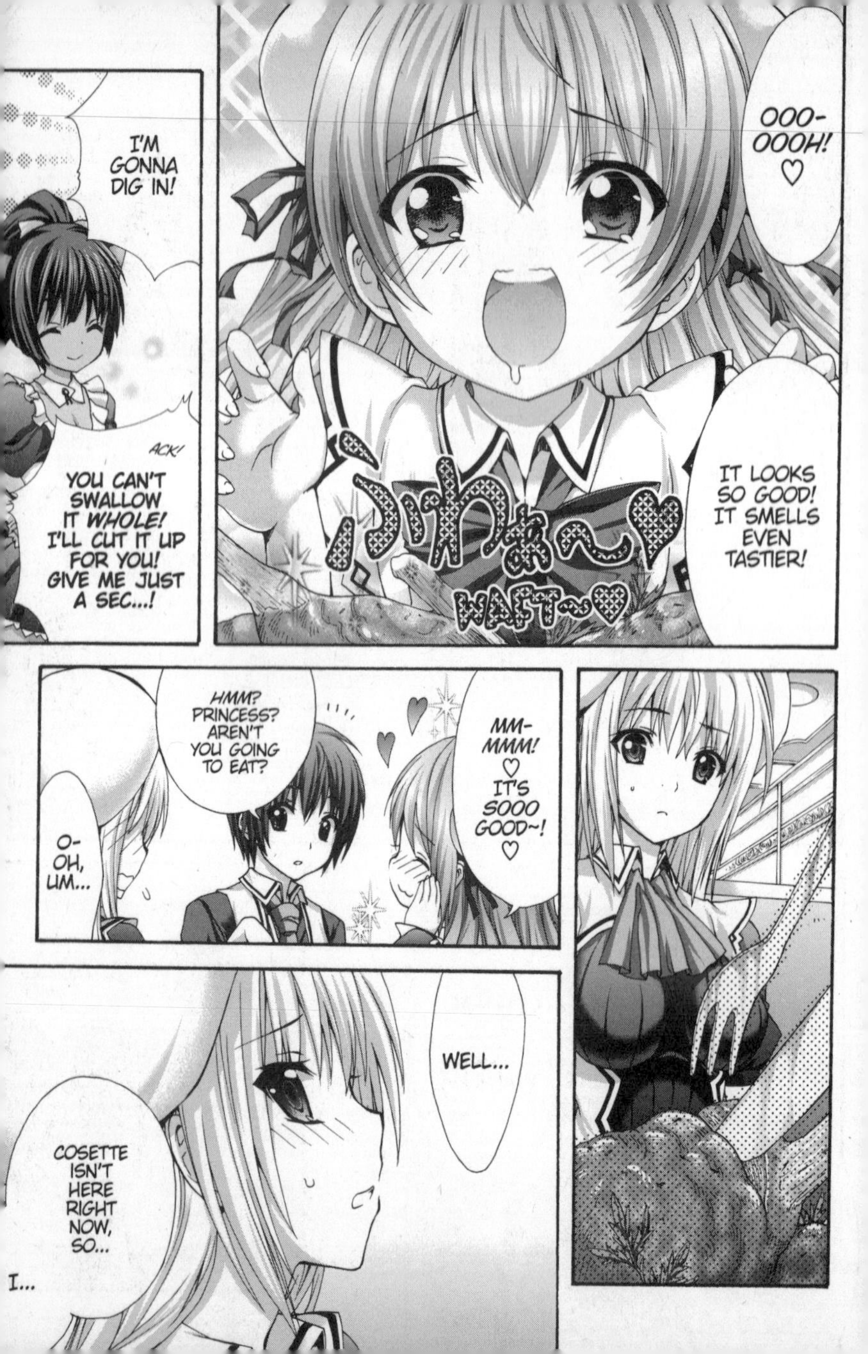
OOO-OOOH! ♡
IT LOOKS SO GOOD! IT SMELLS EVEN TASTIER!
WAFT~♡
I'M GONNA DIG IN!
ACK!
YOU CAN'T SWALLOW IT WHOLE! I'LL CUT IT UP FOR YOU! GIVE ME JUST A SEC...!
MM-MMM! ♡ IT'S SOOO GOOD~! ♡
HMM? PRINCESS? AREN'T YOU GOING TO EAT?
O-OH, UM...
WELL...
COSETTE ISN'T HERE RIGHT NOW, SO...
I...

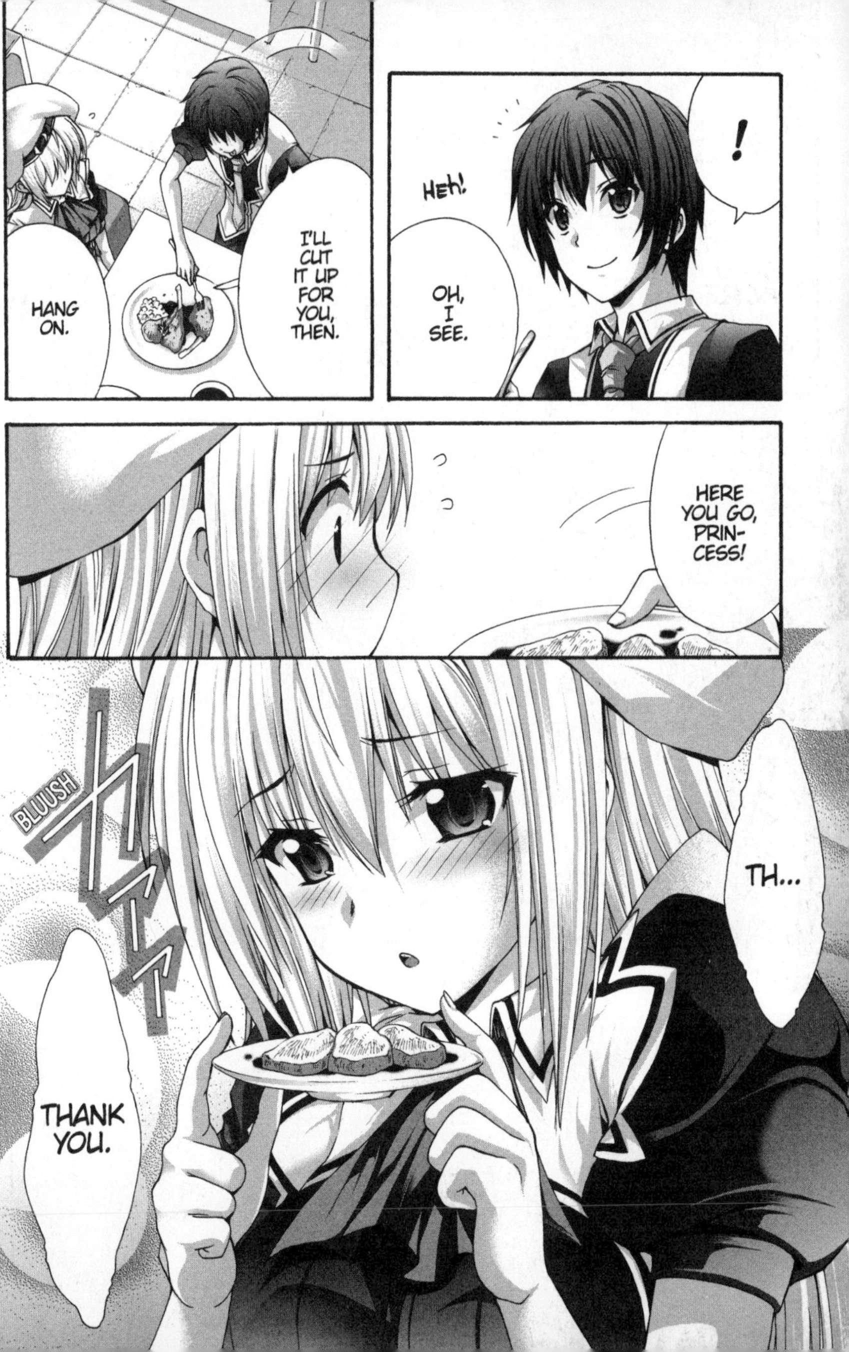
!
Heh!
OH, I SEE.
I'LL CUT IT UP FOR YOU, THEN.
HANG ON.
HERE YOU GO, PRIN-CESS!
TH...
BLUUSH
THANK YOU.

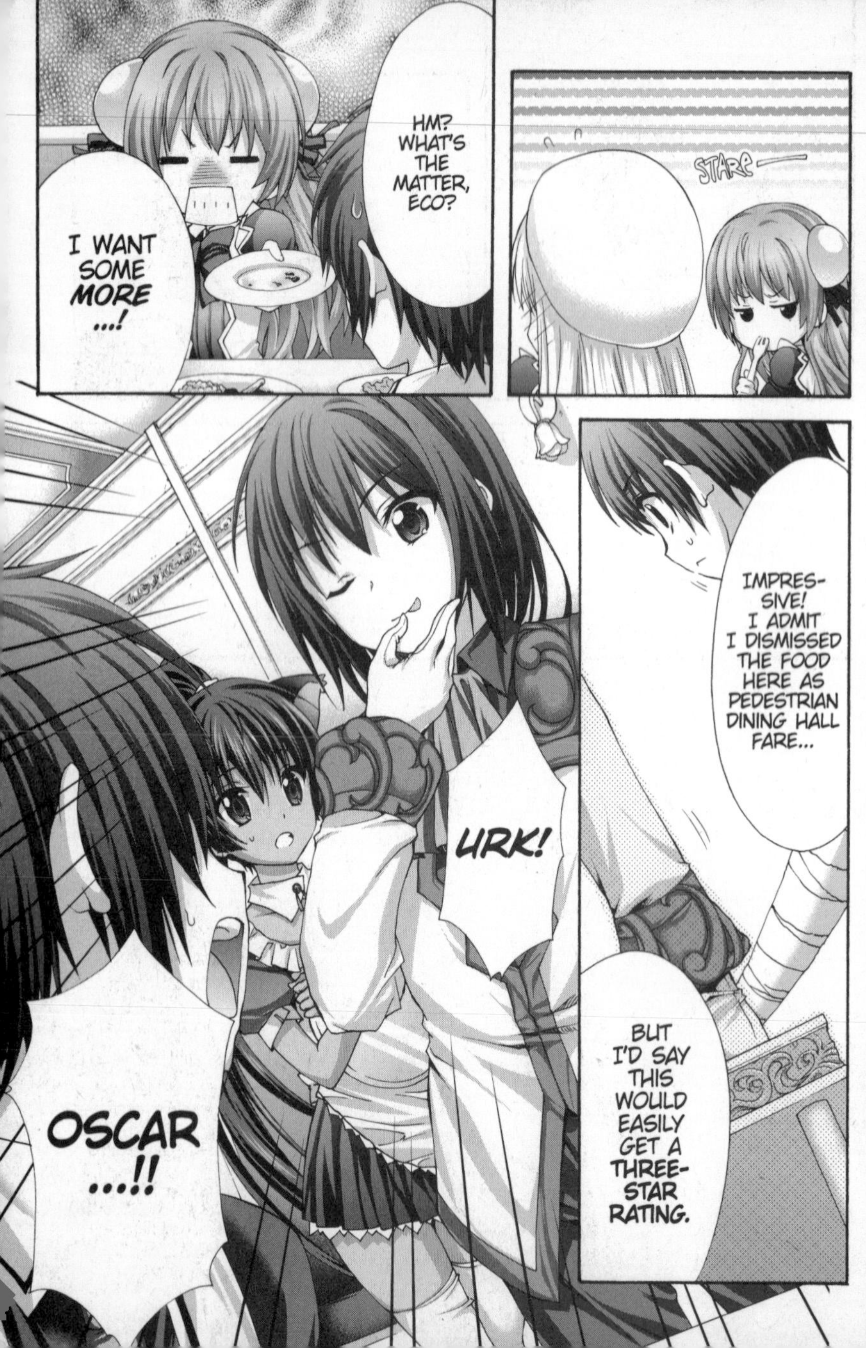
STARE
HM? WHAT'S THE MATTER, ECO?
I WANT SOME MORE ...!
IMPRES-SIVE! I ADMIT I DISMISSED THE FOOD HERE AS PEDESTRIAN DINING HALL FARE...
BUT I'D SAY THIS WOULD EASILY GET A THREE-STAR RATING.
URK!
OSCAR ...!!

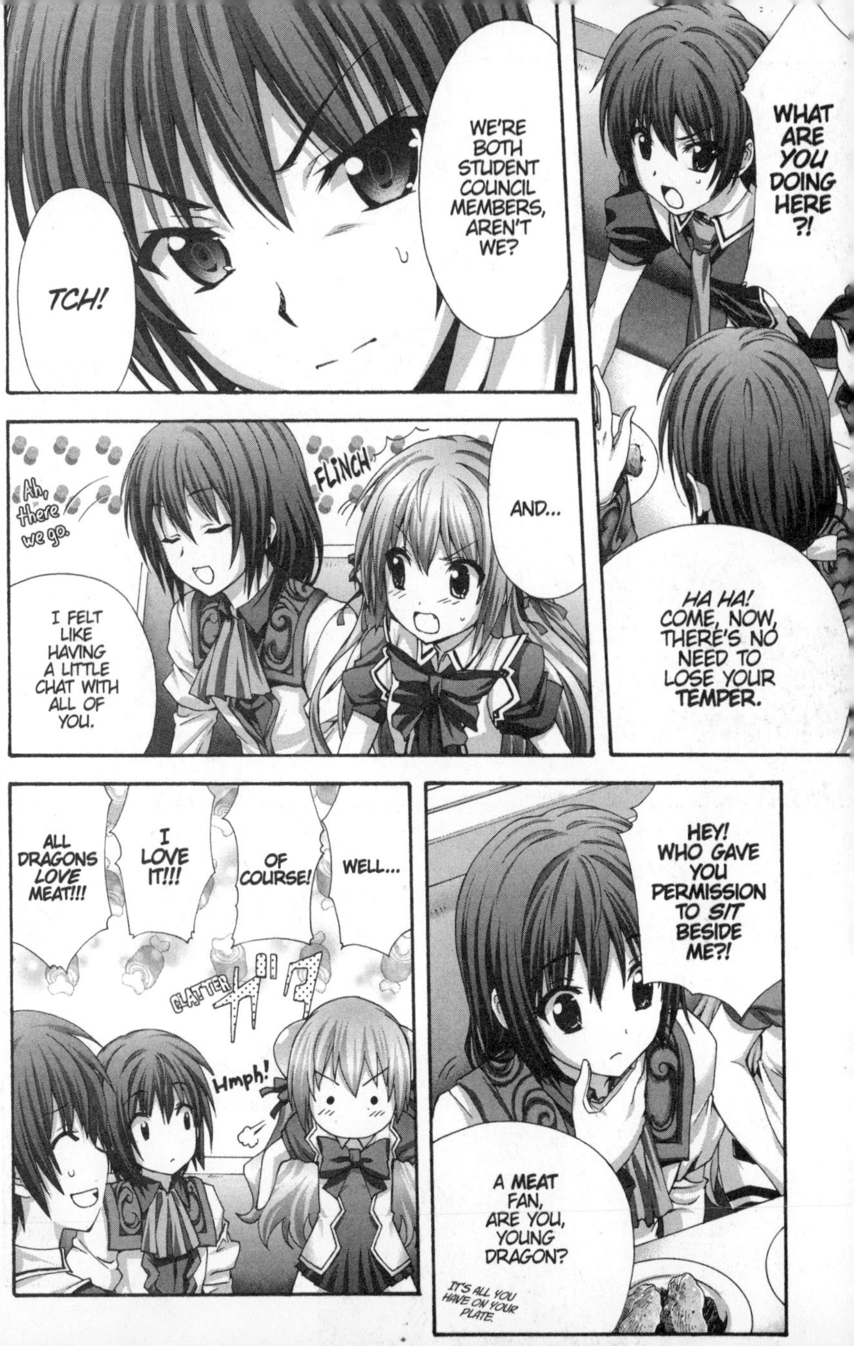
WHAT ARE YOU DOING HERE?!
HA HA! COME, NOW, THERE'S NO NEED TO LOSE YOUR TEMPER.
WE'RE BOTH STUDENT COUNCIL MEMBERS, AREN'T WE?
TCH!
AND...
FLINCH
I FELT LIKE HAVING A LITTLE CHAT WITH ALL OF YOU.
Ah, there we go.
HEY! WHO GAVE YOU PERMISSION TO SIT BESIDE ME?!
A MEAT FAN, ARE YOU, YOUNG DRAGON?
IT'S ALL YOU HAVE ON YOUR PLATE.
WELL...
OF COURSE!
I LOVE IT!!!
ALL DRAGONS LOVE MEAT!!!
CLATTER
Hmph!

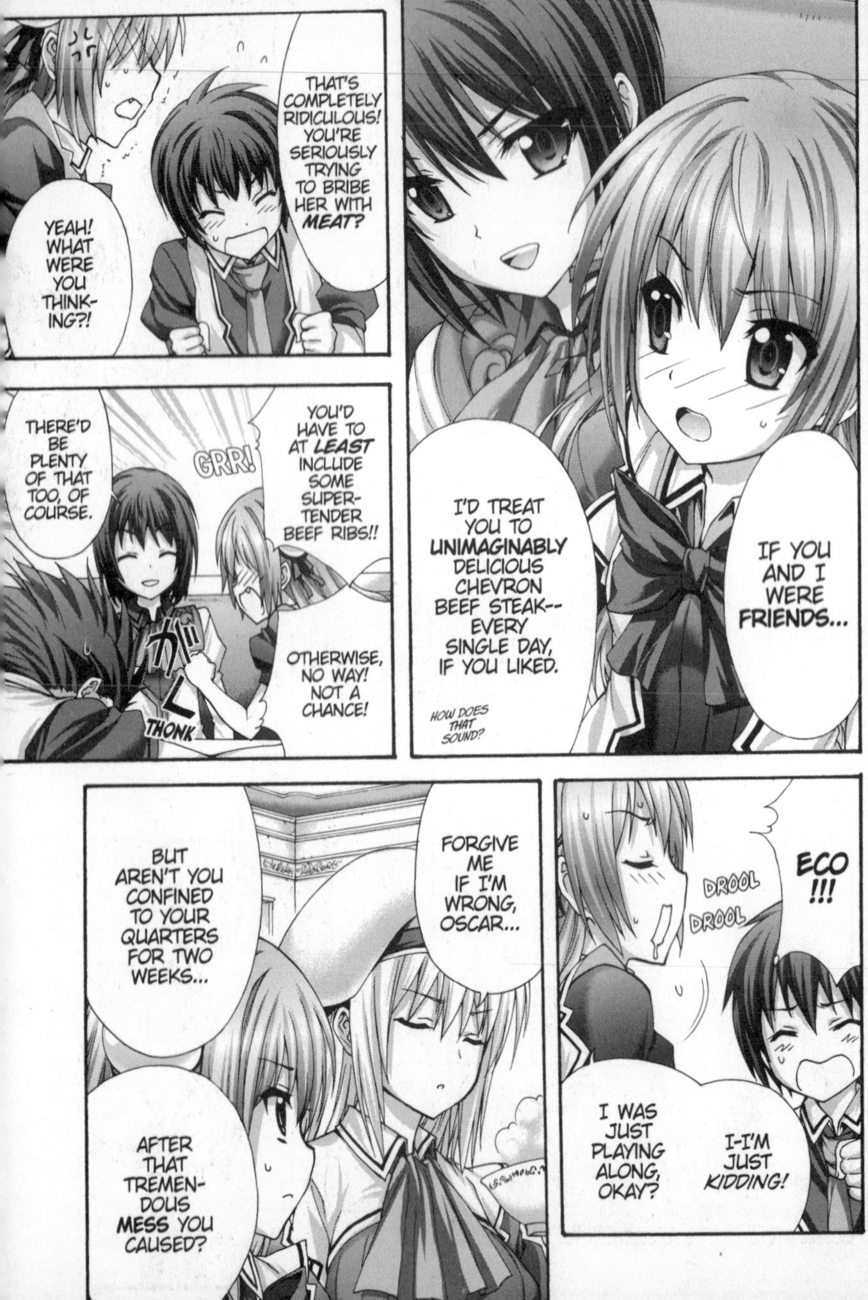
IF YOU AND I WERE FRIENDS...
I'D TREAT YOU TO UNIMAGINABLY DELICIOUS CHEVRON BEEF STEAK--EVERY SINGLE DAY, IF YOU LIKED.
HOW DOES THAT SOUND?
THAT'S COMPLETELY RIDICULOUS! YOU'RE SERIOUSLY TRYING TO BRIBE HER WITH MEAT?
YEAH! WHAT WERE YOU THINKING?!
YOU'D HAVE TO AT LEAST INCLUDE SOME SUPER-TENDER BEEF RIBS!!
GRR!
THERE'D BE PLENTY OF THAT TOO, OF COURSE.
OTHERWISE, NO WAY! NOT A CHANCE!
THONK
ECO!!!
DROOL
DROOL
I-I'M JUST KIDDING!
I WAS JUST PLAYING ALONG, OKAY?
FORGIVE ME IF I'M WRONG, OSCAR...
BUT AREN'T YOU CONFINED TO YOUR QUARTERS FOR TWO WEEKS...
AFTER THAT TREMENDOUS MESS YOU CAUSED?

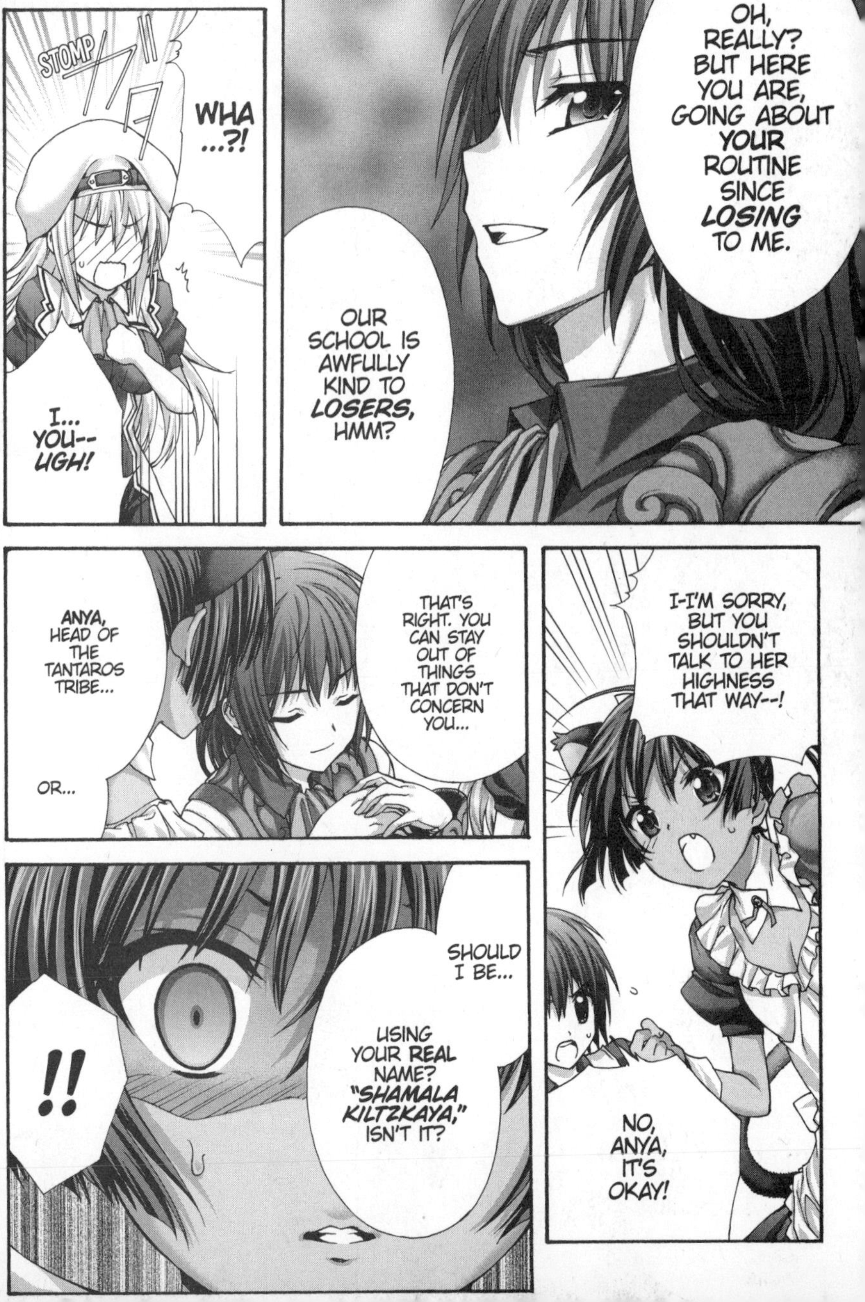
OH, REALLY? BUT HERE YOU ARE, GOING ABOUT YOUR ROUTINE SINCE LOSING TO ME.
OUR SCHOOL IS AWFULLY KIND TO LOSERS, HMM?
STOMP
WHA ...?!
I... YOU-- UGH!
I-I'M SORRY, BUT YOU SHOULDN'T TALK TO HER HIGHNESS THAT WAY--!
NO, ANYA, IT'S OKAY!
THAT'S RIGHT. YOU CAN STAY OUT OF THINGS THAT DON'T CONCERN YOU...
ANYA, HEAD OF THE TANTAROS TRIBE...
OR...
SHOULD I BE...
USING YOUR REAL NAME? "SHAMALA KILTZKAYA," ISN'T IT?
!!

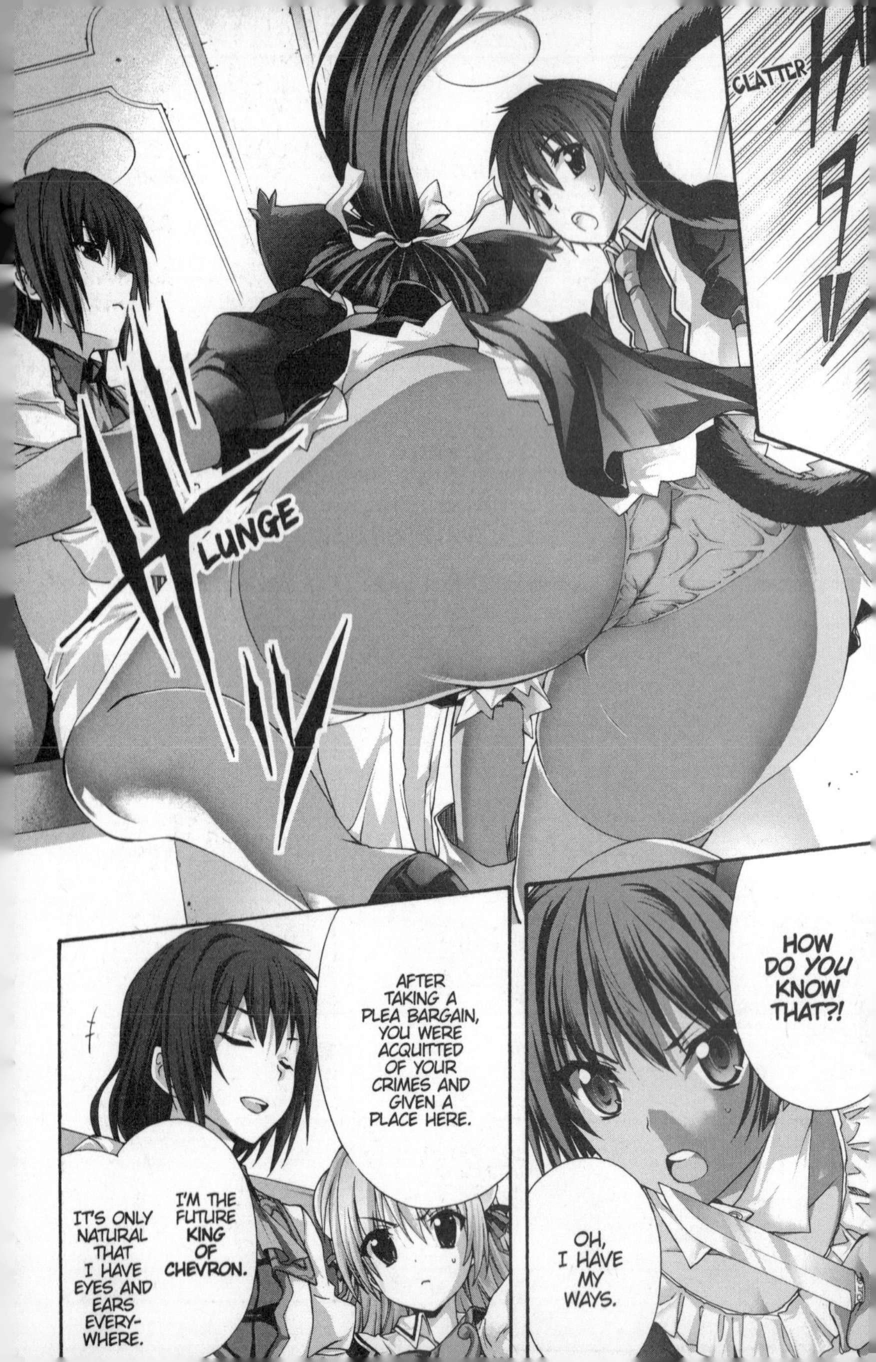
CLATTER
LUNGE
HOW DO YOU KNOW THAT?!
OH, I HAVE MY WAYS.
AFTER TAKING A PLEA BARGAIN, YOU WERE ACQUITTED OF YOUR CRIMES AND GIVEN A PLACE HERE.
I'M THE FUTURE KING OF CHEVRON.
IT'S ONLY NATURAL THAT I HAVE EYES AND EARS EVERY-WHERE.

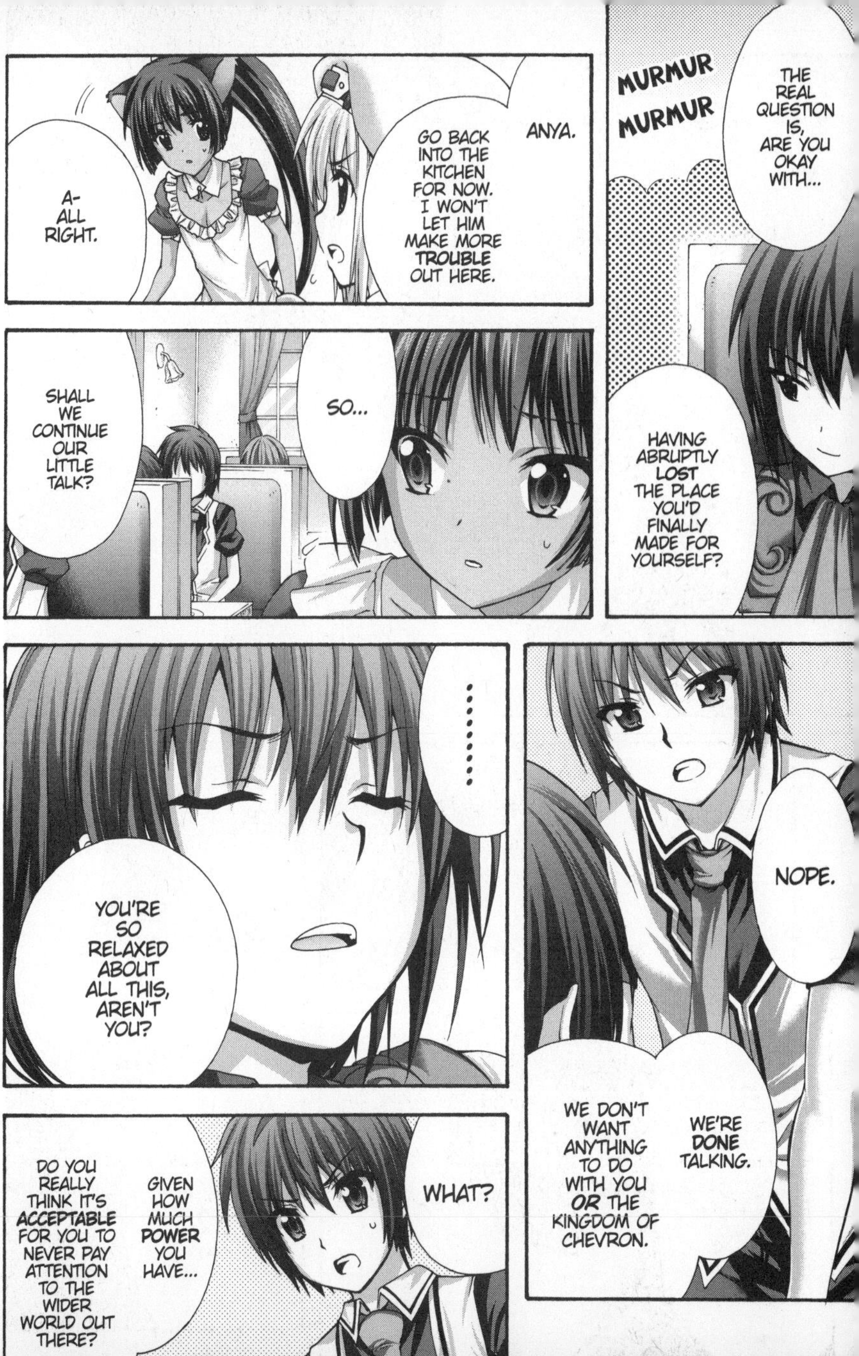
MURMUR
MURMUR
THE REAL QUESTION IS, ARE YOU OKAY WITH...
HAVING ABRUPTLY LOST THE PLACE YOU'D FINALLY MADE FOR YOURSELF?
ANYA.
GO BACK INTO THE KITCHEN FOR NOW. I WON'T LET HIM MAKE MORE TROUBLE OUT HERE.
A- ALL RIGHT.
SO...
SHALL WE CONTINUE OUR LITTLE TALK?
NOPE.
WE'RE DONE TALKING.
WE DON'T WANT ANYTHING TO DO WITH YOU OR THE KINGDOM OF CHEVRON.
....
YOU'RE SO RELAXED ABOUT ALL THIS, AREN'T YOU?
WHAT?
GIVEN HOW MUCH POWER YOU HAVE...
DO YOU REALLY THINK IT'S ACCEPTABLE FOR YOU TO NEVER PAY ATTENTION TO THE WIDER WORLD OUT THERE?

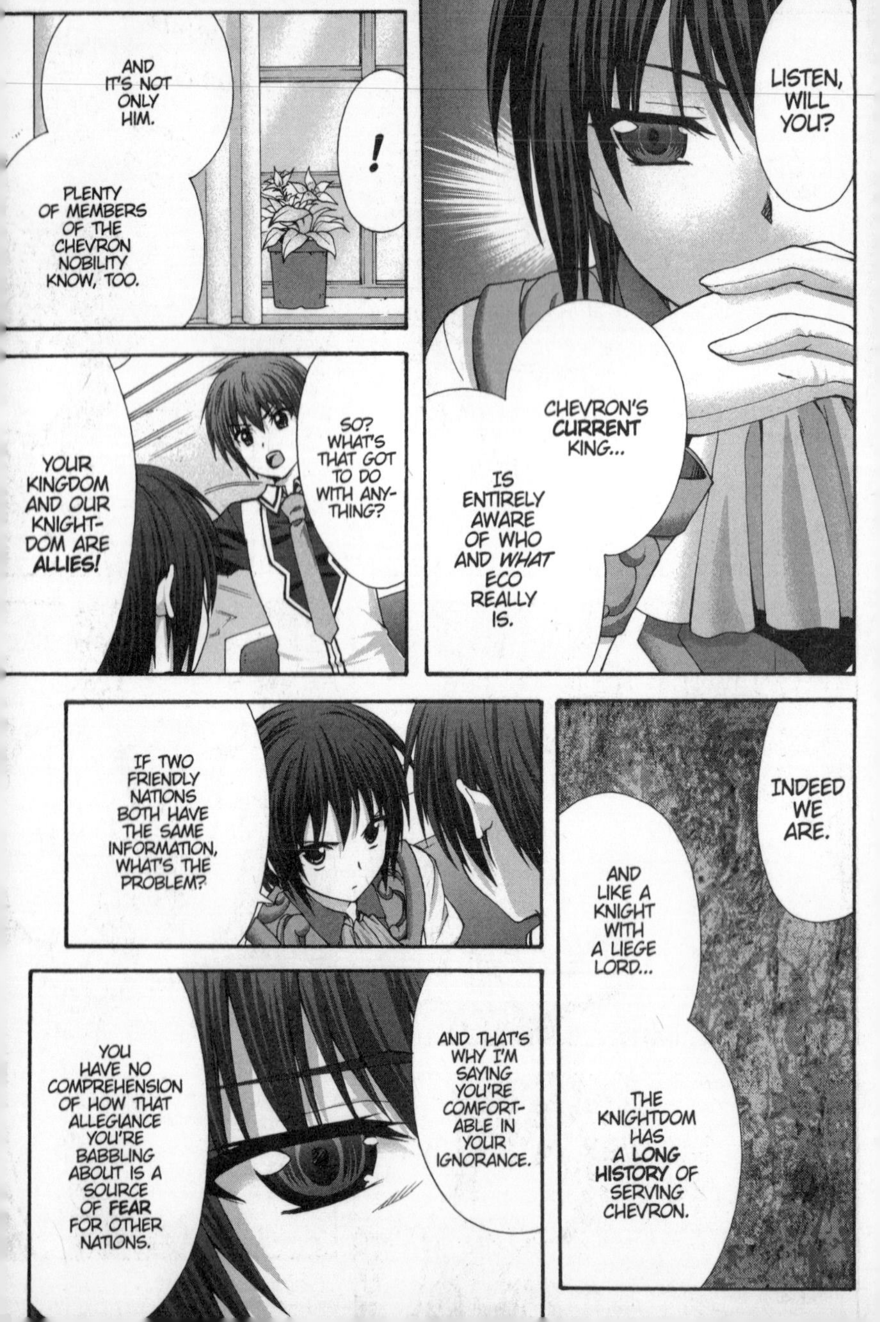
LISTEN, WILL YOU?
CHEVRON'S **CURRENT** KING...
IS ENTIRELY AWARE OF WHO AND *WHAT* ECO REALLY IS.
!
AND IT'S NOT ONLY HIM.
PLENTY OF MEMBERS OF THE CHEVRON NOBILITY KNOW, TOO.
SO? WHAT'S THAT GOT TO DO WITH ANY-THING?
YOUR KINGDOM AND OUR KNIGHT-DOM ARE **ALLIES!**
INDEED WE ARE.
AND LIKE A KNIGHT WITH A LIEGE LORD...
THE KNIGHTDOM HAS A **LONG HISTORY** OF SERVING CHEVRON.
IF TWO FRIENDLY NATIONS BOTH HAVE THE SAME INFORMATION, WHAT'S THE PROBLEM?
AND THAT'S WHY I'M SAYING YOU'RE COMFORT-ABLE IN YOUR IGNORANCE.
YOU HAVE NO COMPREHENSION OF HOW THAT ALLEGIANCE YOU'RE BABBLING ABOUT IS A SOURCE OF **FEAR** FOR OTHER NATIONS.

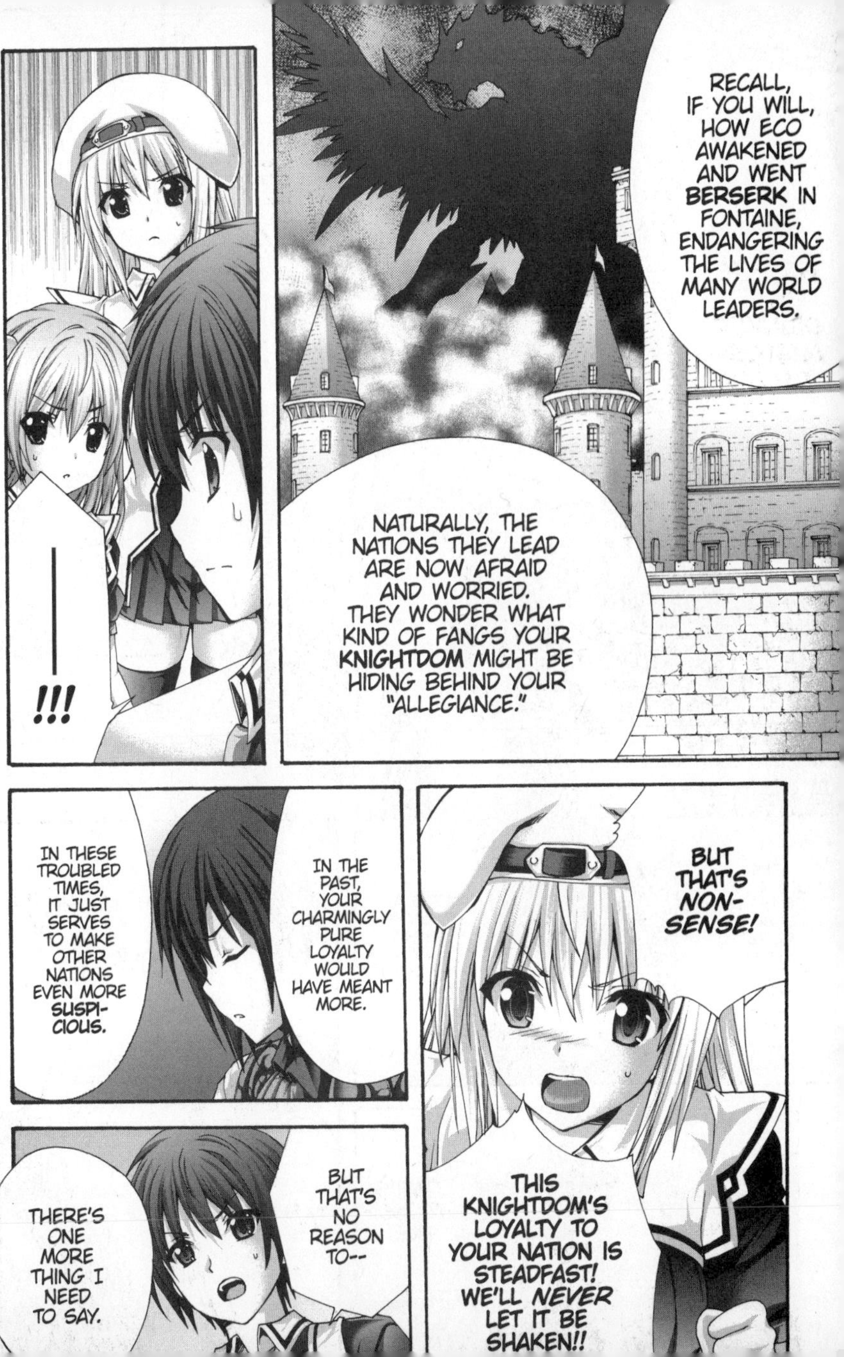
RECALL, IF YOU WILL, HOW ECO AWAKENED AND WENT BERSERK IN FONTAINE, ENDANGERING THE LIVES OF MANY WORLD LEADERS.
NATURALLY, THE NATIONS THEY LEAD ARE NOW AFRAID AND WORRIED. THEY WONDER WHAT KIND OF FANGS YOUR KNIGHTDOM MIGHT BE HIDING BEHIND YOUR "ALLEGIANCE."
—!!!
BUT THAT'S NON-SENSE!
THIS KNIGHTDOM'S LOYALTY TO YOUR NATION IS STEADFAST! WE'LL NEVER LET IT BE SHAKEN!!
IN THE PAST, YOUR CHARMINGLY PURE LOYALTY WOULD HAVE MEANT MORE.
IN THESE TROUBLED TIMES, IT JUST SERVES TO MAKE OTHER NATIONS EVEN MORE SUSPI-CIOUS.
BUT THAT'S NO REASON TO--
THERE'S ONE MORE THING I NEED TO SAY.

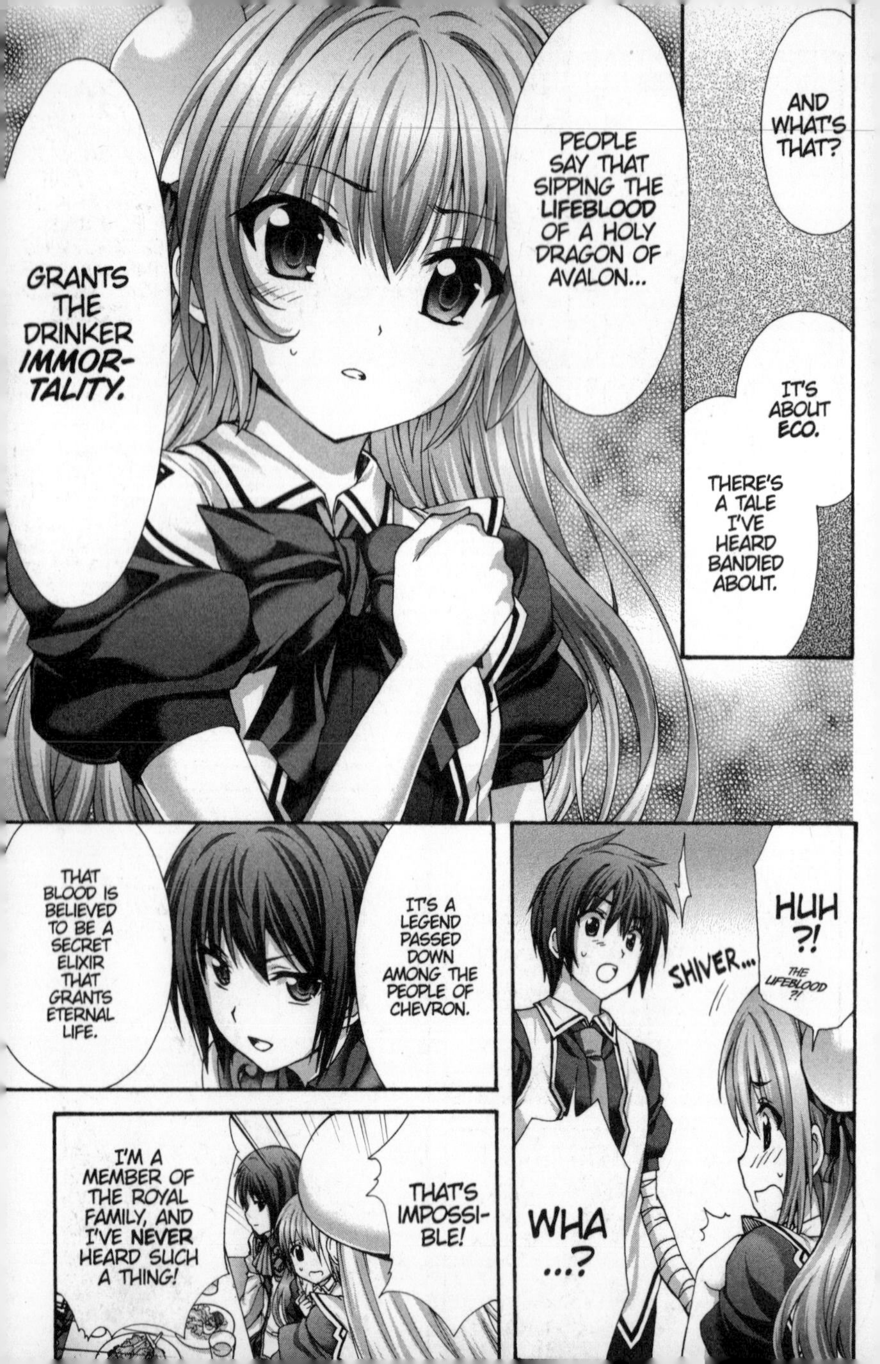
AND WHAT'S THAT?
IT'S ABOUT ECO.
THERE'S A TALE I'VE HEARD BANDIED ABOUT.
PEOPLE SAY THAT SIPPING THE LIFEBLOOD OF A HOLY DRAGON OF AVALON...
GRANTS THE DRINKER IMMORTALITY.
HUH?!
THE LIFEBLOOD?!
SHIVER...
WHA...?
IT'S A LEGEND PASSED DOWN AMONG THE PEOPLE OF CHEVRON.
THAT BLOOD IS BELIEVED TO BE A SECRET ELIXIR THAT GRANTS ETERNAL LIFE.
THAT'S IMPOSSIBLE!
I'M A MEMBER OF THE ROYAL FAMILY, AND I'VE NEVER HEARD SUCH A THING!

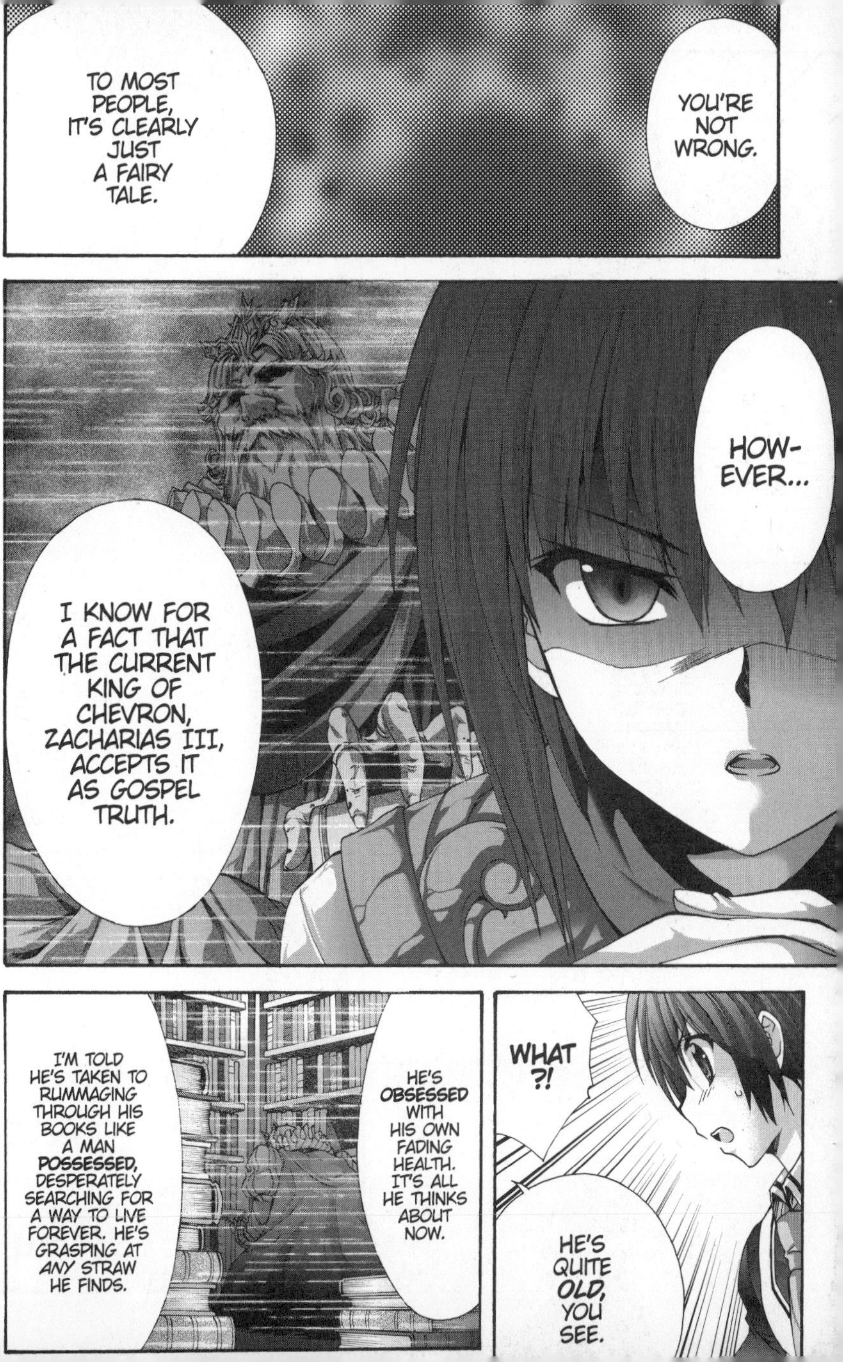
YOU'RE NOT WRONG.
TO MOST PEOPLE, IT'S CLEARLY JUST A FAIRY TALE.
HOW-EVER...
I KNOW FOR A FACT THAT THE CURRENT KING OF CHEVRON, ZACHARIAS III, ACCEPTS IT AS GOSPEL TRUTH.
WHAT ?!
HE'S QUITE OLD, YOU SEE.
HE'S OBSESSED WITH HIS OWN FADING HEALTH. IT'S ALL HE THINKS ABOUT NOW.
I'M TOLD HE'S TAKEN TO RUMMAGING THROUGH HIS BOOKS LIKE A MAN POSSESSED, DESPERATELY SEARCHING FOR A WAY TO LIVE FOREVER. HE'S GRASPING AT ANY STRAW HE FINDS.

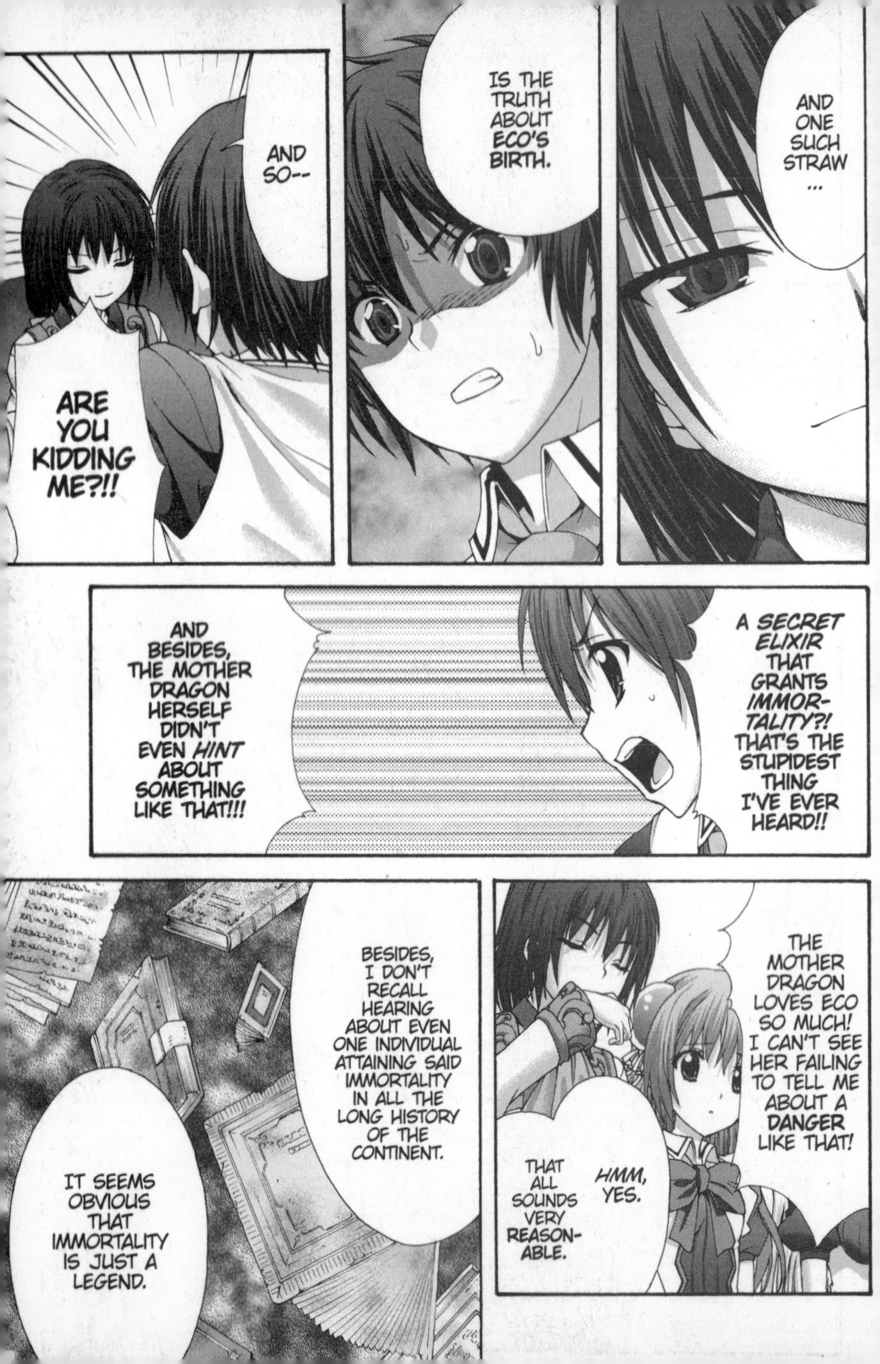
AND ONE SUCH STRAW ...
IS THE TRUTH ABOUT ECO'S BIRTH.
AND SO--
ARE YOU KIDDING ME?!!
A SECRET ELIXIR THAT GRANTS IMMORTALITY?! THAT'S THE STUPIDEST THING I'VE EVER HEARD!!
AND BESIDES, THE MOTHER DRAGON HERSELF DIDN'T EVEN HINT ABOUT SOMETHING LIKE THAT!!!
THE MOTHER DRAGON LOVES ECO SO MUCH! I CAN'T SEE HER FAILING TO TELL ME ABOUT A DANGER LIKE THAT!
HMM, YES.
THAT ALL SOUNDS VERY REASONABLE.
BESIDES, I DON'T RECALL HEARING ABOUT EVEN ONE INDIVIDUAL ATTAINING SAID IMMORTALITY IN ALL THE LONG HISTORY OF THE CONTINENT.
IT SEEMS OBVIOUS THAT IMMORTALITY IS JUST A LEGEND.

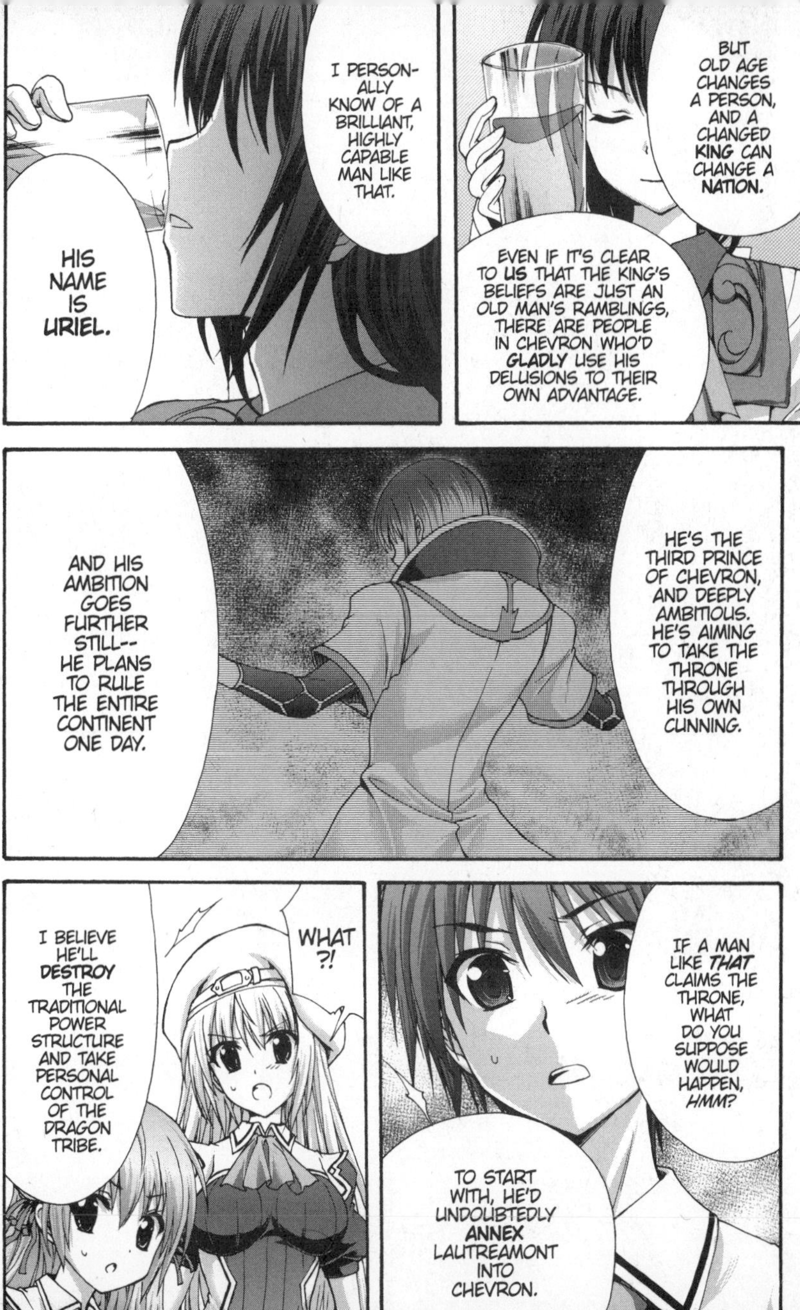
BUT OLD AGE CHANGES A PERSON, AND A CHANGED KING CAN CHANGE A NATION.
EVEN IF IT'S CLEAR TO US THAT THE KING'S BELIEFS ARE JUST AN OLD MAN'S RAMBLINGS, THERE ARE PEOPLE IN CHEVRON WHO'D GLADLY USE HIS DELUSIONS TO THEIR OWN ADVANTAGE.
I PERSONALLY KNOW OF A BRILLIANT, HIGHLY CAPABLE MAN LIKE THAT.
HIS NAME IS URIEL.
HE'S THE THIRD PRINCE OF CHEVRON, AND DEEPLY AMBITIOUS. HE'S AIMING TO TAKE THE THRONE THROUGH HIS OWN CUNNING.
AND HIS AMBITION GOES FURTHER STILL-- HE PLANS TO RULE THE ENTIRE CONTINENT ONE DAY.
IF A MAN LIKE THAT CLAIMS THE THRONE, WHAT DO YOU SUPPOSE WOULD HAPPEN, HMM?
TO START WITH, HE'D UNDOUBTEDLY ANNEX LAUTREAMONT INTO CHEVRON.
WHAT?!
I BELIEVE HE'LL DESTROY THE TRADITIONAL POWER STRUCTURE AND TAKE PERSONAL CONTROL OF THE DRAGON TRIBE.

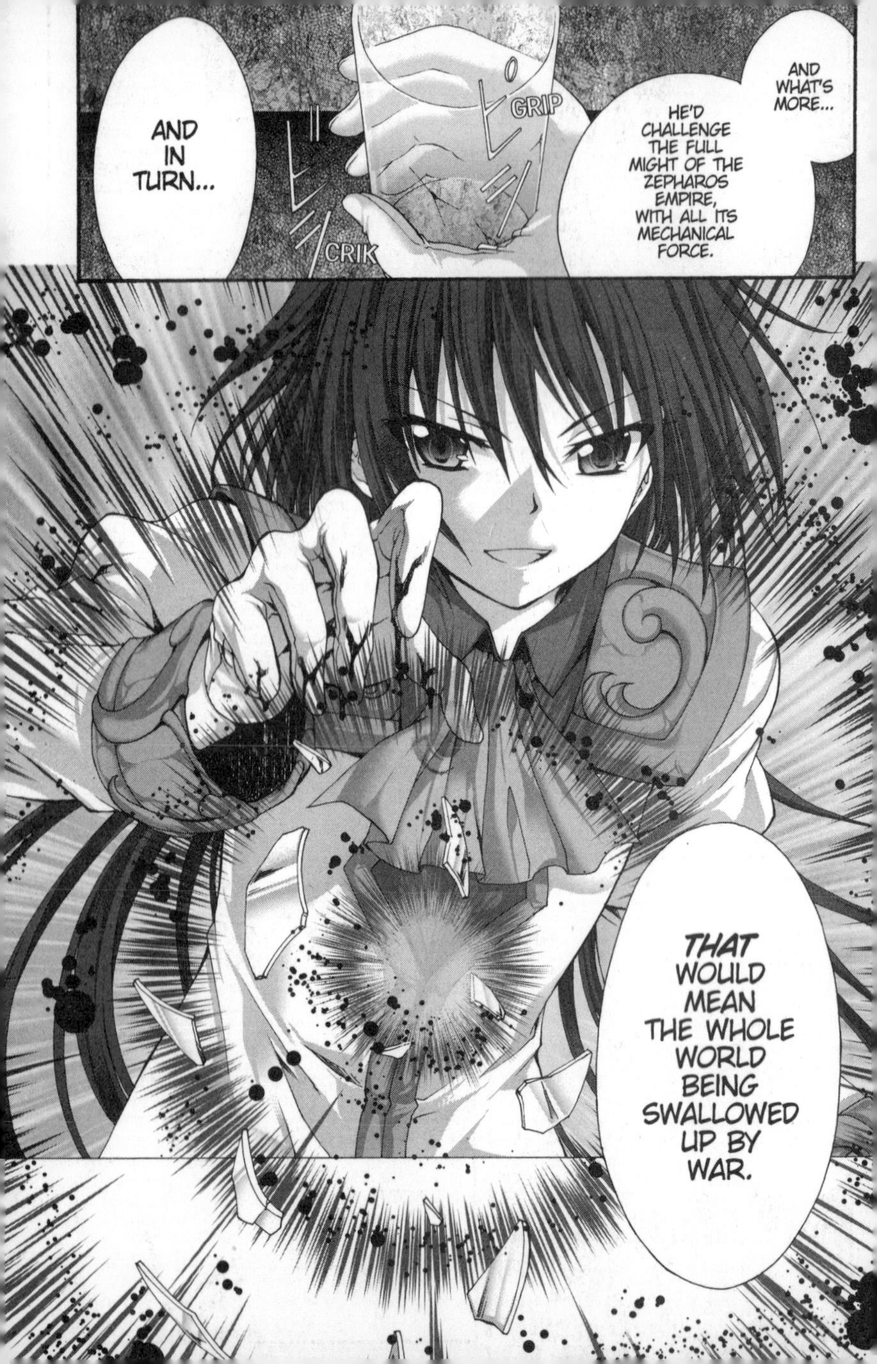
AND WHAT'S MORE...
HE'D CHALLENGE THE FULL MIGHT OF THE ZEPHAROS EMPIRE, WITH ALL ITS MECHANICAL FORCE.
GRIP
CRIK
AND IN TURN...
THAT WOULD MEAN THE WHOLE WORLD BEING SWALLOWED UP BY WAR.

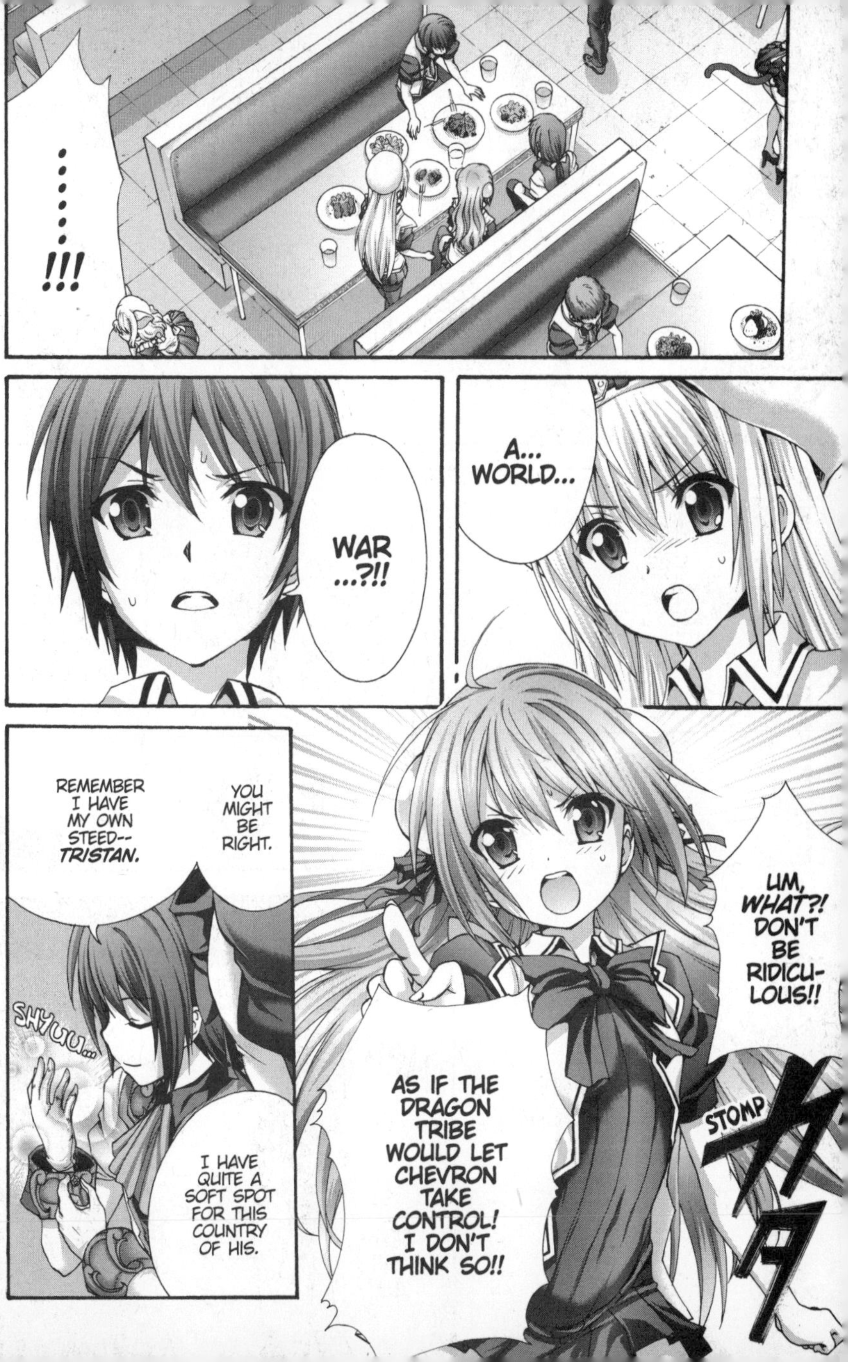
......!!!
A... WORLD...
WAR ...?!!
UM, WHAT?! DON'T BE RIDICU-LOUS!!
STOMP
AS IF THE DRAGON TRIBE WOULD LET CHEVRON TAKE CONTROL! I DON'T THINK SO!!
YOU MIGHT BE RIGHT.
REMEMBER I HAVE MY OWN STEED-- TRISTAN.
SHYUU...
I HAVE QUITE A SOFT SPOT FOR THIS COUNTRY OF HIS.

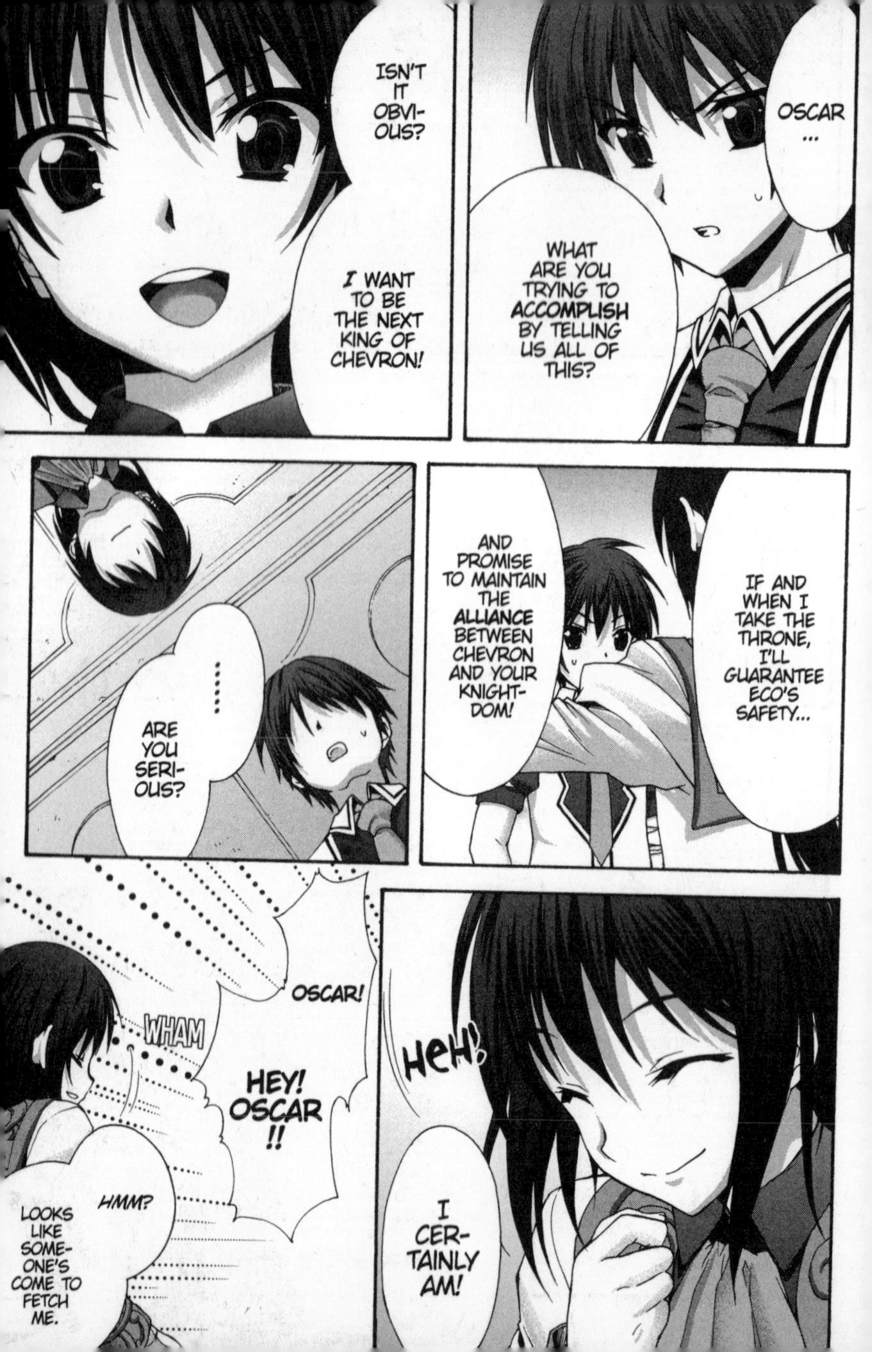
OSCAR...
WHAT ARE YOU TRYING TO ACCOMPLISH BY TELLING US ALL OF THIS?
ISN'T IT OBVI-OUS?
I WANT TO BE THE NEXT KING OF CHEVRON!
IF AND WHEN I TAKE THE THRONE, I'LL GUARANTEE ECO'S SAFETY...
AND PROMISE TO MAINTAIN THE ALLIANCE BETWEEN CHEVRON AND YOUR KNIGHT-DOM!
......
ARE YOU SERI-OUS?
HEH!
I CER-TAINLY AM!
OSCAR!
HEY! OSCAR!!
WHAM
HMM?
LOOKS LIKE SOME-ONE'S COME TO FETCH ME.

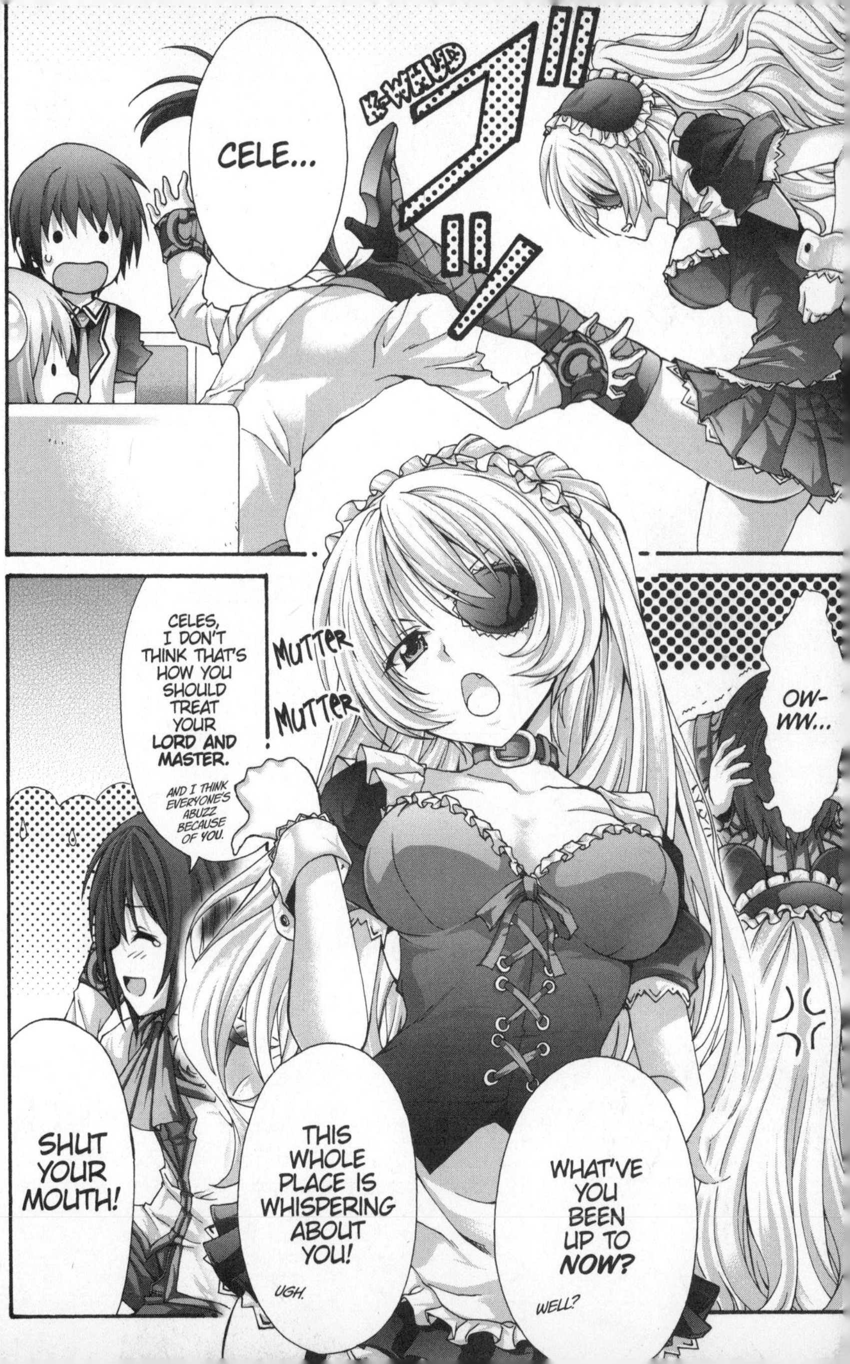
K-WHUD
CELE...
OW-WW...
CELES, I DON'T THINK THAT'S HOW YOU SHOULD TREAT YOUR LORD AND MASTER.
AND I THINK EVERYONE'S ABUZZ BECAUSE OF YOU.
MUTTER
MUTTER
WHAT'VE YOU BEEN UP TO NOW?
WELL?
THIS WHOLE PLACE IS WHISPERING ABOUT YOU!
UGH.
SHUT YOUR MOUTH!

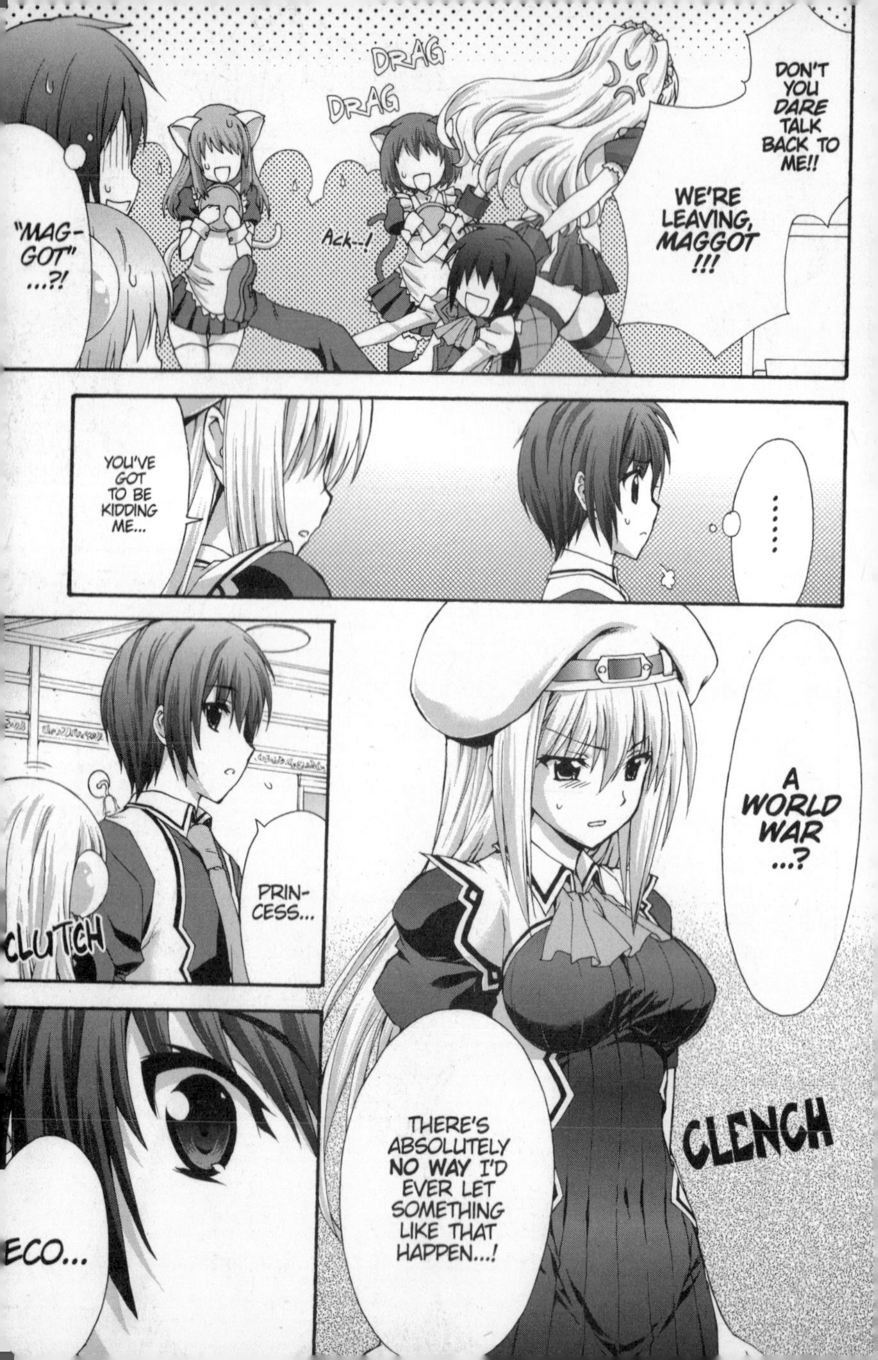
DON'T YOU DARE TALK BACK TO ME!!
WE'RE LEAVING, MAGGOT!!!
DRAG
DRAG
Ack--!
"MAG-GOT" ...?!
......
YOU'VE GOT TO BE KIDDING ME...
A WORLD WAR ...?
THERE'S ABSOLUTELY NO WAY I'D EVER LET SOMETHING LIKE THAT HAPPEN...!
CLENCH
PRIN-CESS...
CLUTCH
ECO...

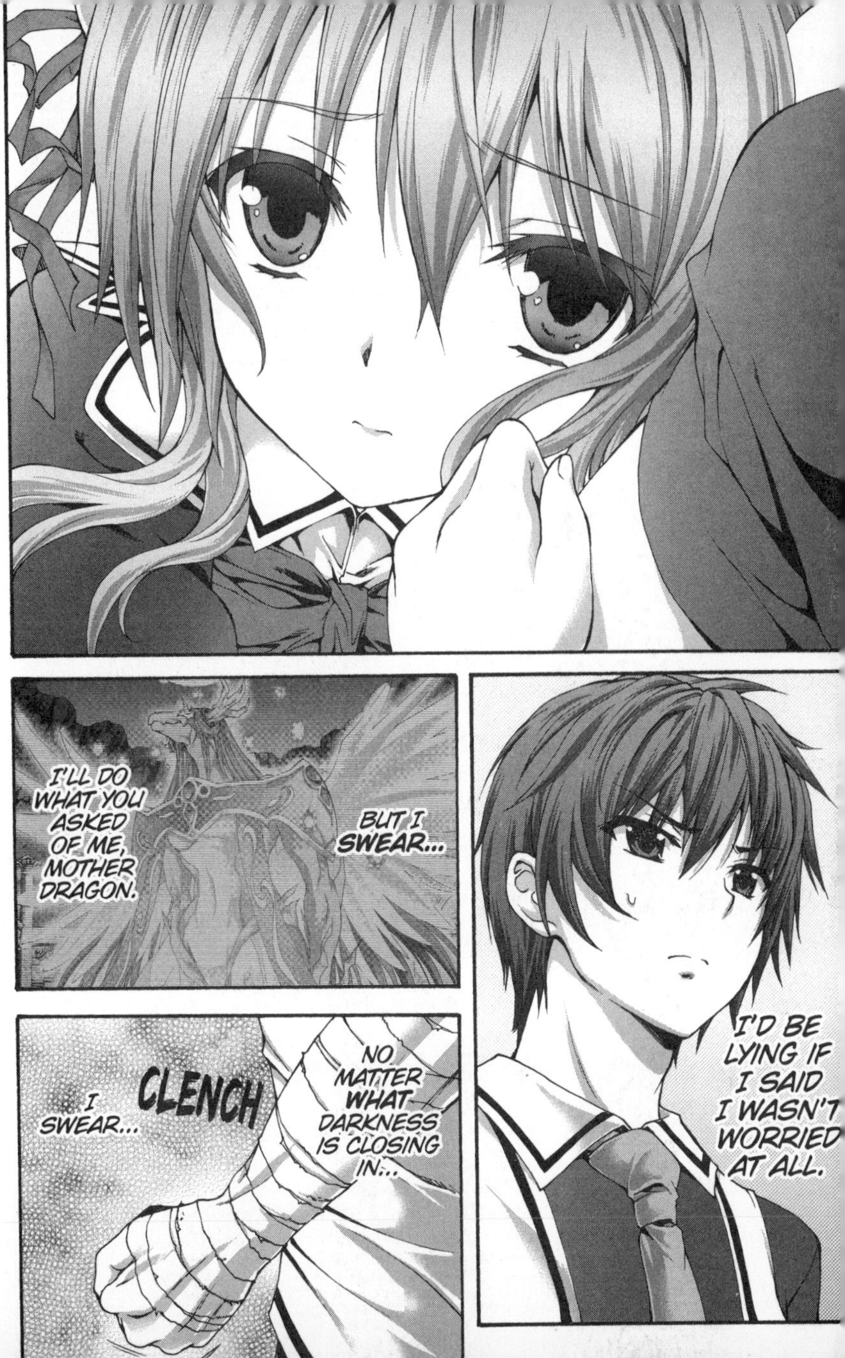
I'D BE LYING IF I SAID I WASN'T WORRIED AT ALL.
I'LL DO WHAT YOU ASKED OF ME, MOTHER DRAGON.
BUT I SWEAR...
NO MATTER WHAT DARKNESS IS CLOSING IN...
CLENCH
I SWEAR...

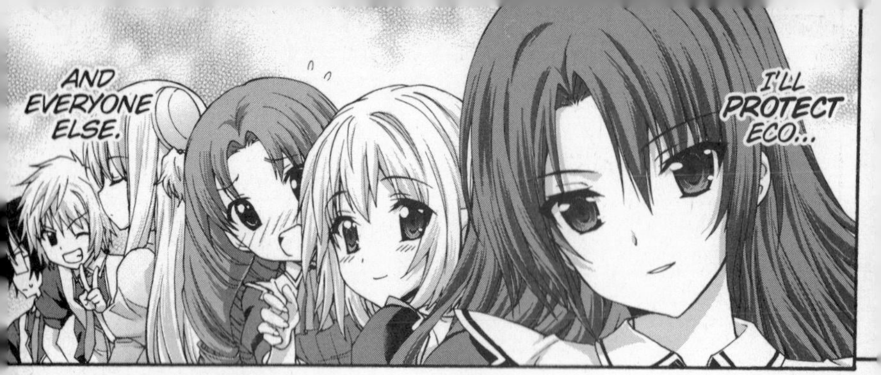
I'LL PROTECT ECO...
AND EVERYONE ELSE.

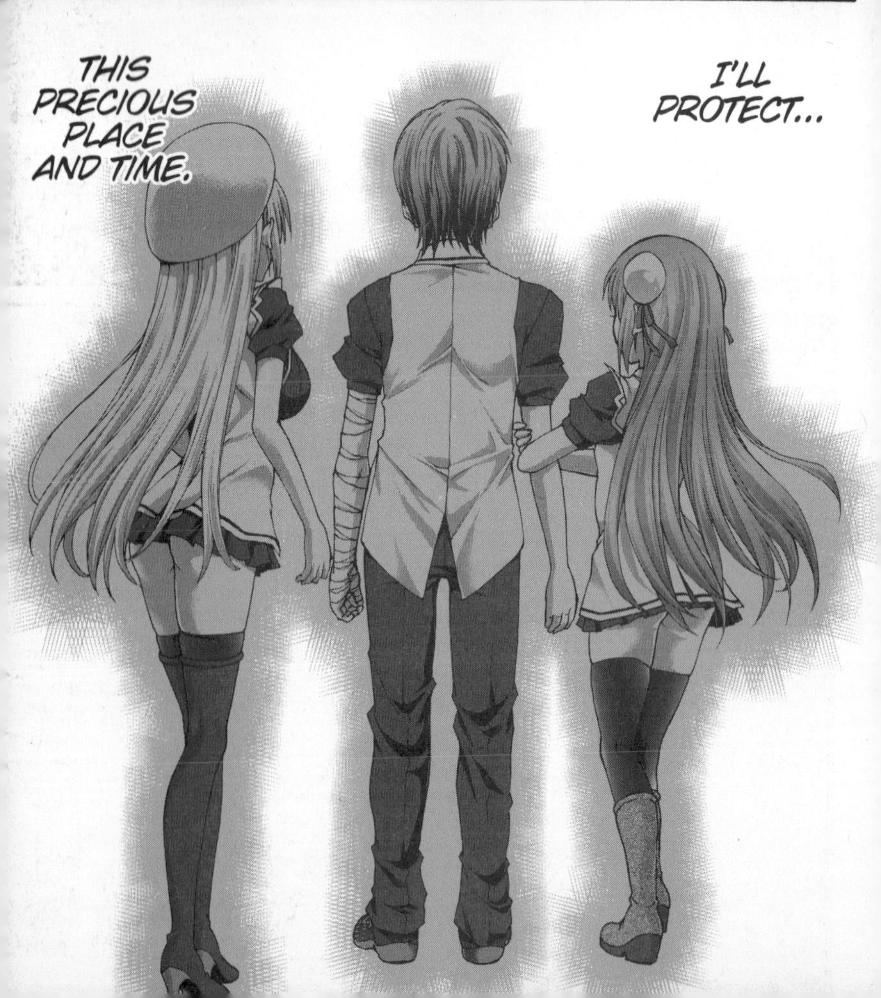
I'LL PROTECT...
THIS PRECIOUS PLACE AND TIME.

DRAGONAR
ACADEMY

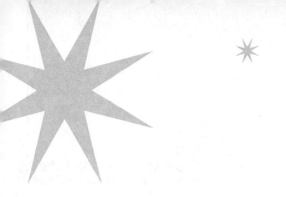

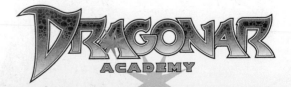

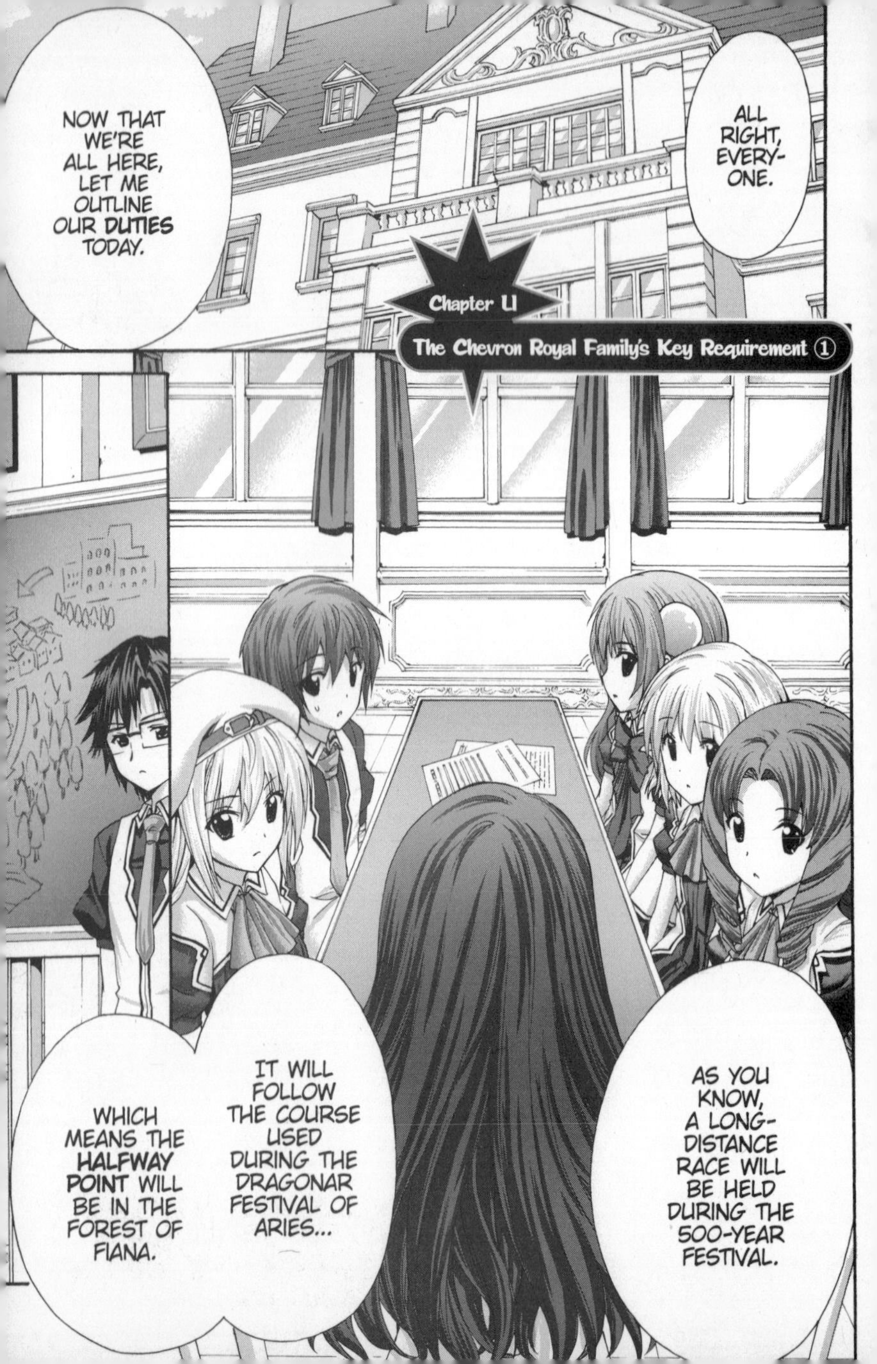
ALL RIGHT, EVERYONE.
NOW THAT WE'RE ALL HERE, LET ME OUTLINE OUR **DUTIES** TODAY.
Chapter 11
The Chevron Royal Family's Key Requirement ①
AS YOU KNOW, A LONG-DISTANCE RACE WILL BE HELD DURING THE 500-YEAR FESTIVAL.
IT WILL FOLLOW THE COURSE USED DURING THE DRAGONAR FESTIVAL OF ARIES...
WHICH MEANS THE **HALFWAY POINT** WILL BE IN THE FOREST OF FIANA.

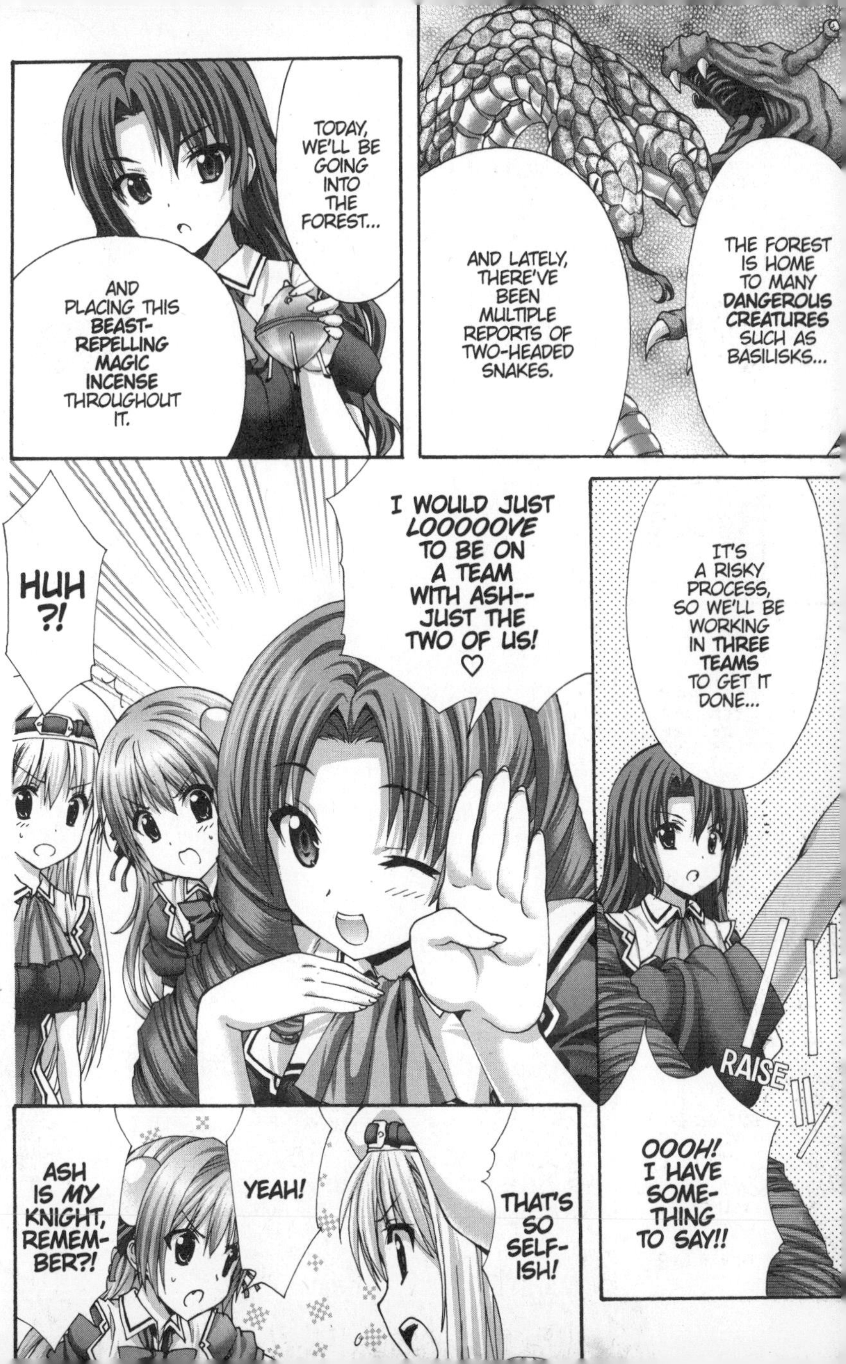
THE FOREST IS HOME TO MANY DANGEROUS CREATURES SUCH AS BASILISKS...
AND LATELY, THERE'VE BEEN MULTIPLE REPORTS OF TWO-HEADED SNAKES.
TODAY, WE'LL BE GOING INTO THE FOREST...
AND PLACING THIS BEAST-REPELLING MAGIC INCENSE THROUGHOUT IT.
IT'S A RISKY PROCESS, SO WE'LL BE WORKING IN THREE TEAMS TO GET IT DONE...
RAISE
OOOH! I HAVE SOME-THING TO SAY!!
I WOULD JUST LOOOOOVE TO BE ON A TEAM WITH ASH-- JUST THE TWO OF US! ♡
HUH?!
THAT'S SO SELF-ISH!
YEAH!
ASH IS MY KNIGHT, REMEM-BER?!

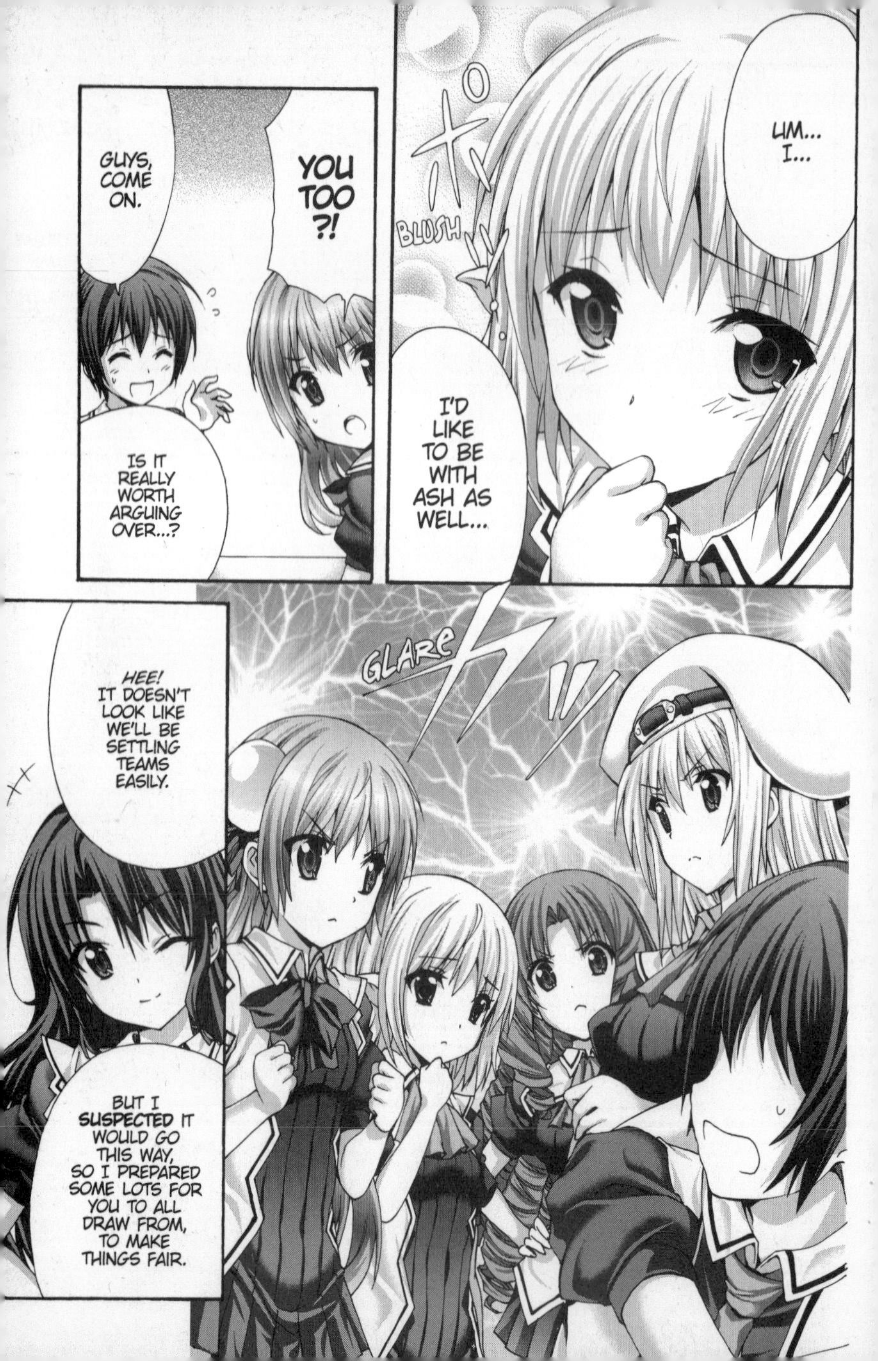
UM... I...
BLUSH
I'D LIKE TO BE WITH ASH AS WELL...
YOU TOO?!
GUYS, COME ON.
IS IT REALLY WORTH ARGUING OVER...?
GLARE
HEE! IT DOESN'T LOOK LIKE WE'LL BE SETTLING TEAMS EASILY.
BUT I **SUSPECTED** IT WOULD GO THIS WAY, SO I PREPARED SOME LOTS FOR YOU TO ALL DRAW FROM, TO MAKE THINGS FAIR.

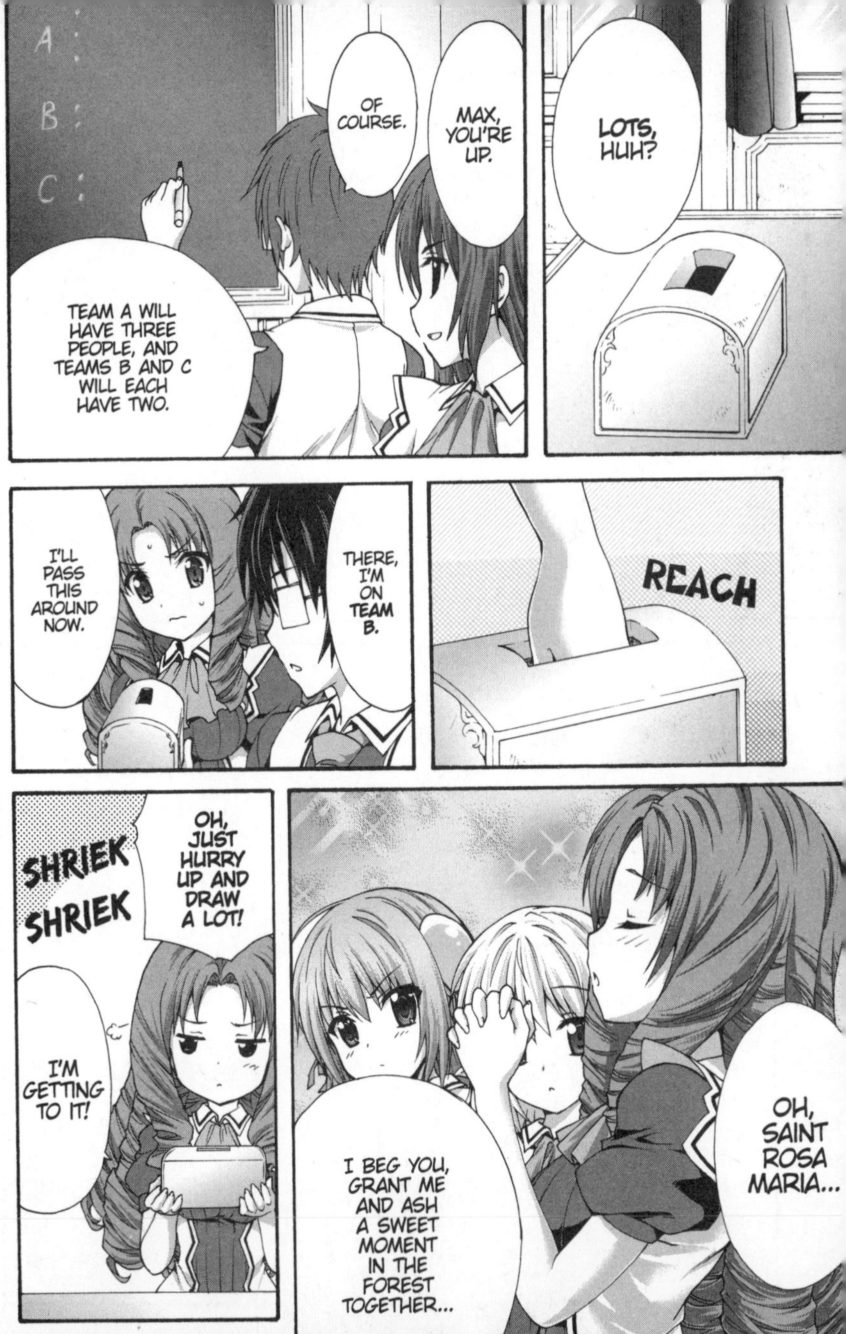
LOTS, HUH?
MAX, YOU'RE UP.
OF COURSE.
TEAM A WILL HAVE THREE PEOPLE, AND TEAMS B AND C WILL EACH HAVE TWO.
A :
B :
C :
REACH
THERE, I'M ON TEAM B.
I'LL PASS THIS AROUND NOW.
OH, SAINT ROSA MARIA...
I BEG YOU, GRANT ME AND ASH A SWEET MOMENT IN THE FOREST TOGETHER...
OH, JUST HURRY UP AND DRAW A LOT!
SHRIEK
SHRIEK
I'M GETTING TO IT!

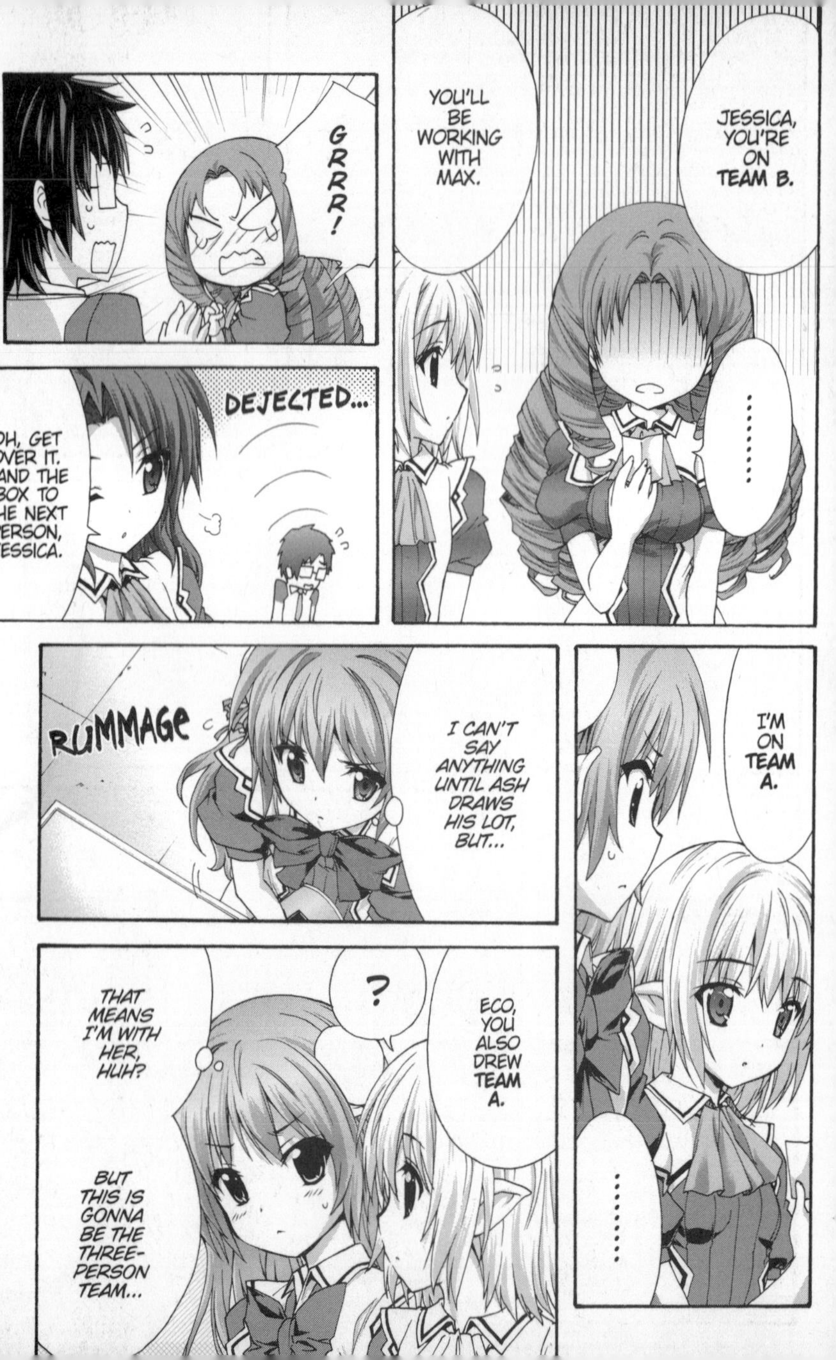
JESSICA, YOU'RE ON TEAM B.
YOU'LL BE WORKING WITH MAX.
......
GRRR!
DEJECTED...
OH, GET OVER IT. HAND THE BOX TO THE NEXT PERSON, JESSICA.
I'M ON TEAM A.
......
I CAN'T SAY ANYTHING UNTIL ASH DRAWS HIS LOT, BUT...
RUMMAGE
ECO, YOU ALSO DREW TEAM A.
?
THAT MEANS I'M WITH HER, HUH?
BUT THIS IS GONNA BE THE THREE-PERSON TEAM...

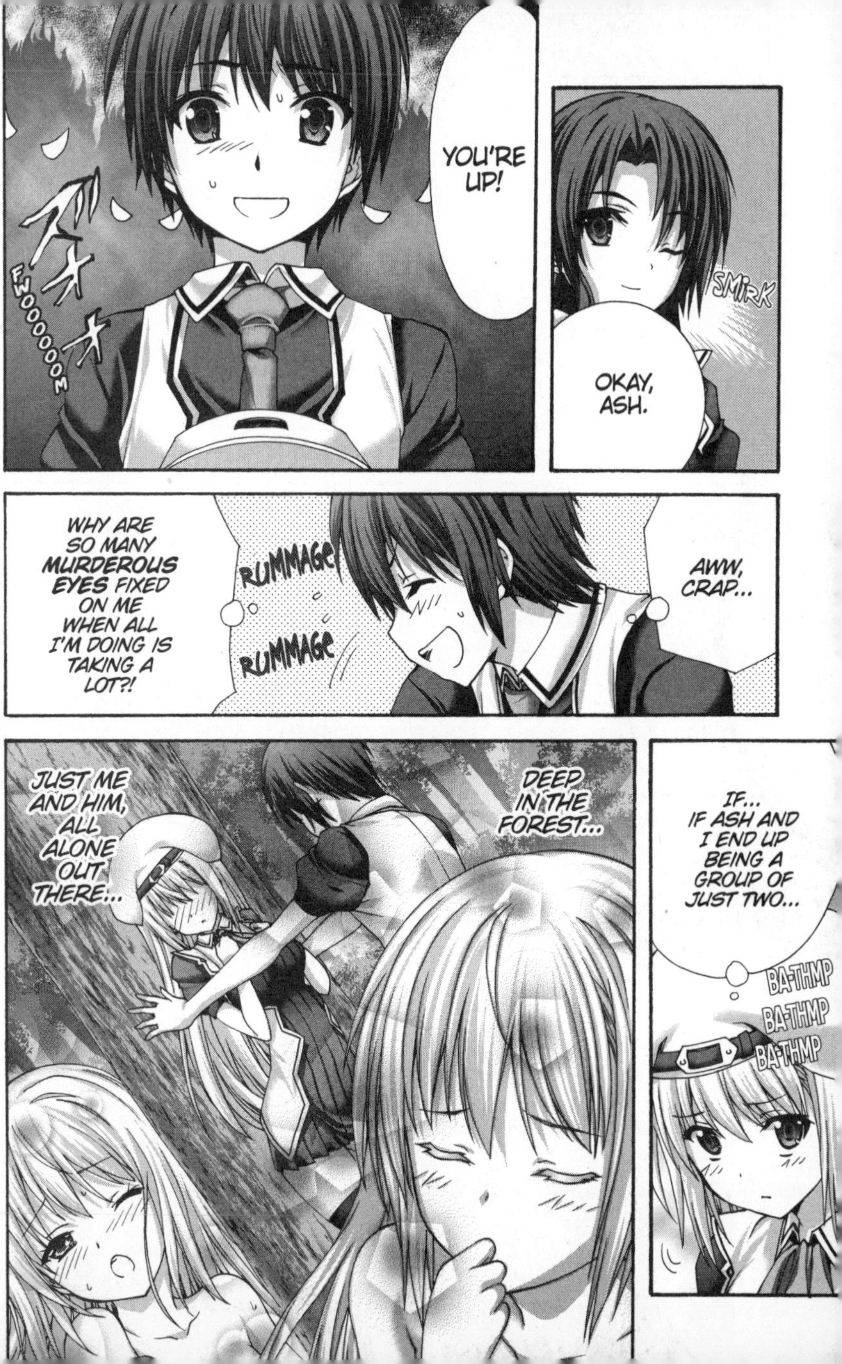
SMIRK
OKAY, ASH.
YOU'RE UP!
FWOOOOOOM
AWW, CRAP...
RUMMAGE
RUMMAGE
WHY ARE SO MANY MURDEROUS EYES FIXED ON ME WHEN ALL I'M DOING IS TAKING A LOT?!
IF... IF ASH AND I END UP BEING A GROUP OF JUST TWO...
BA-THMP
BA-THMP
BA-THMP
DEEP IN THE FOREST...
JUST ME AND HIM, ALL ALONE OUT THERE...

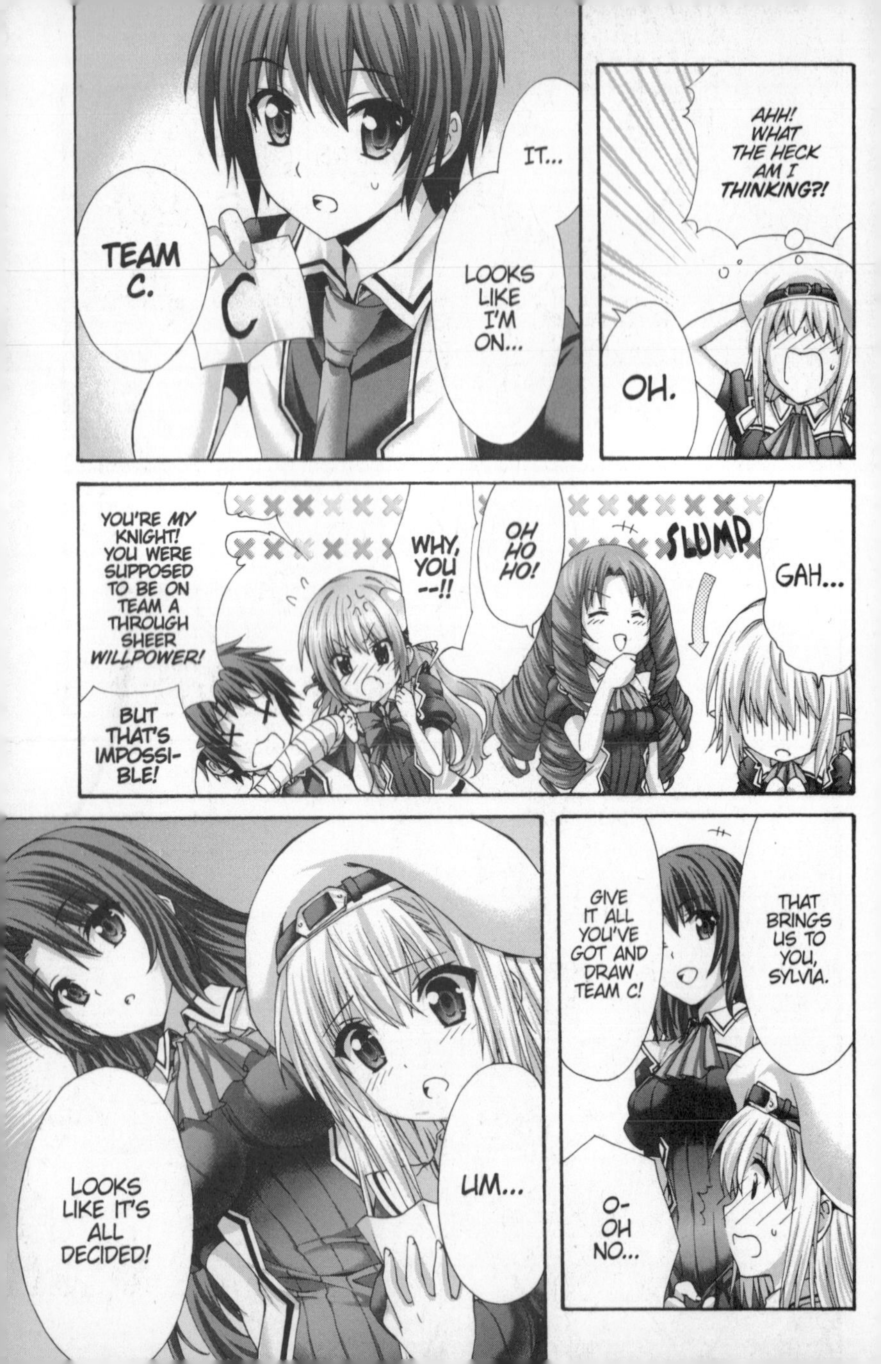
AHH! WHAT THE HECK AM I THINKING?!
OH.
IT...
LOOKS LIKE I'M ON...
TEAM C.
GAH...
SLUMP
OH HO HO!
WHY, YOU --!!
YOU'RE MY KNIGHT! YOU WERE SUPPOSED TO BE ON TEAM A THROUGH SHEER WILLPOWER!
BUT THAT'S IMPOSSI-BLE!
THAT BRINGS US TO YOU, SYLVIA.
GIVE IT ALL YOU'VE GOT AND DRAW TEAM C!
O-OH NO...
UM...
LOOKS LIKE IT'S ALL DECIDED!

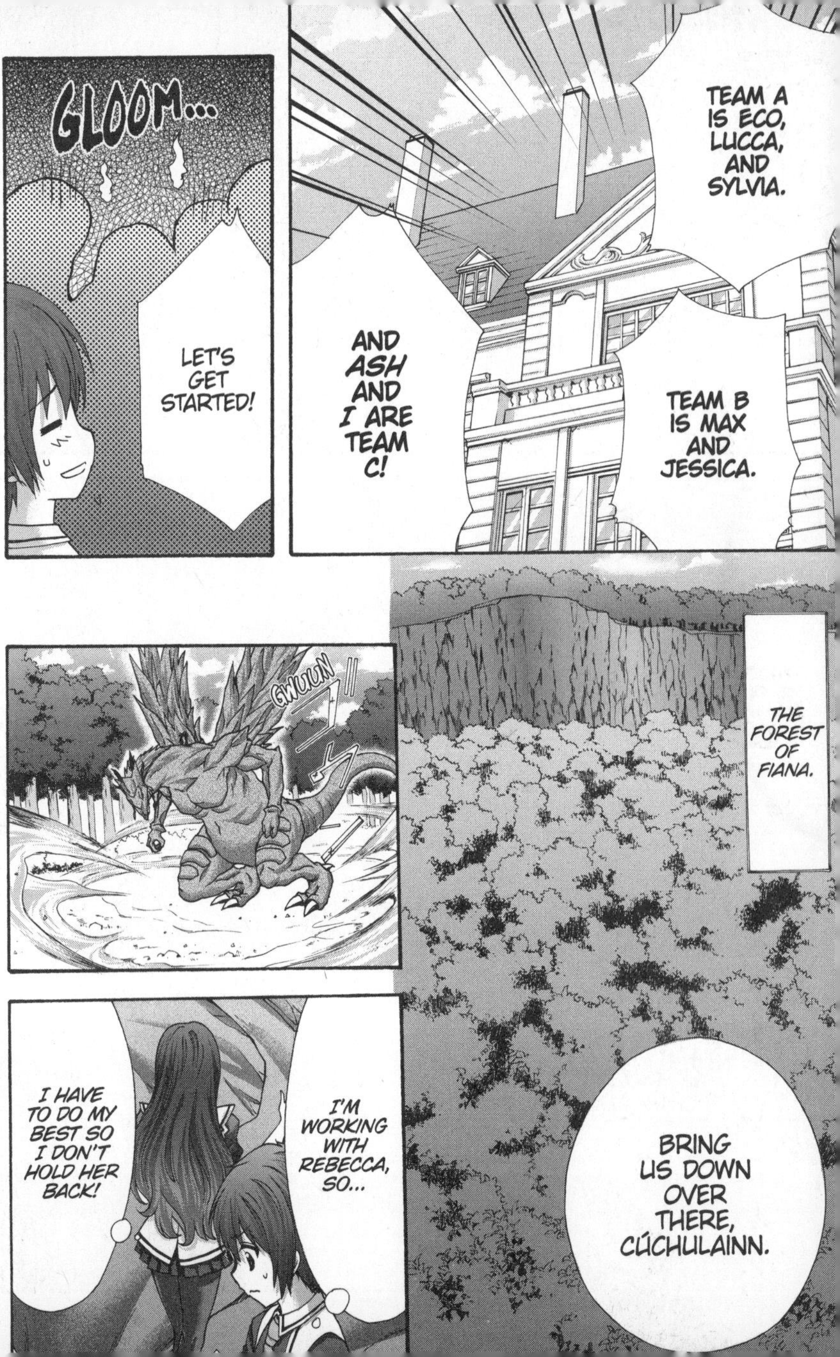
TEAM A IS ECO, LUCCA, AND SYLVIA.
TEAM B IS MAX AND JESSICA.
AND ASH AND I ARE TEAM C!
GLOOM...
LET'S GET STARTED!
THE FOREST OF FIANA.
BRING US DOWN OVER THERE, CÚCHULAINN.
GWUUN
I'M WORKING WITH REBECCA, SO...
I HAVE TO DO MY BEST SO I DON'T HOLD HER BACK!

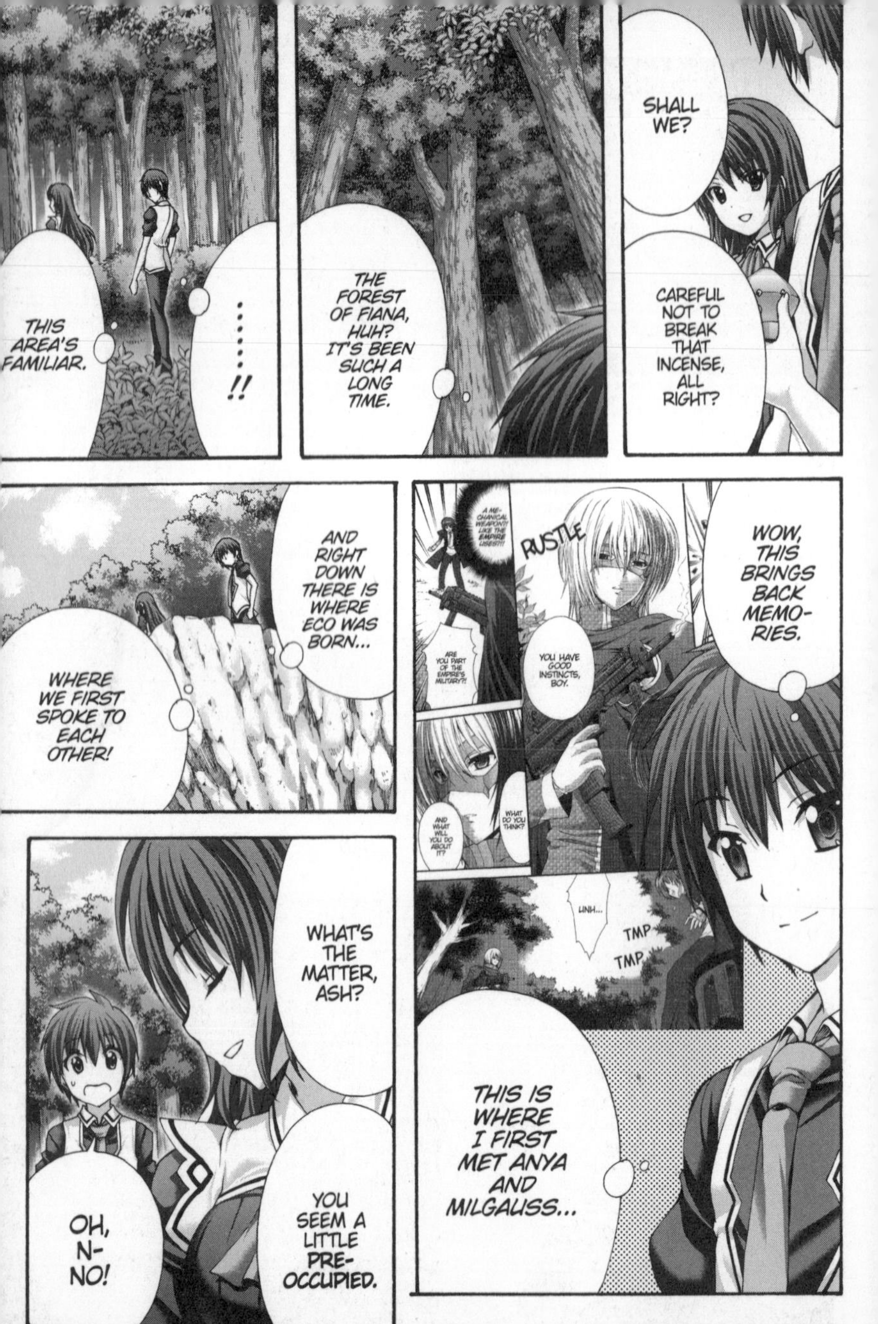
SHALL WE?
CAREFUL NOT TO BREAK THAT INCENSE, ALL RIGHT?
THE FOREST OF FIANA, HUH? IT'S BEEN SUCH A LONG TIME.
......!!
THIS AREA'S FAMILIAR.
WOW, THIS BRINGS BACK MEMORIES.
RUSTLE
YOU HAVE GOOD INSTINCTS, BOY.
A MECHANICAL WEAPON!? LIKE THE EMPIRE USES!?!?
ARE YOU PART OF THE EMPIRE'S MILITARY?!
WHAT DO YOU THINK?
AND WHAT WILL YOU DO ABOUT IT?
UNH...
TMP
TMP
THIS IS WHERE I FIRST MET ANYA AND MILGAUSS...
AND RIGHT DOWN THERE IS WHERE ECO WAS BORN...
WHERE WE FIRST SPOKE TO EACH OTHER!
WHAT'S THE MATTER, ASH?
YOU SEEM A LITTLE PREOCCUPIED.
OH, N-NO!

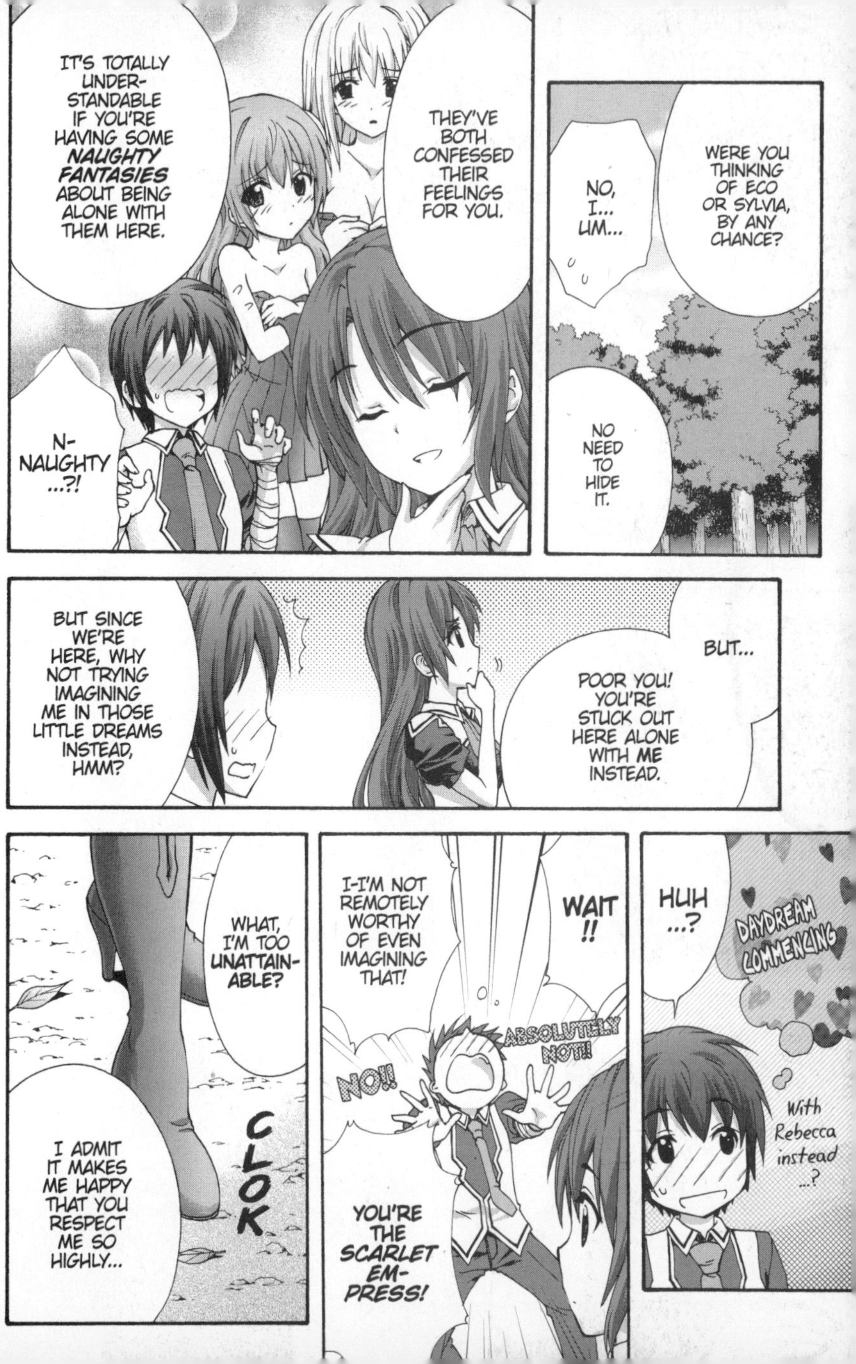
WERE YOU THINKING OF ECO OR SYLVIA, BY ANY CHANCE?
NO, I... UM...
NO NEED TO HIDE IT.
THEY'VE BOTH CONFESSED THEIR FEELINGS FOR YOU.
IT'S TOTALLY UNDER-STANDABLE IF YOU'RE HAVING SOME NAUGHTY FANTASIES ABOUT BEING ALONE WITH THEM HERE.
N-NAUGHTY ...?!
BUT...
POOR YOU! YOU'RE STUCK OUT HERE ALONE WITH ME INSTEAD.
BUT SINCE WE'RE HERE, WHY NOT TRYING IMAGINING ME IN THOSE LITTLE DREAMS INSTEAD, HMM?
HUH ...?
DAYDREAM COMMENCING
With Rebecca instead ...?
WAIT !!
I-I'M NOT REMOTELY WORTHY OF EVEN IMAGINING THAT!
ABSOLUTELY NOT!!
NO!!
YOU'RE THE SCARLET EM-PRESS!
WHAT, I'M TOO UNATTAIN-ABLE?
CLOK
I ADMIT IT MAKES ME HAPPY THAT YOU RESPECT ME SO HIGHLY...

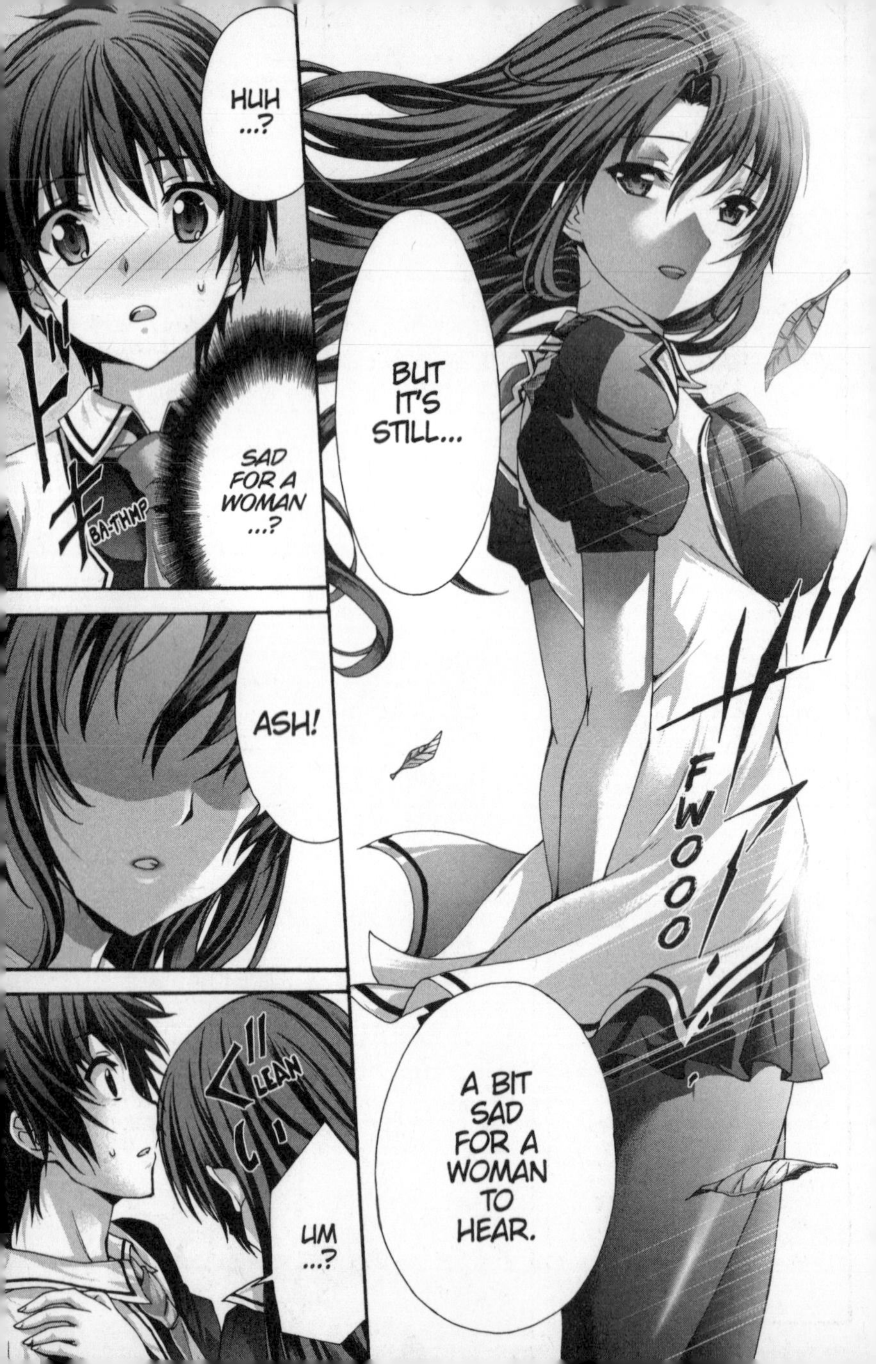
BUT IT'S STILL...
A BIT SAD FOR A WOMAN TO HEAR.
FWOOO
HUH ...?
SAD FOR A WOMAN ...?
BA-THMP
ASH!
LEAN
UM ...?

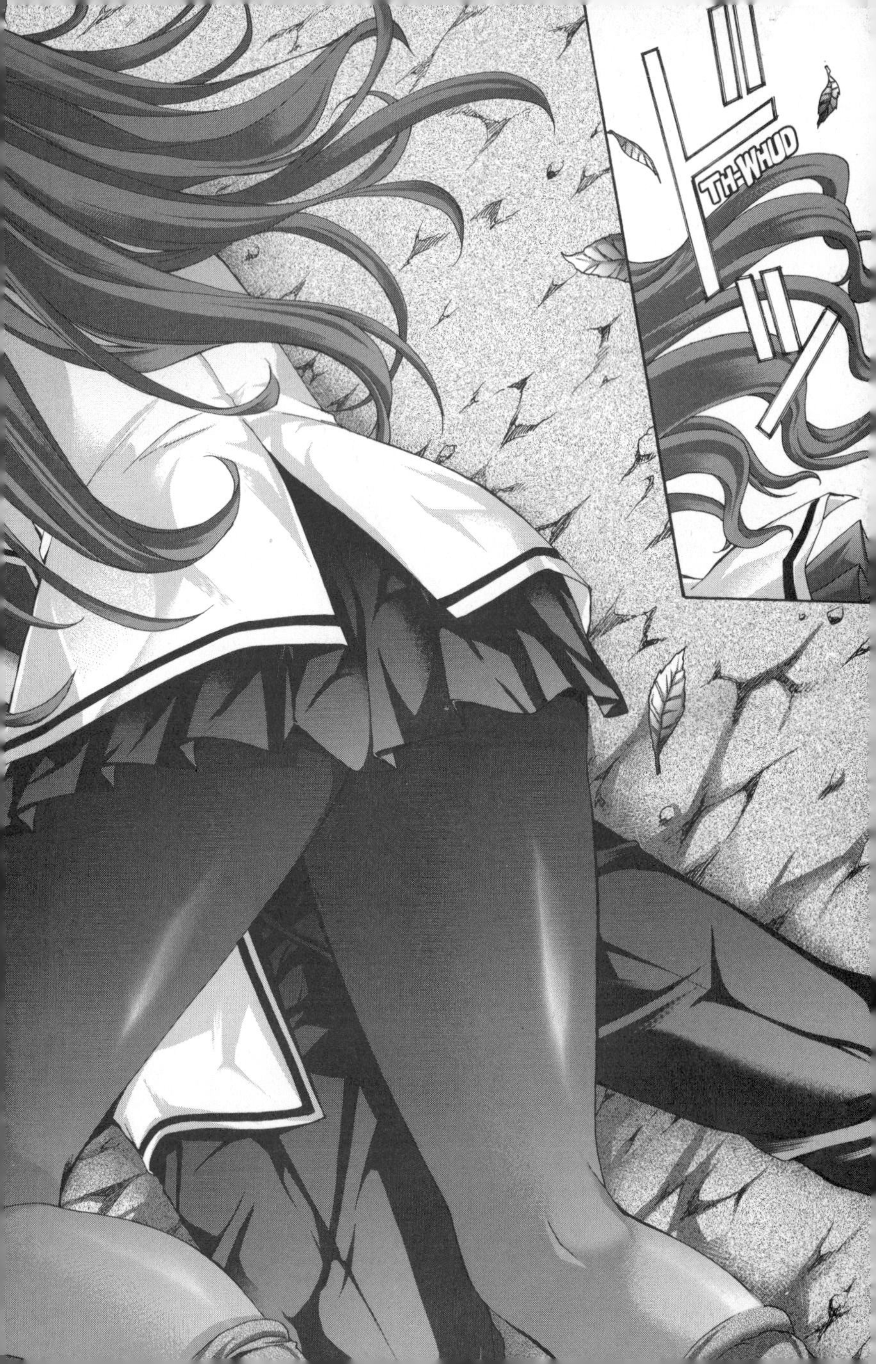
TH-WHUD

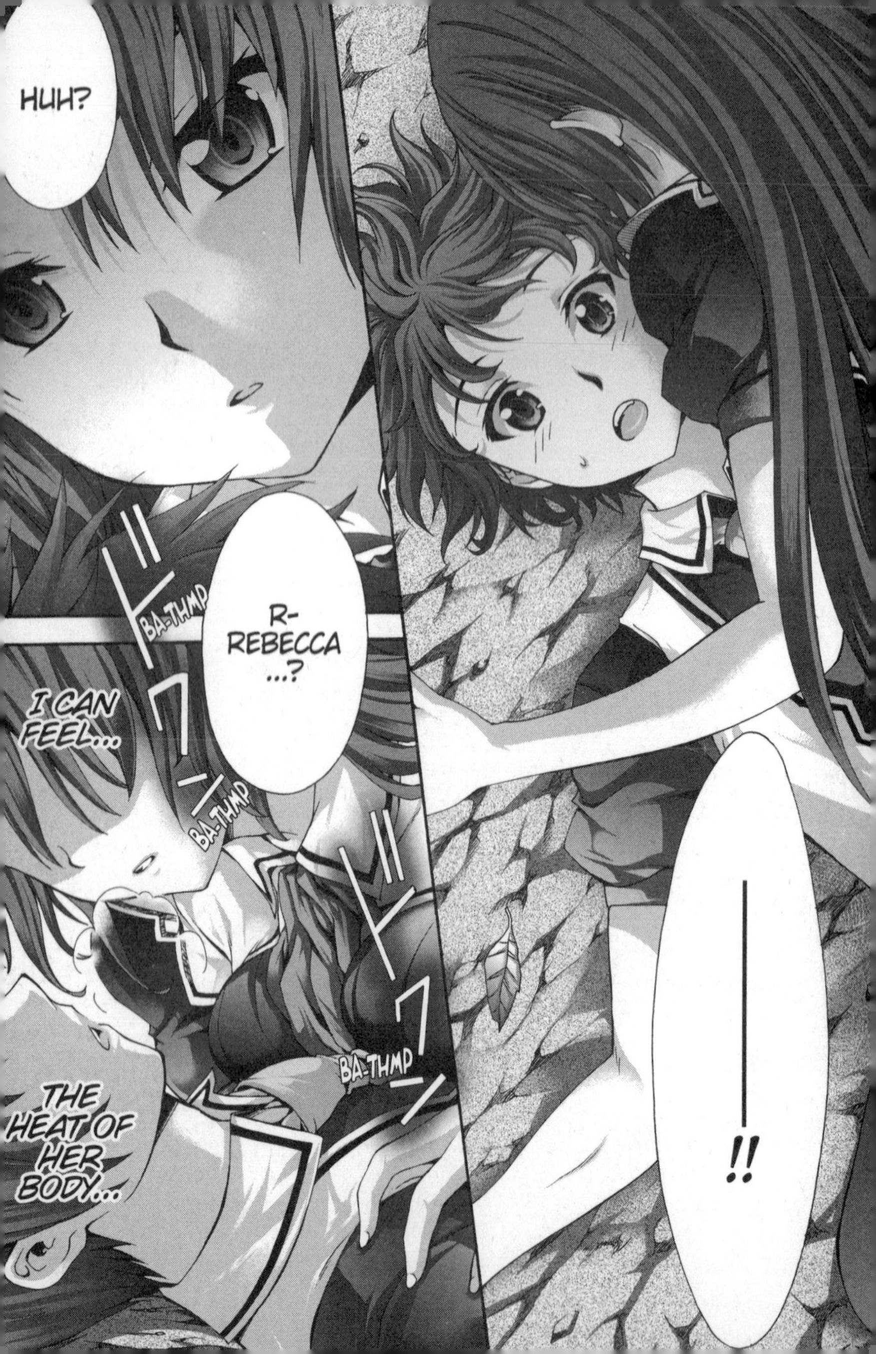
——!!
HUH?
BA-THMP
R-REBECCA...?
BA-THMP
I CAN FEEL...
BA-THMP
THE HEAT OF HER BODY...

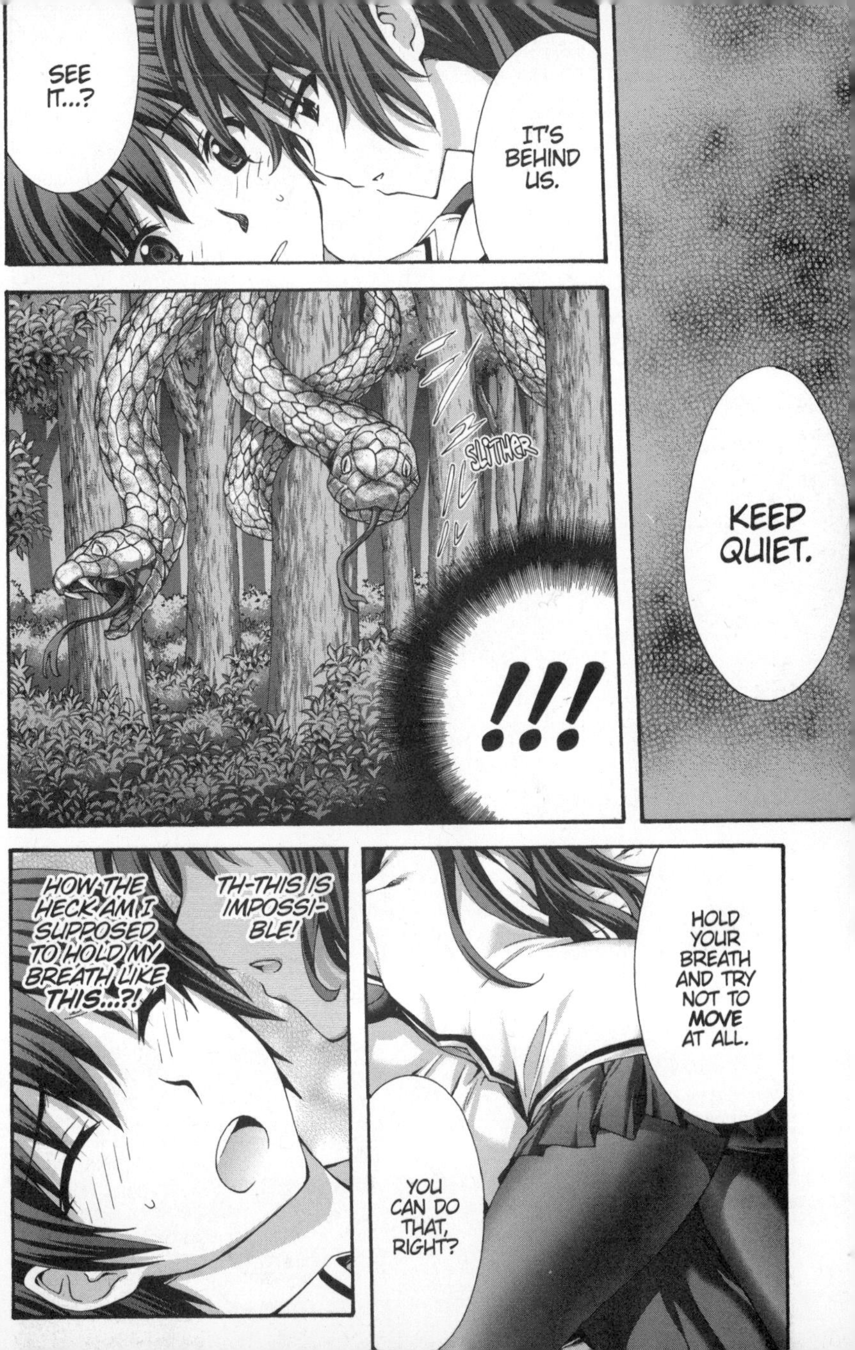
KEEP QUIET.
IT'S BEHIND US.
SEE IT...?
SLITHER
!!!
HOLD YOUR BREATH AND TRY NOT TO MOVE AT ALL.
YOU CAN DO THAT, RIGHT?
TH-THIS IS IMPOSSI-BLE!
HOW THE HECK AM I SUPPOSED TO HOLD MY BREATH LIKE THIS...?!

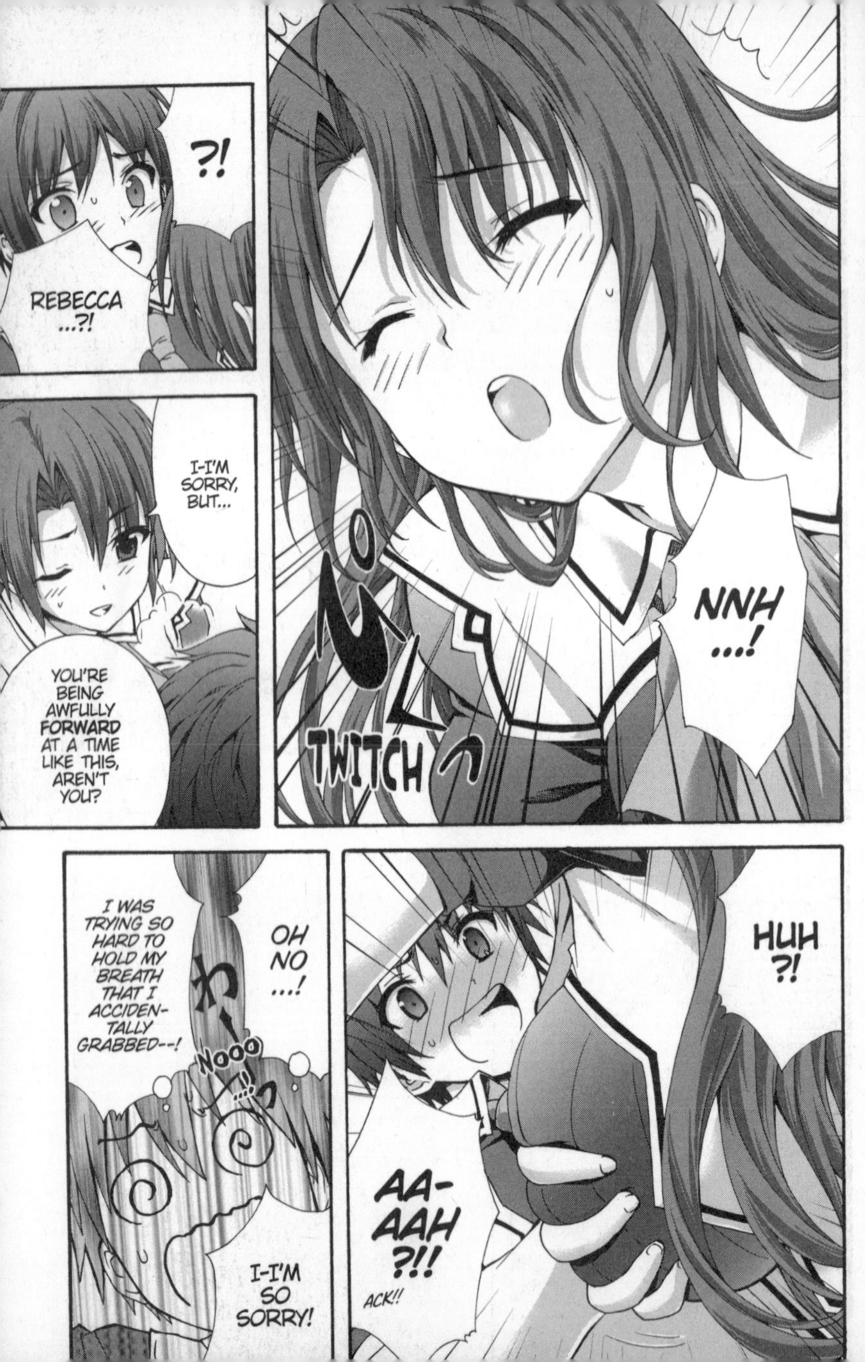
NNH ...!
TWITCH
?!
REBECCA ...?!
I-I'M SORRY, BUT...
YOU'RE BEING AWFULLY FORWARD AT A TIME LIKE THIS, AREN'T YOU?
HUH ?!
AA-AAH ?!!
ACK!!
OH NO ...!
I WAS TRYING SO HARD TO HOLD MY BREATH THAT I ACCIDENTALLY GRABBED--!
NOOO ...!!
I-I'M SO SORRY!

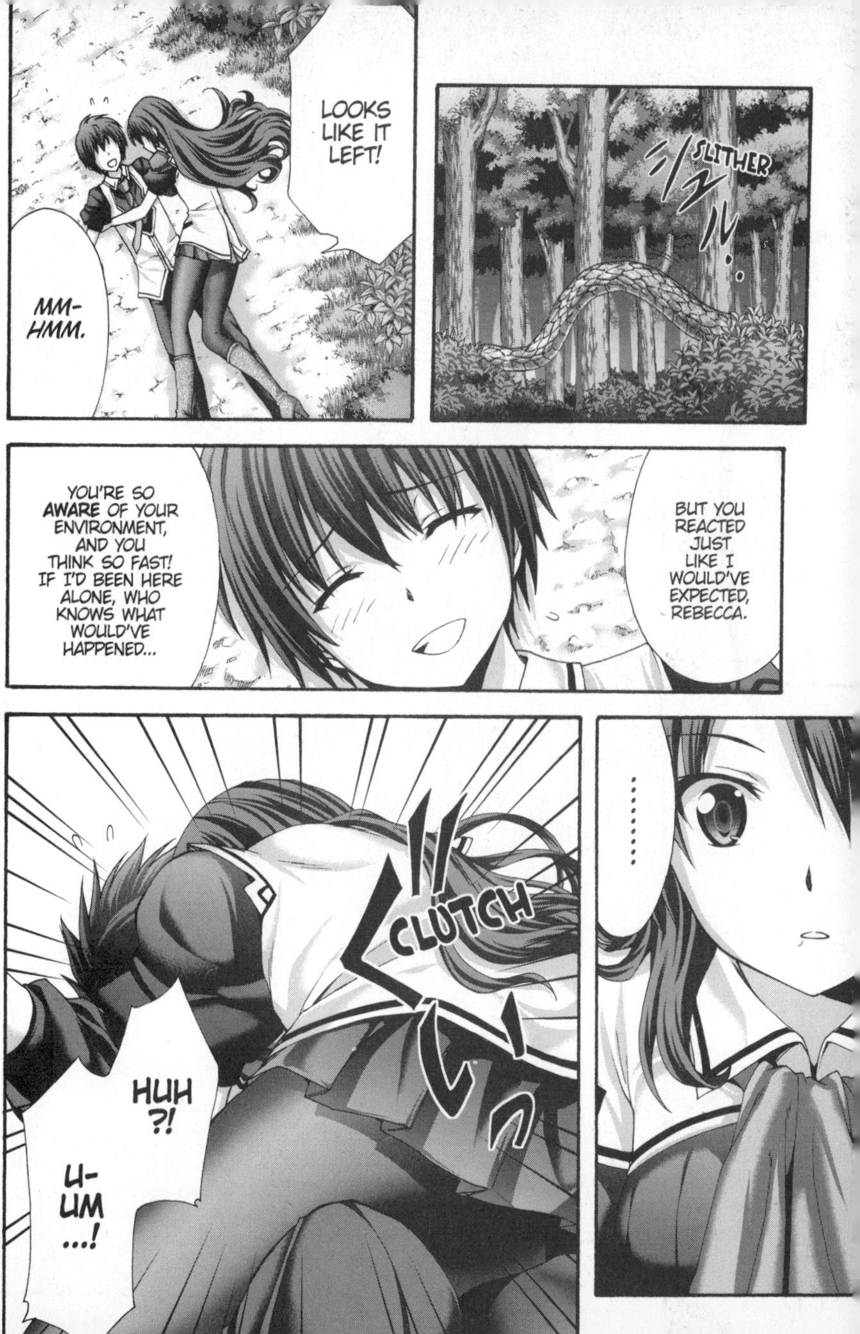
SLITHER
LOOKS LIKE IT LEFT!
MM-HMM.
BUT YOU REACTED JUST LIKE I WOULD'VE EXPECTED, REBECCA.
YOU'RE SO **AWARE** OF YOUR ENVIRONMENT, AND YOU THINK SO FAST! IF I'D BEEN HERE ALONE, WHO KNOWS WHAT WOULD'VE HAPPENED...
......
CLUTCH
HUH?!
U-UM...!

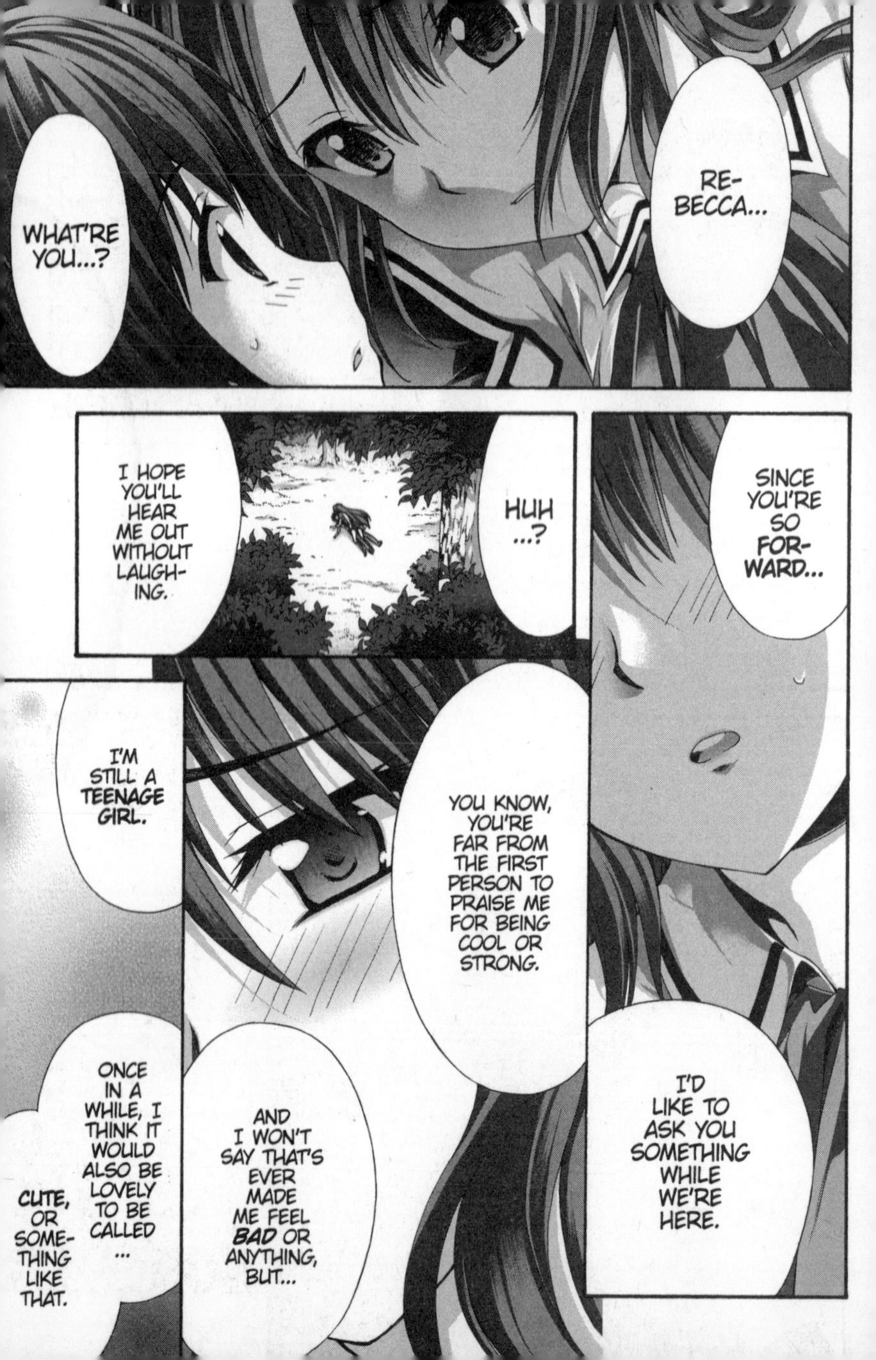
RE-BECCA...
WHAT'RE YOU...?
SINCE YOU'RE SO FOR-WARD...
I'D LIKE TO ASK YOU SOMETHING WHILE WE'RE HERE.
HUH ...?
I HOPE YOU'LL HEAR ME OUT WITHOUT LAUGH-ING.
YOU KNOW, YOU'RE FAR FROM THE FIRST PERSON TO PRAISE ME FOR BEING COOL OR STRONG.
AND I WON'T SAY THAT'S EVER MADE ME FEEL *BAD* OR ANYTHING, BUT...
I'M STILL A TEENAGE GIRL.
ONCE IN A WHILE, I THINK IT WOULD ALSO BE LOVELY TO BE CALLED ...
CUTE, OR SOME-THING LIKE THAT.

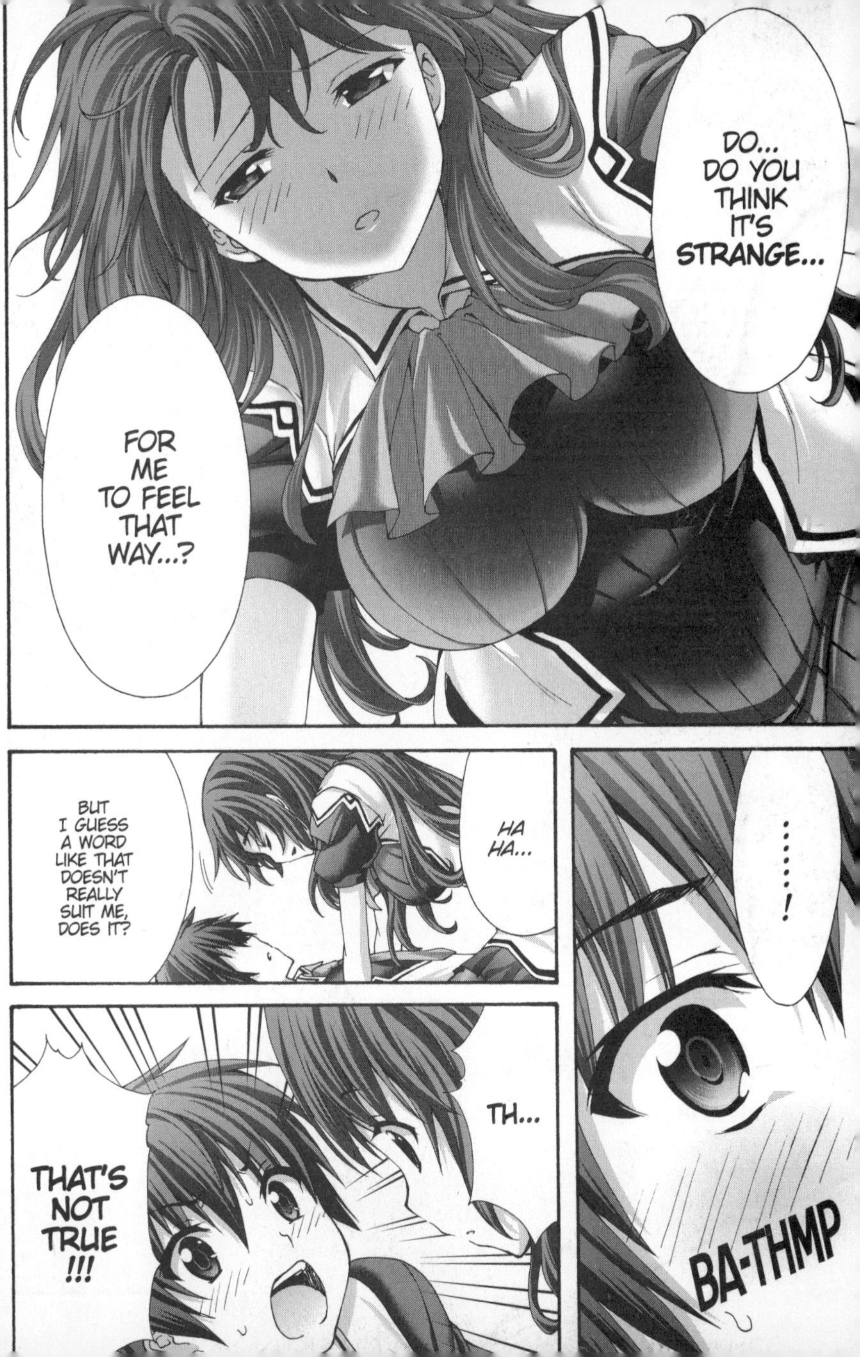
DO... DO YOU THINK IT'S STRANGE...
FOR ME TO FEEL THAT WAY...?
......!
BA-THMP
HA HA...
BUT I GUESS A WORD LIKE THAT DOESN'T REALLY SUIT ME, DOES IT?
TH...
THAT'S NOT TRUE!!!

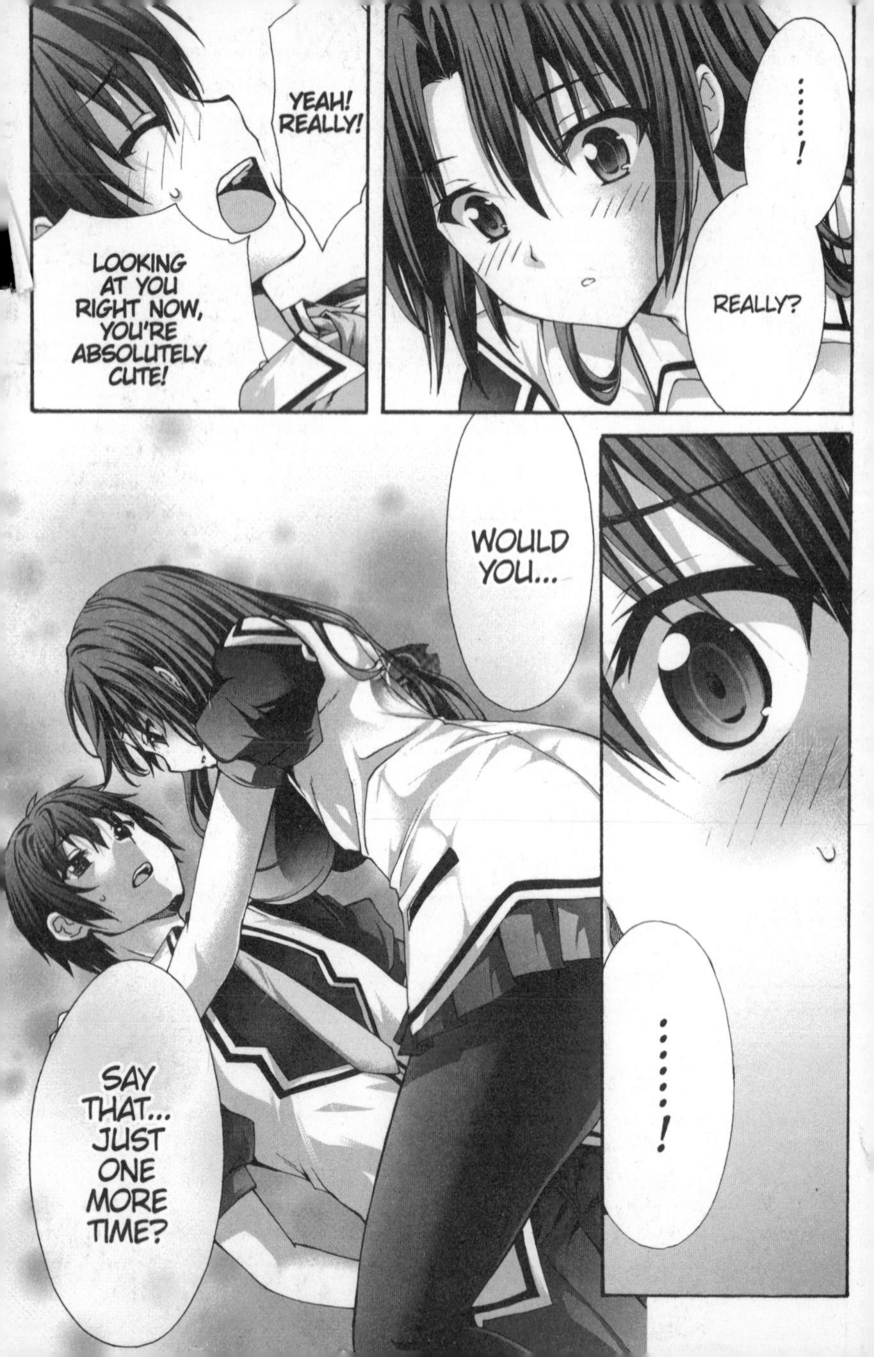
......!
REALLY?
YEAH! REALLY!
LOOKING AT YOU RIGHT NOW, YOU'RE ABSOLUTELY CUTE!
......!
WOULD YOU...
SAY THAT... JUST ONE MORE TIME?

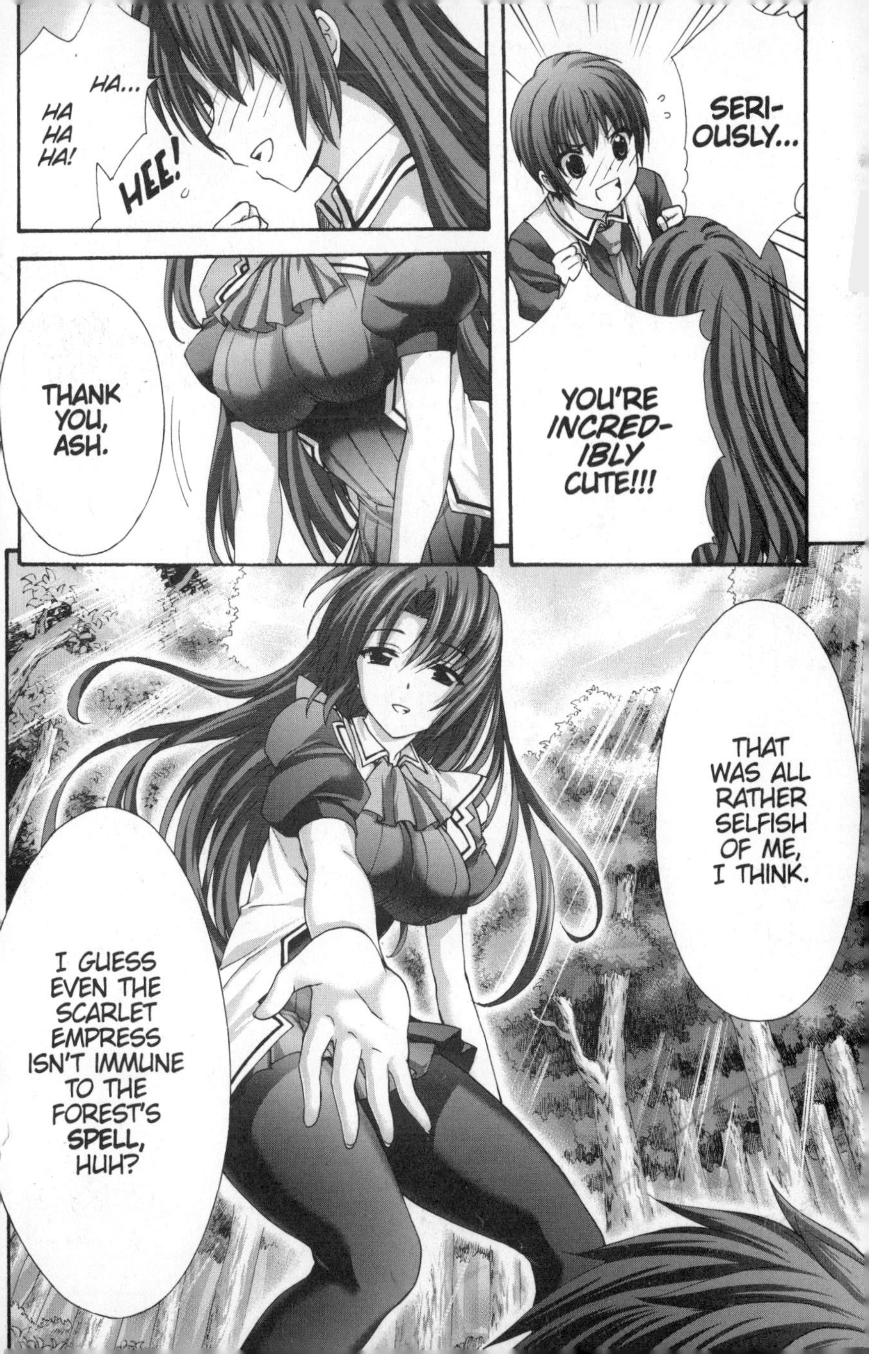
SERI-
OUSLY...
YOU'RE INCRED-IBLY CUTE!!!
HA...
HA HA HA!
HEE!
THANK YOU, ASH.
THAT WAS ALL RATHER SELFISH OF ME, I THINK.
I GUESS EVEN THE SCARLET EMPRESS ISN'T IMMUNE TO THE FOREST'S SPELL, HUH?

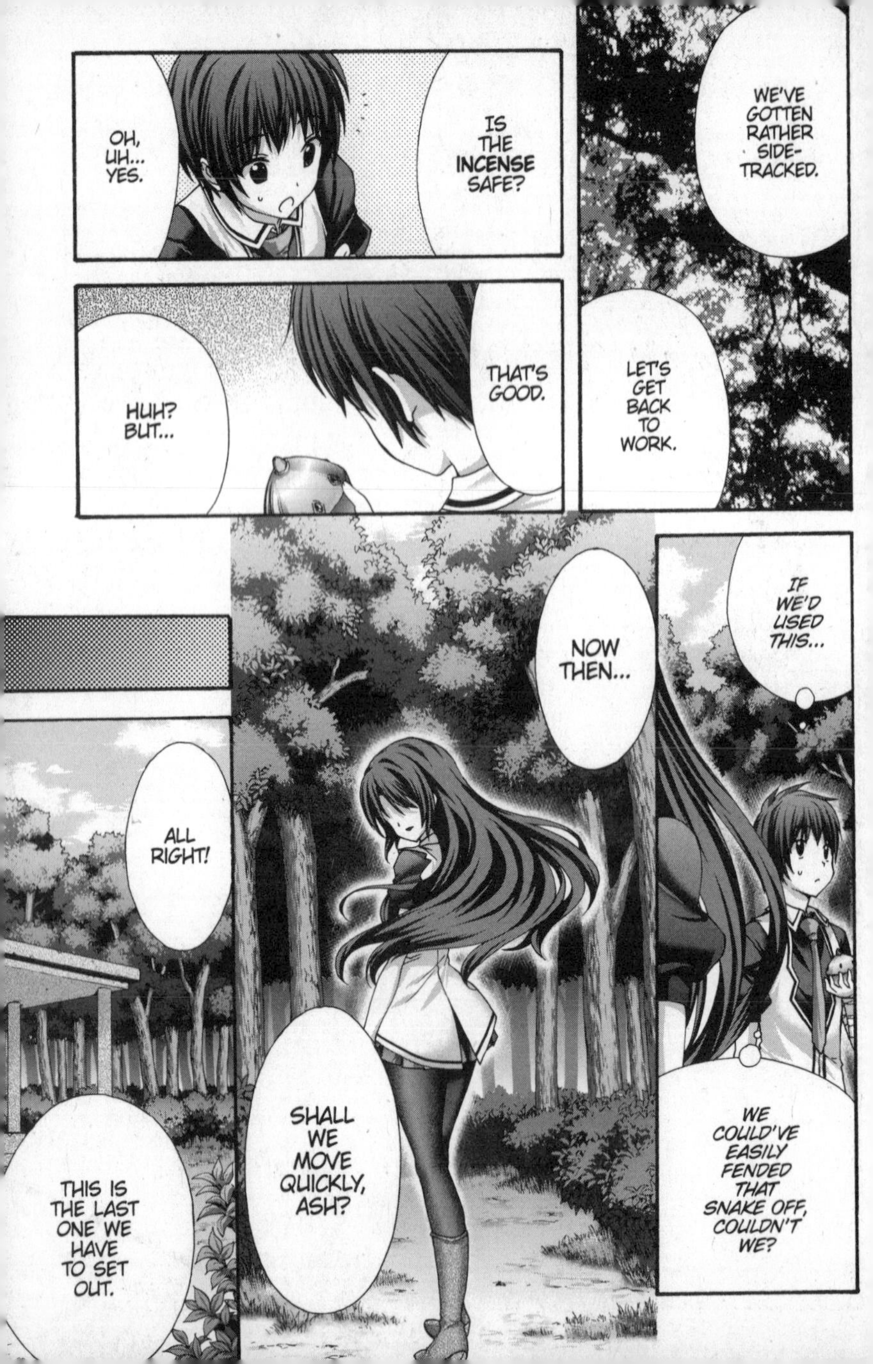
WE'VE GOTTEN RATHER SIDE-TRACKED.
LET'S GET BACK TO WORK.
IS THE INCENSE SAFE?
OH, UH... YES.
THAT'S GOOD.
HUH? BUT...
IF WE'D USED THIS...
WE COULD'VE EASILY FENDED THAT SNAKE OFF, COULDN'T WE?
NOW THEN...
SHALL WE MOVE QUICKLY, ASH?
ALL RIGHT!
THIS IS THE LAST ONE WE HAVE TO SET OUT.

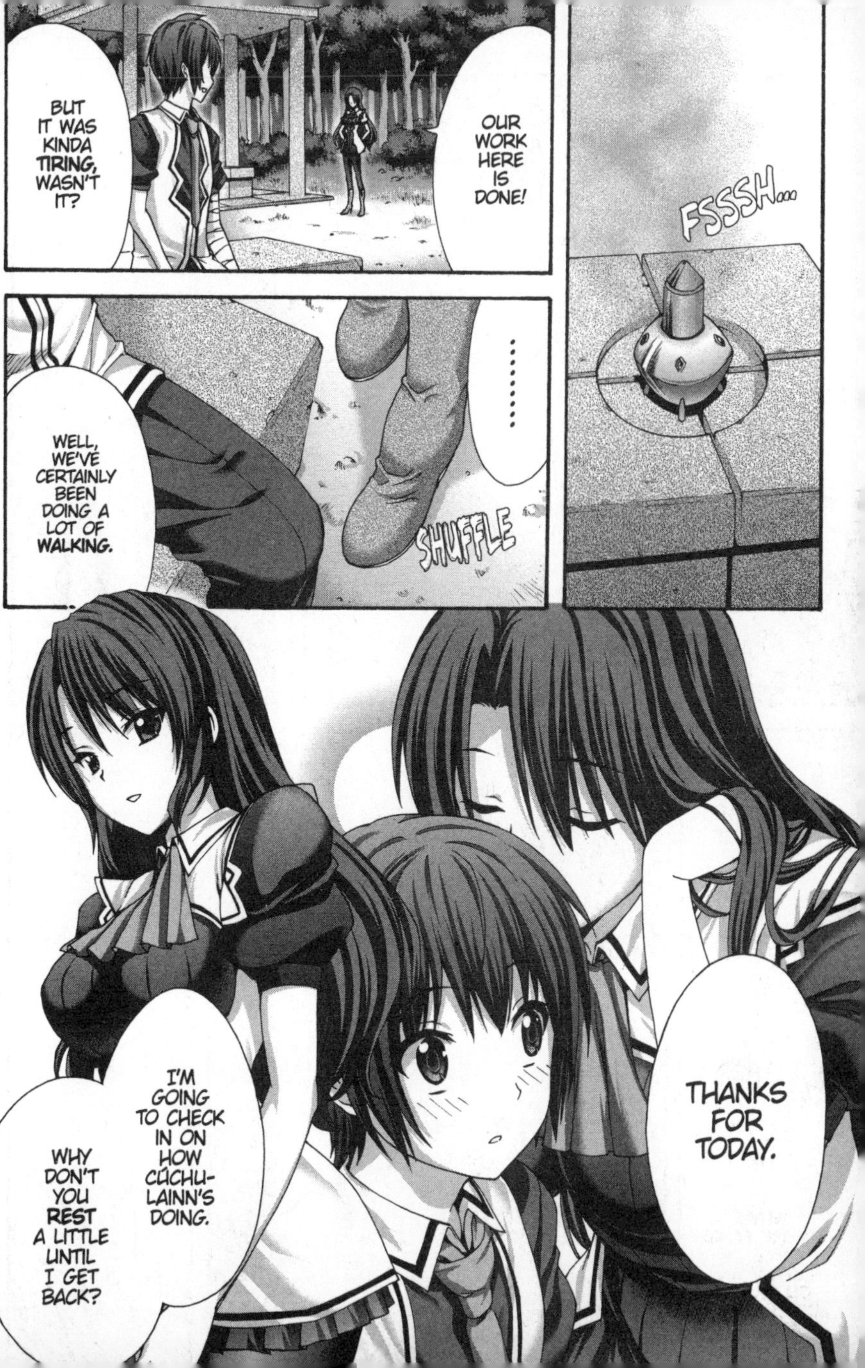
FSSSH...
OUR WORK HERE IS DONE!
BUT IT WAS KINDA TIRING, WASN'T IT?
......
SHUFFLE
WELL, WE'VE CERTAINLY BEEN DOING A LOT OF WALKING.
THANKS FOR TODAY.
I'M GOING TO CHECK IN ON HOW CÚCHULAINN'S DOING.
WHY DON'T YOU REST A LITTLE UNTIL I GET BACK?

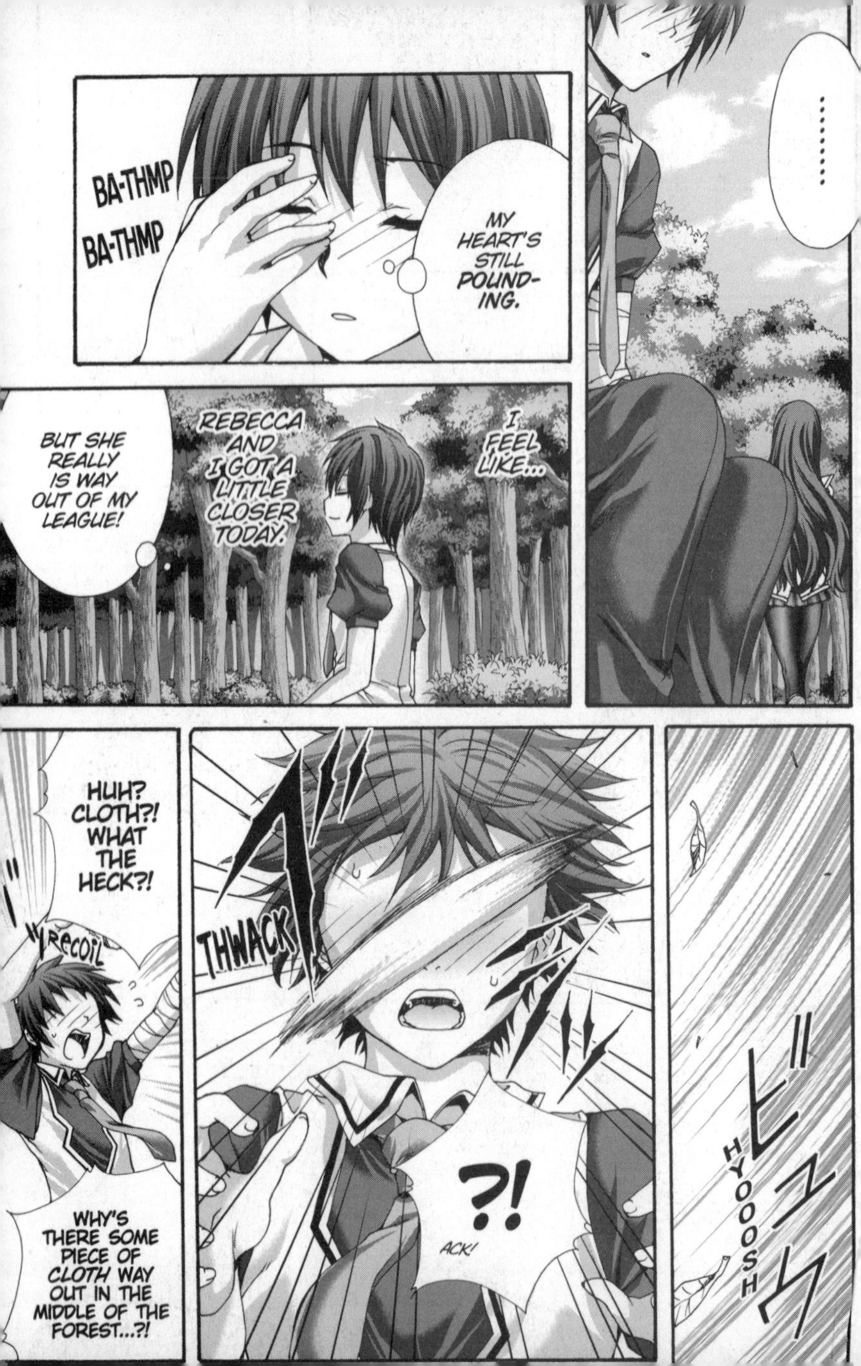
……
BA-THMP
BA-THMP
MY HEART'S STILL POUNDING.
I FEEL LIKE...
REBECCA AND I GOT A LITTLE CLOSER TODAY.
BUT SHE REALLY IS WAY OUT OF MY LEAGUE!
HYOOOSH
THWACK
?!
ACK!
HUH? CLOTH?! WHAT THE HECK?!
recoil
WHY'S THERE SOME PIECE OF CLOTH WAY OUT IN THE MIDDLE OF THE FOREST...?!

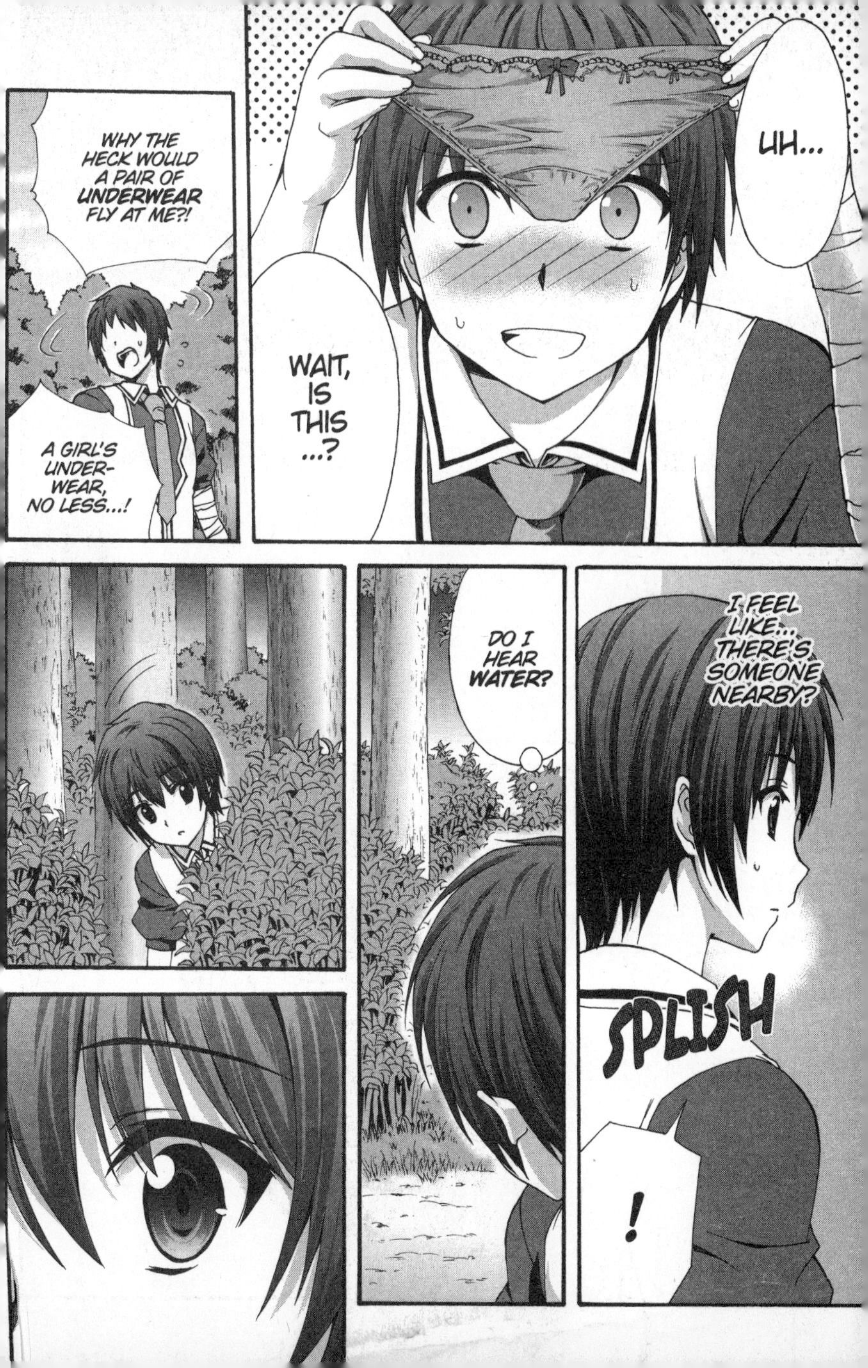
UH...
WAIT, IS THIS ...?
WHY THE HECK WOULD A PAIR OF UNDERWEAR FLY AT ME?!
A GIRL'S UNDER-WEAR, NO LESS...!
I FEEL LIKE... THERE'S SOMEONE NEARBY?
SPLISH
!
DO I HEAR WATER?

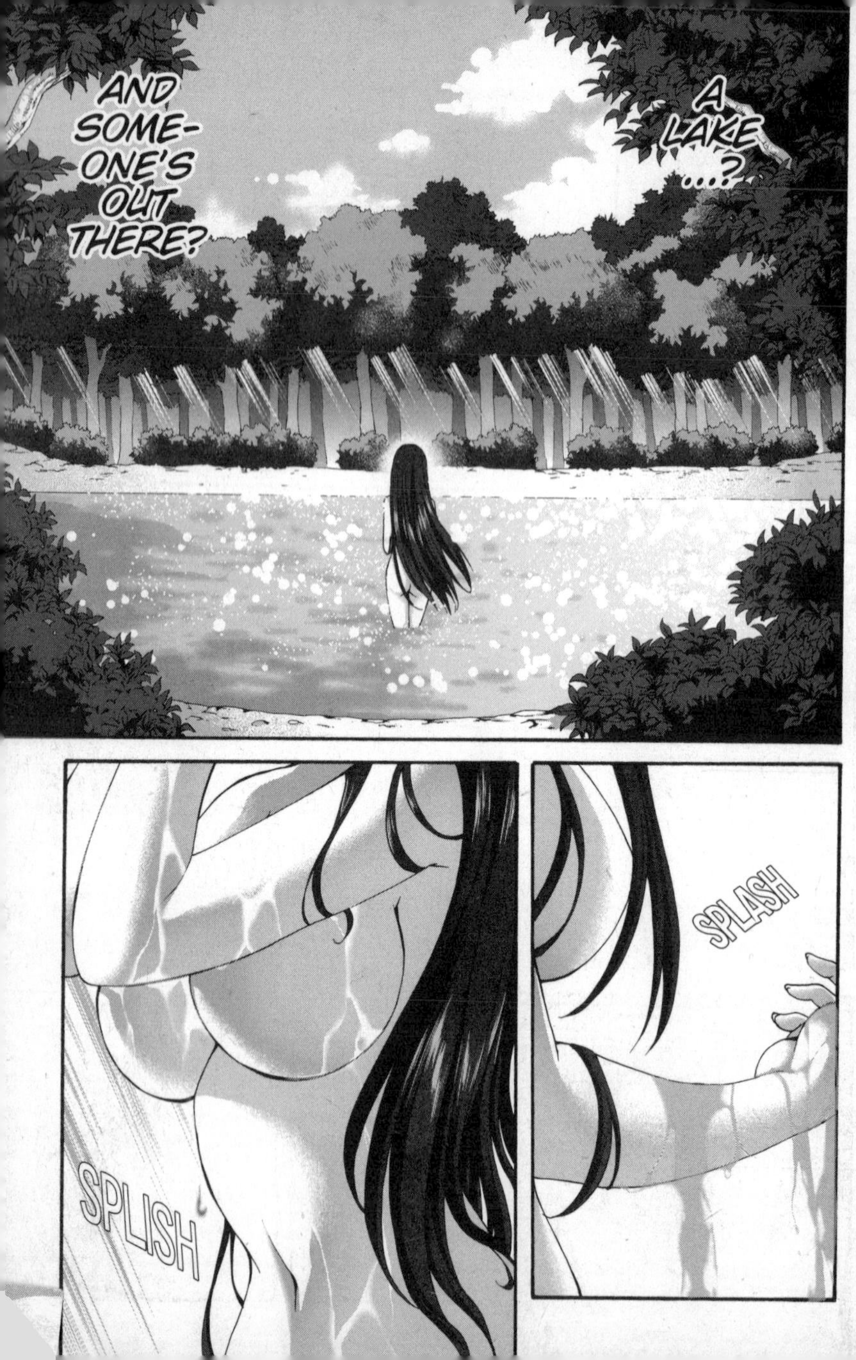
A LAKE...?
AND SOME-ONE'S OUT THERE?
SPLASH
SPLISH

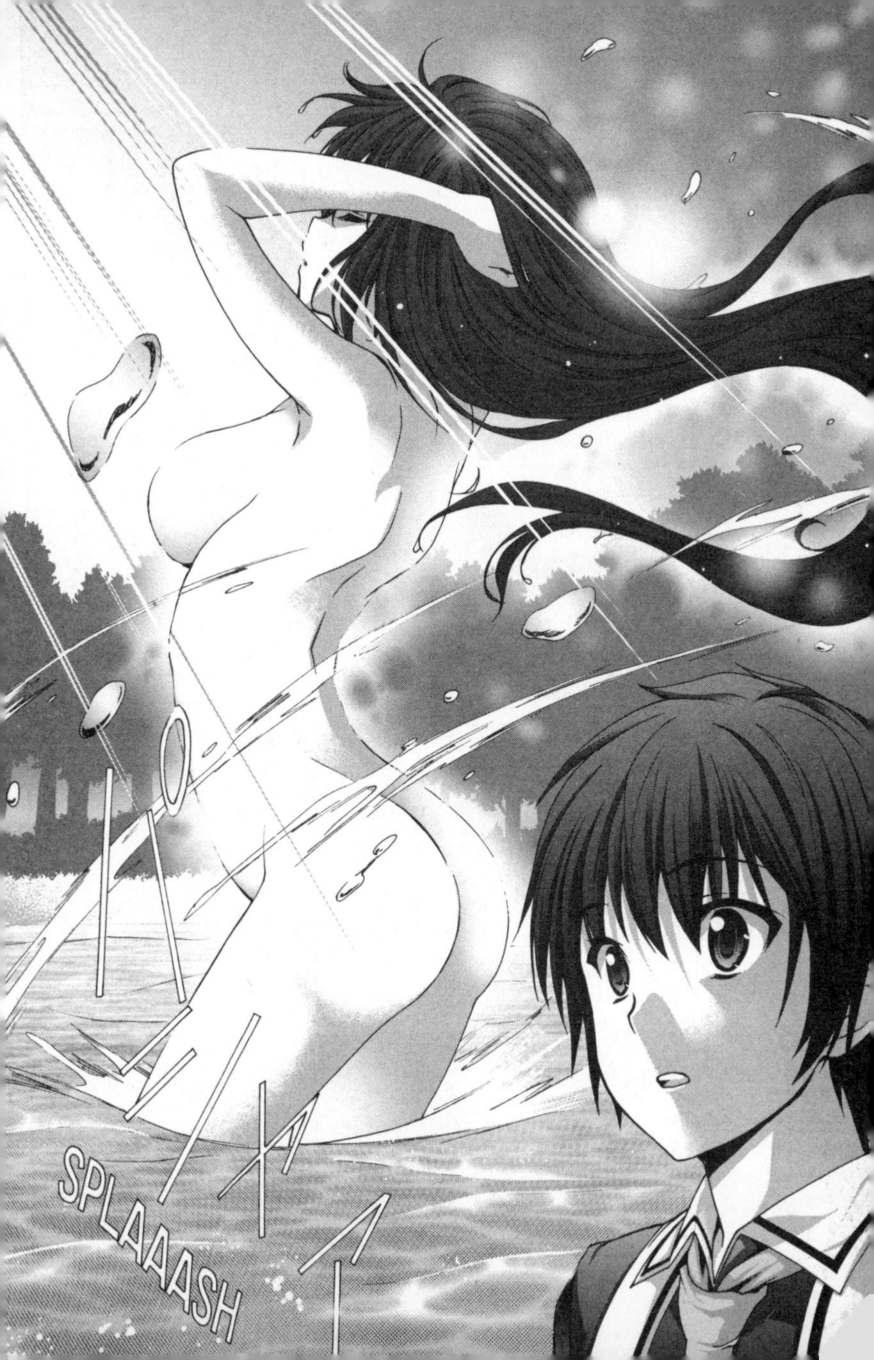
SPLAAASH

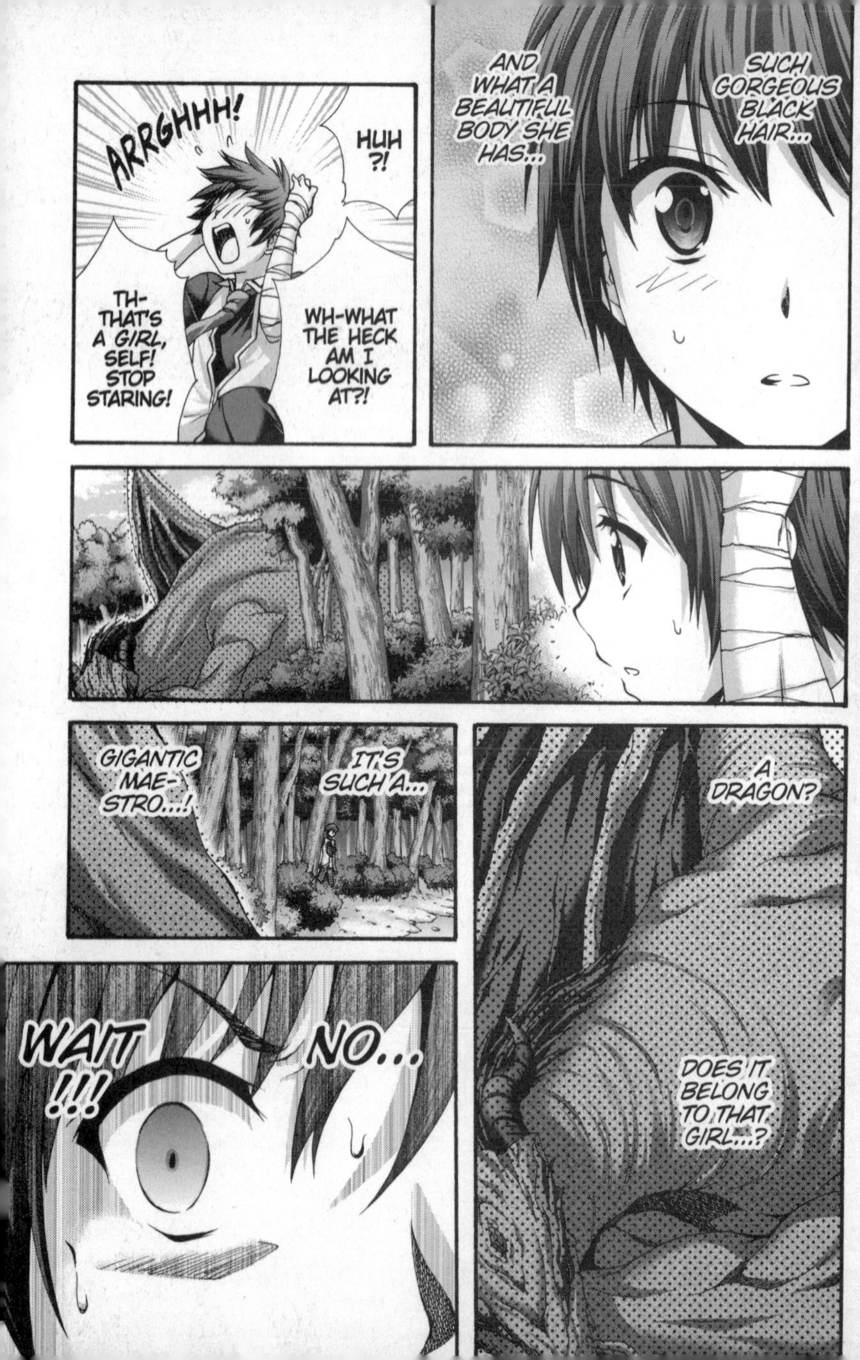
SUCH GORGEOUS BLACK HAIR...
AND WHAT A BEAUTIFUL BODY SHE HAS...
HUH ?!
ARRGHHH!
WH-WHAT THE HECK AM I LOOKING AT?!
TH-THAT'S A *GIRL*, SELF! STOP STARING!
A DRAGON?
DOES IT BELONG TO THAT GIRL...?
IT'S SUCH A...
GIGANTIC MAE-STRO...!
NO...
WAIT !!!

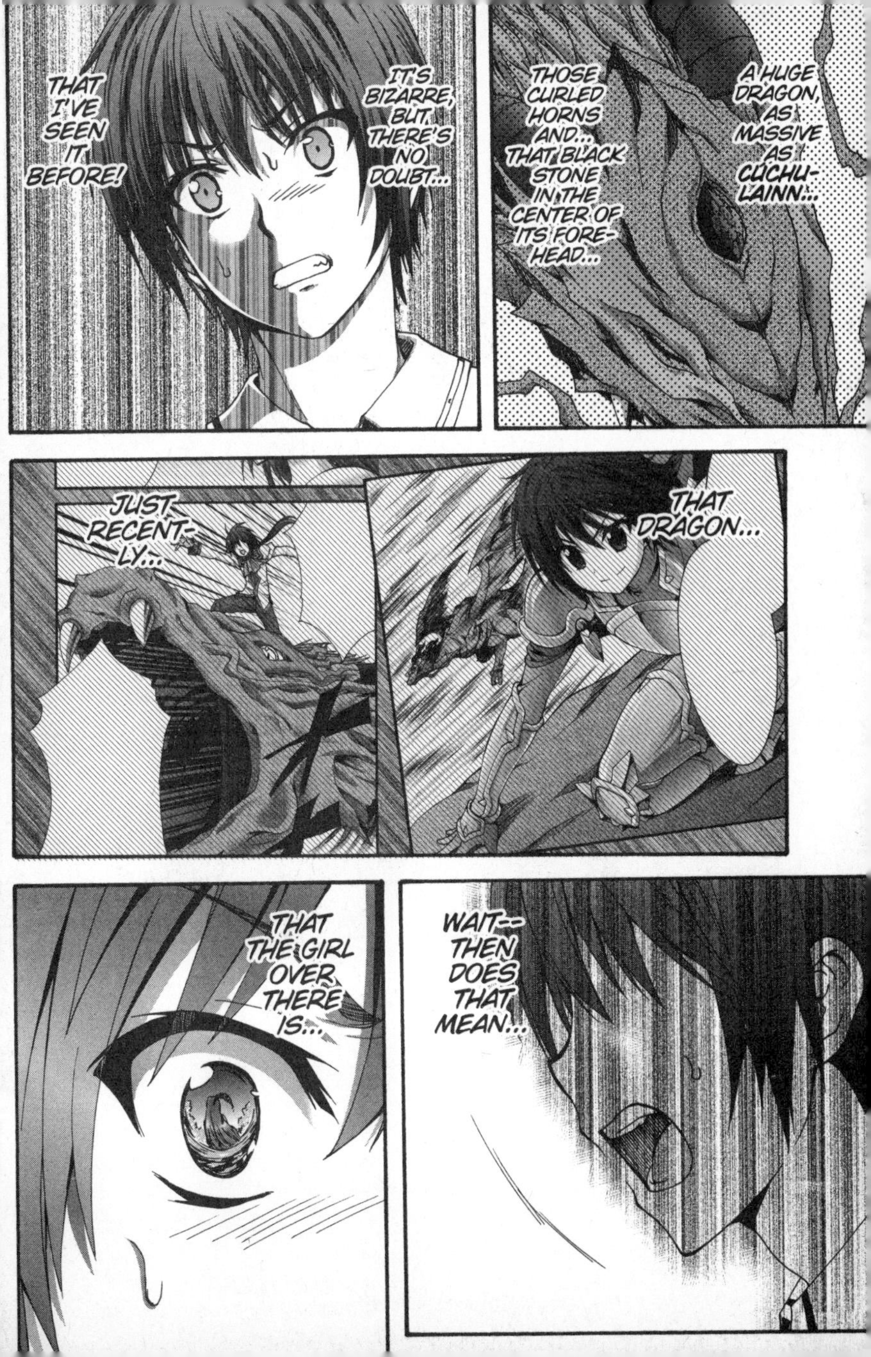
A HUGE DRAGON, AS MASSIVE AS CÚCHULAINN...
THOSE CURLED HORNS AND... THAT BLACK STONE IN THE CENTER OF ITS FORE-HEAD...
IT'S BIZARRE, BUT THERE'S NO DOUBT...
THAT I'VE SEEN IT BEFORE!
THAT DRAGON...
JUST RECENT-LY...
WAIT-- THEN DOES THAT MEAN...
THAT THE GIRL OVER THERE IS...

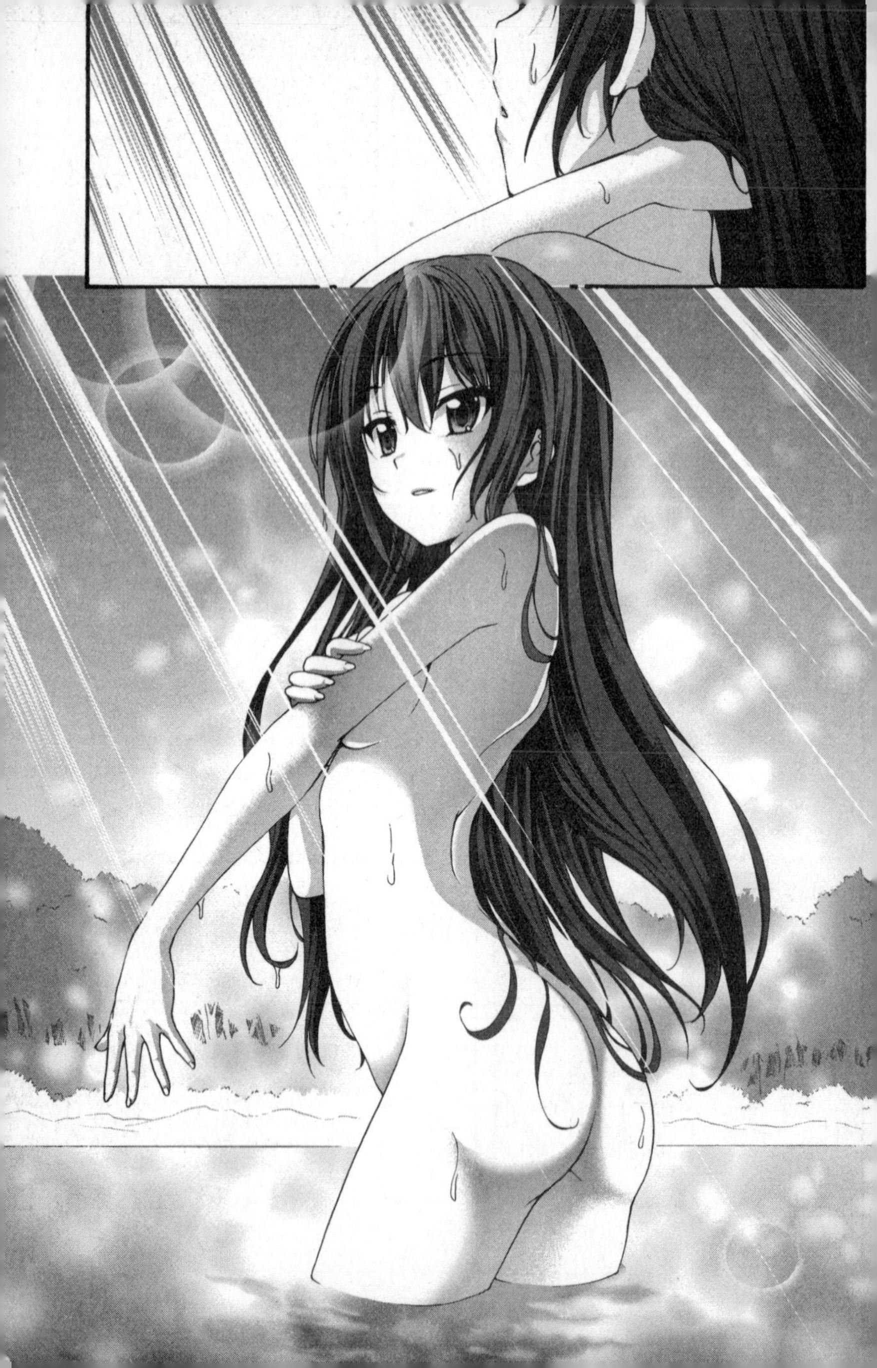

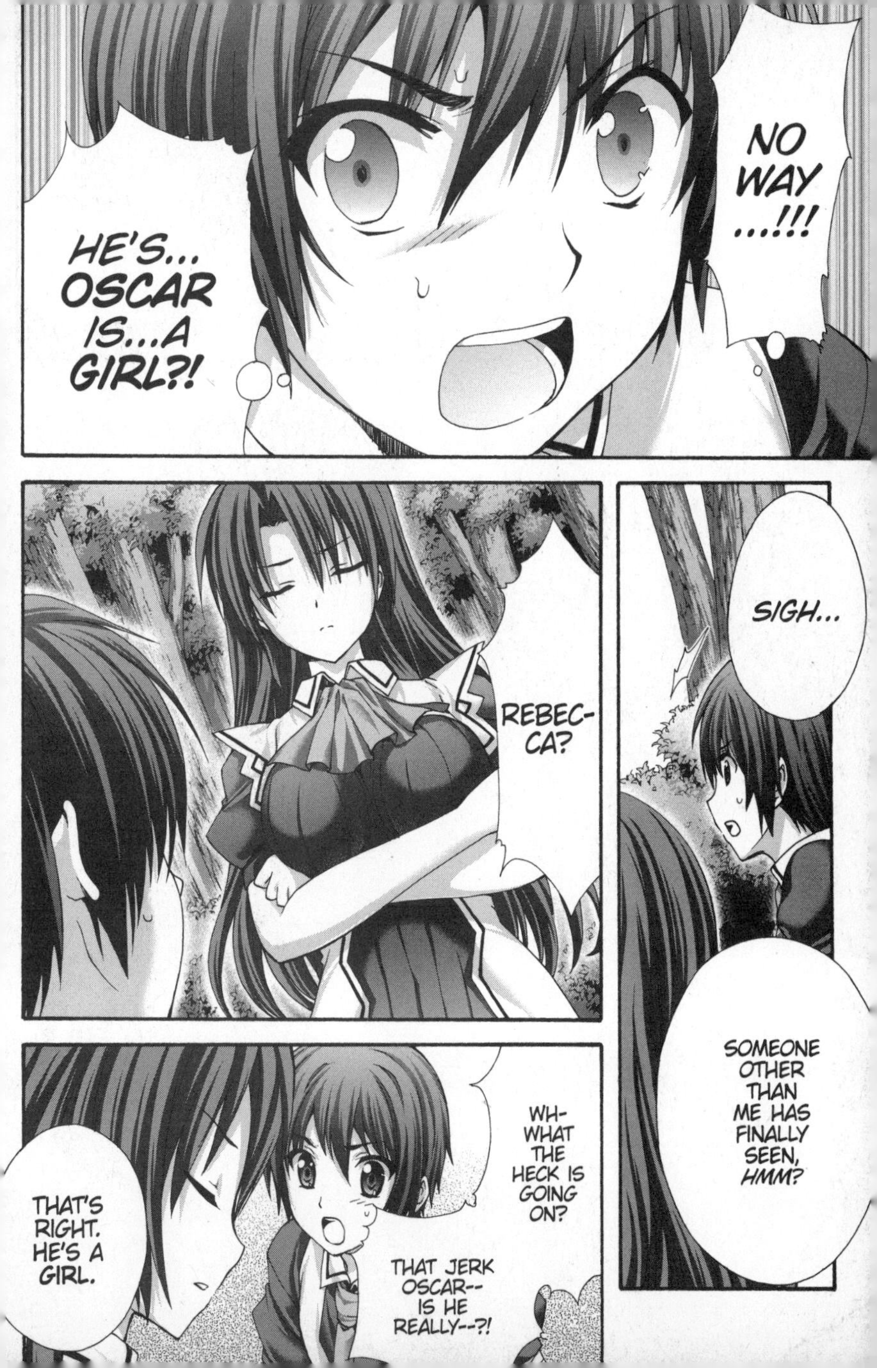
NO WAY ...!!!
HE'S... OSCAR IS...A GIRL?!
SIGH...
SOMEONE OTHER THAN ME HAS FINALLY SEEN, HMM?
REBEC-CA?
WH-WHAT THE HECK IS GOING ON?
THAT JERK OSCAR-- IS HE REALLY--?!
THAT'S RIGHT. HE'S A GIRL.

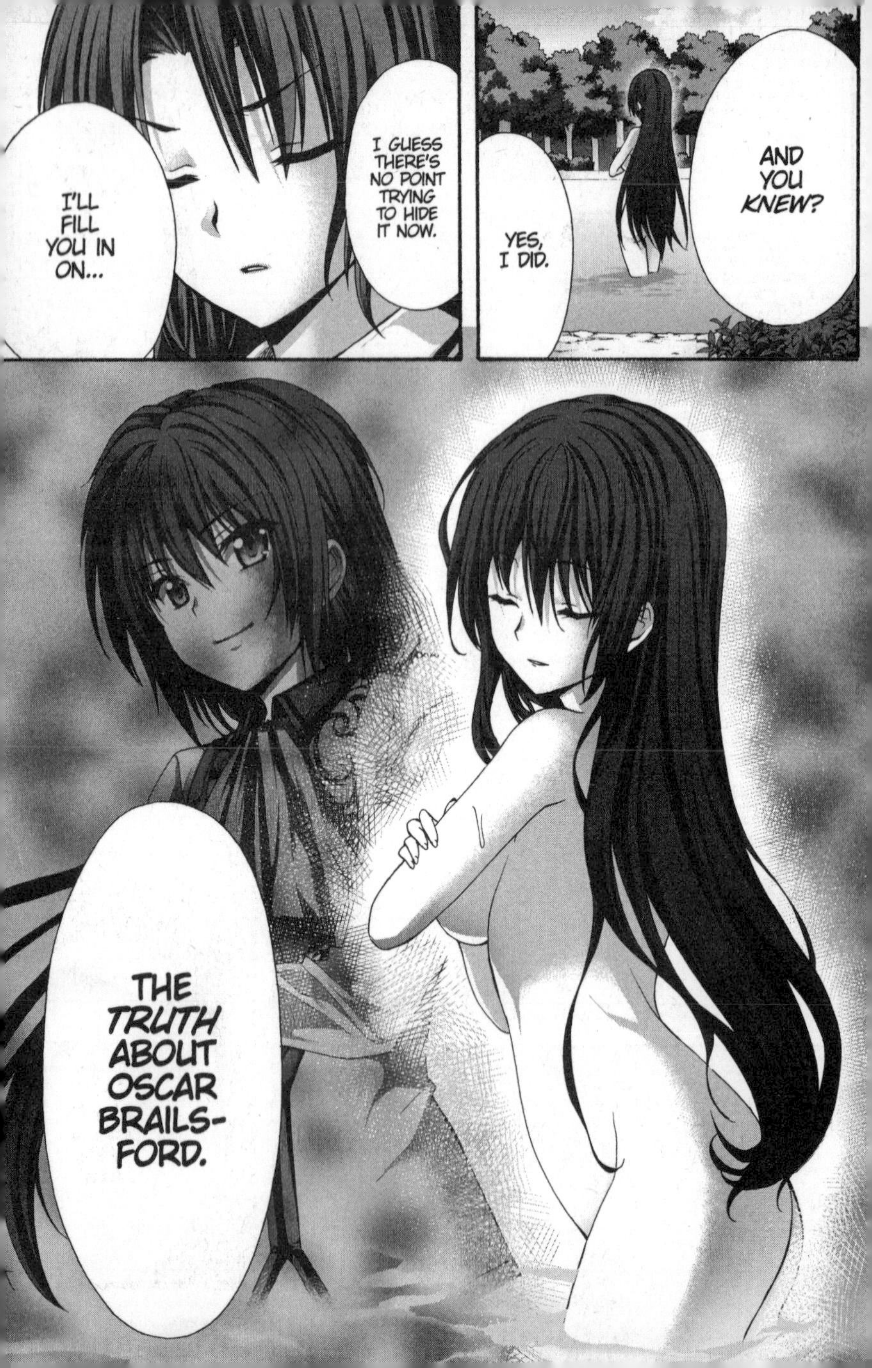
AND YOU KNEW?
YES, I DID.
I GUESS THERE'S NO POINT TRYING TO HIDE IT NOW.
I'LL FILL YOU IN ON...
THE *TRUTH* ABOUT OSCAR BRAILS-FORD.

DRAGONAR ACADEMY

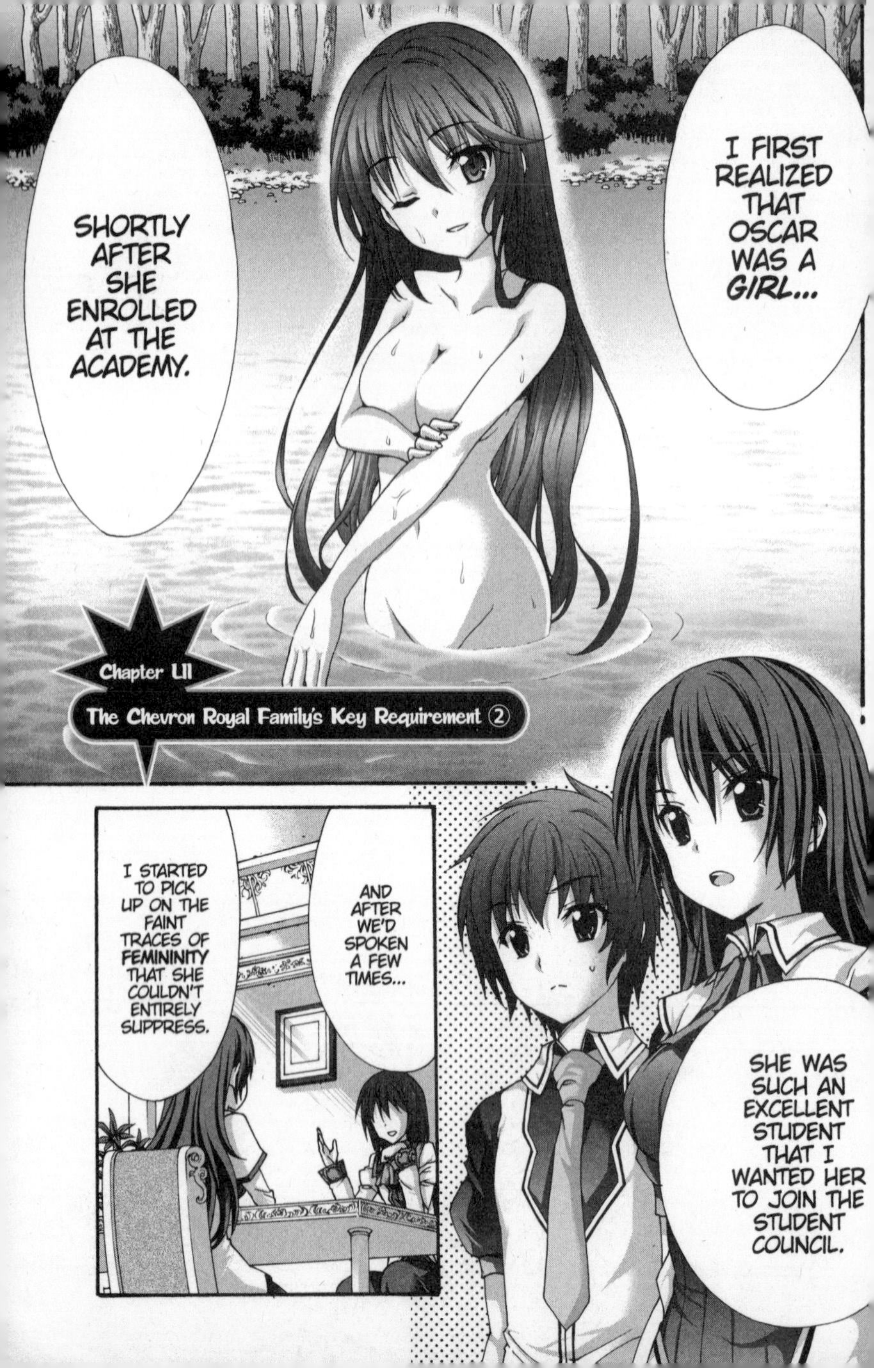
I FIRST REALIZED THAT OSCAR WAS A GIRL...
SHORTLY AFTER SHE ENROLLED AT THE ACADEMY.
Chapter LII
The Chevron Royal Family's Key Requirement ②
SHE WAS SUCH AN EXCELLENT STUDENT THAT I WANTED HER TO JOIN THE STUDENT COUNCIL.
AND AFTER WE'D SPOKEN A FEW TIMES...
I STARTED TO PICK UP ON THE FAINT TRACES OF FEMININITY THAT SHE COULDN'T ENTIRELY SUPPRESS.

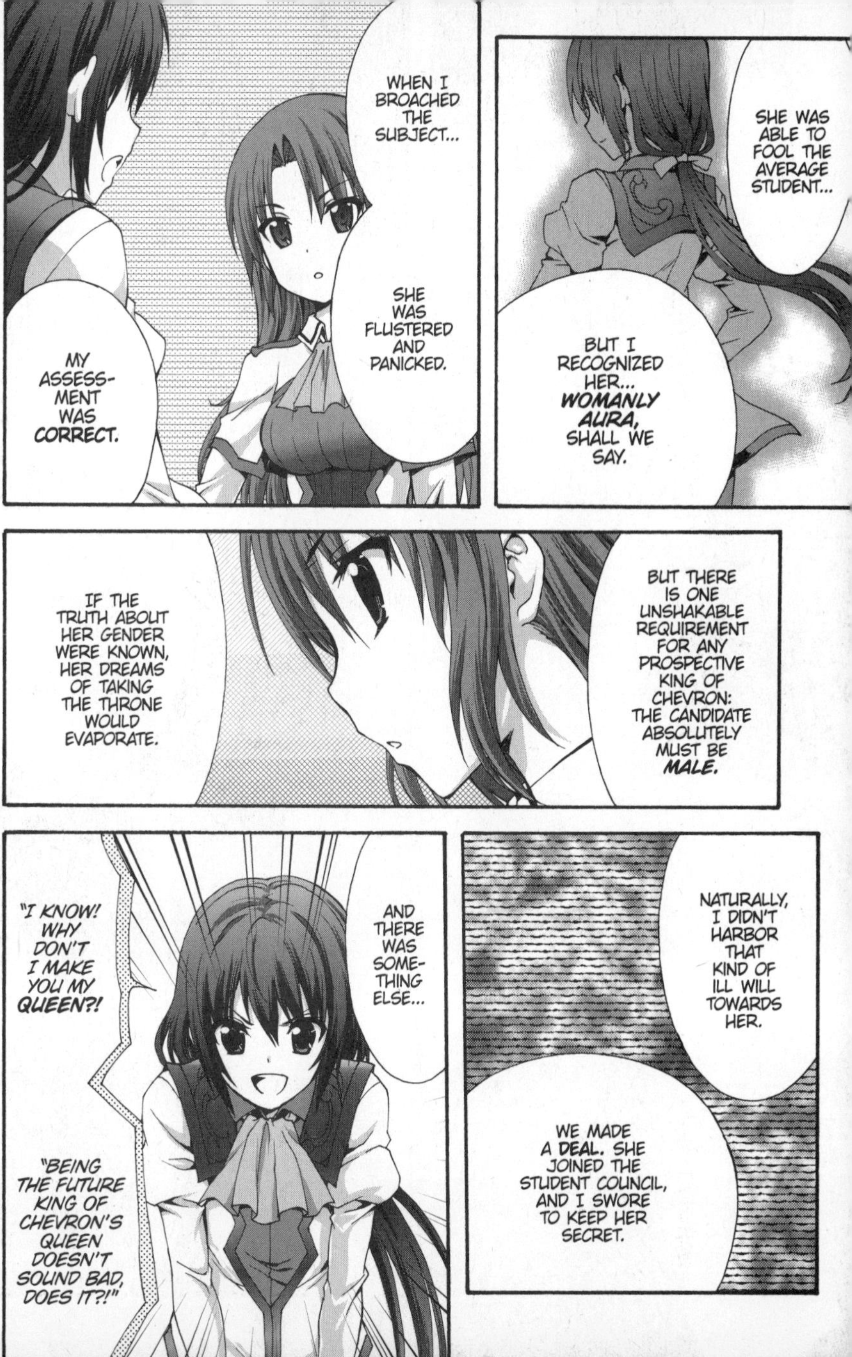
SHE WAS ABLE TO FOOL THE AVERAGE STUDENT...
BUT I RECOGNIZED HER... WOMANLY AURA, SHALL WE SAY.
WHEN I BROACHED THE SUBJECT...
SHE WAS FLUSTERED AND PANICKED.
MY ASSESSMENT WAS CORRECT.
BUT THERE IS ONE UNSHAKABLE REQUIREMENT FOR ANY PROSPECTIVE KING OF CHEVRON: THE CANDIDATE ABSOLUTELY MUST BE MALE.
IF THE TRUTH ABOUT HER GENDER WERE KNOWN, HER DREAMS OF TAKING THE THRONE WOULD EVAPORATE.
NATURALLY, I DIDN'T HARBOR THAT KIND OF ILL WILL TOWARDS HER.
WE MADE A DEAL. SHE JOINED THE STUDENT COUNCIL, AND I SWORE TO KEEP HER SECRET.
AND THERE WAS SOMETHING ELSE...
"I KNOW! WHY DON'T I MAKE YOU MY QUEEN?!
"BEING THE FUTURE KING OF CHEVRON'S QUEEN DOESN'T SOUND BAD, DOES IT?!"

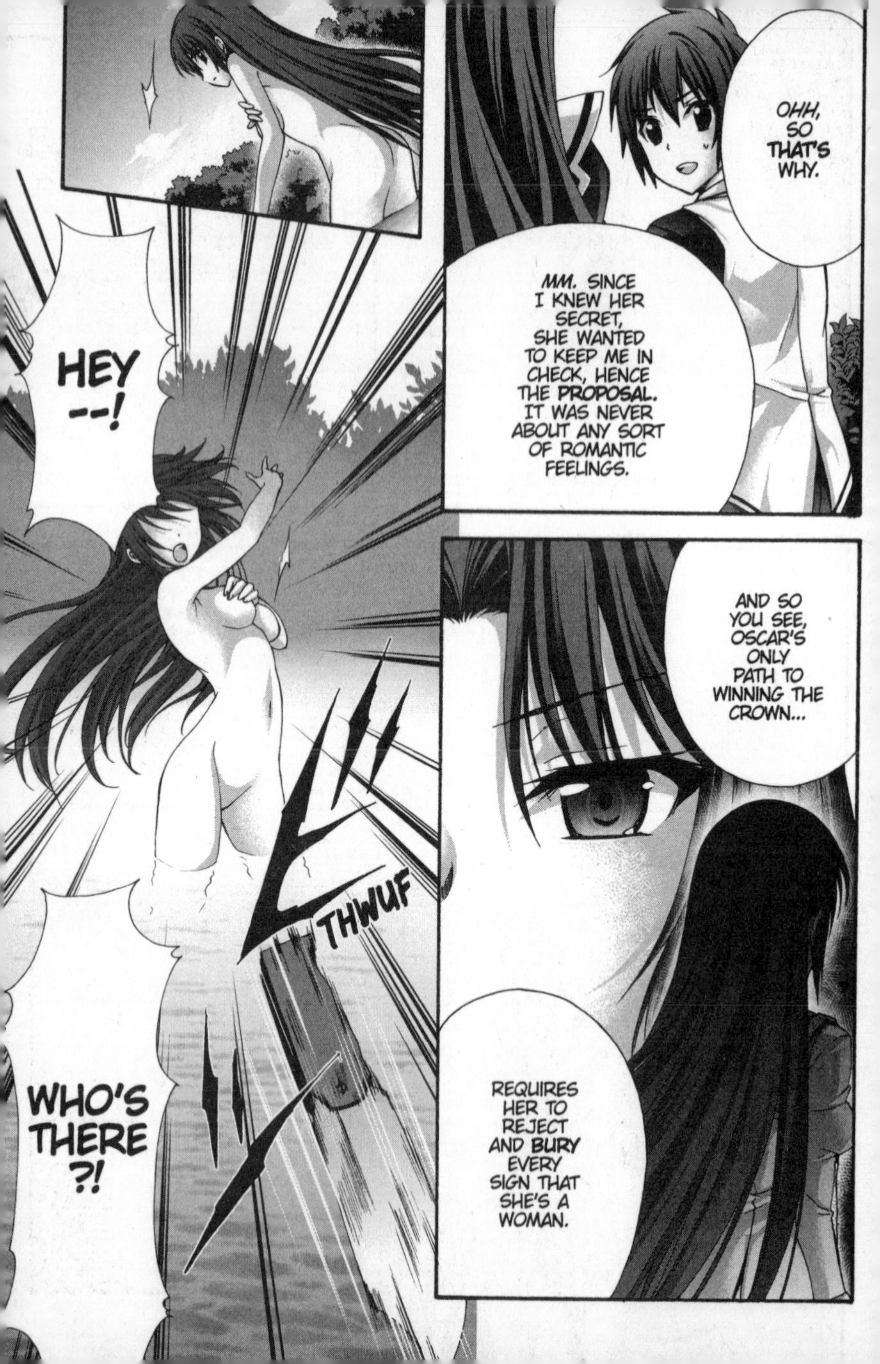
OHH, SO THAT'S WHY.
MM. SINCE I KNEW HER SECRET, SHE WANTED TO KEEP ME IN CHECK, HENCE THE PROPOSAL. IT WAS NEVER ABOUT ANY SORT OF ROMANTIC FEELINGS.
AND SO YOU SEE, OSCAR'S ONLY PATH TO WINNING THE CROWN...
REQUIRES HER TO REJECT AND BURY EVERY SIGN THAT SHE'S A WOMAN.
HEY --!
THWUF
WHO'S THERE ?!

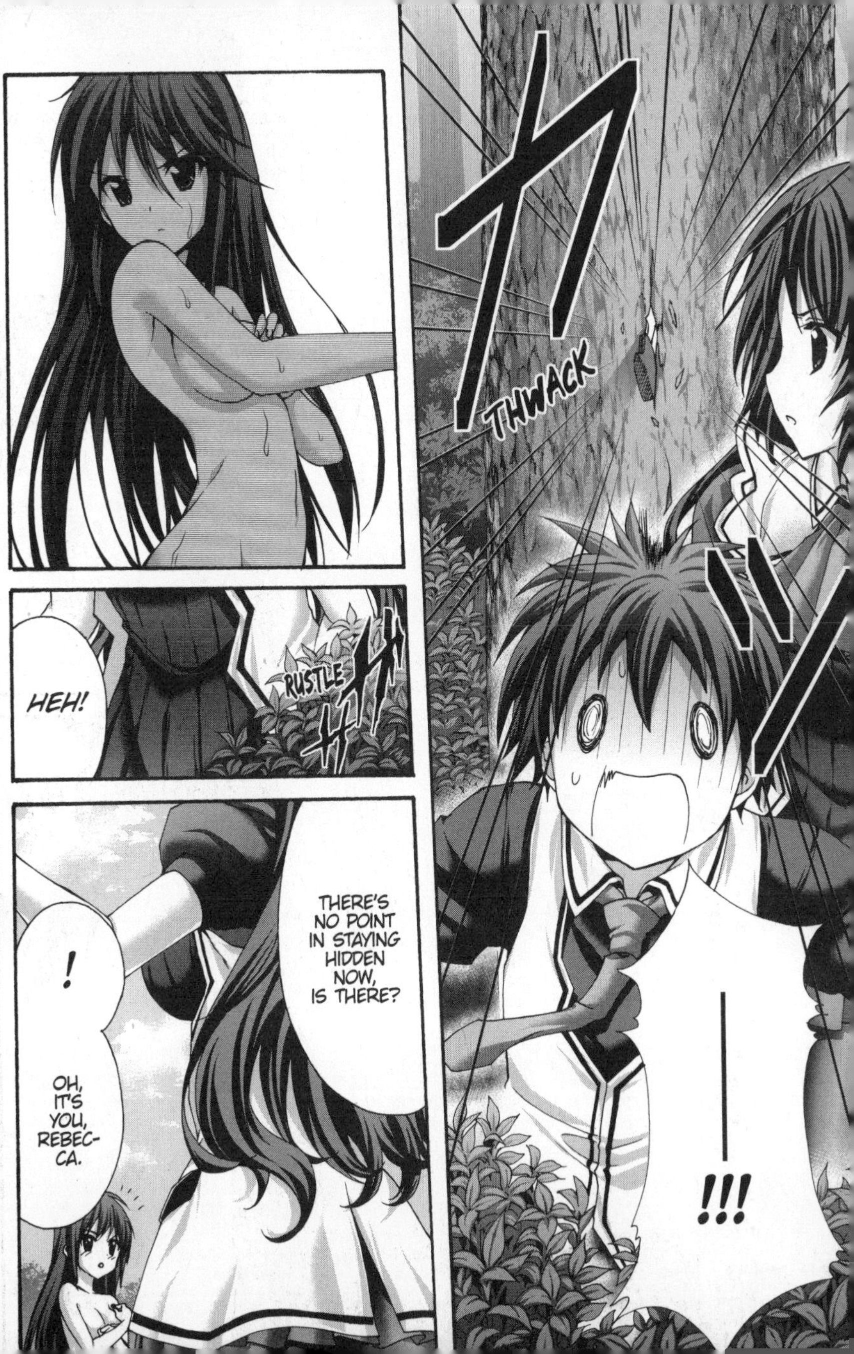
THWACK
—!!!
RUSTLE
HEH!
THERE'S NO POINT IN STAYING HIDDEN NOW, IS THERE?
!
OH, IT'S YOU, REBECCA.

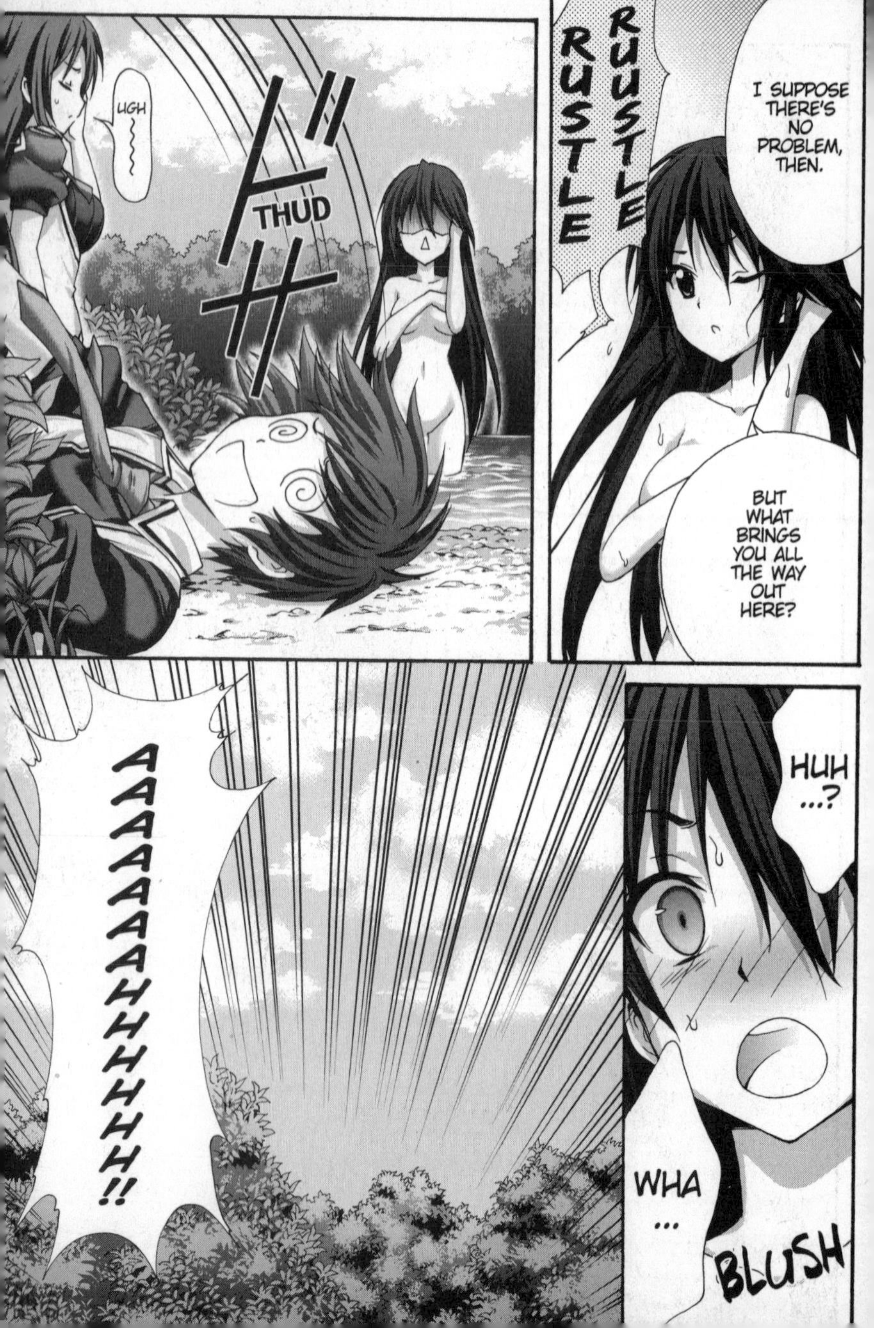
I SUPPOSE THERE'S NO PROBLEM, THEN.
RUUSTLE
RUSTLE
BUT WHAT BRINGS YOU ALL THE WAY OUT HERE?
THUD
UGH ~~~
HUH ...?
WHA ...
BLUSH
AAAAAAAAHHHHHHH!!

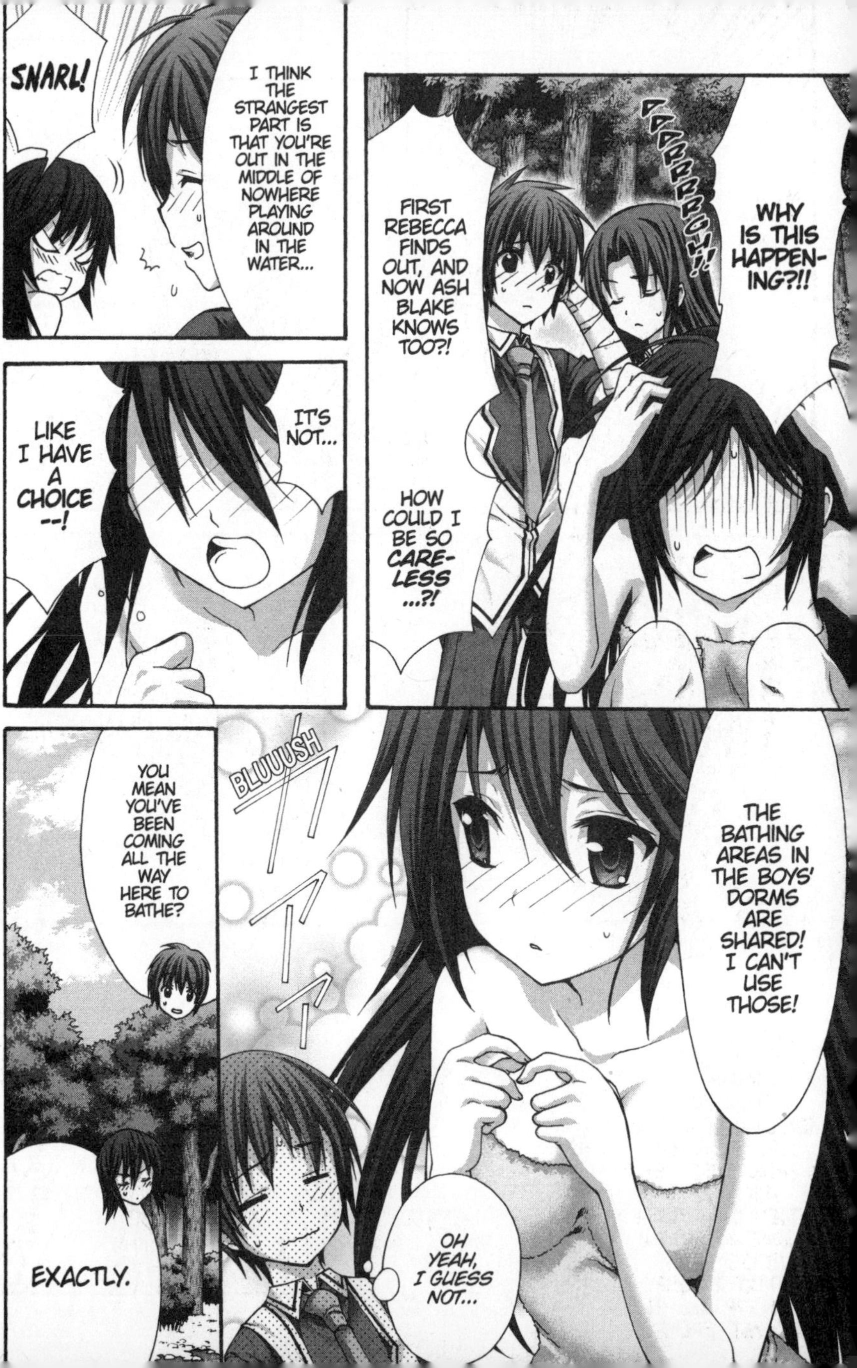
WHY IS THIS HAPPENING?!!
DRRRRRRGH!!
FIRST REBECCA FINDS OUT, AND NOW ASH BLAKE KNOWS TOO?!
HOW COULD I BE SO CARELESS...?!
I THINK THE STRANGEST PART IS THAT YOU'RE OUT IN THE MIDDLE OF NOWHERE PLAYING AROUND IN THE WATER...
SNARL!
IT'S NOT...
LIKE I HAVE A CHOICE--!
THE BATHING AREAS IN THE BOYS' DORMS ARE SHARED! I CAN'T USE THOSE!
BLUUUSH
OH YEAH, I GUESS NOT...
YOU MEAN YOU'VE BEEN COMING ALL THE WAY HERE TO BATHE?
EXACTLY.

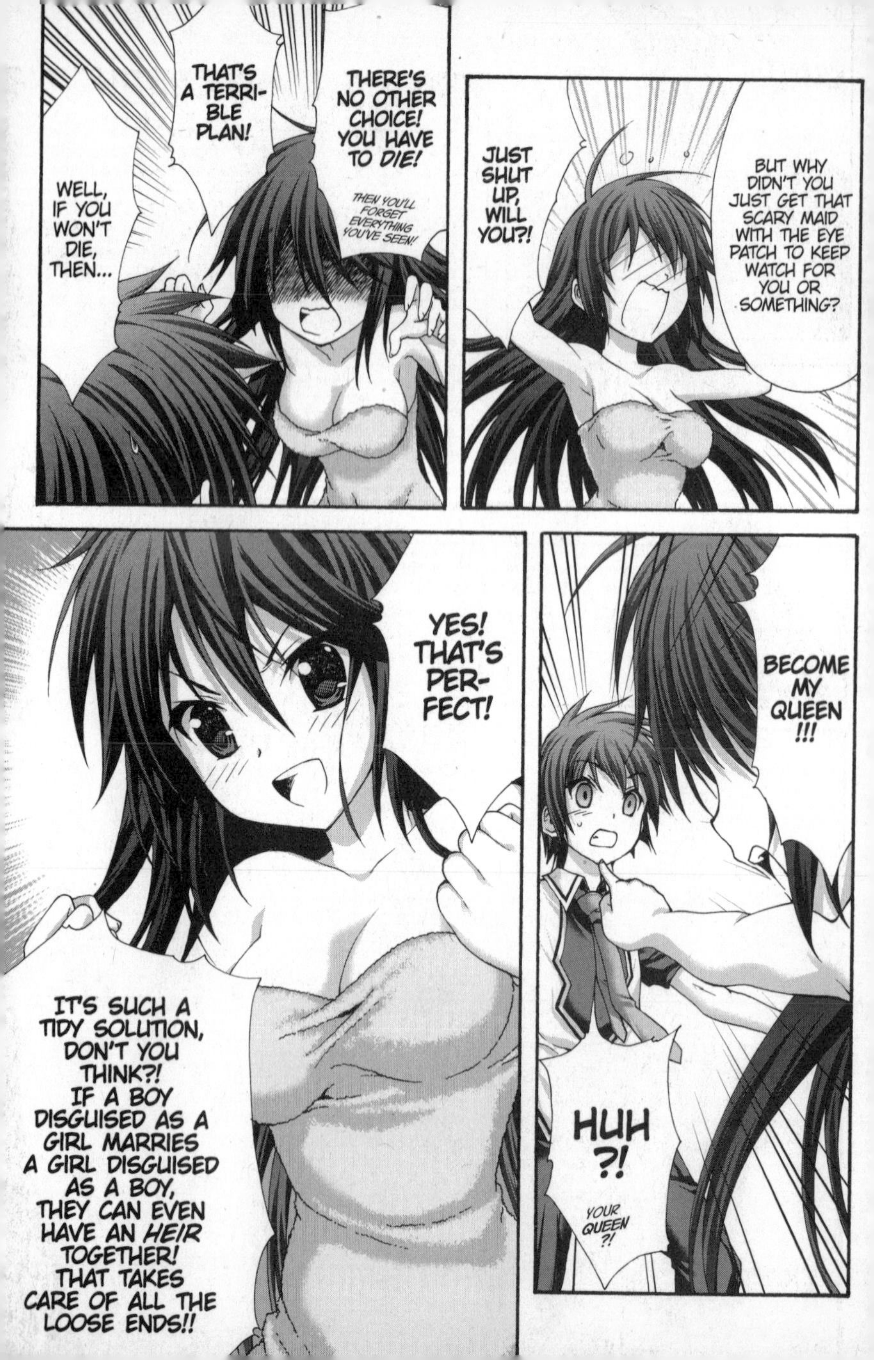
BUT WHY DIDN'T YOU JUST GET THAT SCARY MAID WITH THE EYE PATCH TO KEEP WATCH FOR YOU OR SOMETHING?
JUST SHUT UP, WILL YOU?!
THERE'S NO OTHER CHOICE! YOU HAVE TO *DIE!*
THEN YOU'LL FORGET EVERYTHING YOU'VE SEEN!
THAT'S A TERRI-BLE PLAN!
WELL, IF YOU WON'T DIE, THEN...
BECOME MY QUEEN!!!
HUH?!
YOUR QUEEN?!
YES! THAT'S PER-FECT!
IT'S SUCH A TIDY SOLUTION, DON'T YOU THINK?! IF A BOY DISGUISED AS A GIRL MARRIES A GIRL DISGUISED AS A BOY, THEY CAN EVEN HAVE AN *HEIR* TOGETHER! THAT TAKES CARE OF ALL THE LOOSE ENDS!!

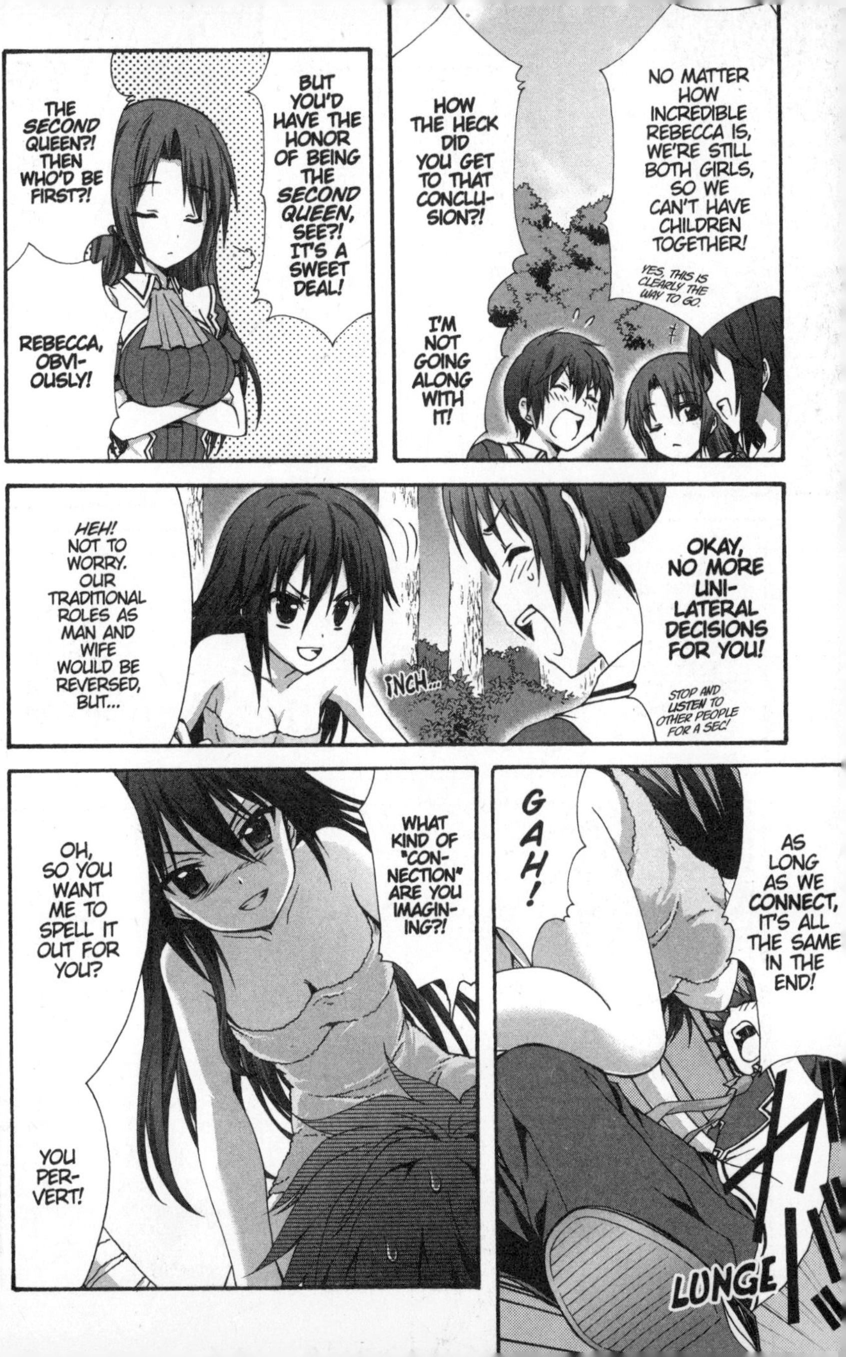
NO MATTER HOW INCREDIBLE REBECCA IS, WE'RE STILL BOTH GIRLS, SO WE CAN'T HAVE CHILDREN TOGETHER!
YES, THIS IS CLEARLY THE WAY TO GO.
HOW THE HECK DID YOU GET TO THAT CONCLU-SION?!
I'M NOT GOING ALONG WITH IT!
BUT YOU'D HAVE THE HONOR OF BEING THE SECOND QUEEN, SEE?! IT'S A SWEET DEAL!
THE SECOND QUEEN?! THEN WHO'D BE FIRST?!
REBECCA, OBVI-OUSLY!
OKAY, NO MORE UNI-LATERAL DECISIONS FOR YOU!
STOP AND LISTEN TO OTHER PEOPLE FOR A SEC!
INCH...
HEH! NOT TO WORRY. OUR TRADITIONAL ROLES AS MAN AND WIFE WOULD BE REVERSED, BUT...
AS LONG AS WE CONNECT, IT'S ALL THE SAME IN THE END!
GAH!
LUNGE
WHAT KIND OF "CON-NECTION" ARE YOU IMAGIN-ING?!
OH, SO YOU WANT ME TO SPELL IT OUT FOR YOU?
YOU PER-VERT!

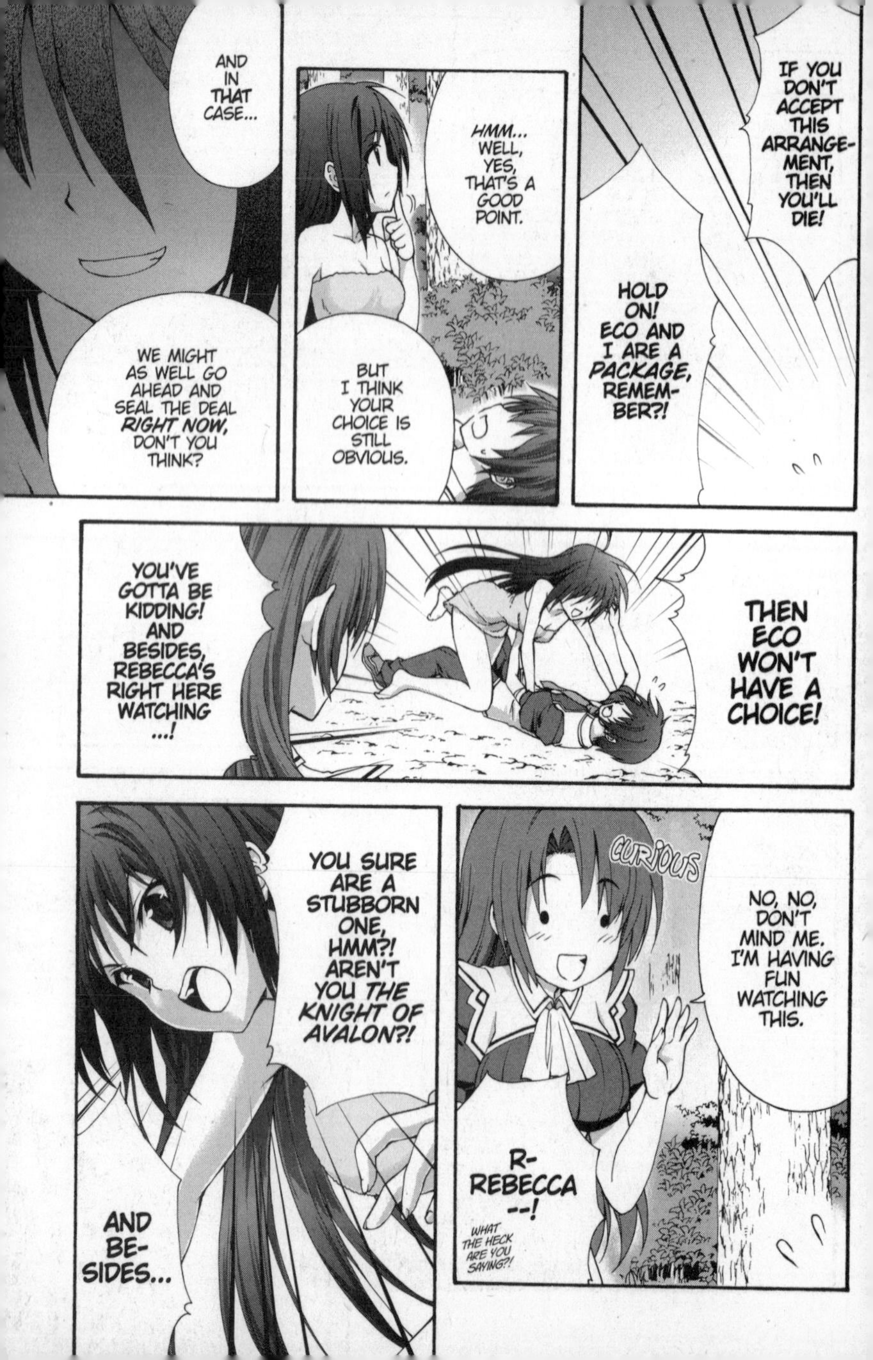
IF YOU DON'T ACCEPT THIS ARRANGEMENT, THEN YOU'LL DIE!
HOLD ON! ECO AND I ARE A PACKAGE, REMEMBER?!
HMM... WELL, YES, THAT'S A GOOD POINT.
BUT I THINK YOUR CHOICE IS STILL OBVIOUS.
AND IN THAT CASE...
WE MIGHT AS WELL GO AHEAD AND SEAL THE DEAL RIGHT NOW, DON'T YOU THINK?
THEN ECO WON'T HAVE A CHOICE!
YOU'VE GOTTA BE KIDDING! AND BESIDES, REBECCA'S RIGHT HERE WATCHING...!
CURIOUS
NO, NO, DON'T MIND ME. I'M HAVING FUN WATCHING THIS.
R-REBECCA--!
WHAT THE HECK ARE YOU SAYING?!
YOU SURE ARE A STUBBORN ONE, HMM?! AREN'T YOU THE KNIGHT OF AVALON?!
AND BESIDES...

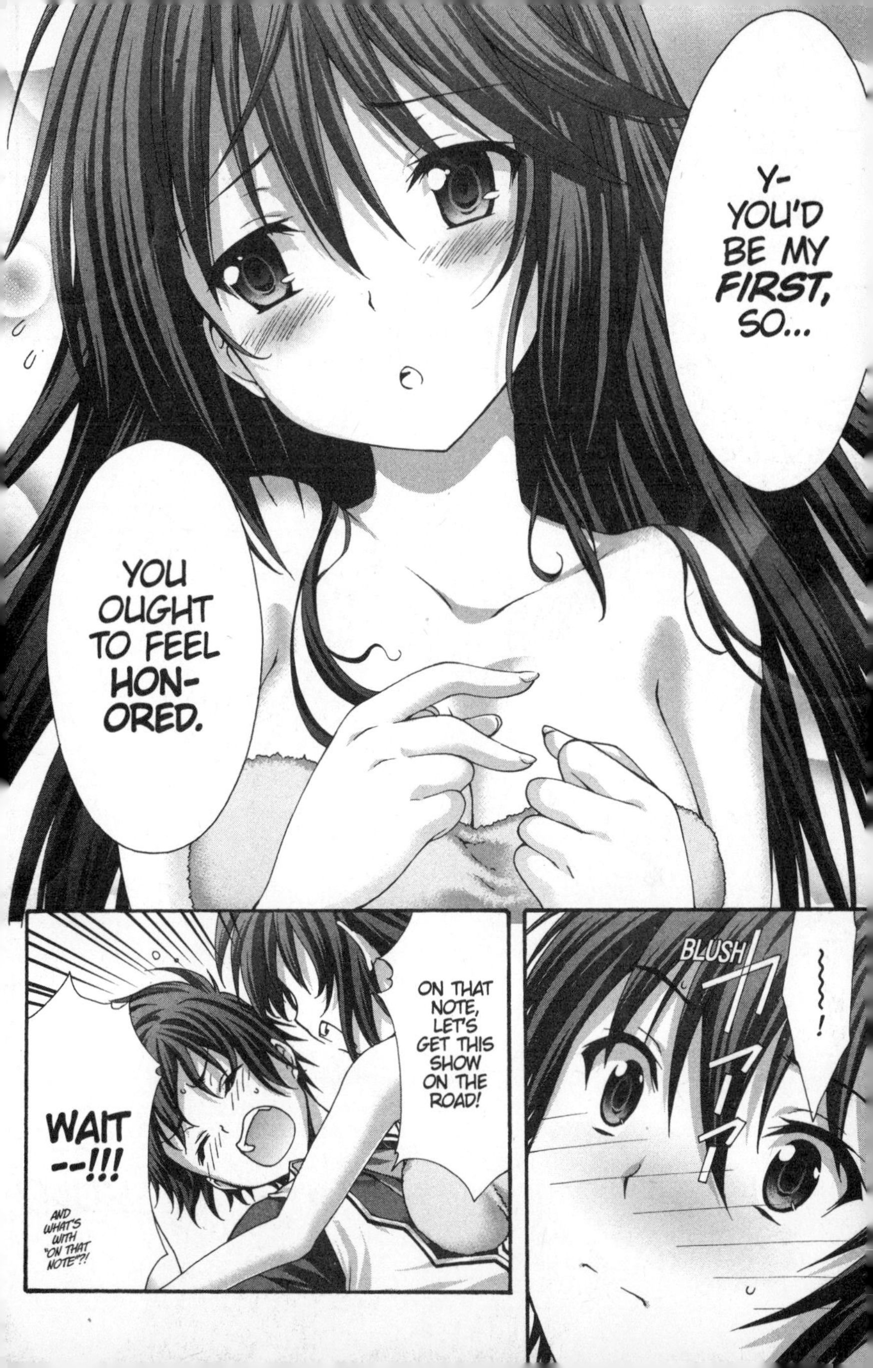
Y-YOU'D BE MY FIRST, SO...
YOU OUGHT TO FEEL HON-ORED.
BLUSH
~~~!
ON THAT NOTE, LET'S GET THIS SHOW ON THE ROAD!
WAIT--!!!
AND WHAT'S WITH "ON THAT NOTE"?!
~~~

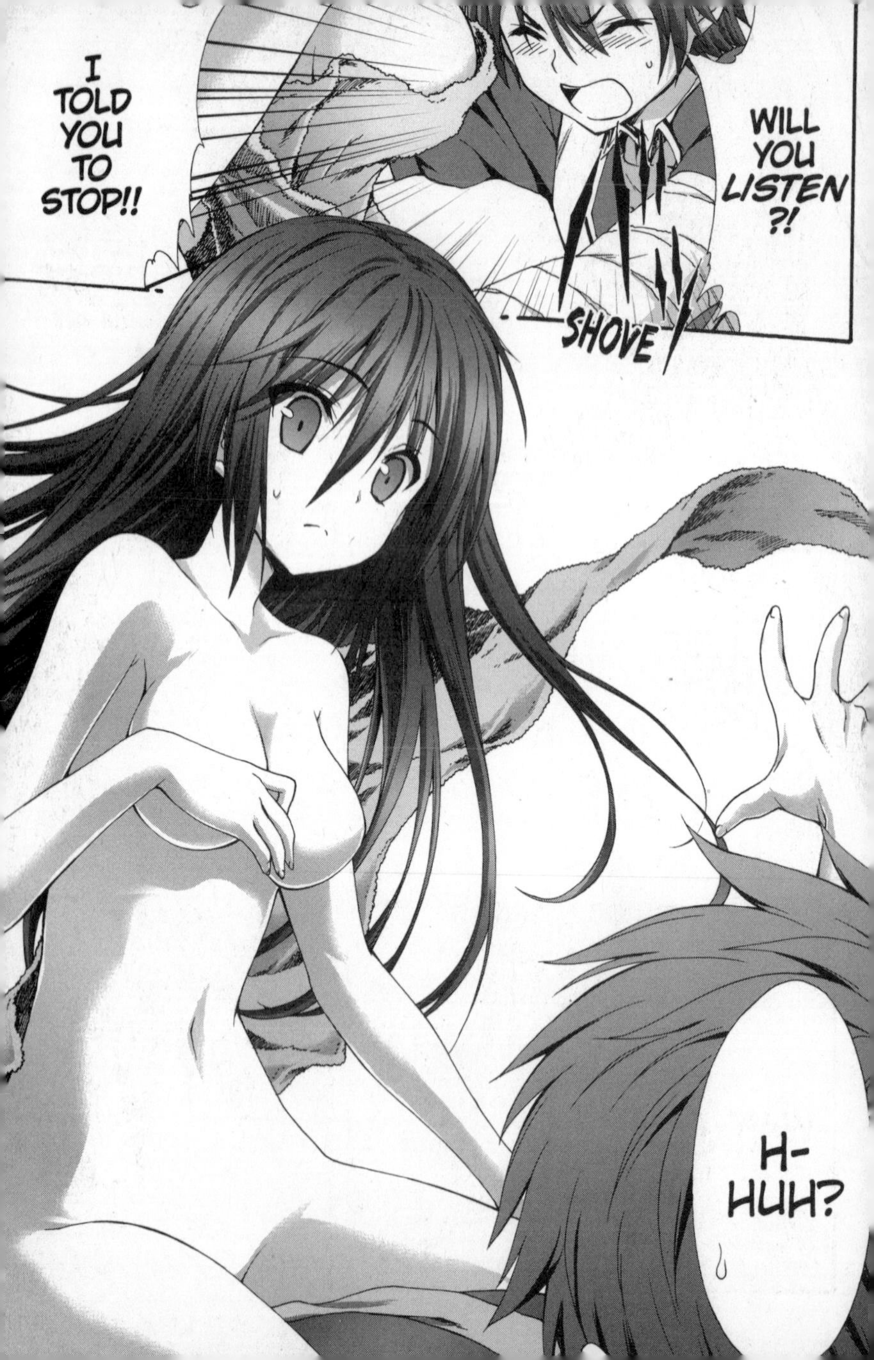
WILL YOU LISTEN?!
I TOLD YOU TO STOP!!
SHOVE
H-HUH?

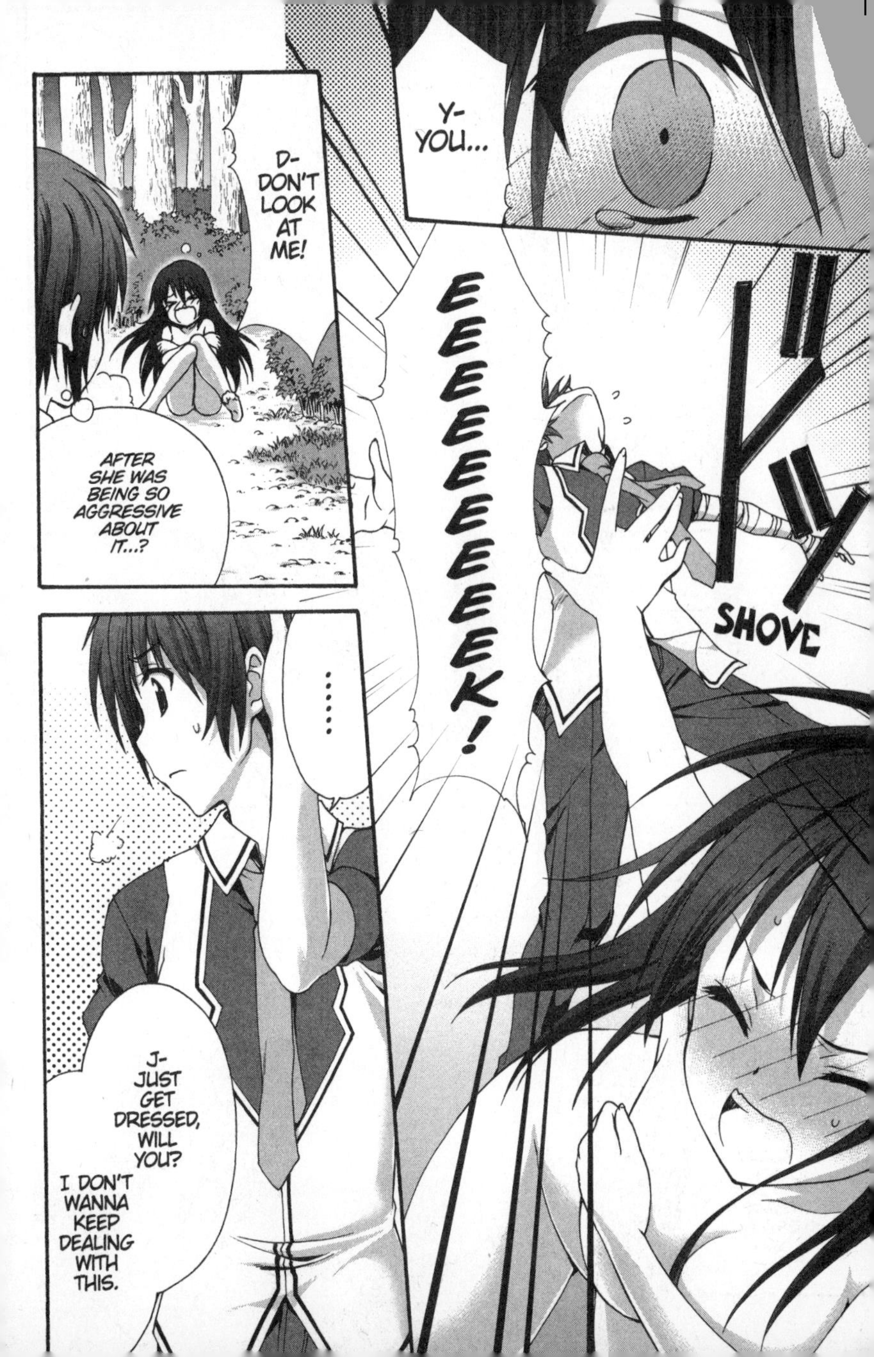
Y-
YOU...
EEEEEEEEEEK!
SHOVE
D-
DON'T LOOK AT ME!
AFTER SHE WAS BEING SO AGGRESSIVE ABOUT IT...?
......
J-
JUST GET DRESSED, WILL YOU?
I DON'T WANNA KEEP DEALING WITH THIS.

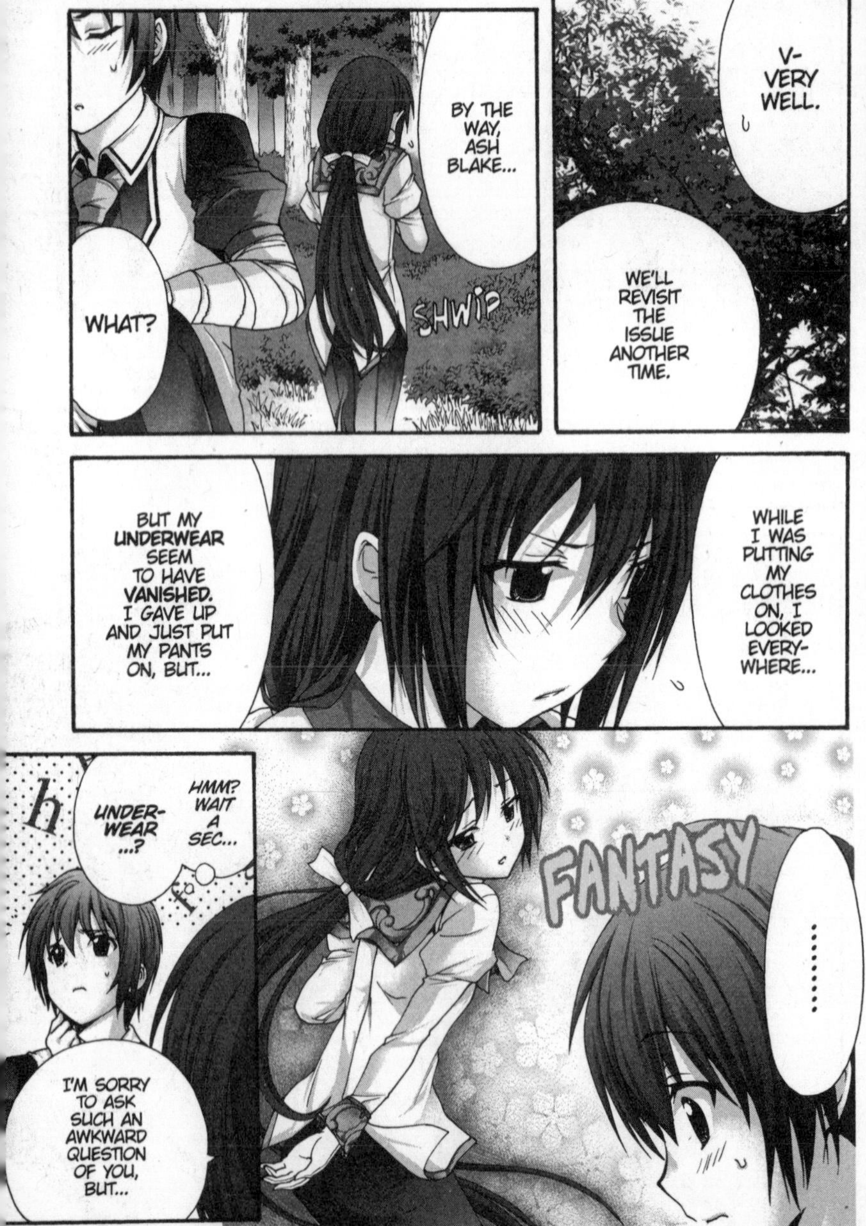
V-VERY WELL.
WE'LL REVISIT THE ISSUE ANOTHER TIME.
BY THE WAY, ASH BLAKE...
SHWIP
WHAT?
WHILE I WAS PUTTING MY CLOTHES ON, I LOOKED EVERYWHERE...
BUT MY **UNDERWEAR** SEEM TO HAVE **VANISHED.** I GAVE UP AND JUST PUT MY PANTS ON, BUT...
FANTASY
......
I'M SORRY TO ASK SUCH AN AWKWARD QUESTION OF YOU, BUT...
HMM? WAIT A SEC...
UNDER-WEAR ...?

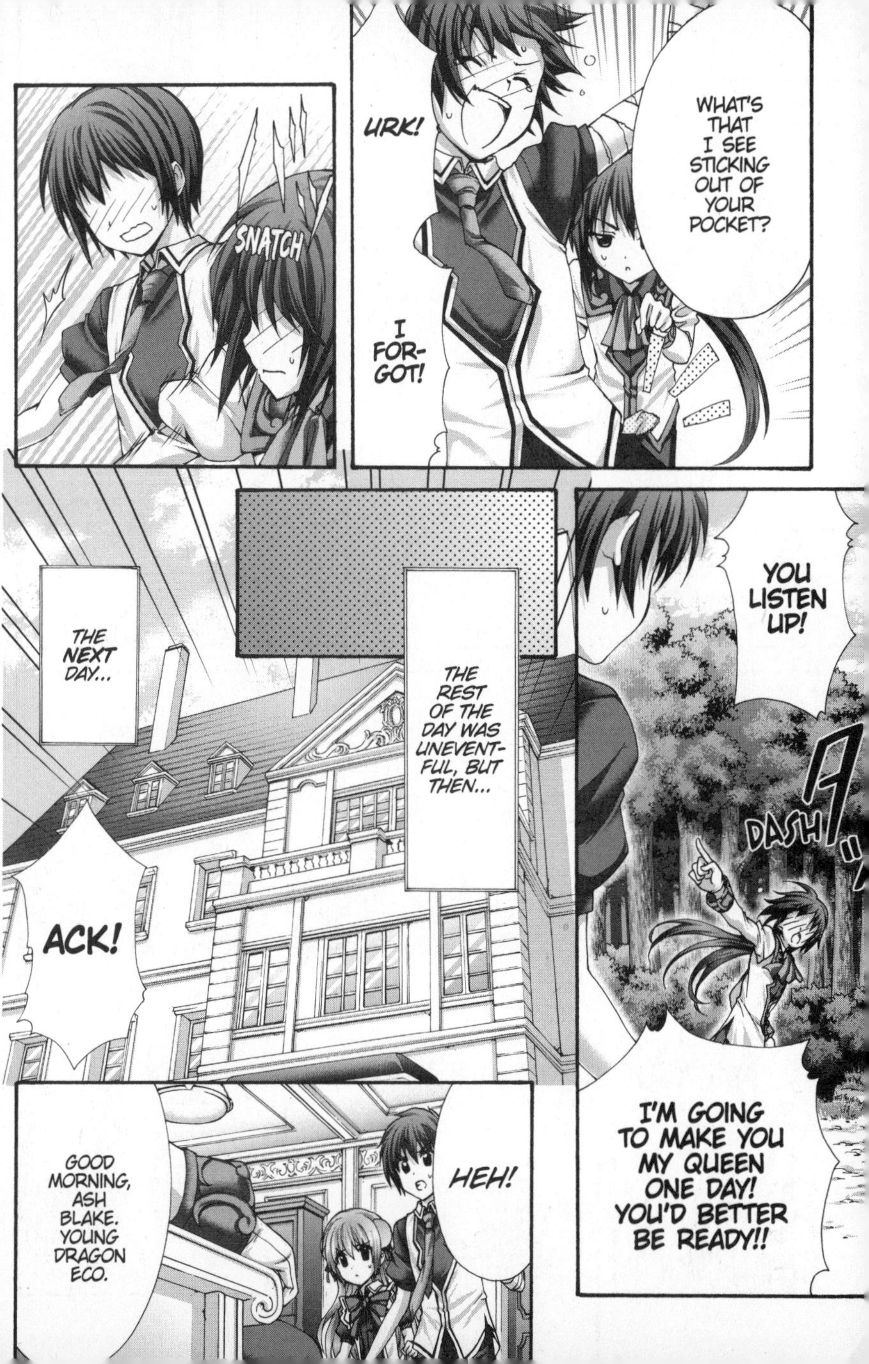
WHAT'S THAT I SEE STICKING OUT OF YOUR POCKET?
URK!
I FOR-GOT!
SNATCH
YOU LISTEN UP!
DASH
I'M GOING TO MAKE YOU MY QUEEN ONE DAY! YOU'D BETTER BE READY!!
THE REST OF THE DAY WAS UNEVENT-FUL, BUT THEN...
THE NEXT DAY...
ACK!
HEH!
GOOD MORNING, ASH BLAKE. YOUNG DRAGON ECO.

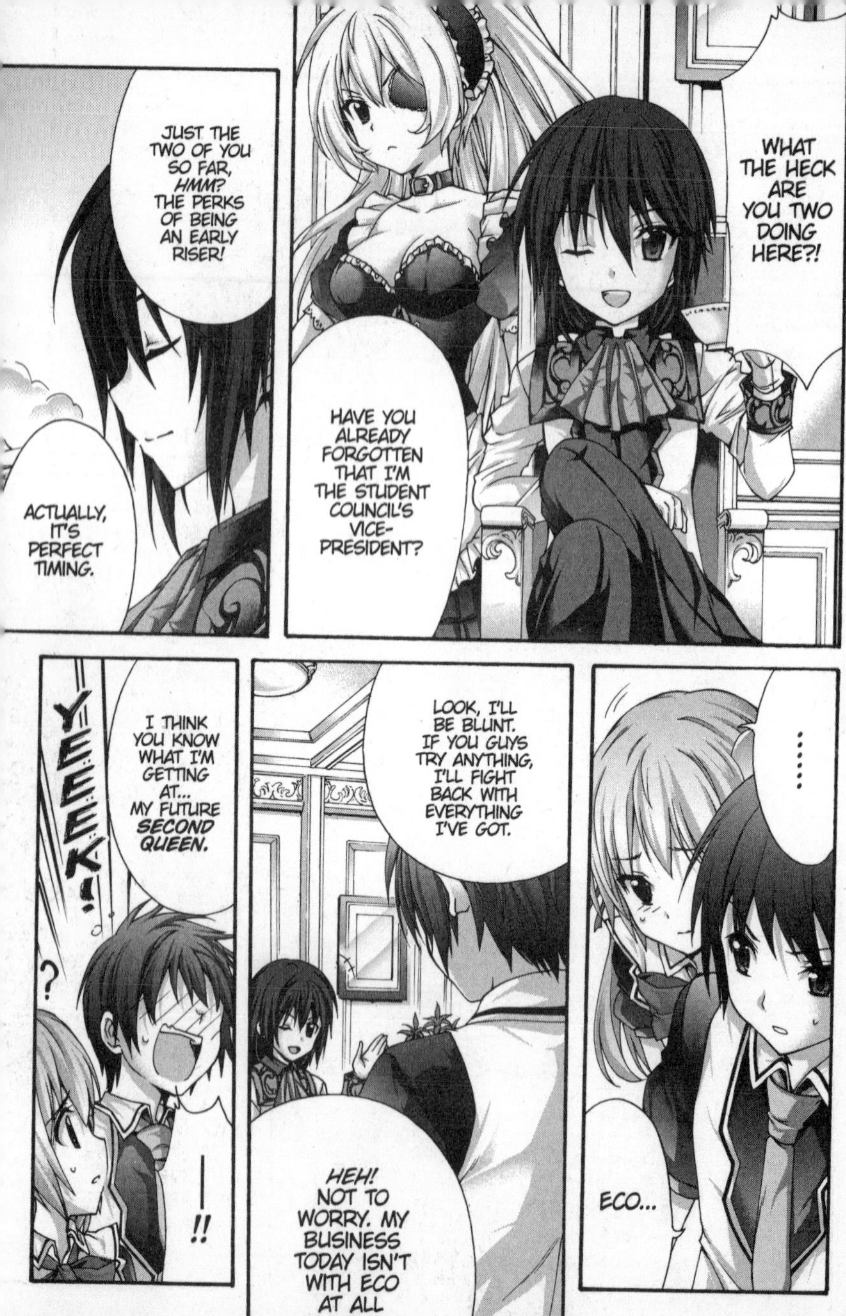
WHAT THE HECK ARE YOU TWO DOING HERE?!
HAVE YOU ALREADY FORGOTTEN THAT I'M THE STUDENT COUNCIL'S VICE-PRESIDENT?
JUST THE TWO OF YOU SO FAR, *HMM?* THE PERKS OF BEING AN EARLY RISER!
ACTUALLY, IT'S PERFECT TIMING.
......
ECO...
LOOK, I'LL BE BLUNT. IF YOU GUYS TRY ANYTHING, I'LL FIGHT BACK WITH EVERYTHING I'VE GOT.
HEH! NOT TO WORRY. MY BUSINESS TODAY ISN'T WITH ECO AT ALL
I THINK YOU KNOW WHAT I'M GETTING AT... MY FUTURE *SECOND QUEEN.*
YEEEK!
?
—!!

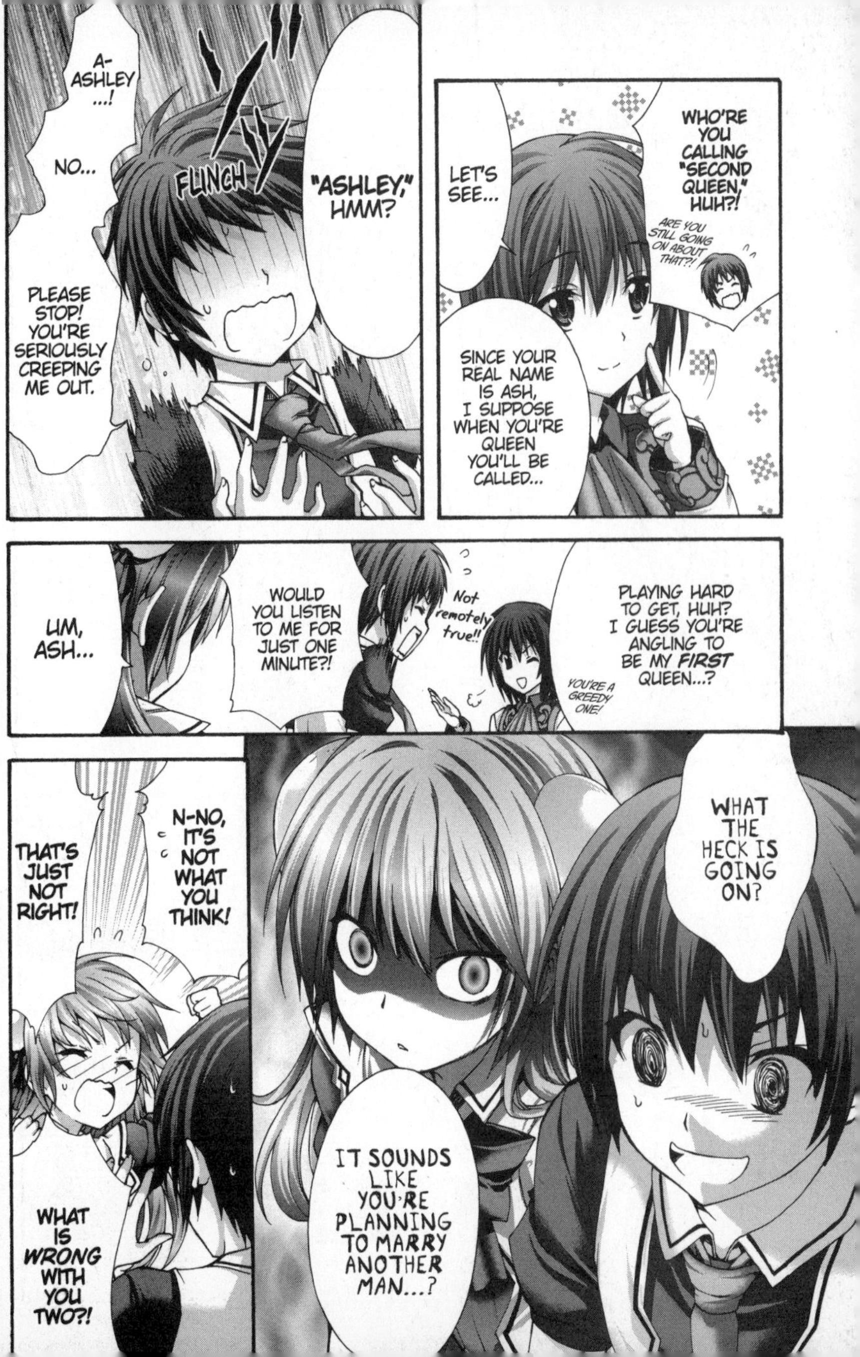
WHO'RE YOU CALLING "SECOND QUEEN," HUH?!
ARE YOU STILL GOING ON ABOUT THAT?!
LET'S SEE...
SINCE YOUR REAL NAME IS ASH, I SUPPOSE WHEN YOU'RE QUEEN YOU'LL BE CALLED...
"ASHLEY," HMM?
FLINCH
A-ASHLEY ...!
NO...
PLEASE STOP! YOU'RE SERIOUSLY CREEPING ME OUT.
PLAYING HARD TO GET, HUH? I GUESS YOU'RE ANGLING TO BE MY *FIRST* QUEEN...?
YOU'RE A GREEDY ONE!
Not remotely true!!
WOULD YOU LISTEN TO ME FOR JUST ONE MINUTE?!
UM, ASH...
WHAT THE HECK IS GOING ON?
IT SOUNDS LIKE YOU'RE PLANNING TO MARRY ANOTHER MAN...?
N-NO, IT'S NOT WHAT YOU THINK!
THAT'S JUST NOT RIGHT!
WHAT IS *WRONG* WITH YOU TWO?!

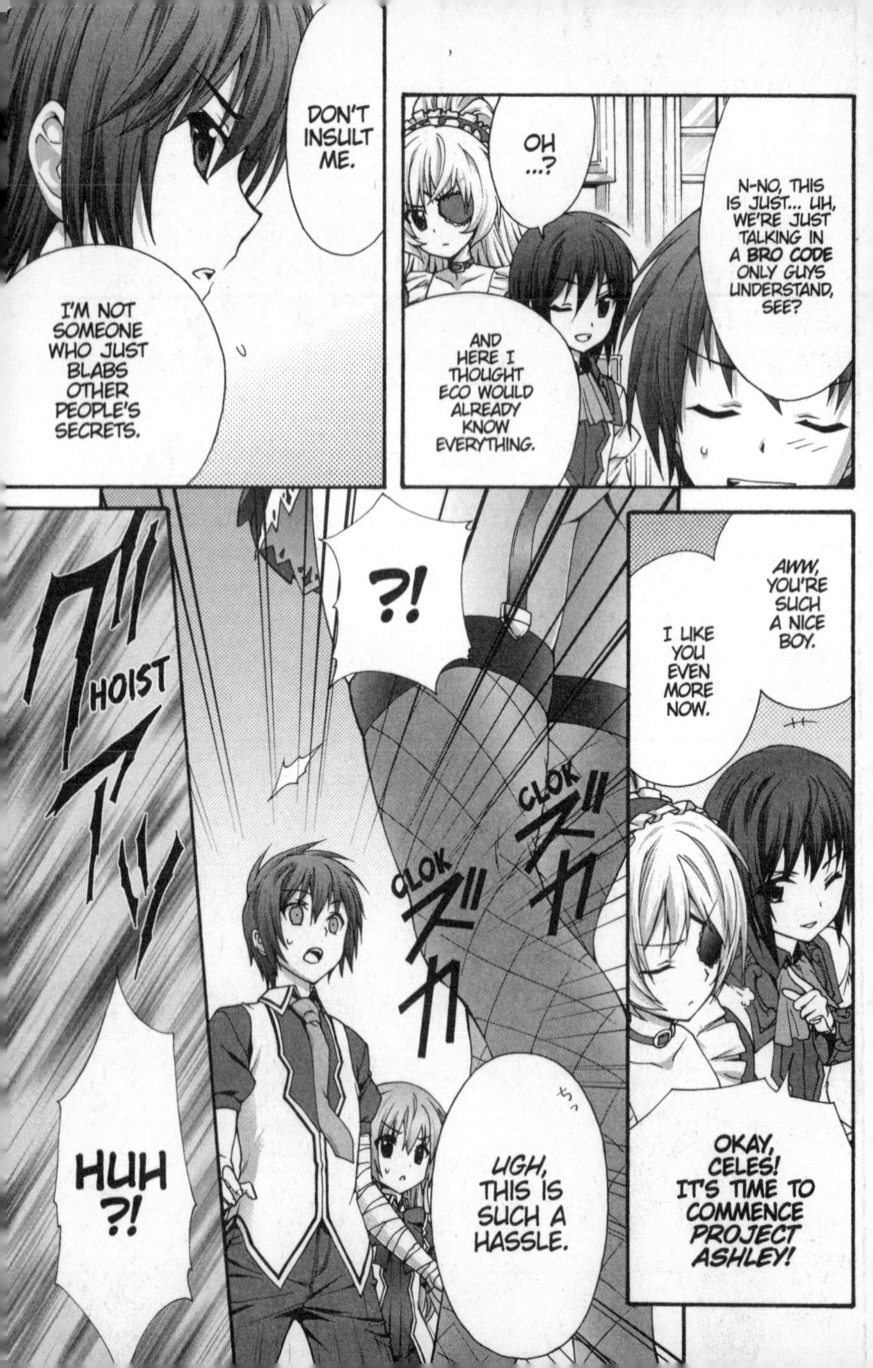
N-NO, THIS IS JUST... UH, WE'RE JUST TALKING IN A BRO CODE ONLY GUYS UNDERSTAND, SEE?
OH ...?
AND HERE I THOUGHT ECO WOULD ALREADY KNOW EVERYTHING.
DON'T INSULT ME.
I'M NOT SOMEONE WHO JUST BLABS OTHER PEOPLE'S SECRETS.
AWW, YOU'RE SUCH A NICE BOY.
I LIKE YOU EVEN MORE NOW.
OKAY, CELES! IT'S TIME TO COMMENCE PROJECT ASHLEY!
?!
CLOK
CLOK
UGH, THIS IS SUCH A HASSLE.
HOIST
HUH ?!

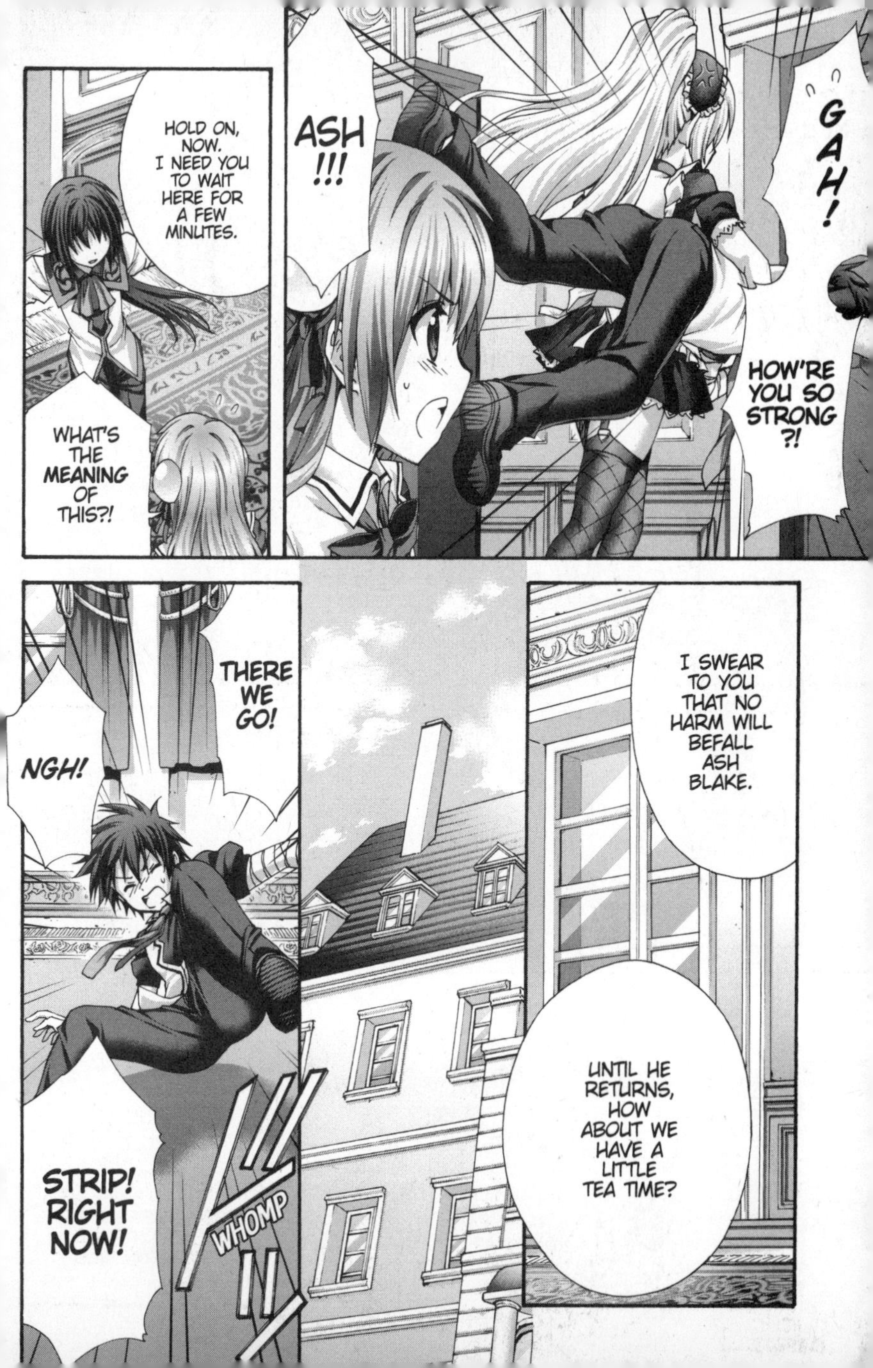
GAH!
HOW'RE YOU SO STRONG?!
ASH!!!
HOLD ON, NOW. I NEED YOU TO WAIT HERE FOR A FEW MINUTES.
WHAT'S THE MEANING OF THIS?!
I SWEAR TO YOU THAT NO HARM WILL BEFALL ASH BLAKE.
UNTIL HE RETURNS, HOW ABOUT WE HAVE A LITTLE TEA TIME?
THERE WE GO!
NGH!
STRIP! RIGHT NOW!
WHOMP

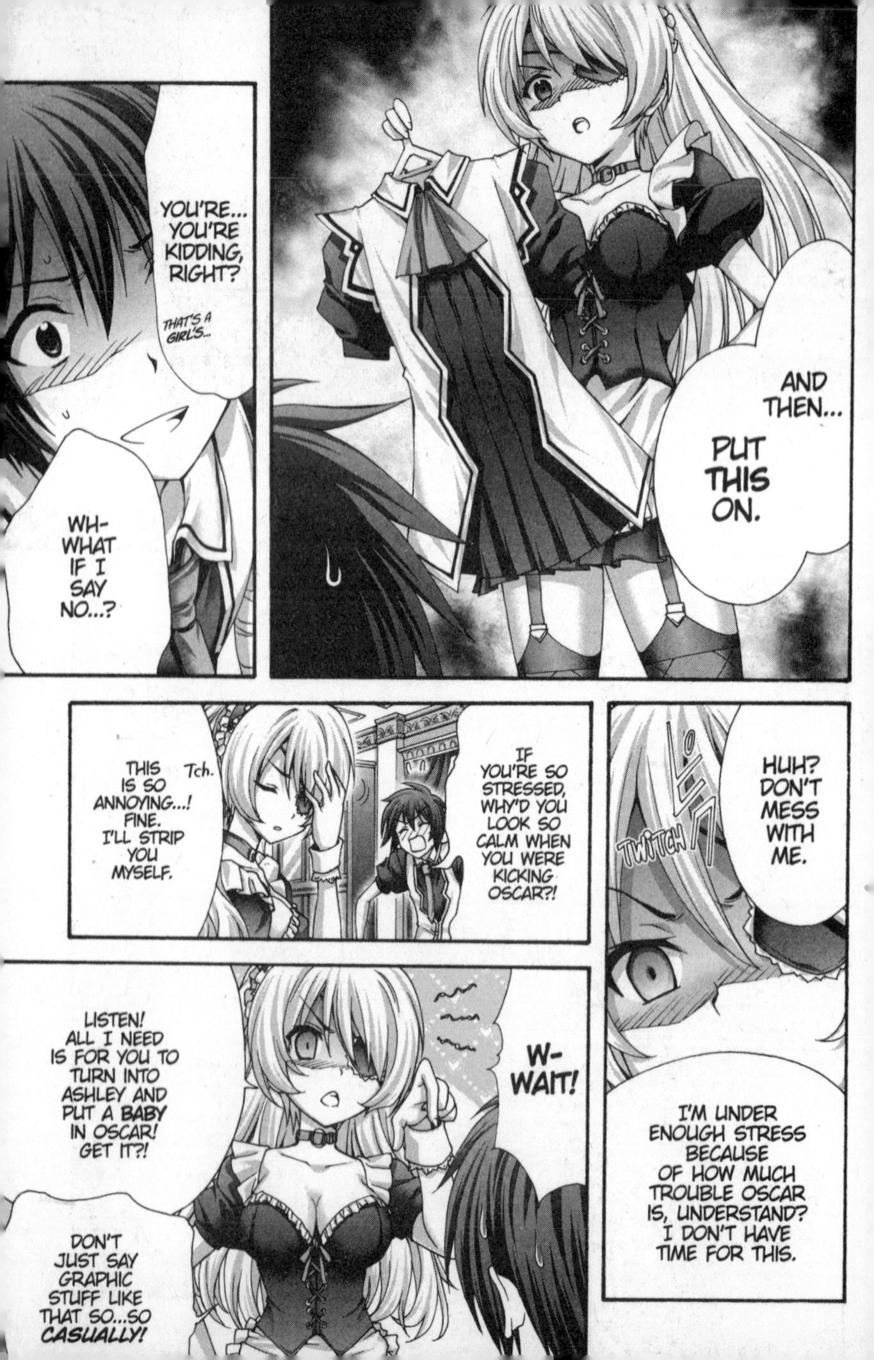
AND THEN...
PUT THIS ON.
YOU'RE... YOU'RE KIDDING, RIGHT?
THAT'S A GIRL'S...
WH- WHAT IF I SAY NO...?
HUH? DON'T MESS WITH ME.
TWITCH
I'M UNDER ENOUGH STRESS BECAUSE OF HOW MUCH TROUBLE OSCAR IS, UNDERSTAND? I DON'T HAVE TIME FOR THIS.
IF YOU'RE SO STRESSED, WHY'D YOU LOOK SO CALM WHEN YOU WERE KICKING OSCAR?!
Tch.
THIS IS SO ANNOYING...! FINE. I'LL STRIP YOU MYSELF.
W- WAIT!
LISTEN! ALL I NEED IS FOR YOU TO TURN INTO ASHLEY AND PUT A BABY IN OSCAR! GET IT?!
DON'T JUST SAY GRAPHIC STUFF LIKE THAT SO...SO CASUALLY!

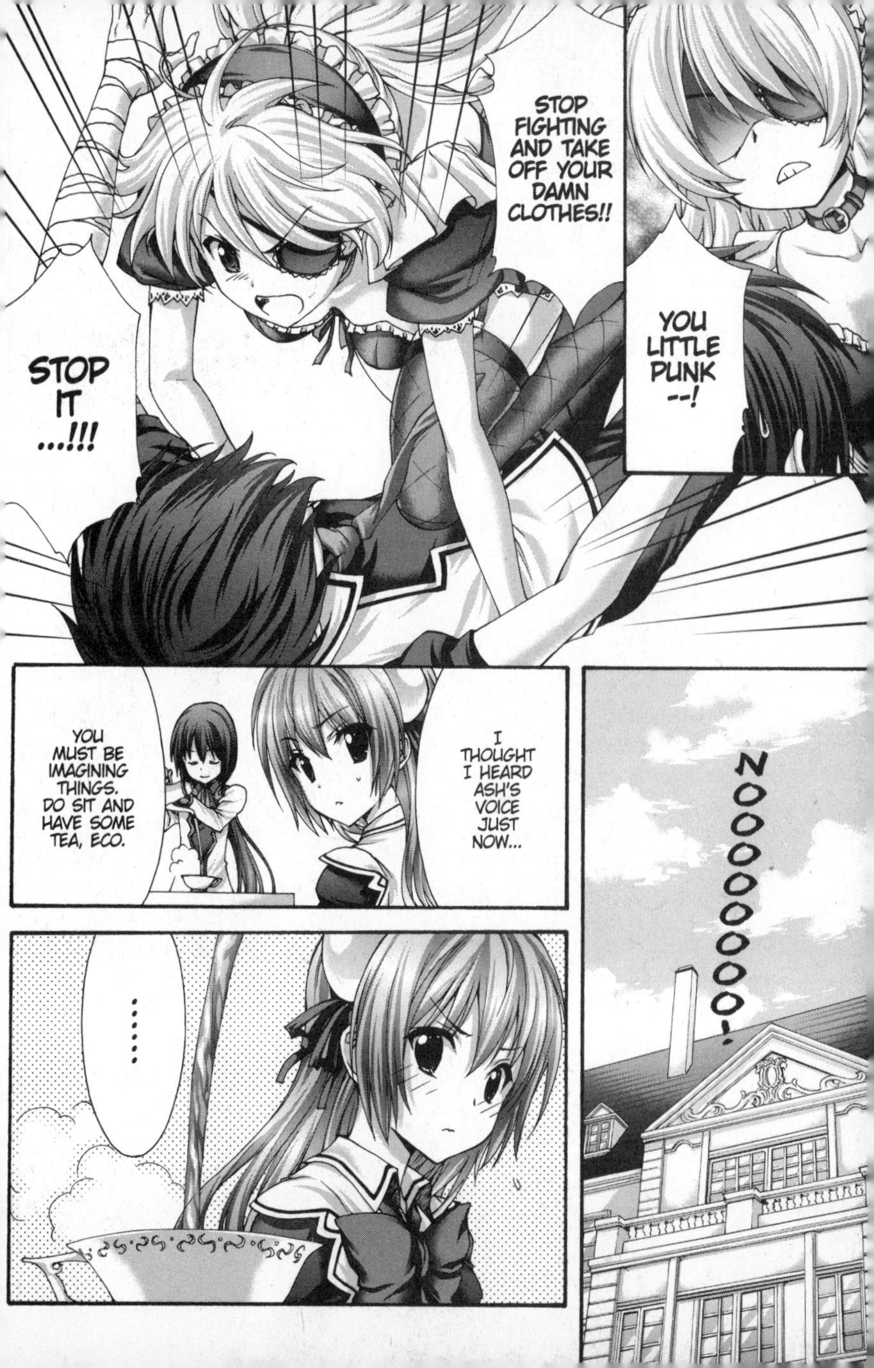
STOP FIGHTING AND TAKE OFF YOUR DAMN CLOTHES!!
YOU LITTLE PUNK --!
STOP IT ...!!!
NOOOOOOOOO!
I THOUGHT I HEARD ASH'S VOICE JUST NOW...
YOU MUST BE IMAGINING THINGS. DO SIT AND HAVE SOME TEA, ECO.
......

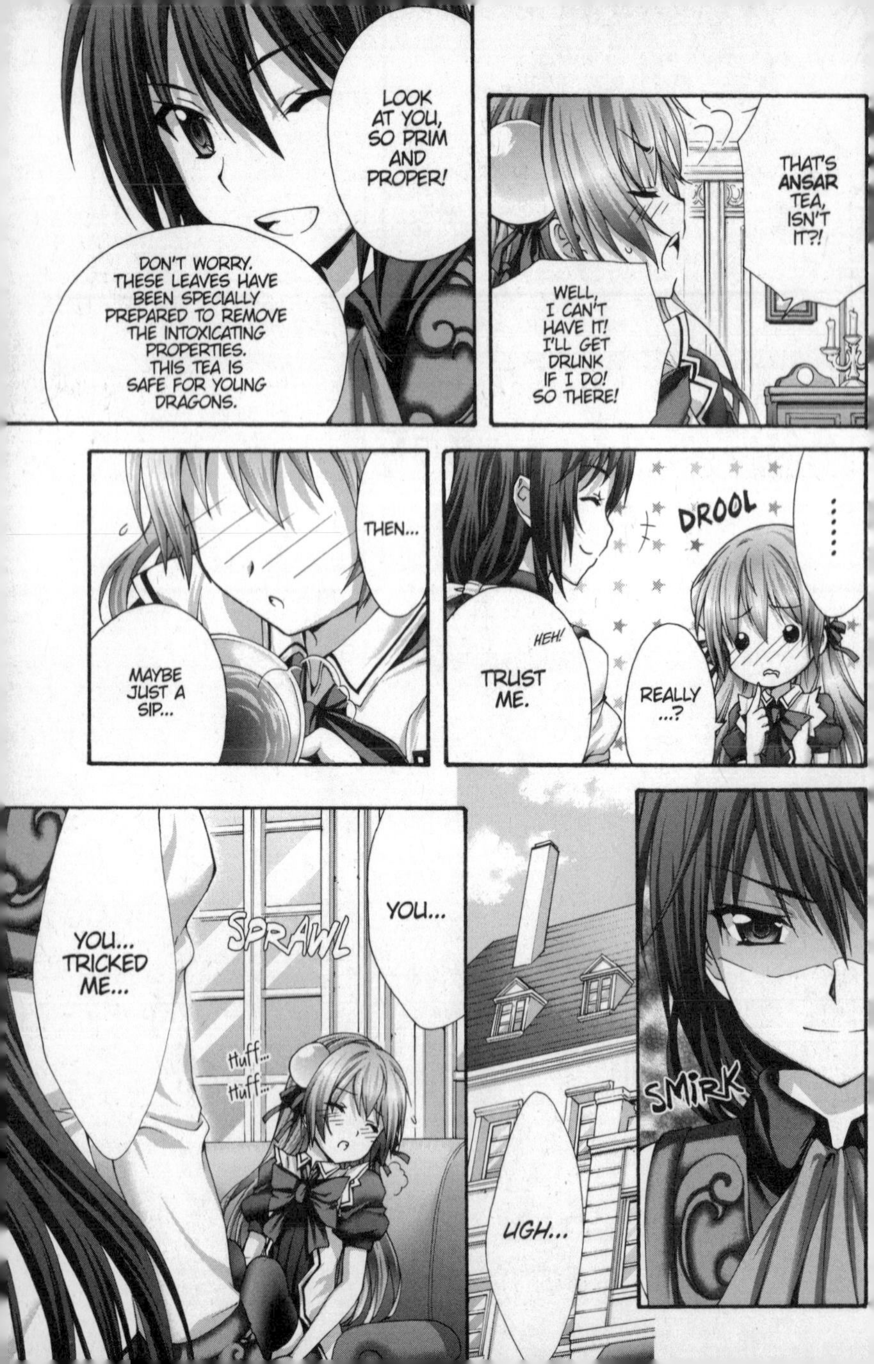
THAT'S ANSAR TEA, ISN'T IT?!
WELL, I CAN'T HAVE IT! I'LL GET DRUNK IF I DO! SO THERE!
LOOK AT YOU, SO PRIM AND PROPER!
DON'T WORRY. THESE LEAVES HAVE BEEN SPECIALLY PREPARED TO REMOVE THE INTOXICATING PROPERTIES. THIS TEA IS SAFE FOR YOUNG DRAGONS.
.....
DROOL
REALLY ...?
HEH!
TRUST ME.
THEN...
MAYBE JUST A SIP...
SMIRK
UGH...
YOU...
SPRAWL
Huff... Huff...
YOU... TRICKED ME...

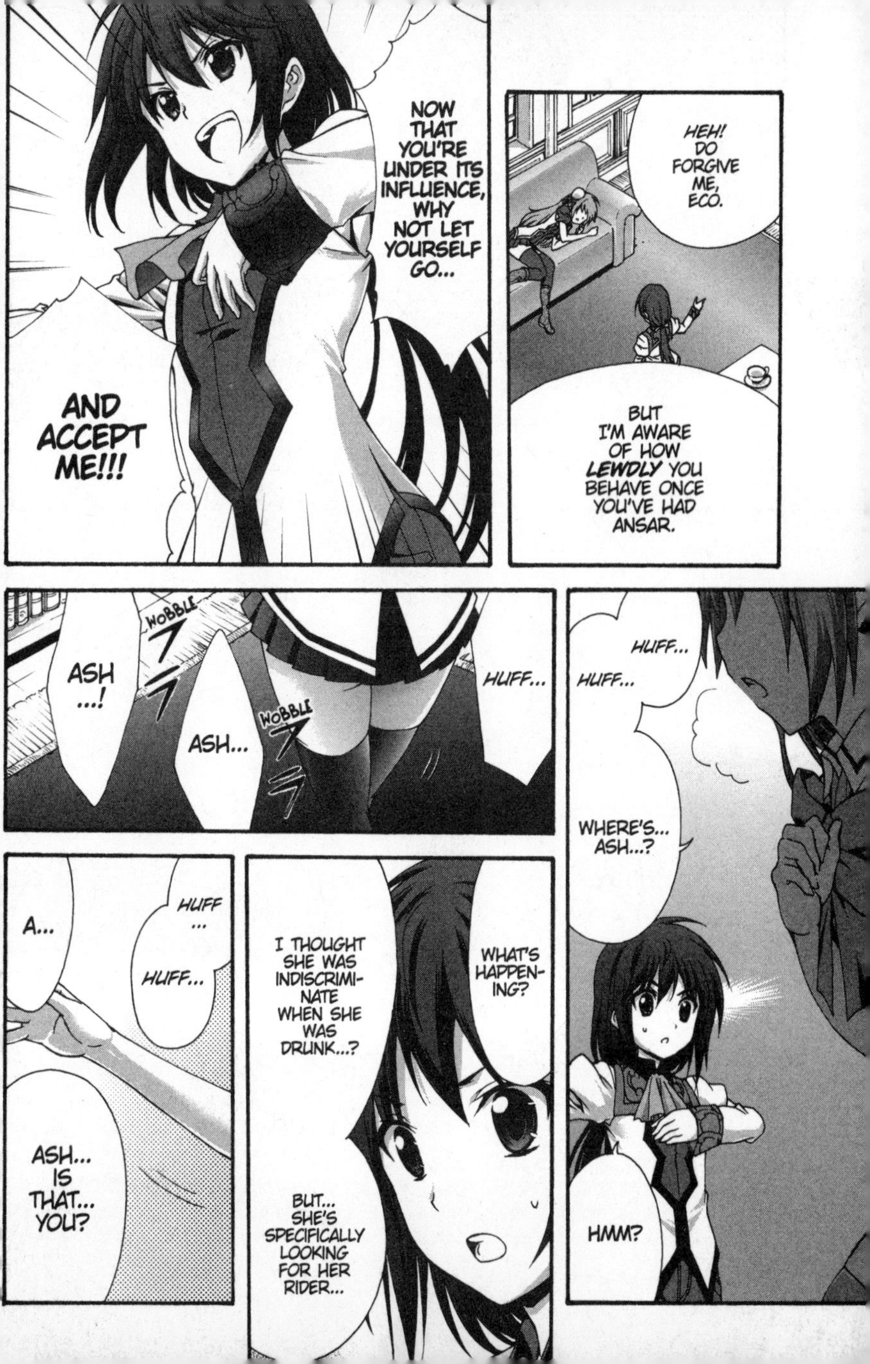
HEH! DO FORGIVE ME, ECO.
BUT I'M AWARE OF HOW *LEWDLY* YOU BEHAVE ONCE YOU'VE HAD ANSAR.
NOW THAT YOU'RE UNDER ITS INFLUENCE, WHY NOT LET YOURSELF GO...
AND ACCEPT ME!!!
HUFF...
HUFF...
WHERE'S... ASH...?
HMM?
HUFF...
WOBBLE
ASH ...!
ASH...
WOBBLE
WHAT'S HAPPEN-ING?
I THOUGHT SHE WAS INDISCRIMI-NATE WHEN SHE WAS DRUNK...?
BUT... SHE'S SPECIFICALLY LOOKING FOR HER RIDER...
HUFF ...
HUFF...
A...
ASH... IS THAT... YOU?

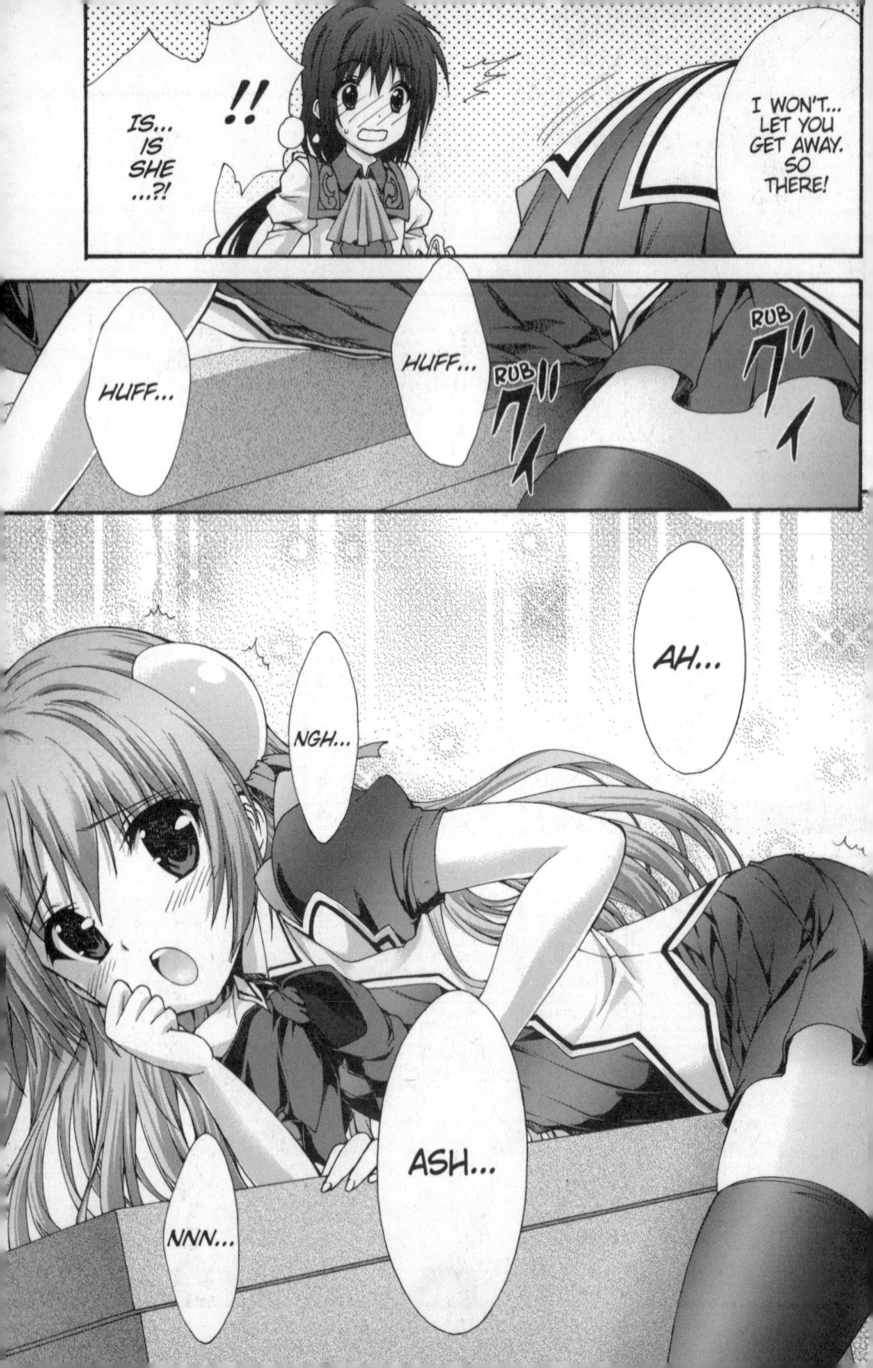
I WON'T... LET YOU GET AWAY. SO THERE!
!!
IS... IS SHE ...?!
RUB
RUB
HUFF...
HUFF...
AH...
NGH...
ASH...
NNN...

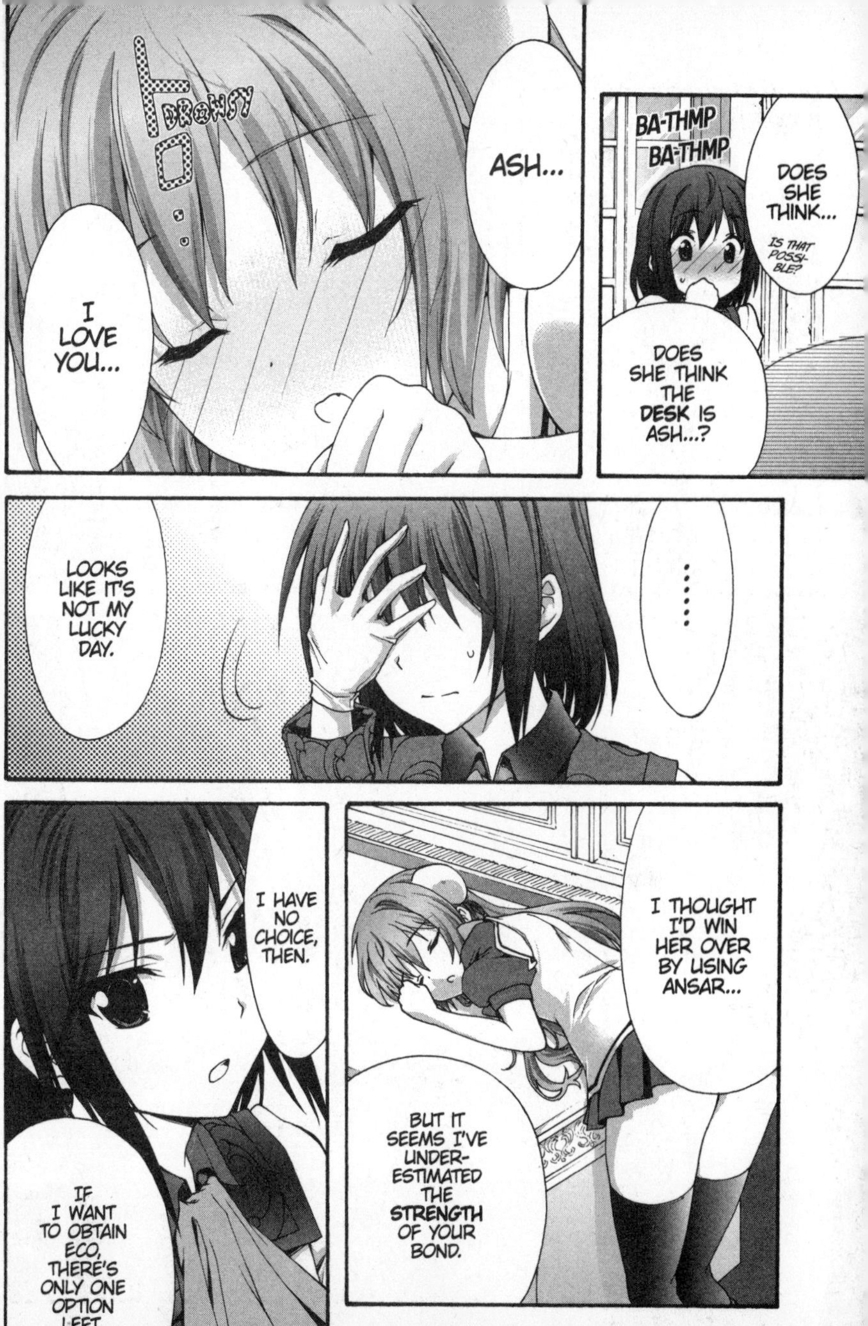
BA-THMP
BA-THMP
DOES SHE THINK...
IS THAT POSSI-BLE?
DOES SHE THINK THE DESK IS ASH...?
ASH...
DROWSY
I LOVE YOU...
......
LOOKS LIKE IT'S NOT MY LUCKY DAY.
I THOUGHT I'D WIN HER OVER BY USING ANSAR...
BUT IT SEEMS I'VE UNDER-ESTIMATED THE STRENGTH OF YOUR BOND.
I HAVE NO CHOICE, THEN.
IF I WANT TO OBTAIN ECO, THERE'S ONLY ONE OPTION LEFT.

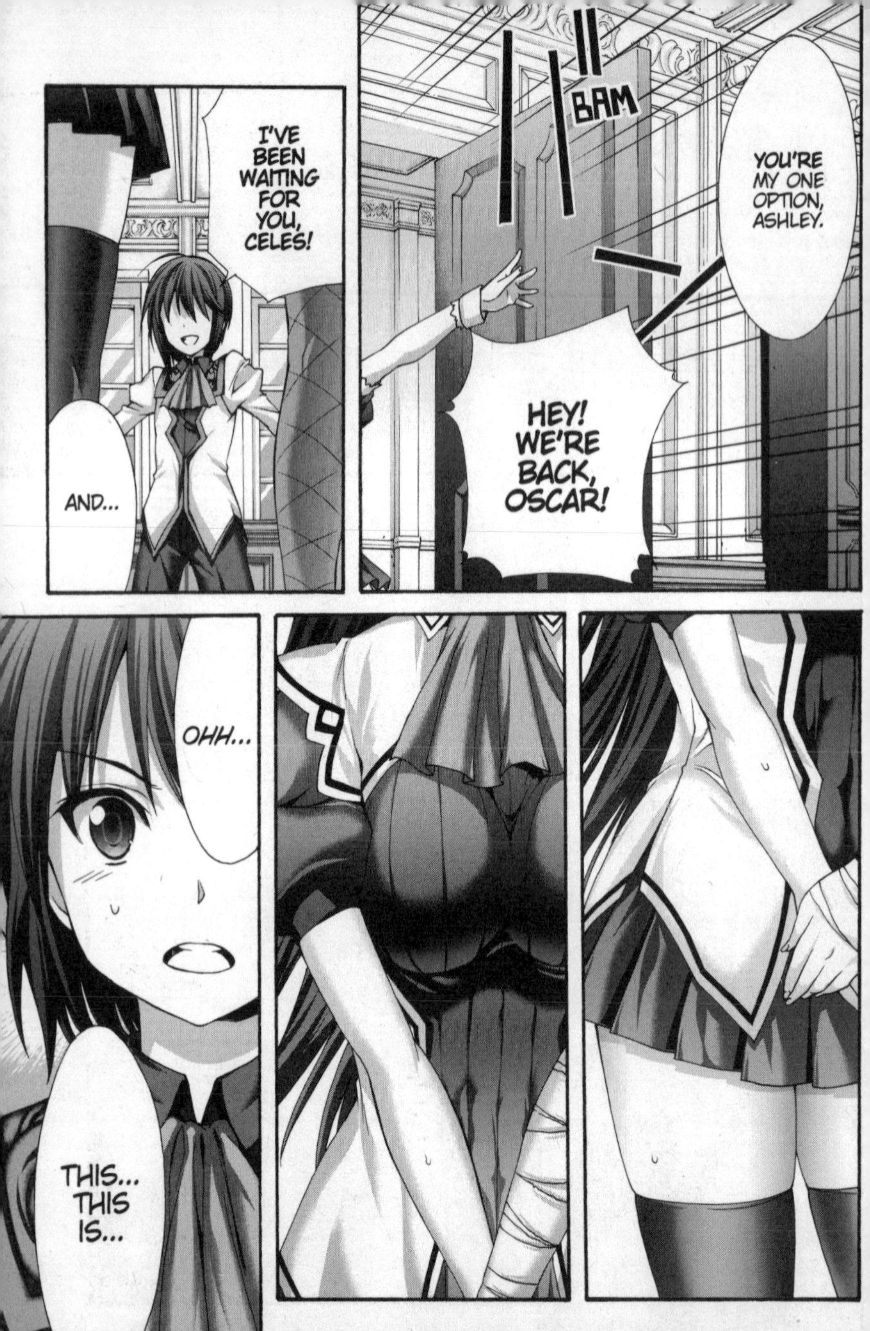
YOU'RE MY ONE OPTION, ASHLEY.
BAM
HEY! WE'RE BACK, OSCAR!
I'VE BEEN WAITING FOR YOU, CELES!
AND...
OHH...
THIS... THIS IS...

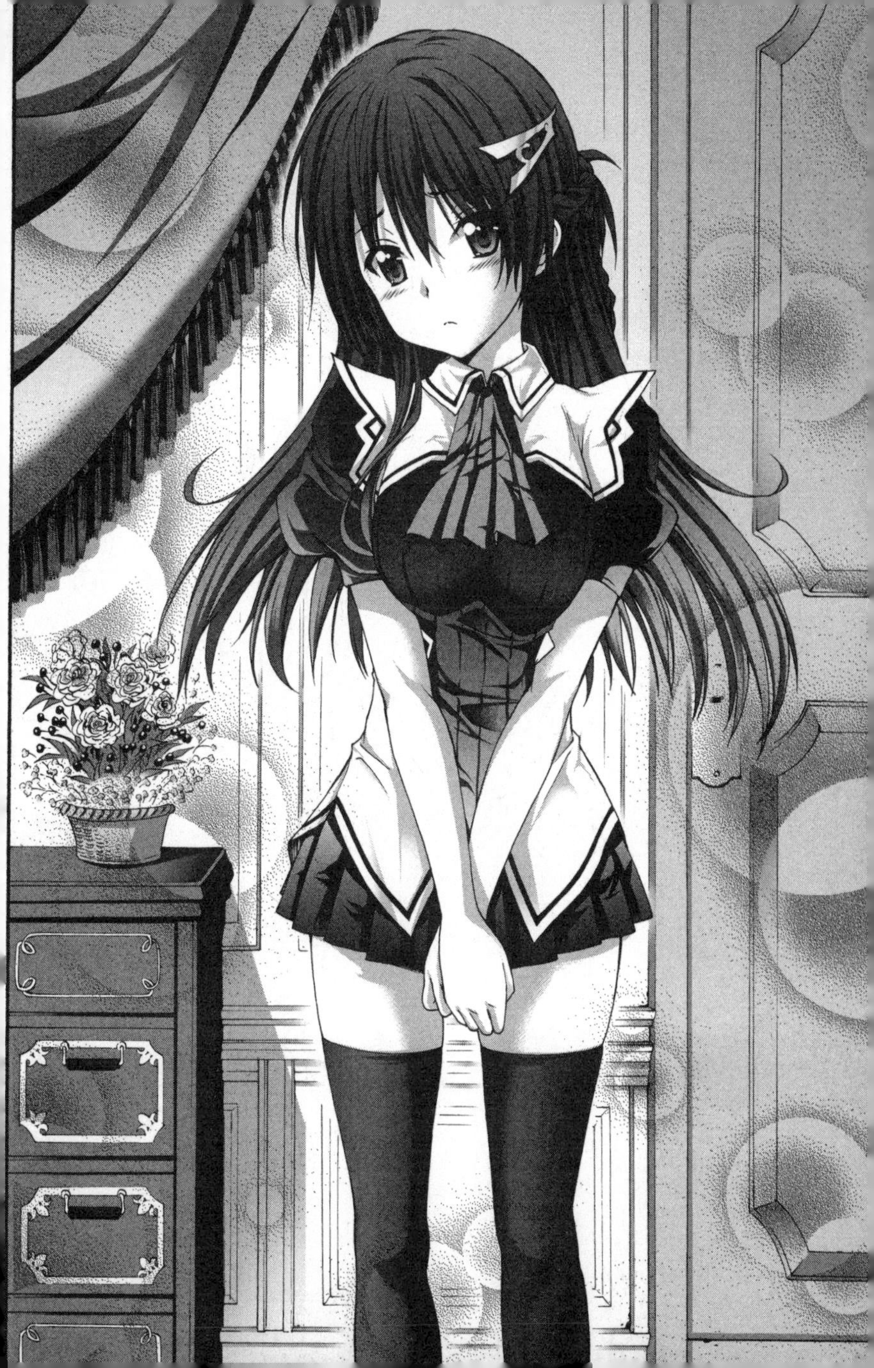

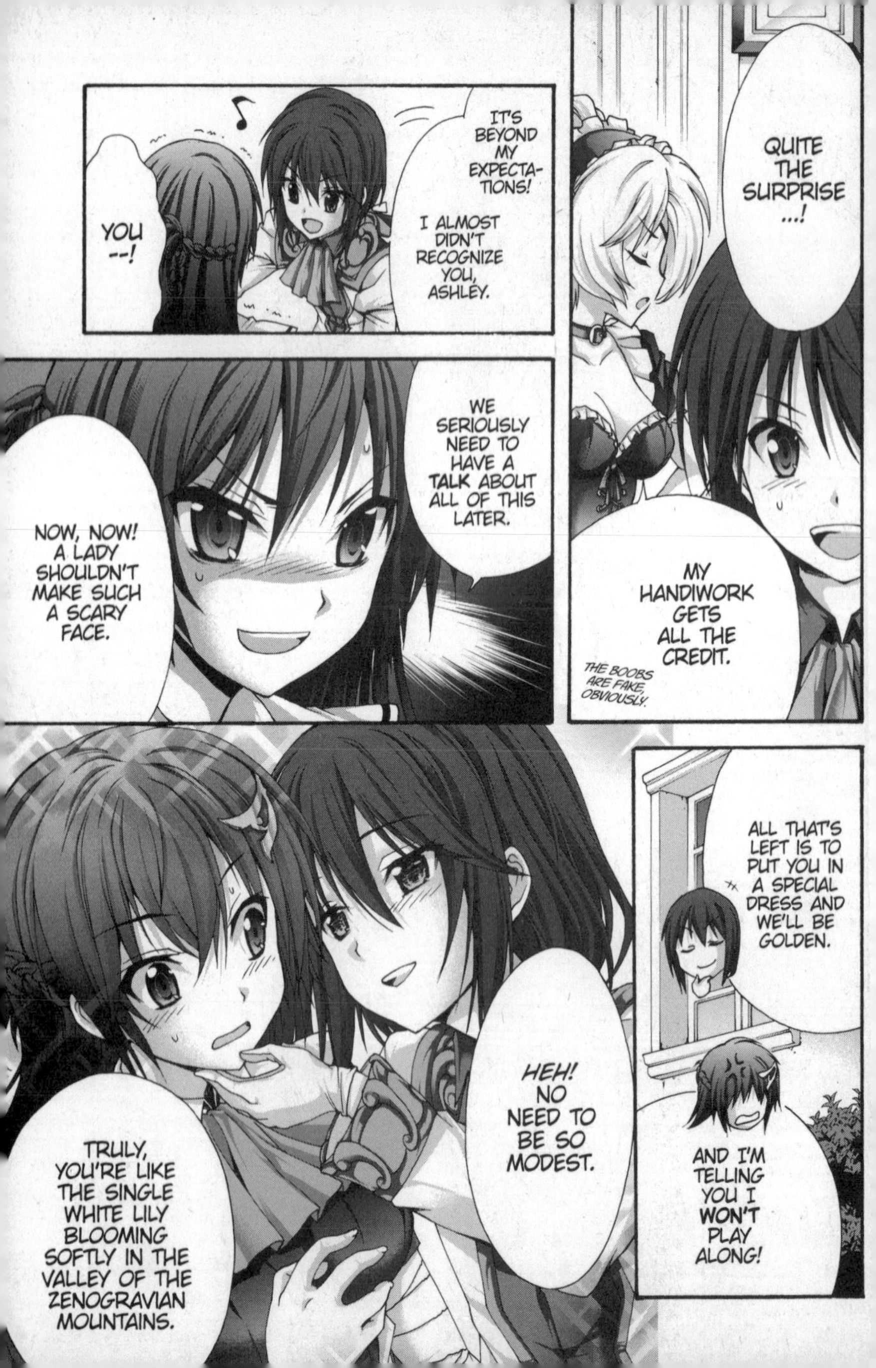
QUITE THE SURPRISE ...!
MY HANDIWORK GETS ALL THE CREDIT.
THE BOOBS ARE FAKE, OBVIOUSLY.
IT'S BEYOND MY EXPECTATIONS!
I ALMOST DIDN'T RECOGNIZE YOU, ASHLEY.
YOU --!
WE SERIOUSLY NEED TO HAVE A TALK ABOUT ALL OF THIS LATER.
NOW, NOW! A LADY SHOULDN'T MAKE SUCH A SCARY FACE.
ALL THAT'S LEFT IS TO PUT YOU IN A SPECIAL DRESS AND WE'LL BE GOLDEN.
AND I'M TELLING YOU I WON'T PLAY ALONG!
HEH! NO NEED TO BE SO MODEST.
TRULY, YOU'RE LIKE THE SINGLE WHITE LILY BLOOMING SOFTLY IN THE VALLEY OF THE ZENOGRAVIAN MOUNTAINS.

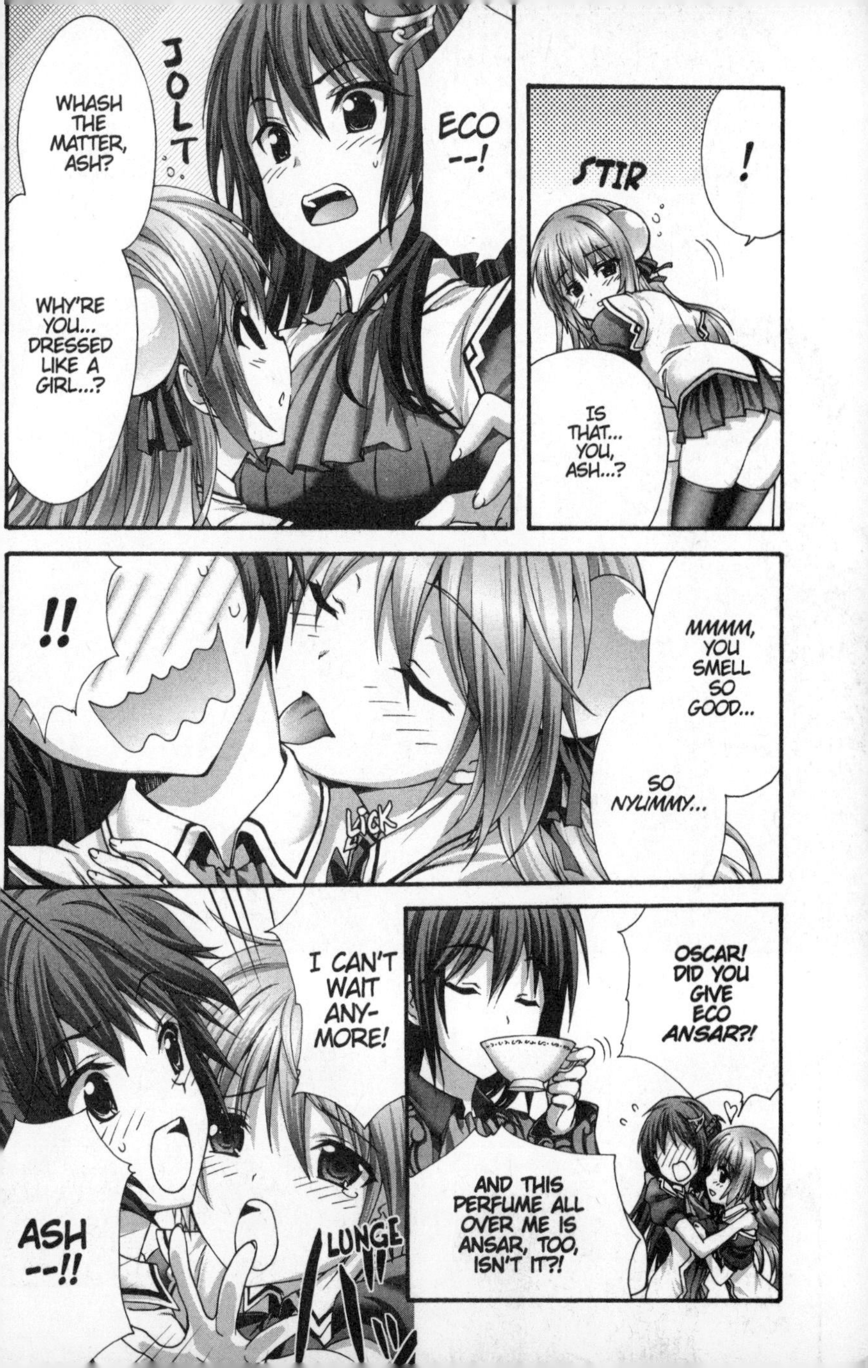
STIR
!
IS THAT... YOU, ASH...?
ECO --!
JOLT
WHASH THE MATTER, ASH?
WHY'RE YOU... DRESSED LIKE A GIRL...?
MMMM, YOU SMELL SO GOOD...
SO NYUMMY...
!!
LICK
OSCAR! DID YOU GIVE ECO ANSAR?!
AND THIS PERFUME ALL OVER ME IS ANSAR, TOO, ISN'T IT?!
I CAN'T WAIT ANY-MORE!
ASH --!!
LUNGE

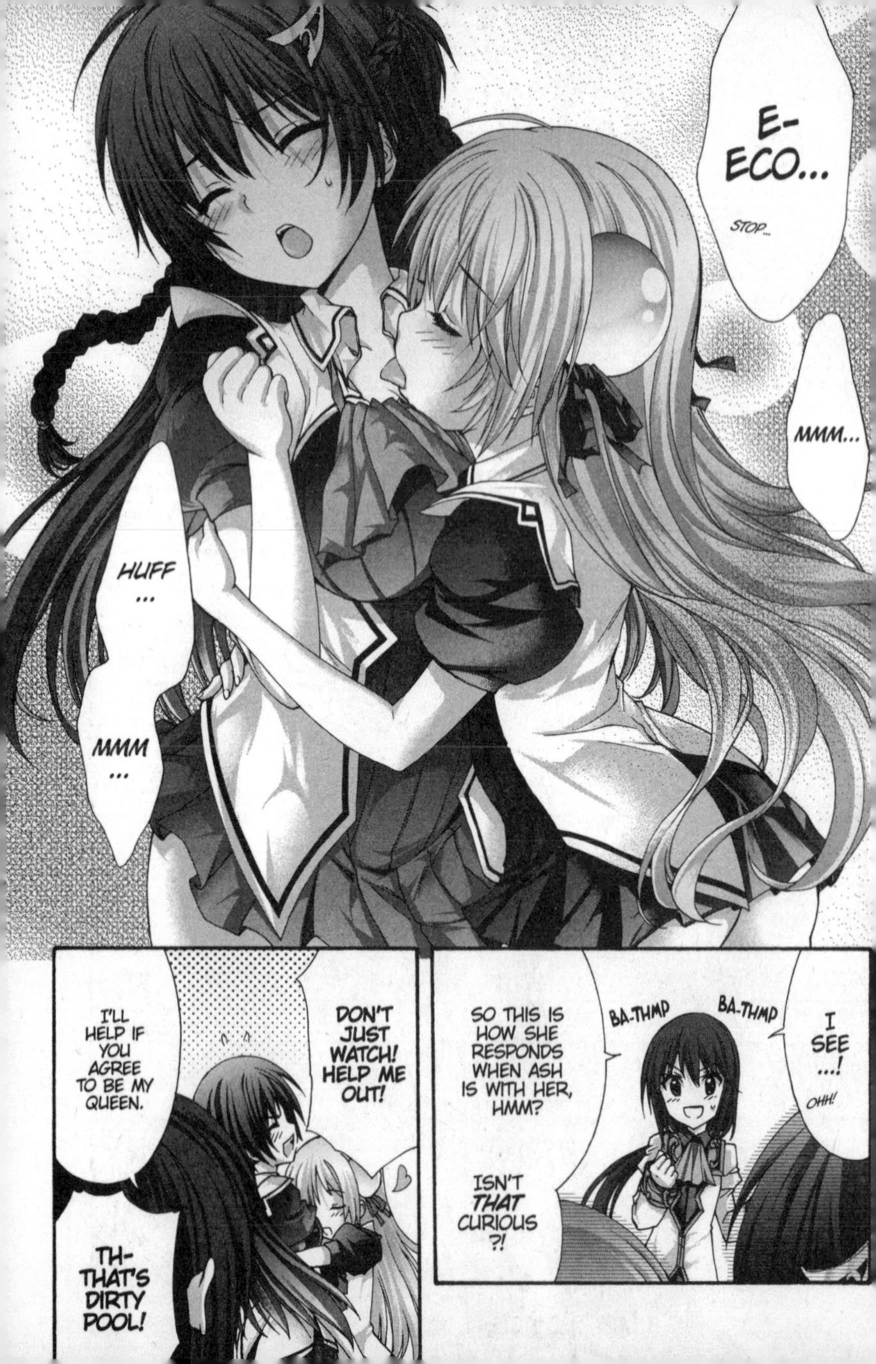
E-ECO...
STOP...
MMM...
HUFF...
MMM...
I SEE...!
OHH!
BA-THMP
BA-THMP
SO THIS IS HOW SHE RESPONDS WHEN ASH IS WITH HER, HMM?
ISN'T *THAT* CURIOUS?!
DON'T JUST WATCH! HELP ME OUT!
I'LL HELP IF YOU AGREE TO BE MY QUEEN.
TH-THAT'S DIRTY POOL!

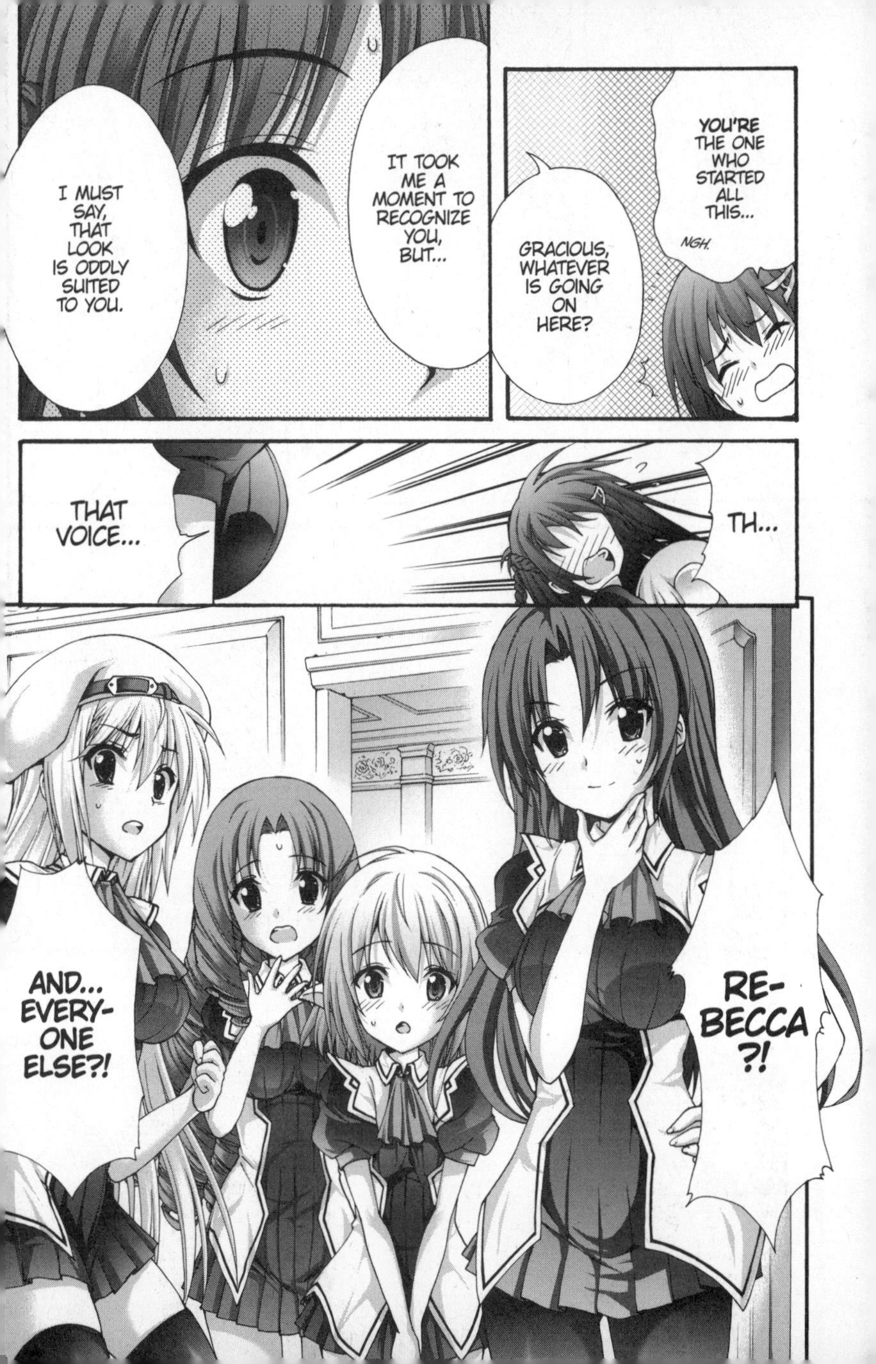
YOU'RE THE ONE WHO STARTED ALL THIS...
NGH.
GRACIOUS, WHATEVER IS GOING ON HERE?
IT TOOK ME A MOMENT TO RECOGNIZE YOU, BUT...
I MUST SAY, THAT LOOK IS ODDLY SUITED TO YOU.
TH...
THAT VOICE...
RE-BECCA?!
AND... EVERY-ONE ELSE?!

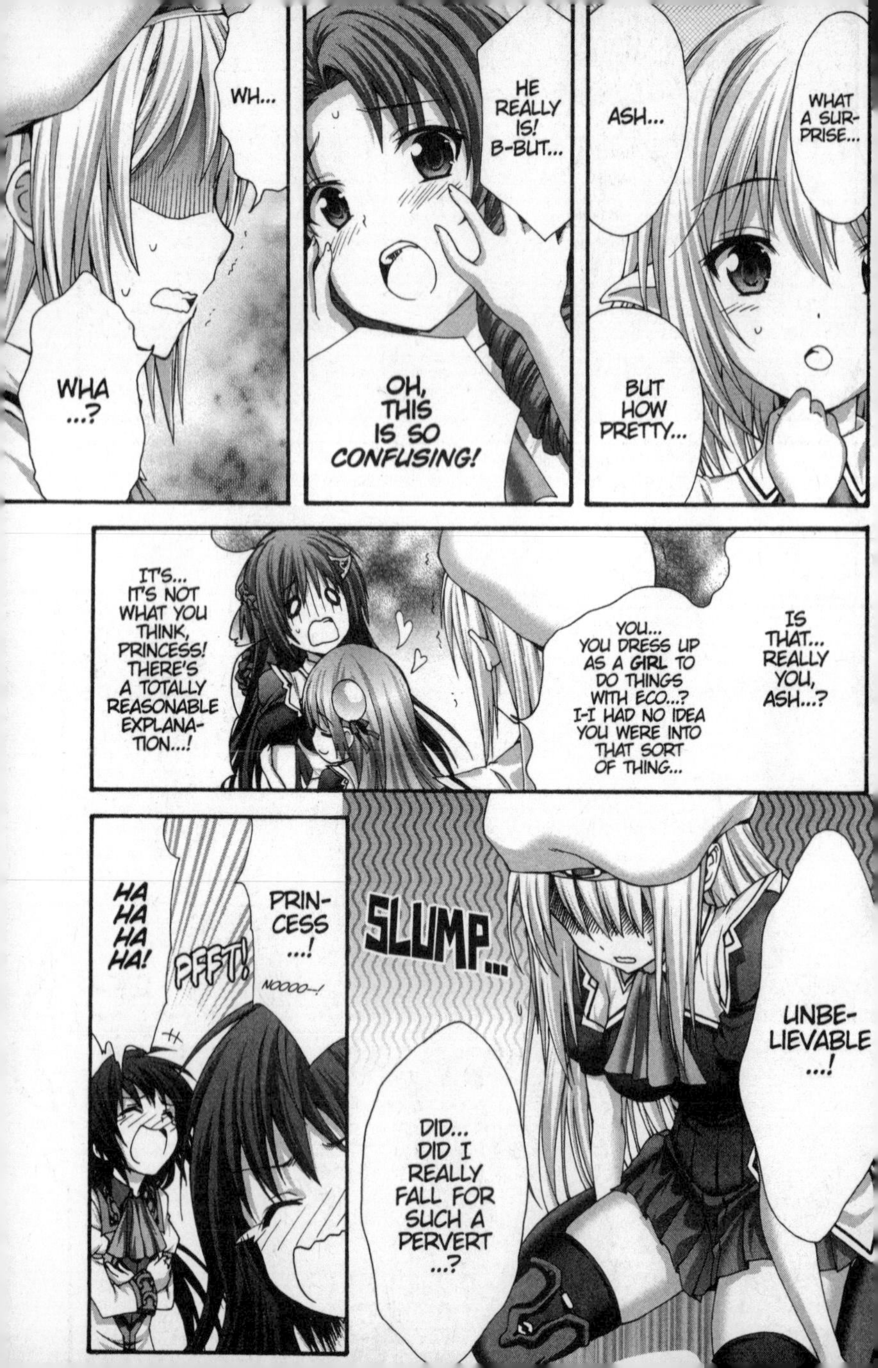
WHAT A SUR-PRISE...
ASH...
BUT HOW PRETTY...
HE REALLY IS! B-BUT...
OH, THIS IS SO CONFUSING!
WH...
WHA ...?
IS THAT... REALLY YOU, ASH...?
YOU... YOU DRESS UP AS A GIRL TO DO THINGS WITH ECO...? I-I HAD NO IDEA YOU WERE INTO THAT SORT OF THING...
IT'S... IT'S NOT WHAT YOU THINK, PRINCESS! THERE'S A TOTALLY REASONABLE EXPLANA-TION...!
UNBE-LIEVABLE ...!
SLUMP...
DID... DID I REALLY FALL FOR SUCH A PERVERT ...?
PRIN-CESS ...!
NOOOO--!
PFFT!
HA HA HA HA!

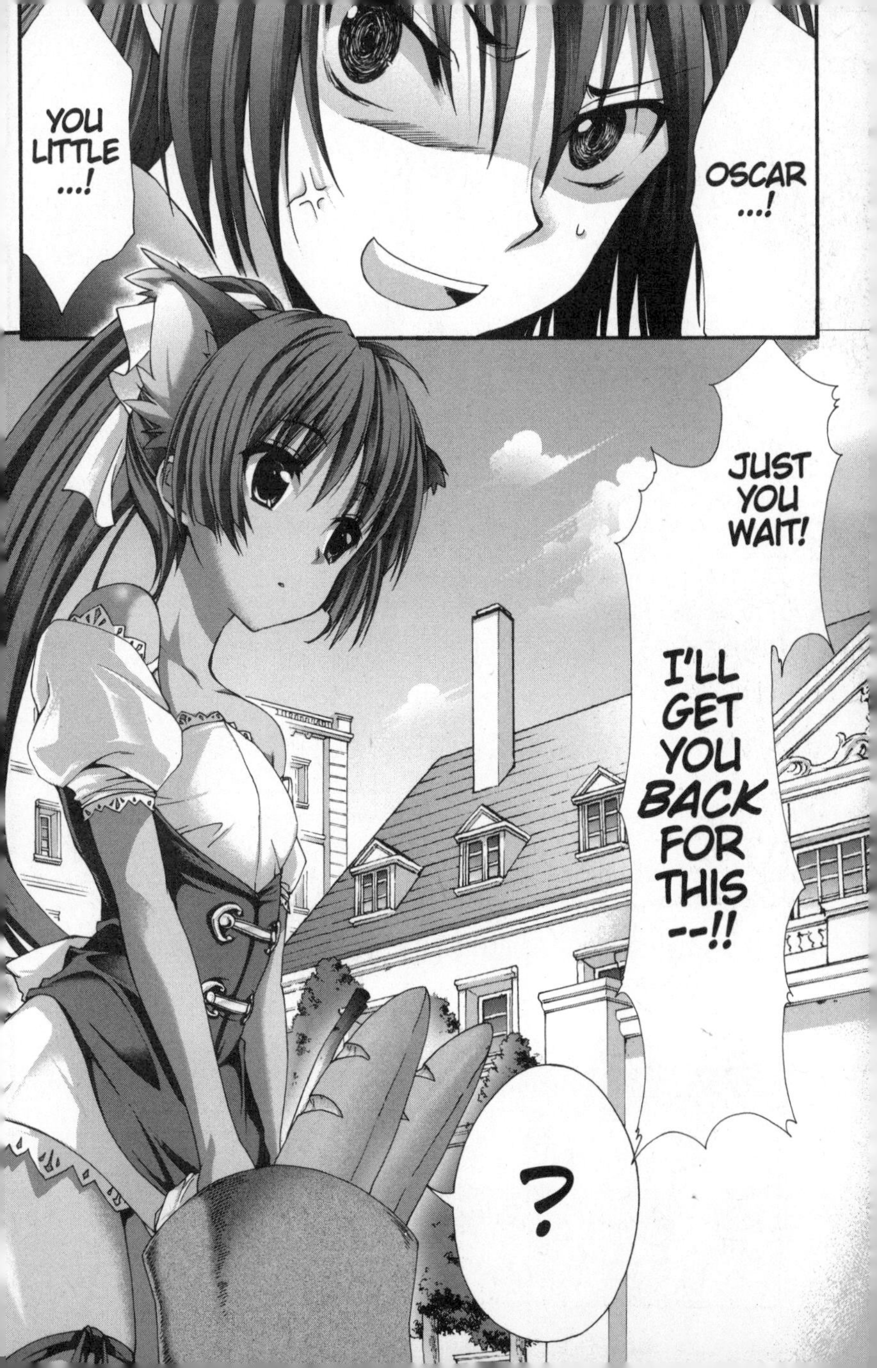
OSCAR ...!
YOU LITTLE ...!
JUST YOU WAIT!
I'LL GET YOU BACK FOR THIS --!!
?

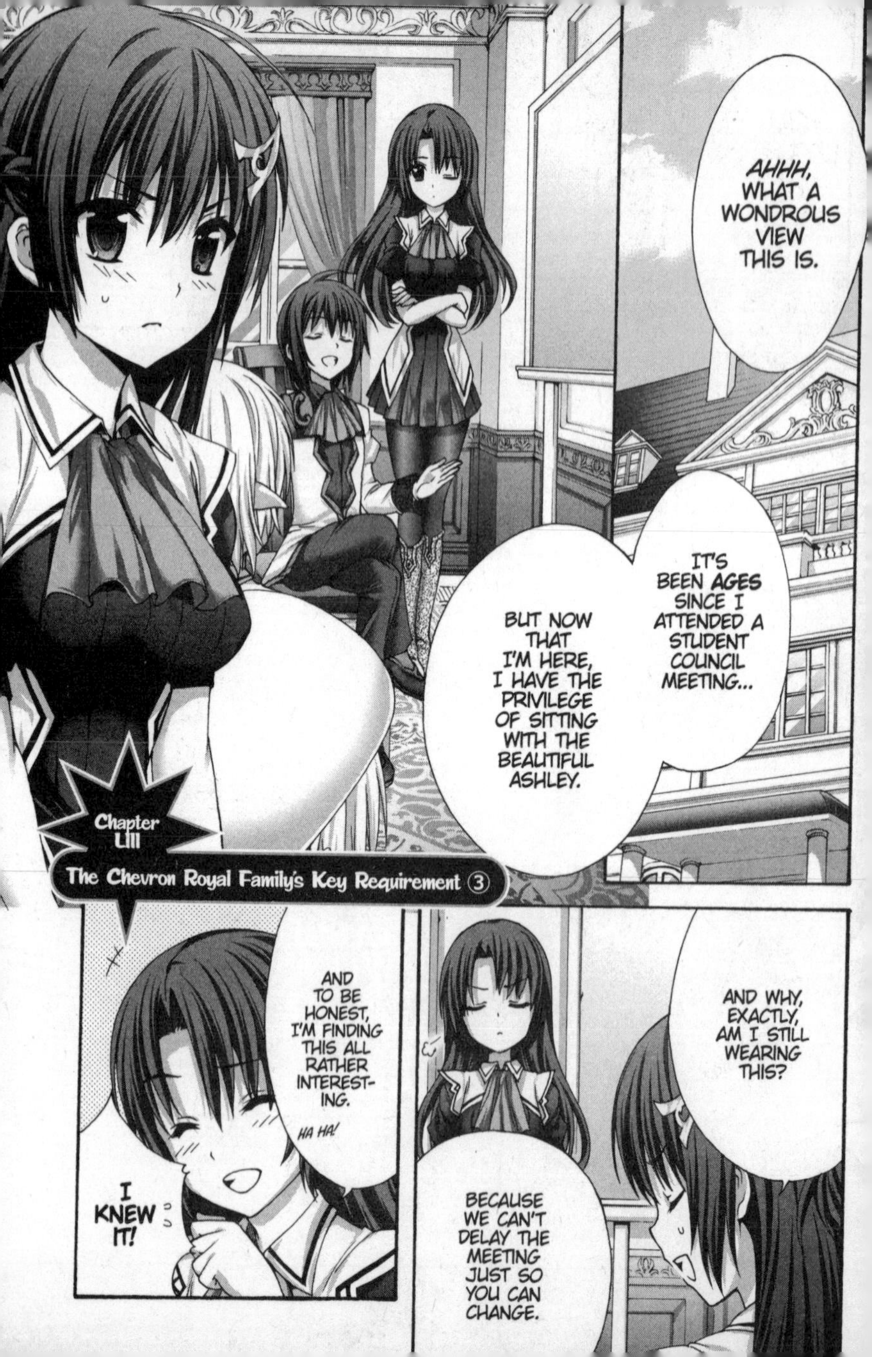
AHHH, WHAT A WONDROUS VIEW THIS IS.
IT'S BEEN AGES SINCE I ATTENDED A STUDENT COUNCIL MEETING...
BUT NOW THAT I'M HERE, I HAVE THE PRIVILEGE OF SITTING WITH THE BEAUTIFUL ASHLEY.
Chapter LIII
The Chevron Royal Family's Key Requirement ③
AND WHY, EXACTLY, AM I STILL WEARING THIS?
BECAUSE WE CAN'T DELAY THE MEETING JUST SO YOU CAN CHANGE.
AND TO BE HONEST, I'M FINDING THIS ALL RATHER INTEREST-ING.
HA HA!
I KNEW IT!

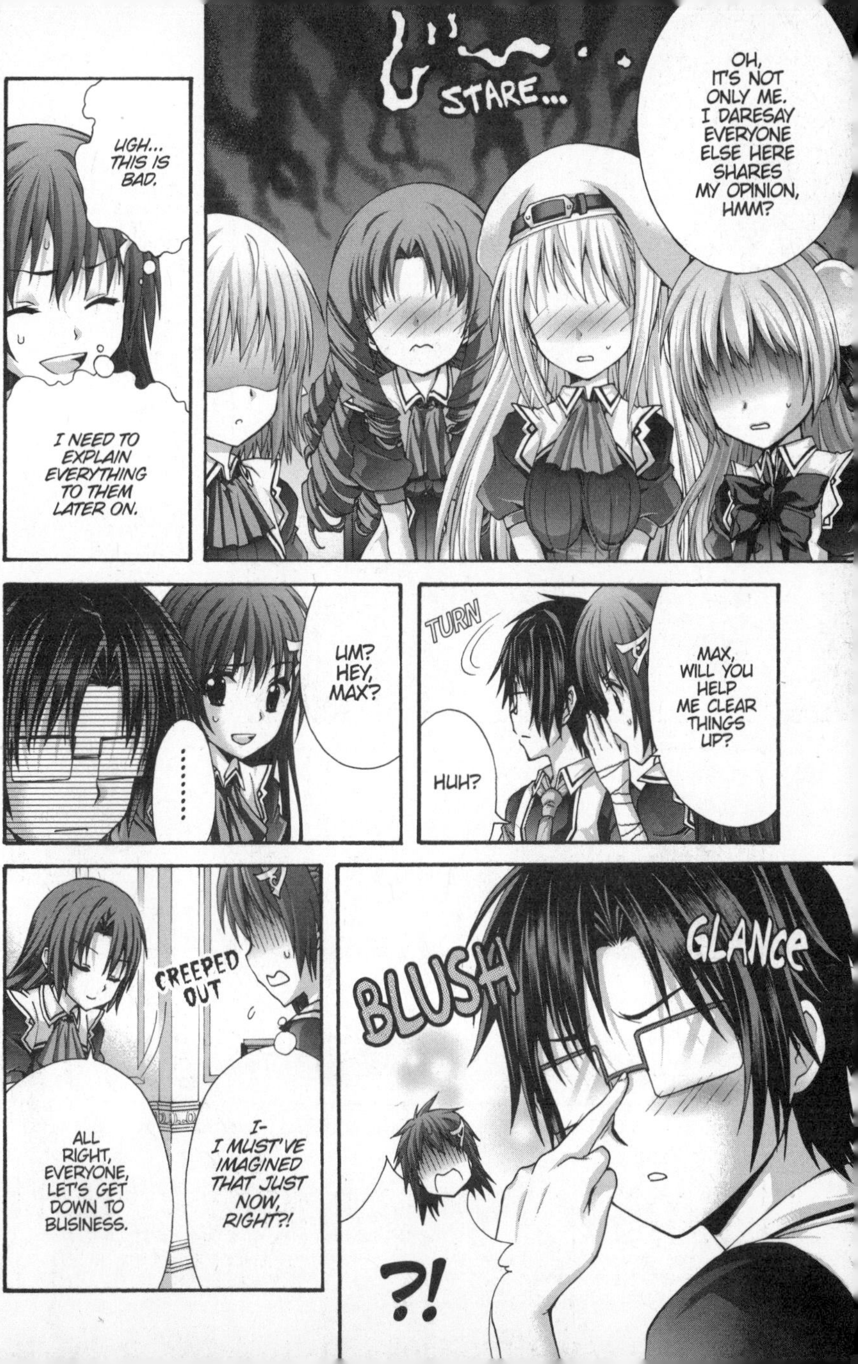
OH, IT'S NOT ONLY ME. I DARESAY EVERYONE ELSE HERE SHARES MY OPINION, HMM?
STARE...
UGH... THIS IS BAD.
I NEED TO EXPLAIN EVERYTHING TO THEM LATER ON.
TURN
MAX, WILL YOU HELP ME CLEAR THINGS UP?
HUH?
UM? HEY, MAX?
......
GLANCE
BLUSH
?!
CREEPED OUT
I- I MUST'VE IMAGINED THAT JUST NOW, RIGHT?!
ALL RIGHT, EVERYONE, LET'S GET DOWN TO BUSINESS.

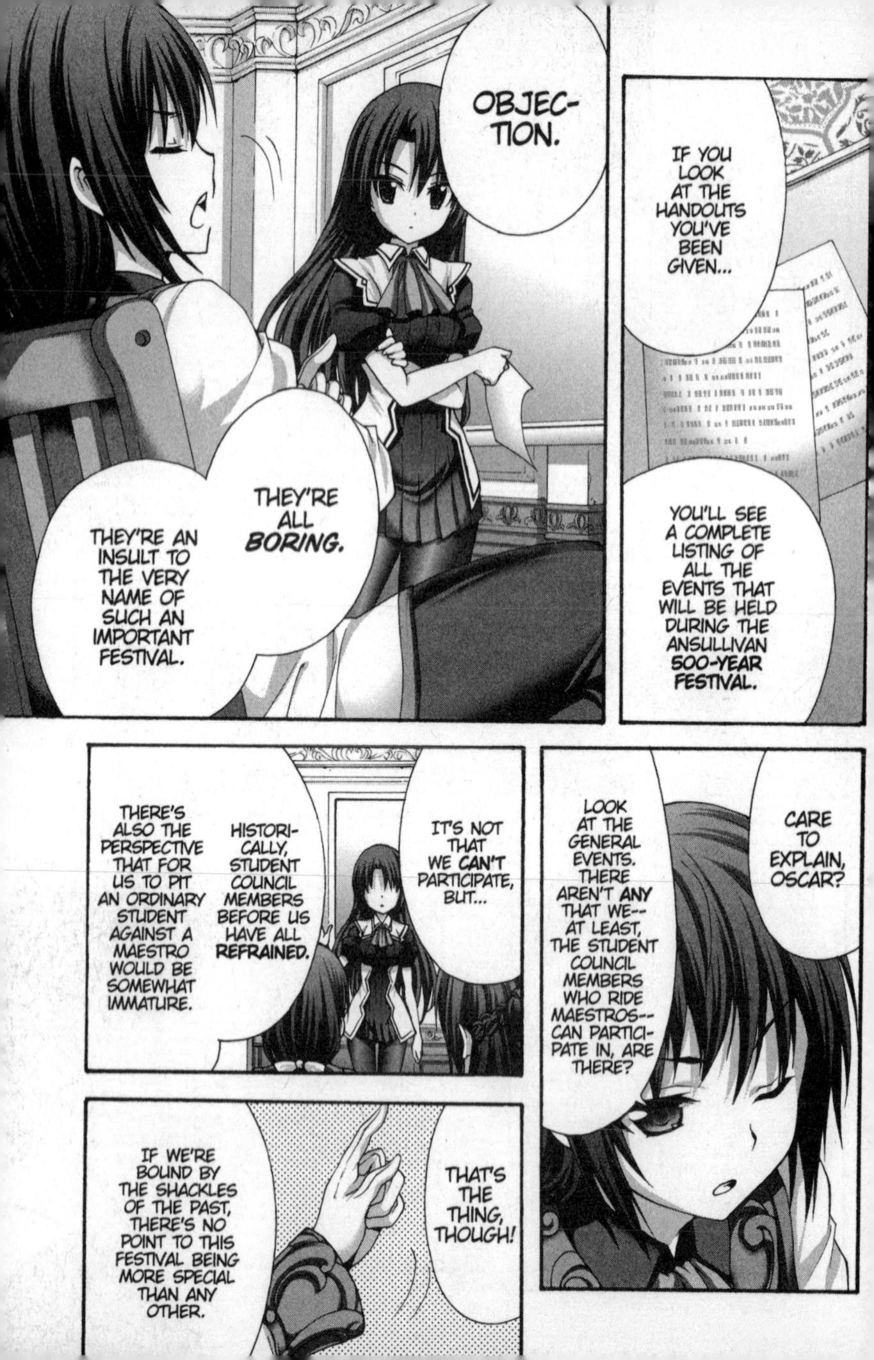
IF YOU LOOK AT THE HANDOUTS YOU'VE BEEN GIVEN...
YOU'LL SEE A COMPLETE LISTING OF ALL THE EVENTS THAT WILL BE HELD DURING THE ANSULLIVAN 500-YEAR FESTIVAL.
OBJECTION.
THEY'RE ALL BORING.
THEY'RE AN INSULT TO THE VERY NAME OF SUCH AN IMPORTANT FESTIVAL.
CARE TO EXPLAIN, OSCAR?
LOOK AT THE GENERAL EVENTS. THERE AREN'T ANY THAT WE-- AT LEAST, THE STUDENT COUNCIL MEMBERS WHO RIDE MAESTROS-- CAN PARTICIPATE IN, ARE THERE?
IT'S NOT THAT WE CAN'T PARTICIPATE, BUT...
HISTORICALLY, STUDENT COUNCIL MEMBERS BEFORE US HAVE ALL REFRAINED.
THERE'S ALSO THE PERSPECTIVE THAT FOR US TO PIT AN ORDINARY STUDENT AGAINST A MAESTRO WOULD BE SOMEWHAT IMMATURE.
THAT'S THE THING, THOUGH!
IF WE'RE BOUND BY THE SHACKLES OF THE PAST, THERE'S NO POINT TO THIS FESTIVAL BEING MORE SPECIAL THAN ANY OTHER.

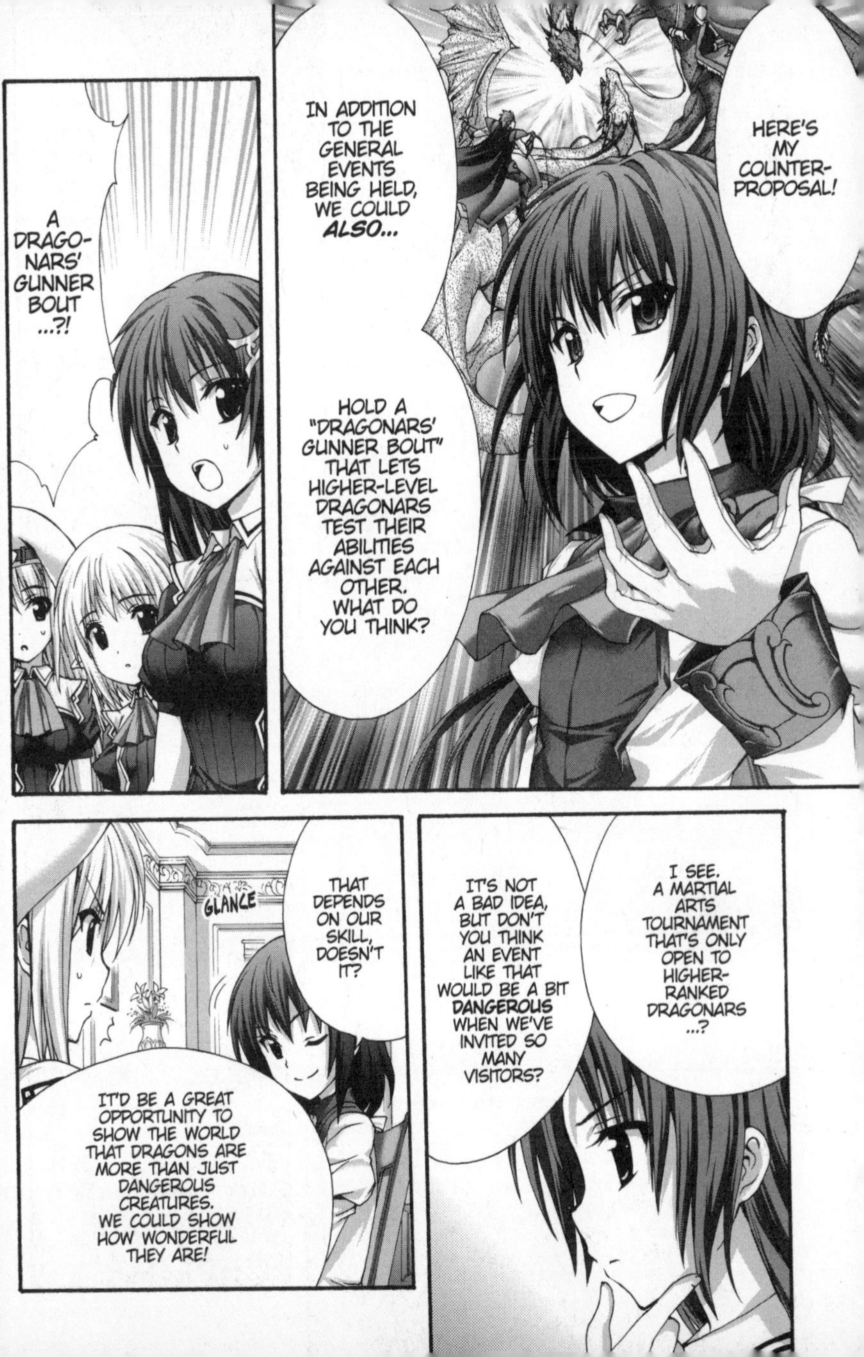
HERE'S MY COUNTER-PROPOSAL!
IN ADDITION TO THE GENERAL EVENTS BEING HELD, WE COULD ALSO...
HOLD A "DRAGONARS' GUNNER BOUT" THAT LETS HIGHER-LEVEL DRAGONARS TEST THEIR ABILITIES AGAINST EACH OTHER. WHAT DO YOU THINK?
A DRAGONARS' GUNNER BOUT ...?!
I SEE. A MARTIAL ARTS TOURNAMENT THAT'S ONLY OPEN TO HIGHER-RANKED DRAGONARS ...?
IT'S NOT A BAD IDEA, BUT DON'T YOU THINK AN EVENT LIKE THAT WOULD BE A BIT DANGEROUS WHEN WE'VE INVITED SO MANY VISITORS?
THAT DEPENDS ON OUR SKILL, DOESN'T IT?
GLANCE
IT'D BE A GREAT OPPORTUNITY TO SHOW THE WORLD THAT DRAGONS ARE MORE THAN JUST DANGEROUS CREATURES. WE COULD SHOW HOW WONDERFUL THEY ARE!

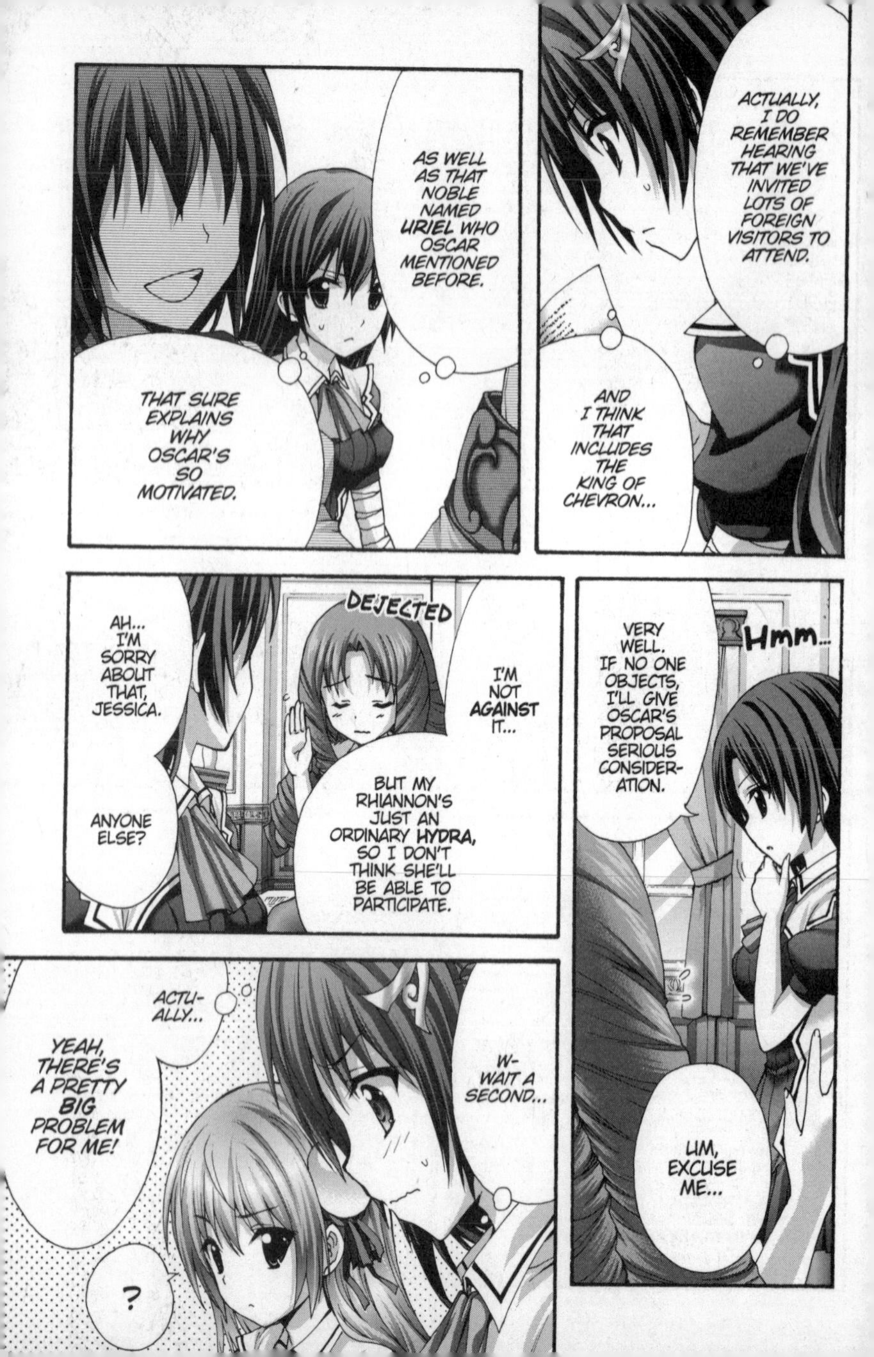
ACTUALLY, I DO REMEMBER HEARING THAT WE'VE INVITED LOTS OF FOREIGN VISITORS TO ATTEND.
AND I THINK THAT INCLUDES THE KING OF CHEVRON...
AS WELL AS THAT NOBLE NAMED **URIEL** WHO OSCAR MENTIONED BEFORE.
THAT SURE EXPLAINS WHY OSCAR'S SO MOTIVATED.
Hmm...
VERY WELL. IF NO ONE OBJECTS, I'LL GIVE OSCAR'S PROPOSAL SERIOUS CONSIDER-ATION.
UM, EXCUSE ME...
DEJECTED
I'M NOT **AGAINST** IT...
BUT MY RHIANNON'S JUST AN ORDINARY **HYDRA**, SO I DON'T THINK SHE'LL BE ABLE TO PARTICIPATE.
AH... I'M SORRY ABOUT THAT, JESSICA.
ANYONE ELSE?
W-WAIT A SECOND...
ACTU-ALLY...
YEAH, THERE'S A PRETTY **BIG** PROBLEM FOR ME!
?

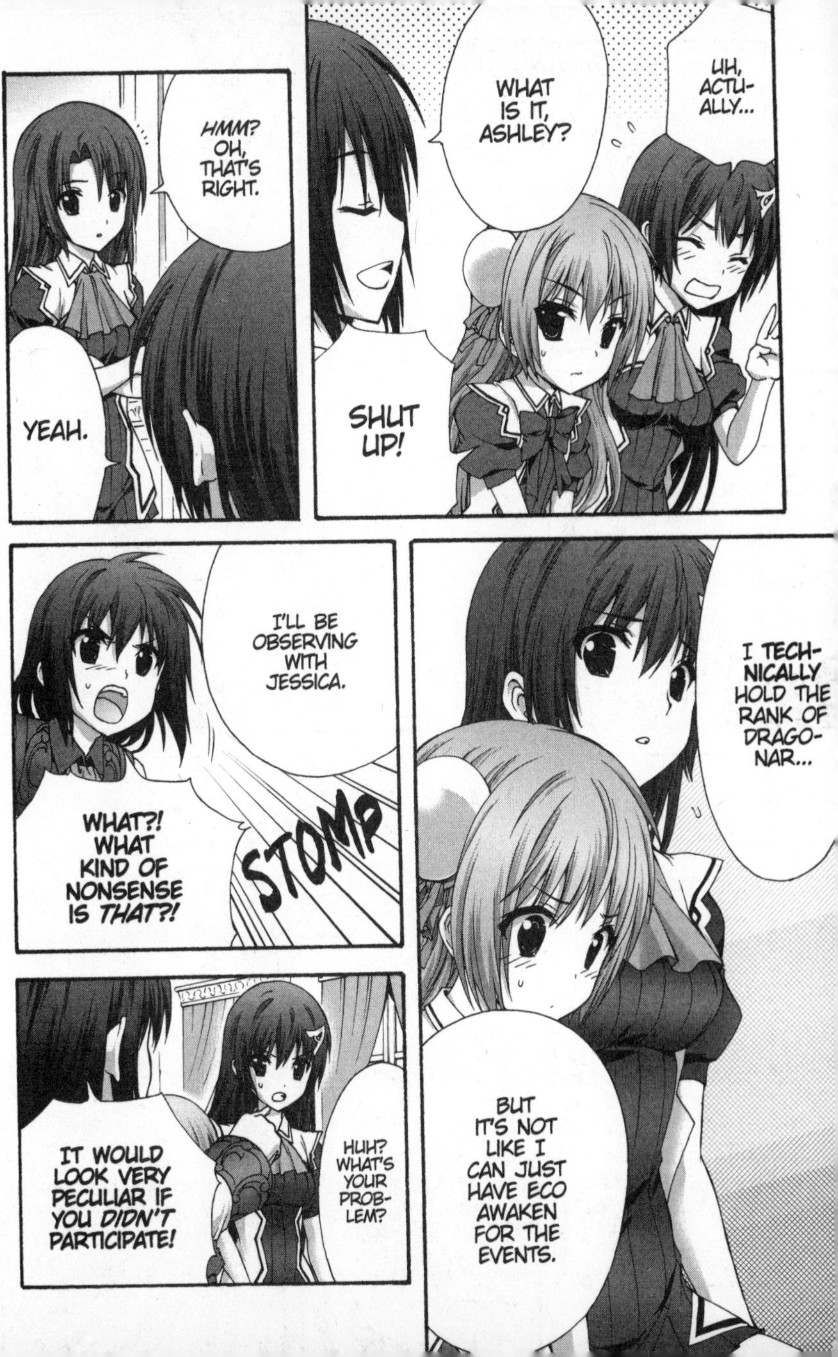
UH, ACTUALLY...
WHAT IS IT, ASHLEY?
SHUT UP!
HMM? OH, THAT'S RIGHT.
YEAH.
I TECHNICALLY HOLD THE RANK OF DRAGONAR...
BUT IT'S NOT LIKE I CAN JUST HAVE ECO AWAKEN FOR THE EVENTS.
I'LL BE OBSERVING WITH JESSICA.
WHAT?! WHAT KIND OF NONSENSE IS *THAT*?!
STOMP
HUH? WHAT'S YOUR PROBLEM?
IT WOULD LOOK VERY PECULIAR IF YOU *DIDN'T* PARTICIPATE!

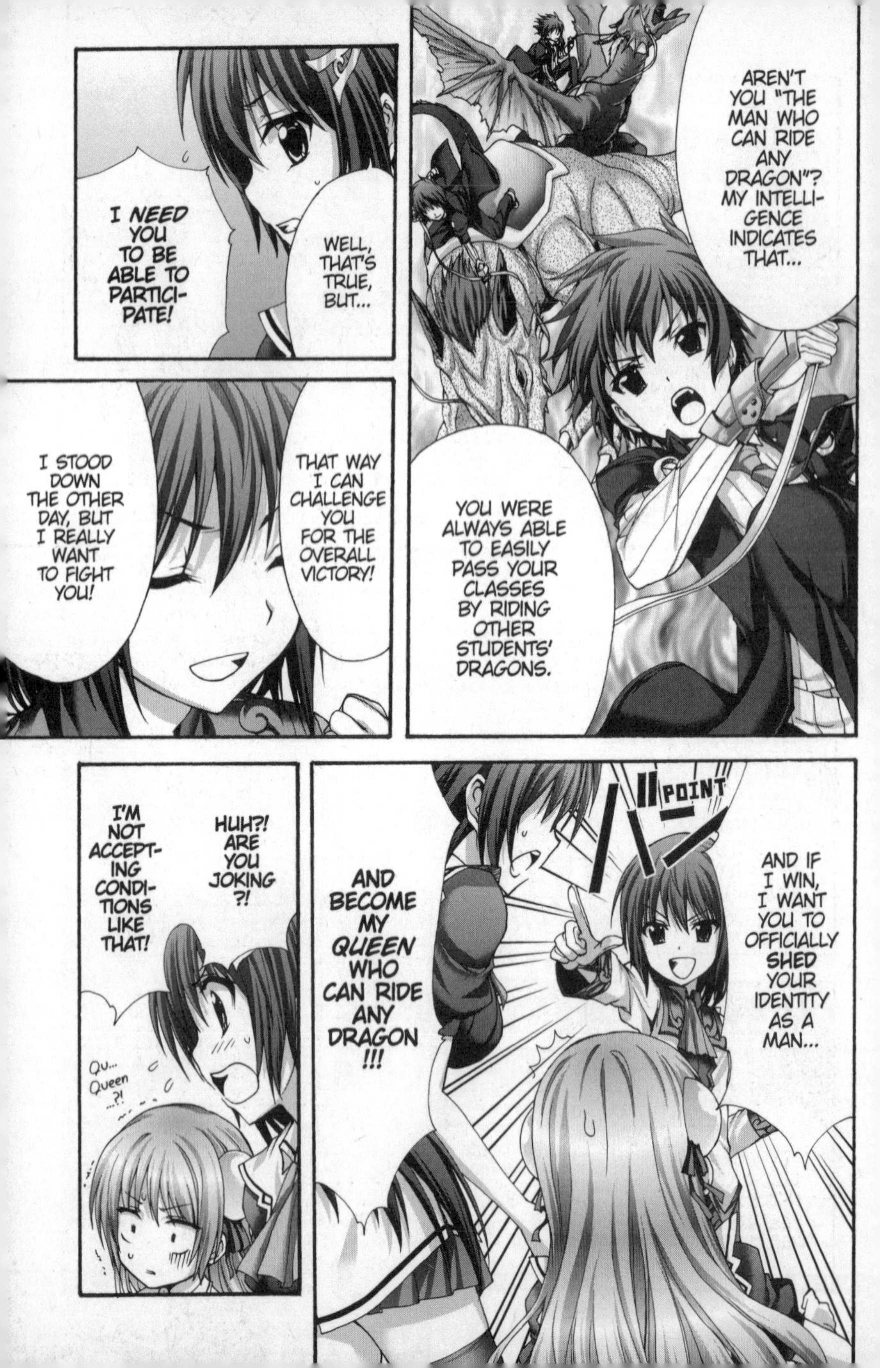
AREN'T YOU "THE MAN WHO CAN RIDE ANY DRAGON"? MY INTELLIGENCE INDICATES THAT...
YOU WERE ALWAYS ABLE TO EASILY PASS YOUR CLASSES BY RIDING OTHER STUDENTS' DRAGONS.
WELL, THAT'S TRUE, BUT...
I *NEED* YOU TO BE ABLE TO PARTICIPATE!
THAT WAY I CAN CHALLENGE YOU FOR THE OVERALL VICTORY!
I STOOD DOWN THE OTHER DAY, BUT I REALLY WANT TO FIGHT YOU!
AND IF I WIN, I WANT YOU TO OFFICIALLY SHED YOUR IDENTITY AS A MAN...
POINT
AND BECOME MY *QUEEN* WHO CAN RIDE ANY DRAGON!!!
HUH?! ARE YOU JOKING?!
I'M NOT ACCEPTING CONDITIONS LIKE THAT!
Qu... Queen ...?!

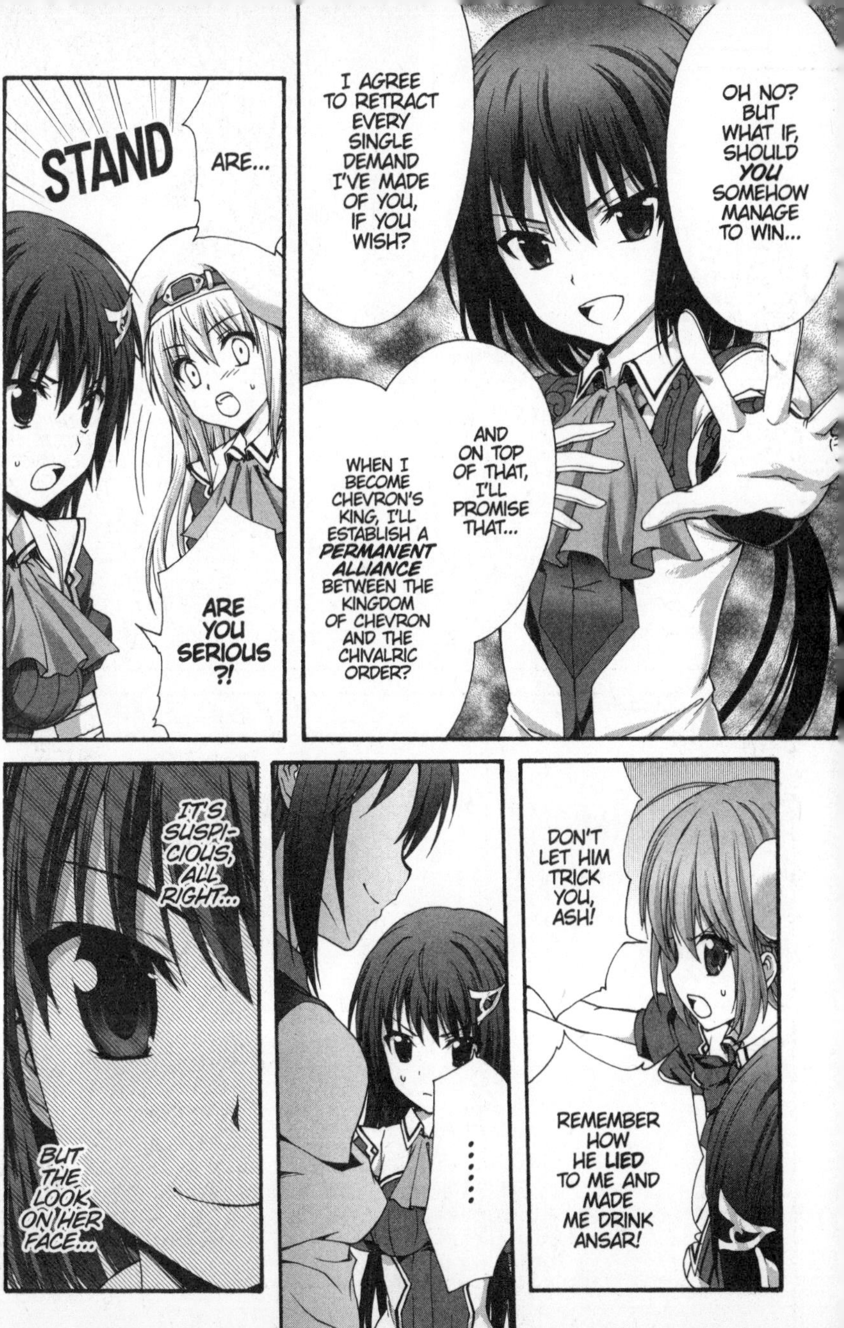
OH NO? BUT WHAT IF, SHOULD YOU SOMEHOW MANAGE TO WIN...
I AGREE TO RETRACT EVERY SINGLE DEMAND I'VE MADE OF YOU, IF YOU WISH?
AND ON TOP OF THAT, I'LL PROMISE THAT...
WHEN I BECOME CHEVRON'S KING, I'LL ESTABLISH A PERMANENT ALLIANCE BETWEEN THE KINGDOM OF CHEVRON AND THE CHIVALRIC ORDER?
STAND
ARE...
ARE YOU SERIOUS?!
DON'T LET HIM TRICK YOU, ASH!
REMEMBER HOW HE LIED TO ME AND MADE ME DRINK ANSAR!
......
IT'S SUSPICIOUS, ALL RIGHT...
BUT THE LOOK ON HER FACE...

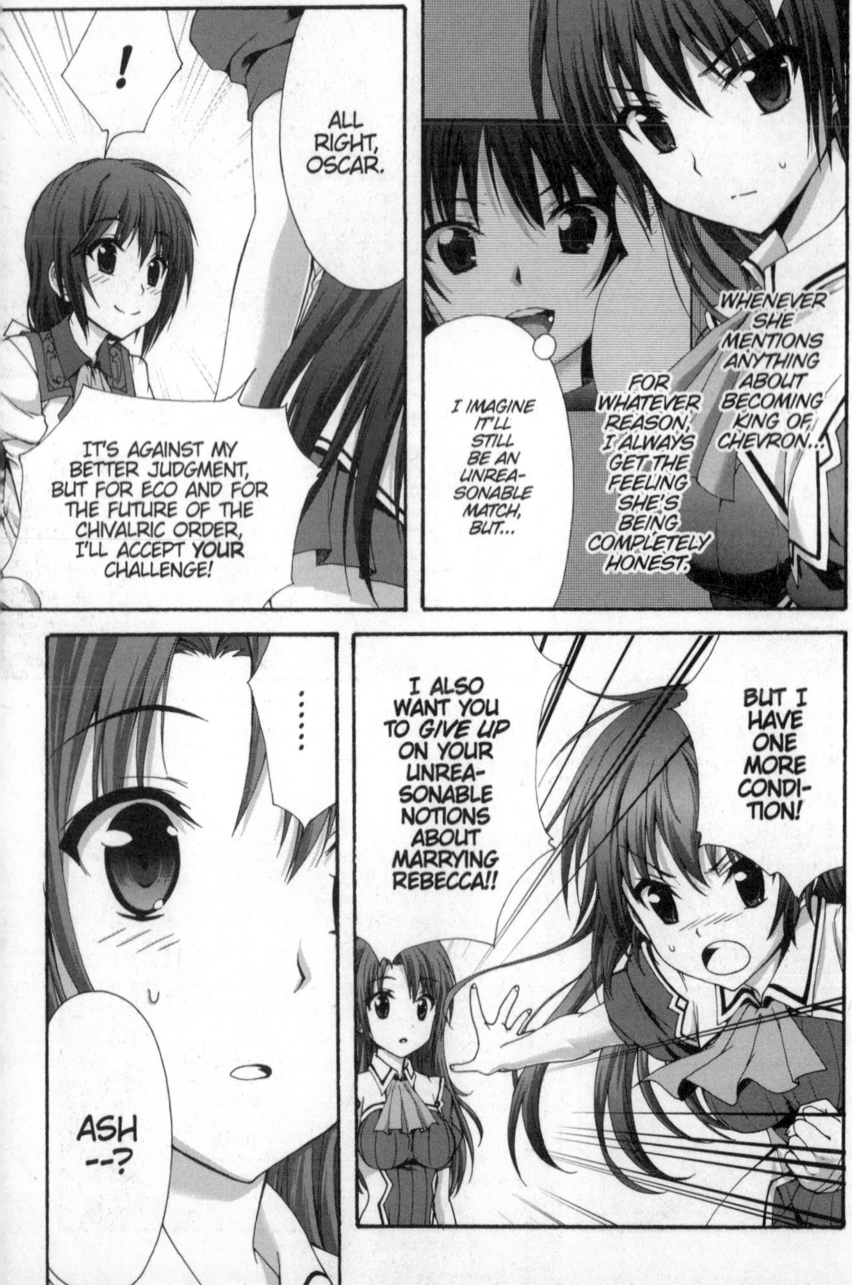
WHENEVER SHE MENTIONS ANYTHING ABOUT BECOMING KING OF CHEVRON...
FOR WHATEVER REASON, I ALWAYS GET THE FEELING SHE'S BEING COMPLETELY HONEST.
I IMAGINE IT'LL STILL BE AN UNREA-SONABLE MATCH, BUT...
ALL RIGHT, OSCAR.
!
IT'S AGAINST MY BETTER JUDGMENT, BUT FOR ECO AND FOR THE FUTURE OF THE CHIVALRIC ORDER, I'LL ACCEPT YOUR CHALLENGE!
BUT I HAVE ONE MORE CONDI-TION!
I ALSO WANT YOU TO GIVE UP ON YOUR UNREA-SONABLE NOTIONS ABOUT MARRYING REBECCA!!
......
ASH --?

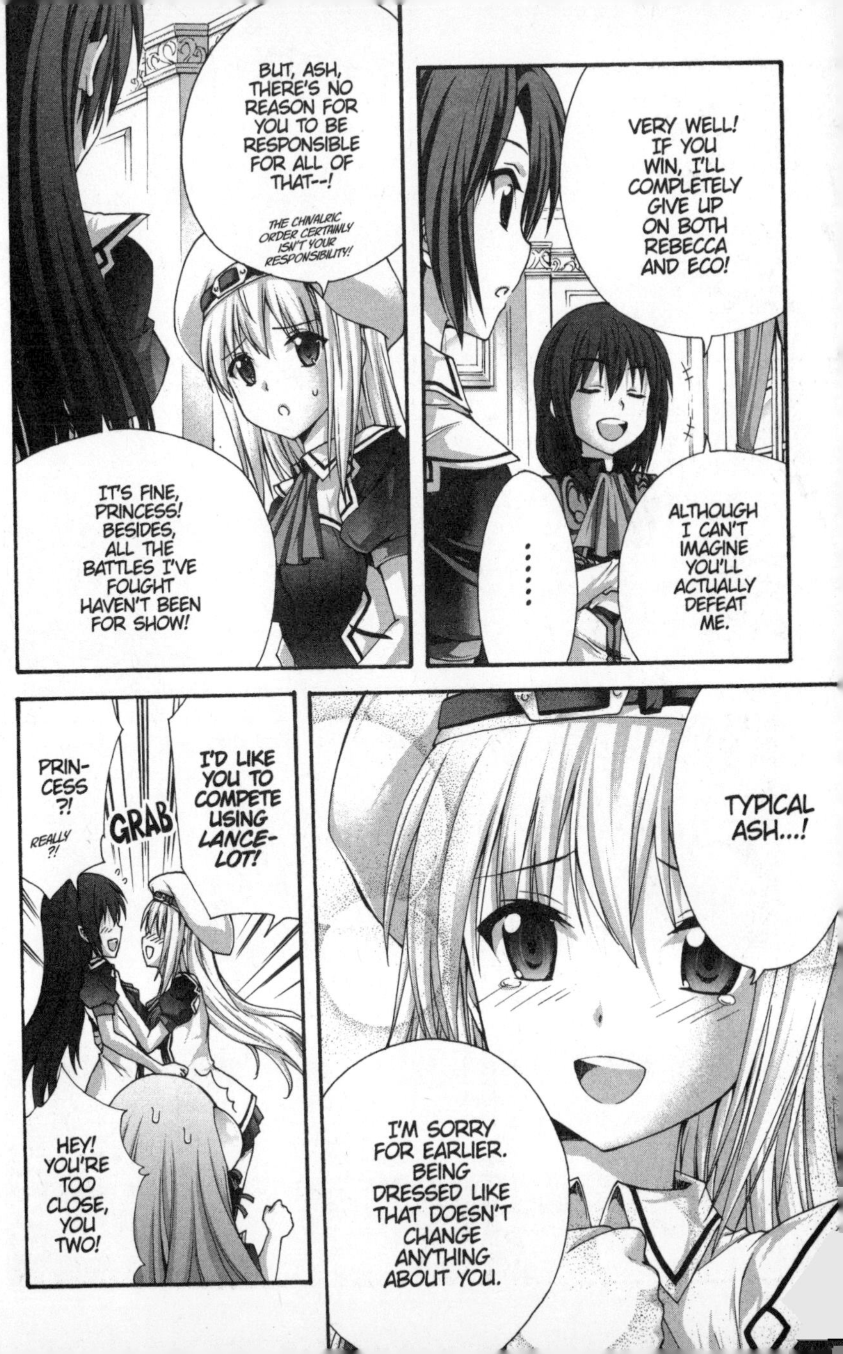
VERY WELL! IF YOU WIN, I'LL COMPLETELY GIVE UP ON BOTH REBECCA AND ECO!
ALTHOUGH I CAN'T IMAGINE YOU'LL ACTUALLY DEFEAT ME.
......
BUT, ASH, THERE'S NO REASON FOR YOU TO BE RESPONSIBLE FOR ALL OF THAT--!
THE CHIVALRIC ORDER CERTAINLY ISN'T YOUR RESPONSIBILITY!
IT'S FINE, PRINCESS! BESIDES, ALL THE BATTLES I'VE FOUGHT HAVEN'T BEEN FOR SHOW!
TYPICAL ASH...!
I'M SORRY FOR EARLIER. BEING DRESSED LIKE THAT DOESN'T CHANGE ANYTHING ABOUT YOU.
I'D LIKE YOU TO COMPETE USING LANCE-LOT!
GRAB
PRIN-CESS?!
REALLY?!
HEY! YOU'RE TOO CLOSE, YOU TWO!

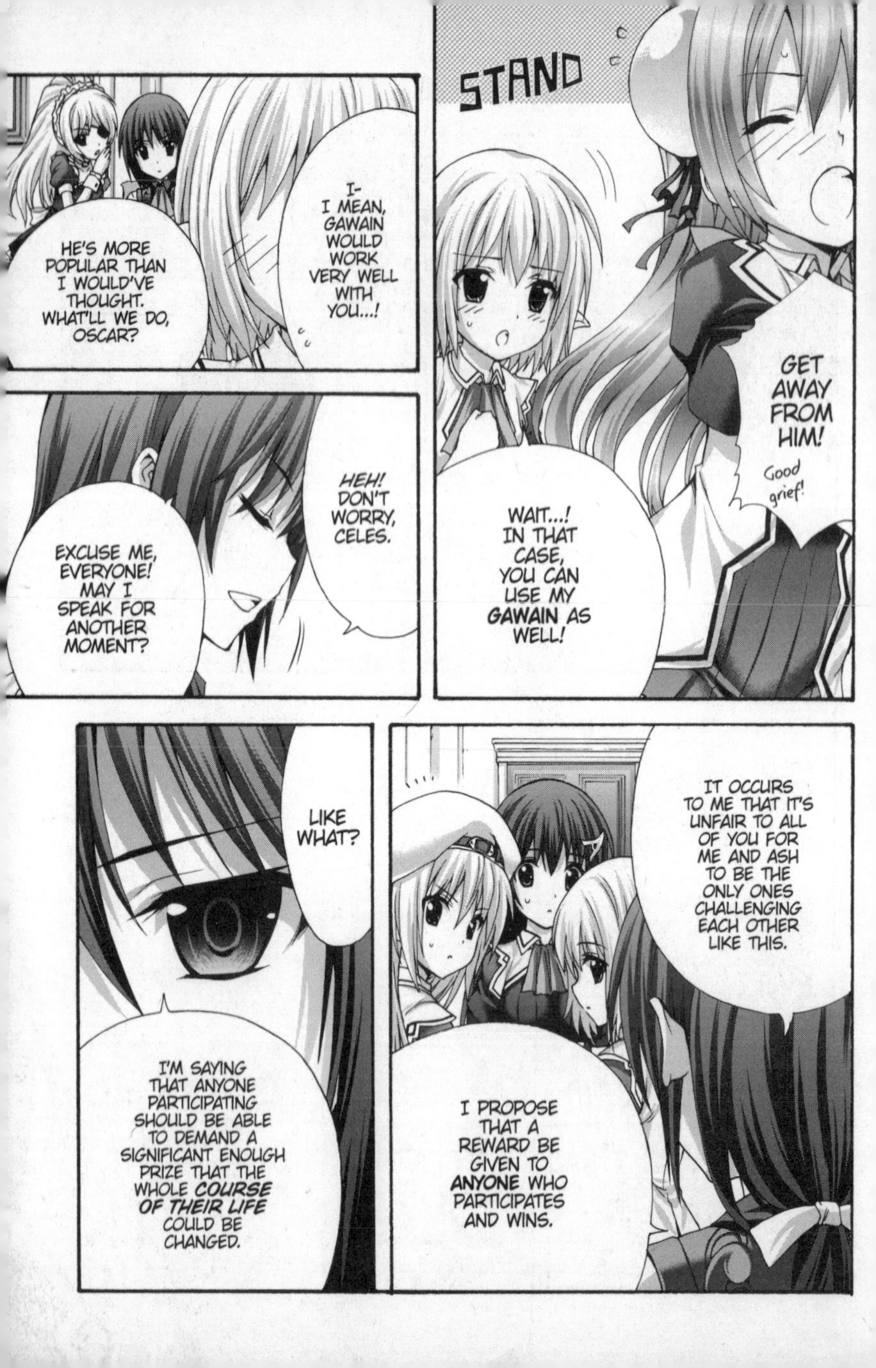
STAND
GET AWAY FROM HIM!
Good grief!
WAIT...! IN THAT CASE, YOU CAN USE MY **GAWAIN** AS WELL!
I- I MEAN, GAWAIN WOULD WORK VERY WELL WITH YOU...!
HE'S MORE POPULAR THAN I WOULD'VE THOUGHT. WHAT'LL WE DO, OSCAR?
HEH! DON'T WORRY, CELES.
EXCUSE ME, EVERYONE! MAY I SPEAK FOR ANOTHER MOMENT?
IT OCCURS TO ME THAT IT'S UNFAIR TO ALL OF YOU FOR ME AND ASH TO BE THE ONLY ONES CHALLENGING EACH OTHER LIKE THIS.
I PROPOSE THAT A REWARD BE GIVEN TO **ANYONE** WHO PARTICIPATES AND WINS.
LIKE WHAT?
I'M SAYING THAT ANYONE PARTICIPATING SHOULD BE ABLE TO DEMAND A SIGNIFICANT ENOUGH PRIZE THAT THE WHOLE ***COURSE OF THEIR LIFE*** COULD BE CHANGED.

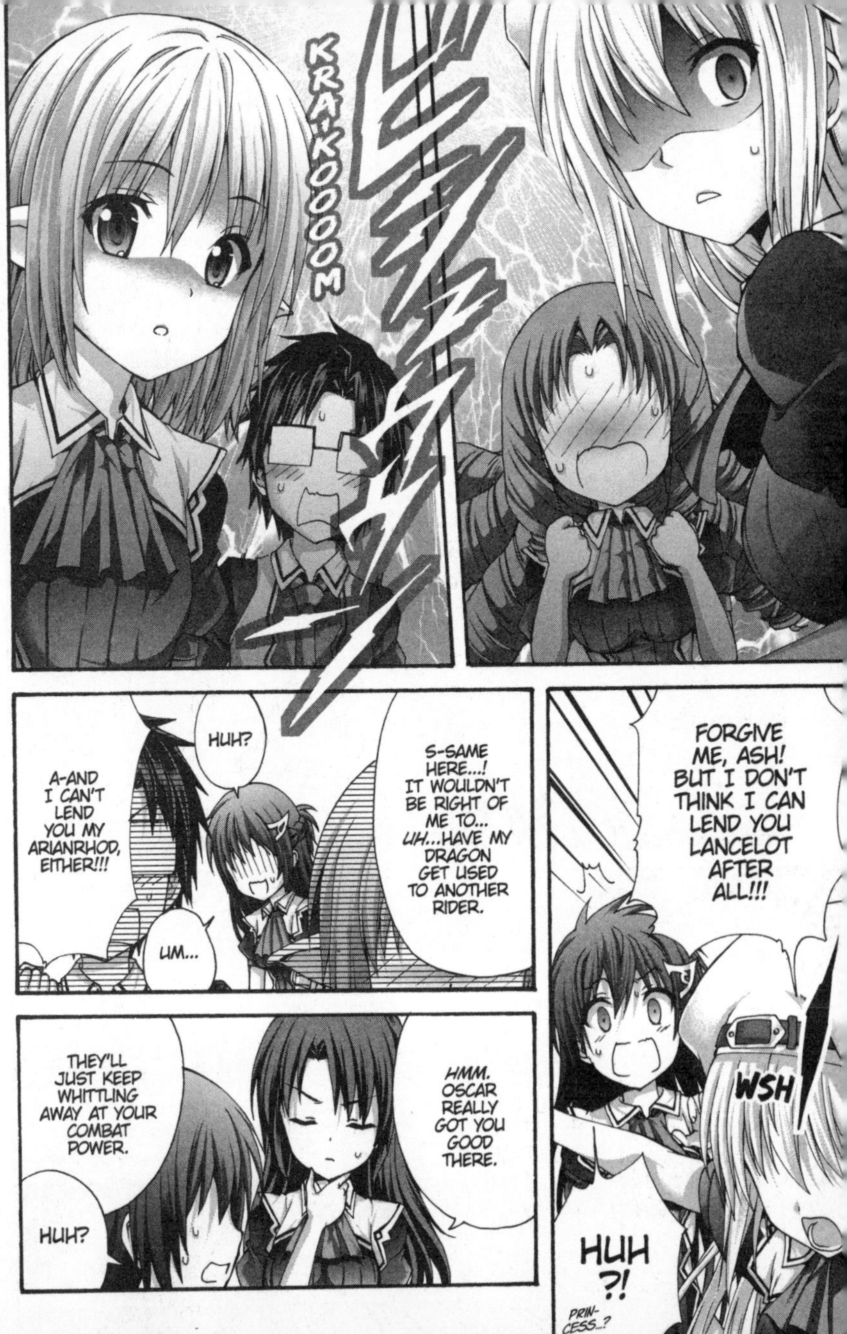
KRAKOOOOOM
FORGIVE ME, ASH! BUT I DON'T THINK I CAN LEND YOU LANCELOT AFTER ALL!!!
WSH
HUH ?!
PRIN- CESS...?
S-SAME HERE...! IT WOULDN'T BE RIGHT OF ME TO... UH...HAVE MY DRAGON GET USED TO ANOTHER RIDER.
HUH?
A-AND I CAN'T LEND YOU MY ARIANRHOD, EITHER!!!
UM...
HMM. OSCAR REALLY GOT YOU GOOD THERE.
THEY'LL JUST KEEP WHITTLING AWAY AT YOUR COMBAT POWER.
HUH?

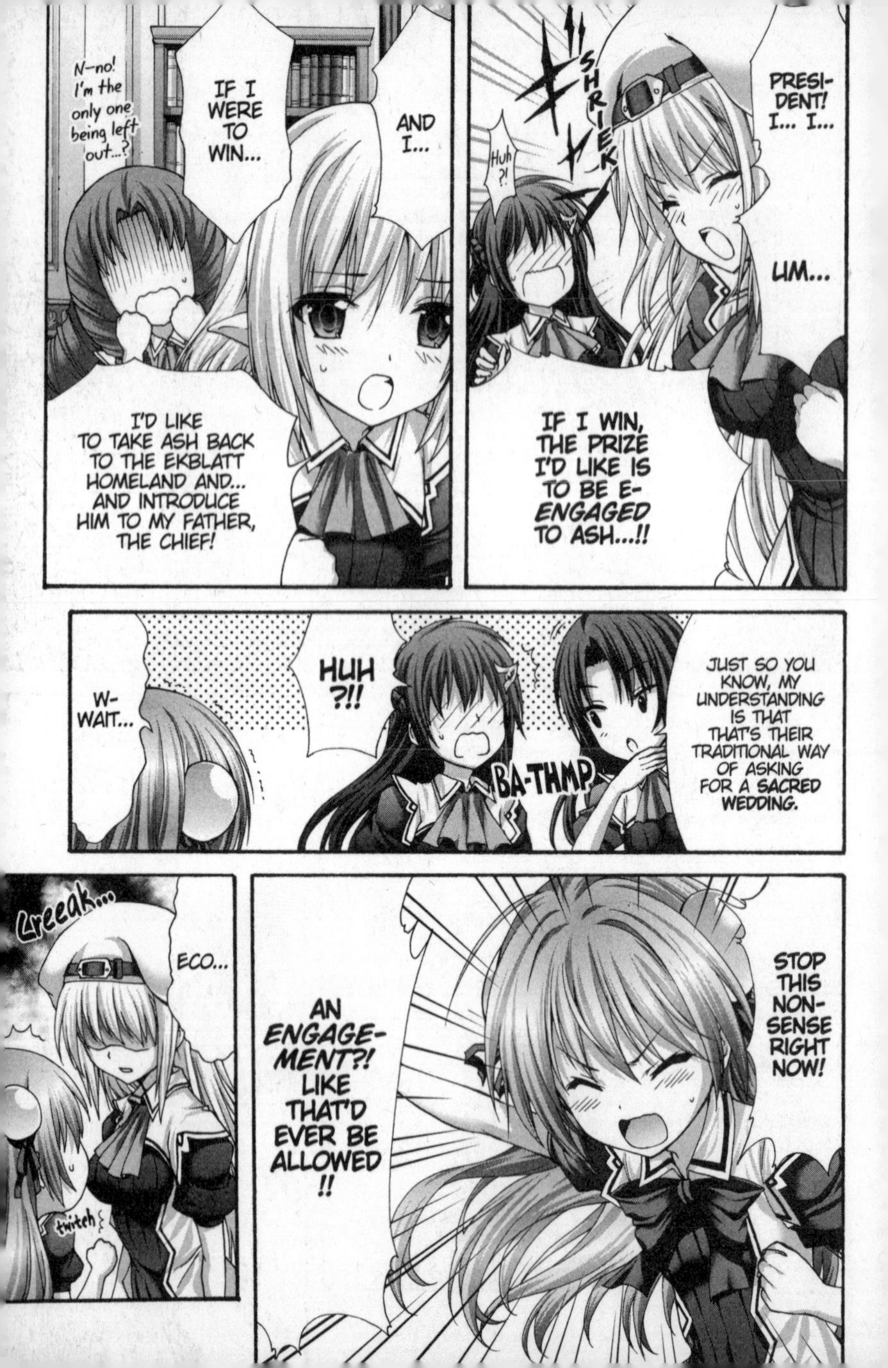

PRESIDENT! I... I...
SHRIEK
Huh ?!
UM...
IF I WIN, THE PRIZE I'D LIKE IS TO BE E-ENGAGED TO ASH...!!
AND I...
IF I WERE TO WIN...
N-no! I'm the only one being left out...?
I'D LIKE TO TAKE ASH BACK TO THE EKBLATT HOMELAND AND... AND INTRODUCE HIM TO MY FATHER, THE CHIEF!
JUST SO YOU KNOW, MY UNDERSTANDING IS THAT THAT'S THEIR TRADITIONAL WAY OF ASKING FOR A SACRED WEDDING.
BA-THMP
HUH ?!!
W-WAIT...
STOP THIS NON-SENSE RIGHT NOW!
AN ENGAGE-MENT?! LIKE THAT'D EVER BE ALLOWED !!
Creeak...
ECO...
twitch

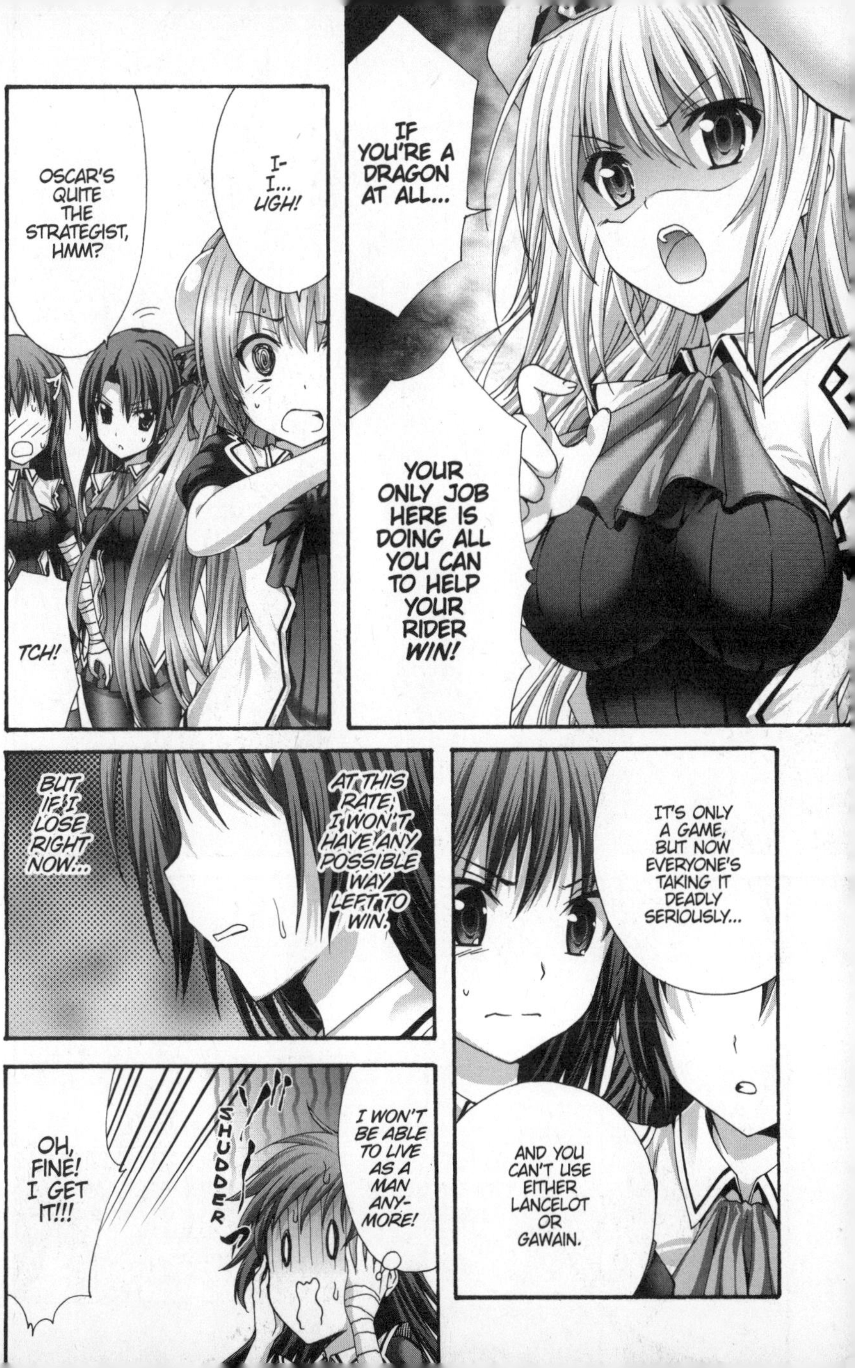
IF YOU'RE A DRAGON AT ALL...
YOUR ONLY JOB HERE IS DOING ALL YOU CAN TO HELP YOUR RIDER WIN!
I- I... UGH!
OSCAR'S QUITE THE STRATEGIST, HMM?
TCH!
IT'S ONLY A GAME, BUT NOW EVERYONE'S TAKING IT DEADLY SERIOUSLY...
AND YOU CAN'T USE EITHER LANCELOT OR GAWAIN.
AT THIS RATE, I WON'T HAVE ANY POSSIBLE WAY LEFT TO WIN.
BUT IF I LOSE RIGHT NOW...
I WON'T BE ABLE TO LIVE AS A MAN ANY-MORE!
SHUDDER
OH, FINE! I GET IT!!!

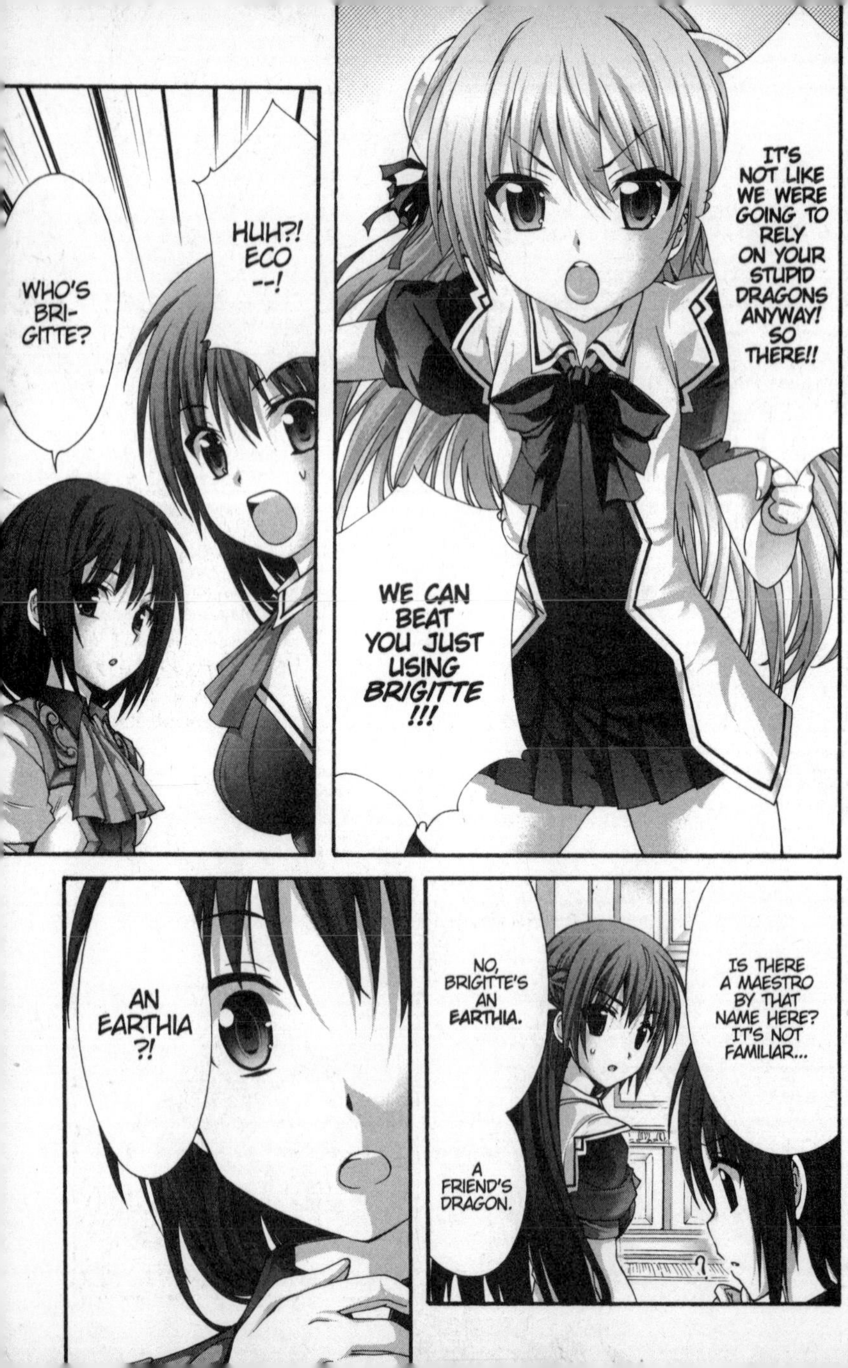
IT'S NOT LIKE WE WERE GOING TO RELY ON YOUR STUPID DRAGONS ANYWAY! SO THERE!!
WE CAN BEAT YOU JUST USING BRIGITTE!!!
HUH?! ECO--!
WHO'S BRI-GITTE?
IS THERE A MAESTRO BY THAT NAME HERE? IT'S NOT FAMILIAR...
NO, BRIGITTE'S AN EARTHIA.
A FRIEND'S DRAGON.
AN EARTHIA?!

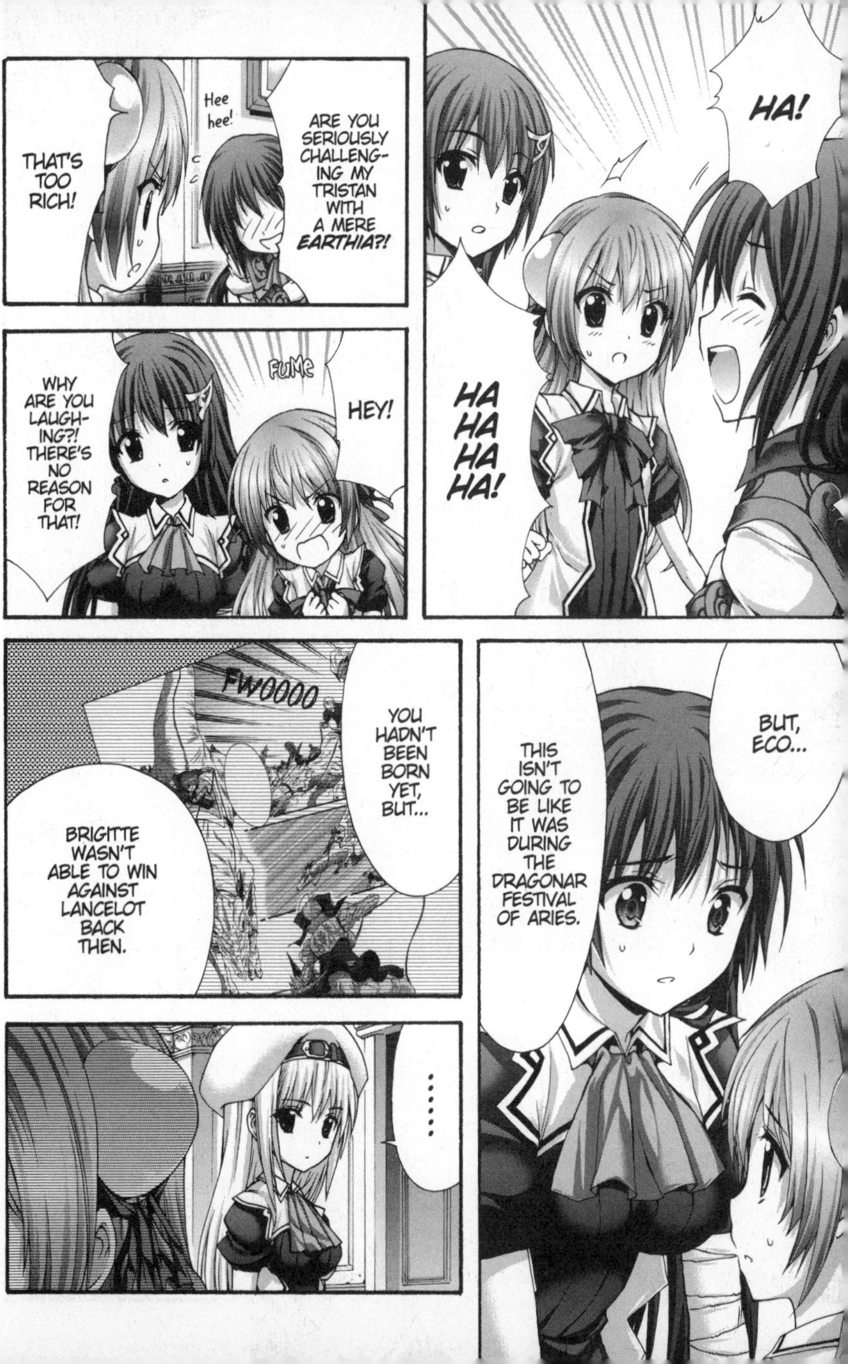
HA!
HA HA HA HA!
ARE YOU SERIOUSLY CHALLENGING MY TRISTAN WITH A MERE EARTHIA?!
Hee hee!
THAT'S TOO RICH!
HEY!
FuMe
WHY ARE YOU LAUGHING?! THERE'S NO REASON FOR THAT!
BUT, ECO...
THIS ISN'T GOING TO BE LIKE IT WAS DURING THE DRAGONAR FESTIVAL OF ARIES.
YOU HADN'T BEEN BORN YET, BUT...
FWOOOO
BRIGITTE WASN'T ABLE TO WIN AGAINST LANCELOT BACK THEN.
......

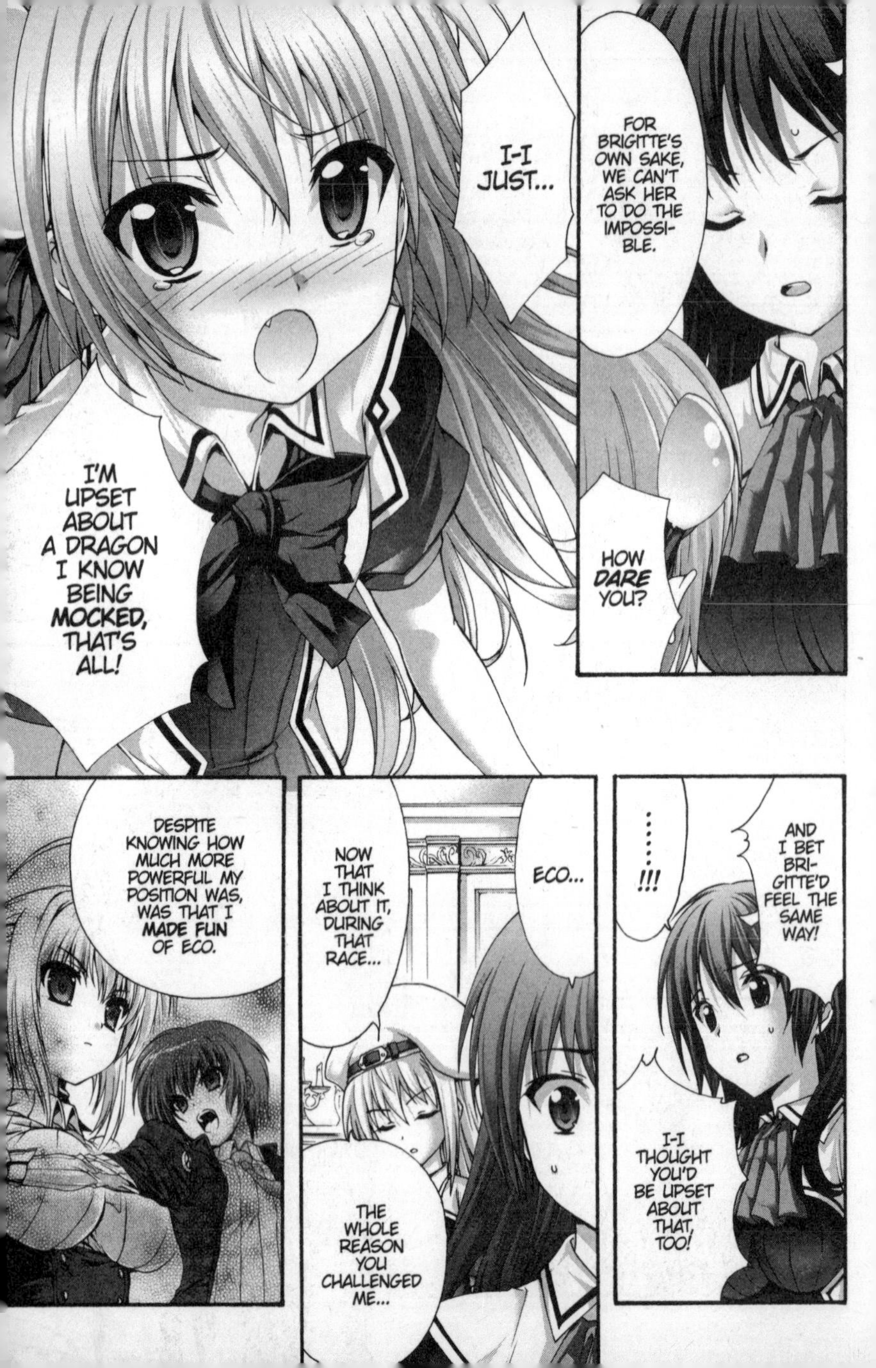
FOR BRIGITTE'S OWN SAKE, WE CAN'T ASK HER TO DO THE IMPOSSIBLE.
HOW **DARE** YOU?
I-I JUST...
I'M UPSET ABOUT A DRAGON I KNOW BEING **MOCKED**, THAT'S ALL!
AND I BET BRIGITTE'D FEEL THE SAME WAY!
......!!!
I-I THOUGHT YOU'D BE UPSET ABOUT THAT, TOO!
ECO...
NOW THAT I THINK ABOUT IT, DURING THAT RACE...
THE WHOLE REASON YOU CHALLENGED ME...
DESPITE KNOWING HOW MUCH MORE POWERFUL MY POSITION WAS, WAS THAT I **MADE FUN** OF ECO.

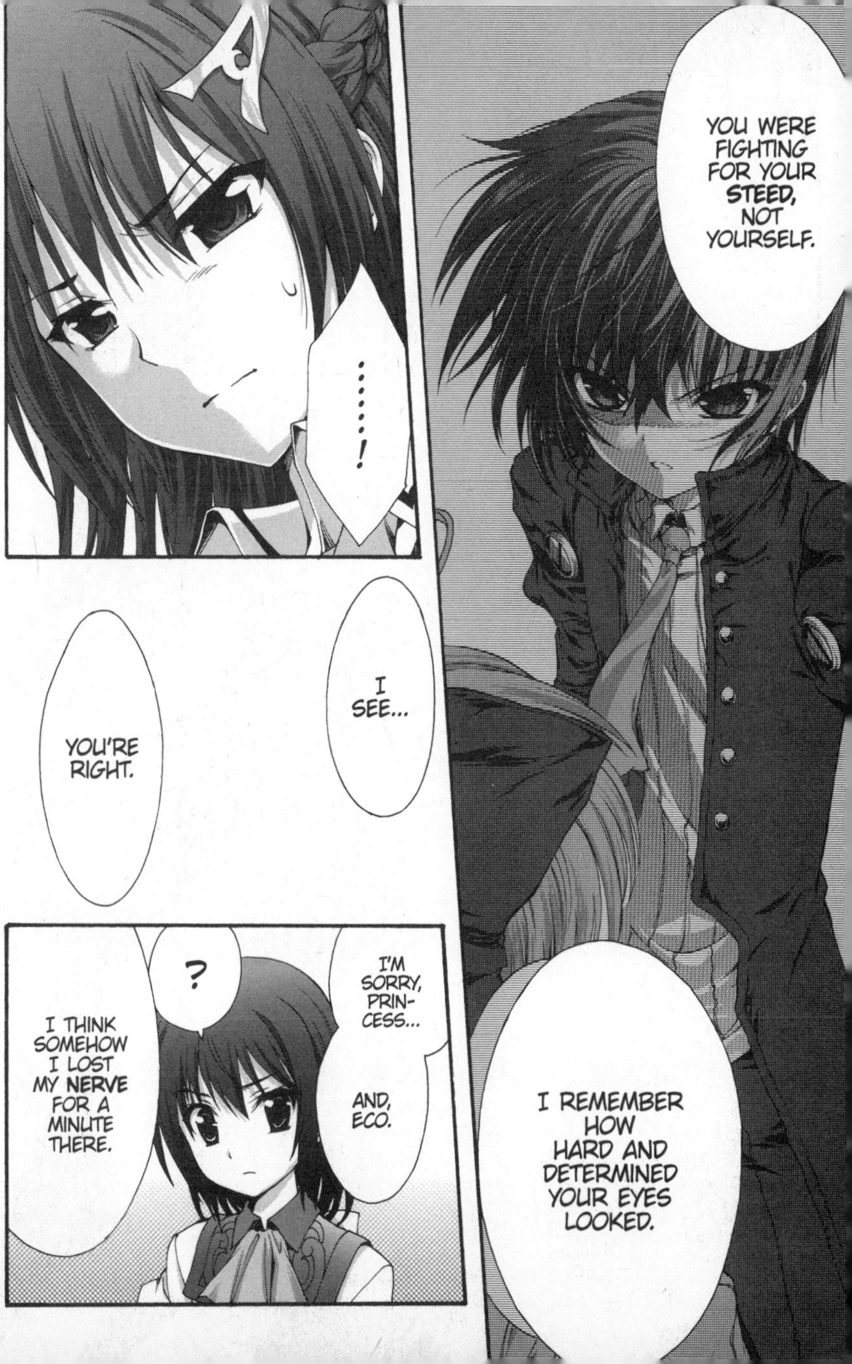
YOU WERE FIGHTING FOR YOUR STEED, NOT YOURSELF.
I REMEMBER HOW HARD AND DETERMINED YOUR EYES LOOKED.
......!
I SEE...
YOU'RE RIGHT.
I'M SORRY, PRINCESS...
AND, ECO.
?
I THINK SOMEHOW I LOST MY NERVE FOR A MINUTE THERE.

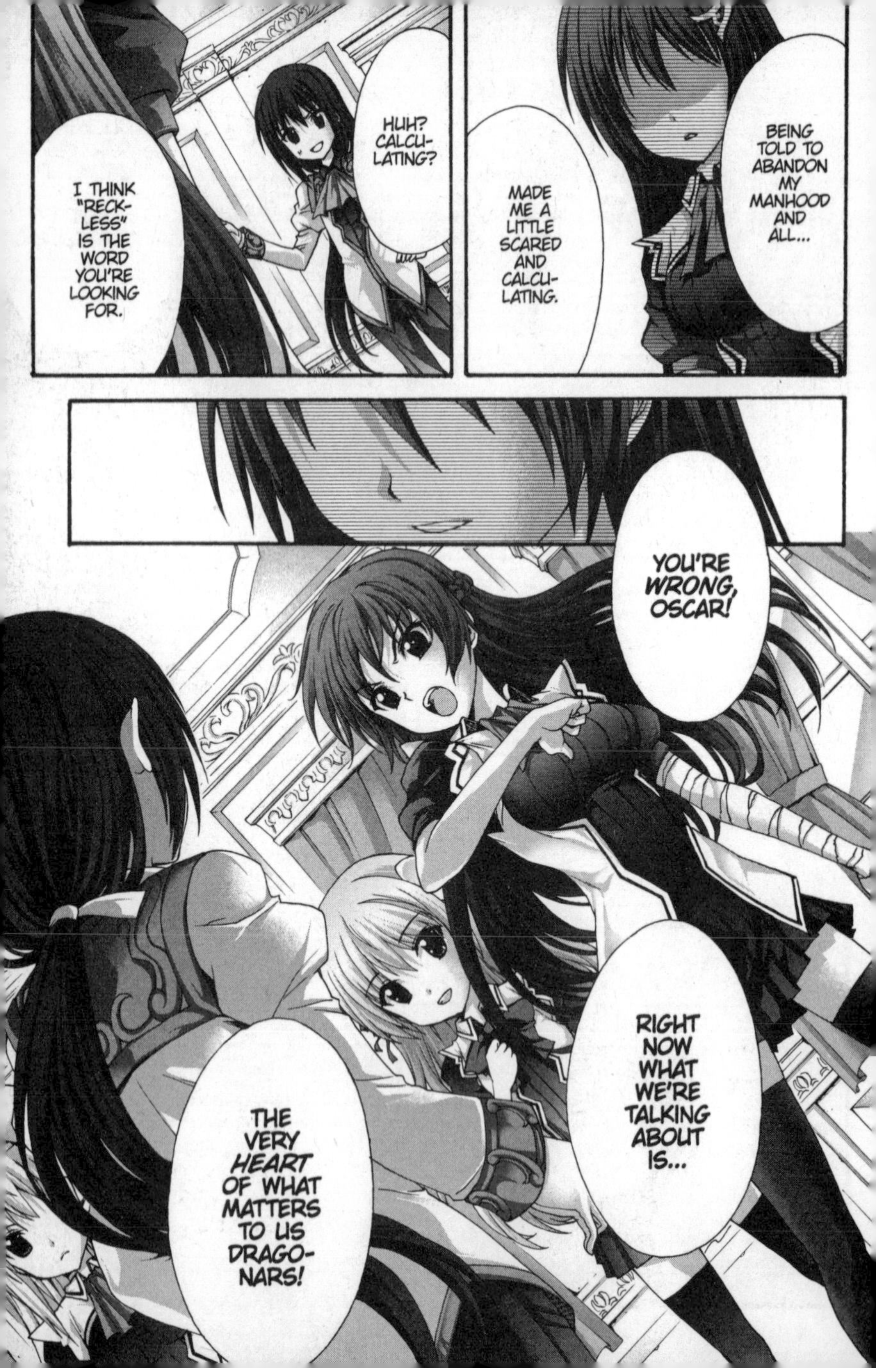
BEING TOLD TO ABANDON MY MANHOOD AND ALL...
MADE ME A LITTLE SCARED AND CALCULATING.
HUH? CALCULATING?
I THINK "RECKLESS" IS THE WORD YOU'RE LOOKING FOR.
YOU'RE *WRONG*, OSCAR!
RIGHT NOW WHAT WE'RE TALKING ABOUT IS...
THE VERY *HEART* OF WHAT MATTERS TO US DRAGONARS!

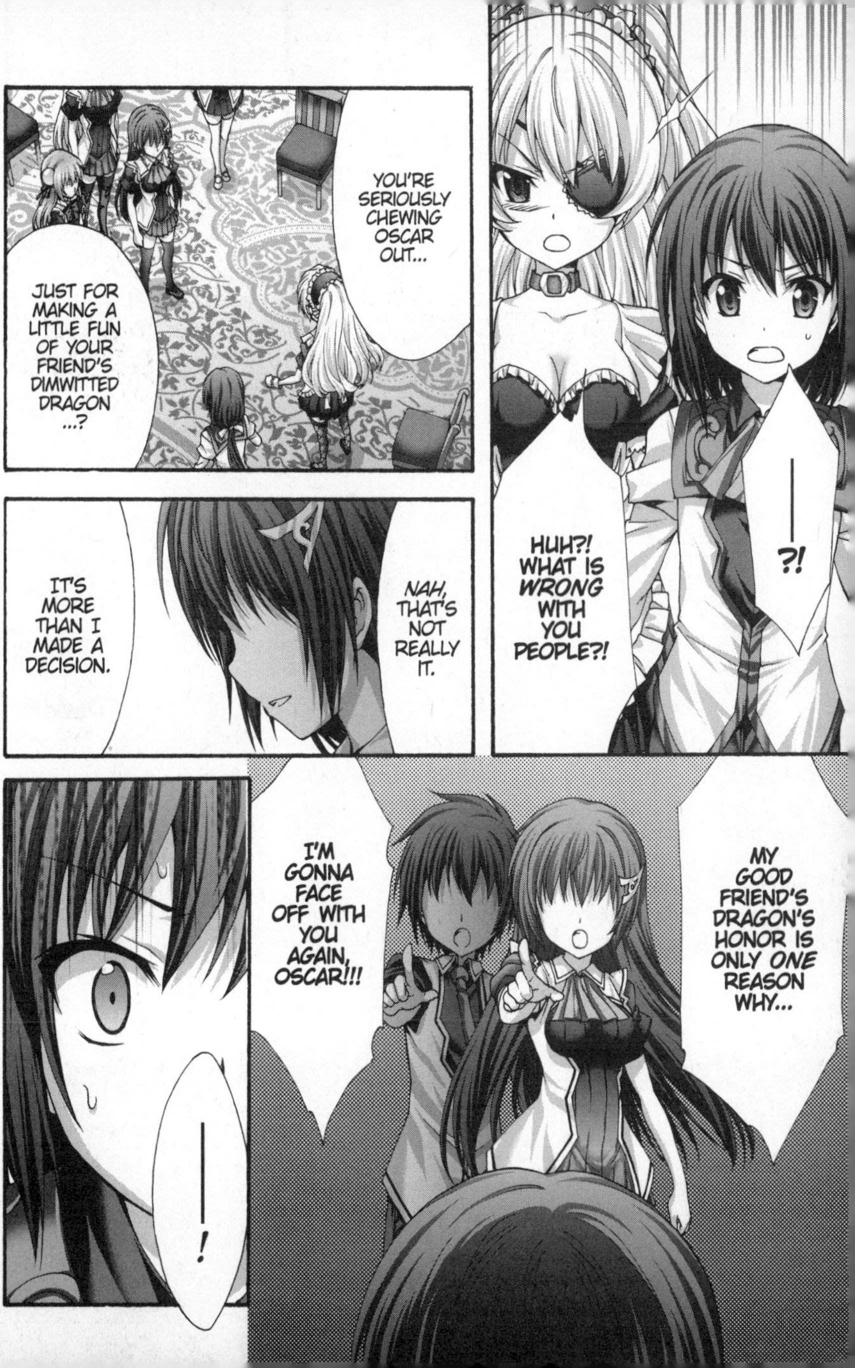
—?!
HUH?! WHAT IS *WRONG* WITH YOU PEOPLE?!
YOU'RE SERIOUSLY CHEWING OSCAR OUT...
JUST FOR MAKING A LITTLE FUN OF YOUR FRIEND'S DIMWITTED DRAGON ...?
NAH, THAT'S NOT REALLY IT.
IT'S MORE THAN I MADE A DECISION.
MY GOOD FRIEND'S DRAGON'S HONOR IS ONLY *ONE* REASON WHY...
I'M GONNA FACE OFF WITH YOU AGAIN, OSCAR!!!
—!

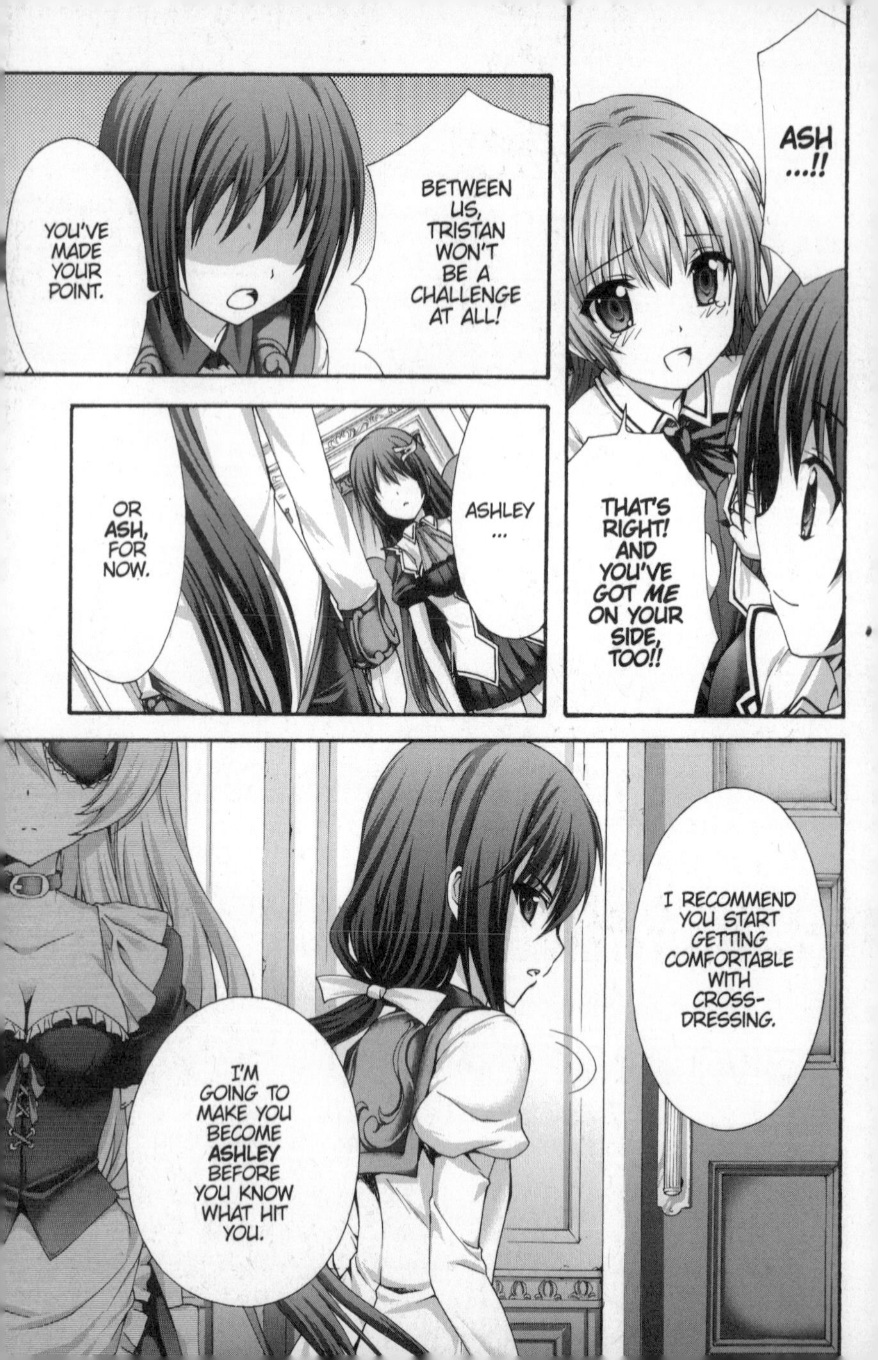
ASH ...!!
THAT'S RIGHT! AND YOU'VE GOT ME ON YOUR SIDE, TOO!!
BETWEEN US, TRISTAN WON'T BE A CHALLENGE AT ALL!
YOU'VE MADE YOUR POINT.
ASHLEY ...
OR ASH, FOR NOW.
I RECOMMEND YOU START GETTING COMFORTABLE WITH CROSS-DRESSING.
I'M GOING TO MAKE YOU BECOME ASHLEY BEFORE YOU KNOW WHAT HIT YOU.

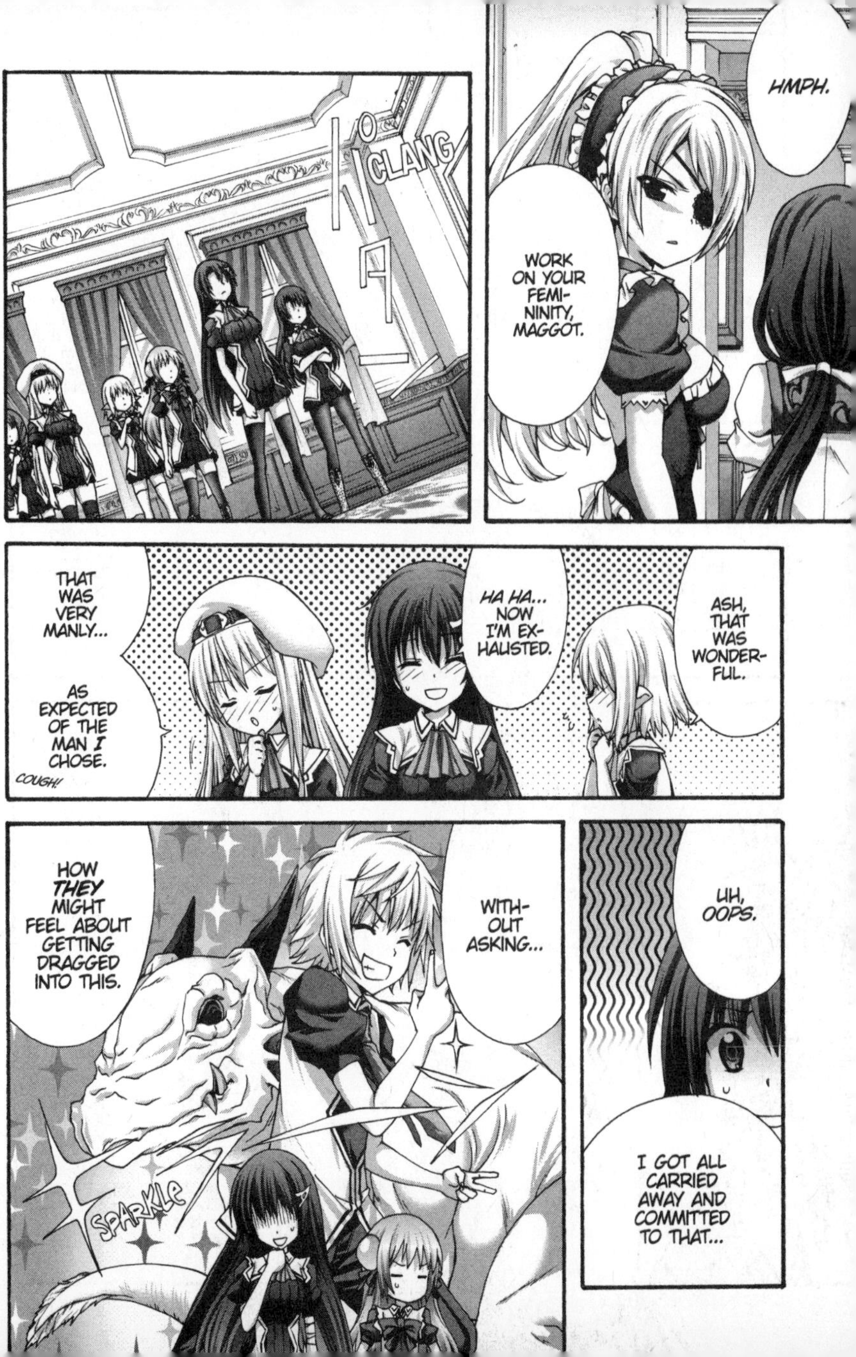
HMPH.
WORK ON YOUR FEMININITY, MAGGOT.
CLANG
ASH, THAT WAS WONDERFUL.
HA HA... NOW I'M EXHAUSTED.
THAT WAS VERY MANLY...
AS EXPECTED OF THE MAN *I* CHOSE.
COUGH!
UH, OOPS.
I GOT ALL CARRIED AWAY AND COMMITTED TO THAT...
WITHOUT ASKING...
HOW **THEY** MIGHT FEEL ABOUT GETTING DRAGGED INTO THIS.
SPARKLE

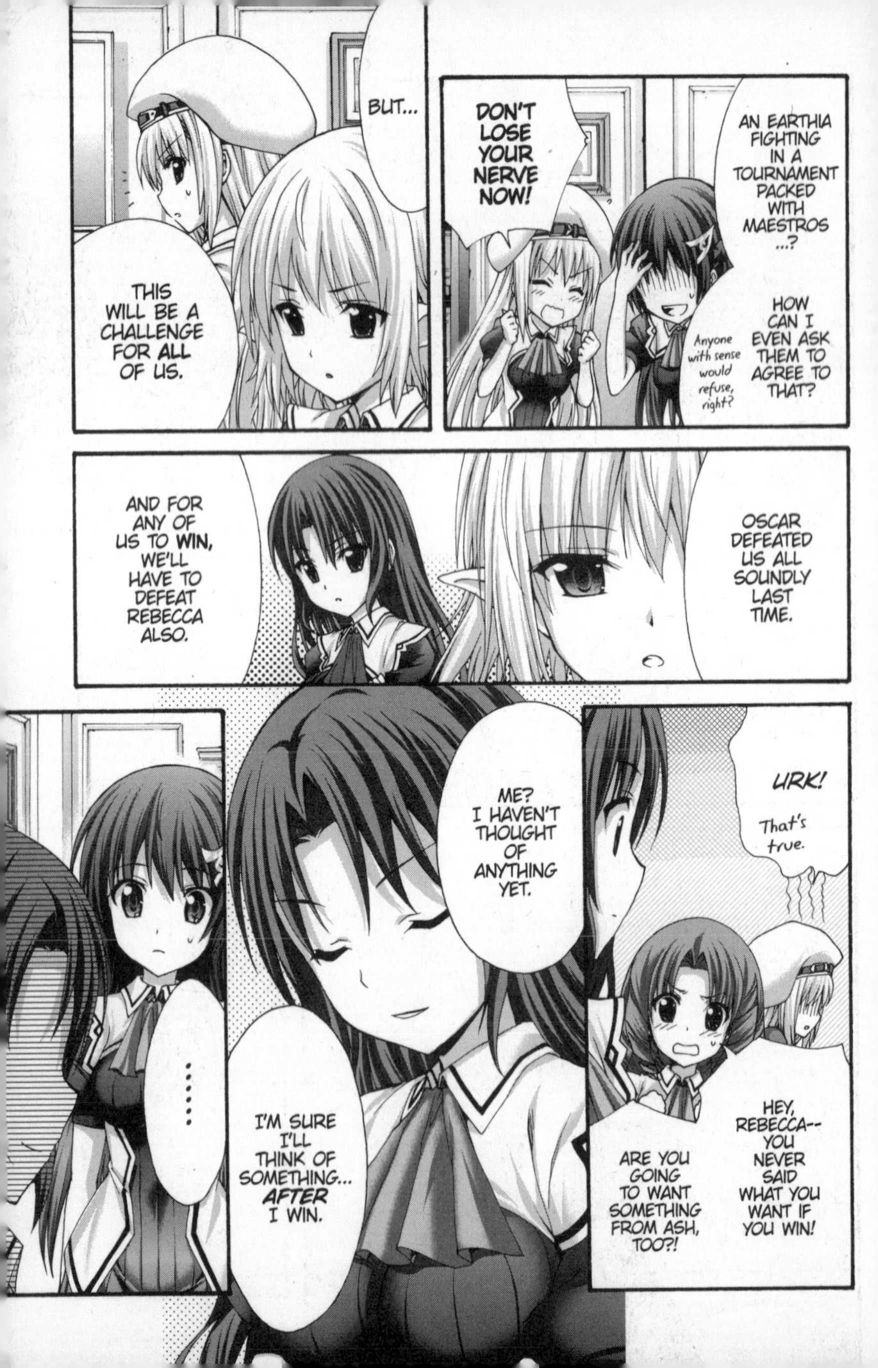
AN EARTHIA FIGHTING IN A TOURNAMENT PACKED WITH MAESTROS ...?
HOW CAN I EVEN ASK THEM TO AGREE TO THAT?
Anyone with sense would refuse, right?
DON'T LOSE YOUR NERVE NOW!
BUT...
THIS WILL BE A CHALLENGE FOR **ALL** OF US.
OSCAR DEFEATED US ALL SOUNDLY LAST TIME.
AND FOR ANY OF US TO **WIN**, WE'LL HAVE TO DEFEAT REBECCA ALSO.
URK!
That's true.
HEY, REBECCA-- YOU NEVER SAID WHAT YOU WANT IF YOU WIN!
ARE YOU GOING TO WANT SOMETHING FROM ASH, TOO?!
ME? I HAVEN'T THOUGHT OF ANYTHING YET.
I'M SURE I'LL THINK OF SOMETHING... ***AFTER*** I WIN.
......

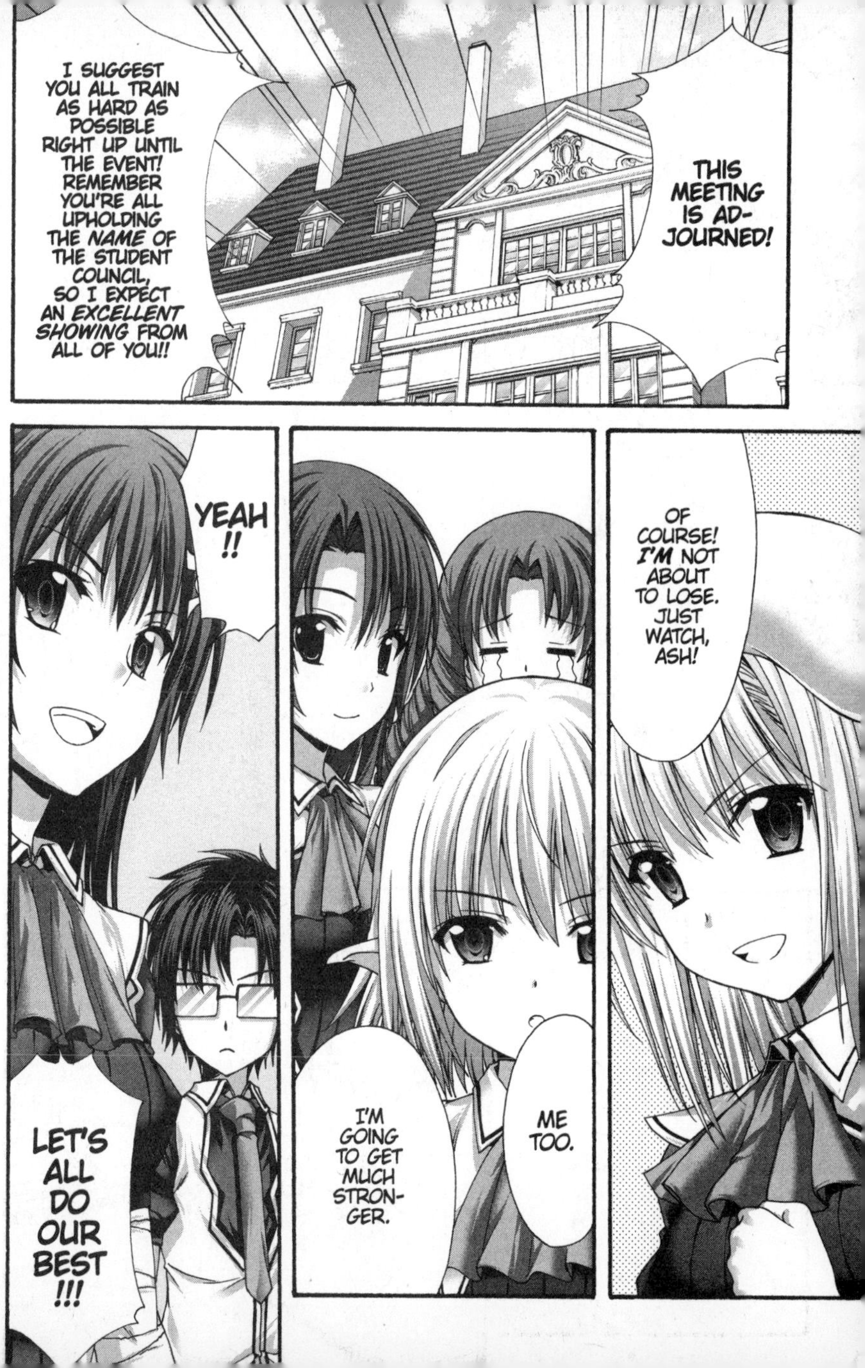

I SUGGEST YOU ALL TRAIN AS HARD AS POSSIBLE RIGHT UP UNTIL THE EVENT! REMEMBER YOU'RE ALL UPHOLDING THE *NAME* OF THE STUDENT COUNCIL, SO I EXPECT AN *EXCELLENT SHOWING* FROM ALL OF YOU!!
THIS MEETING IS AD-JOURNED!
OF COURSE! ***I'M*** NOT ABOUT TO LOSE. JUST WATCH, ASH!
ME TOO.
I'M GOING TO GET MUCH STRON-GER.
YEAH!!
LET'S ALL DO OUR BEST!!!

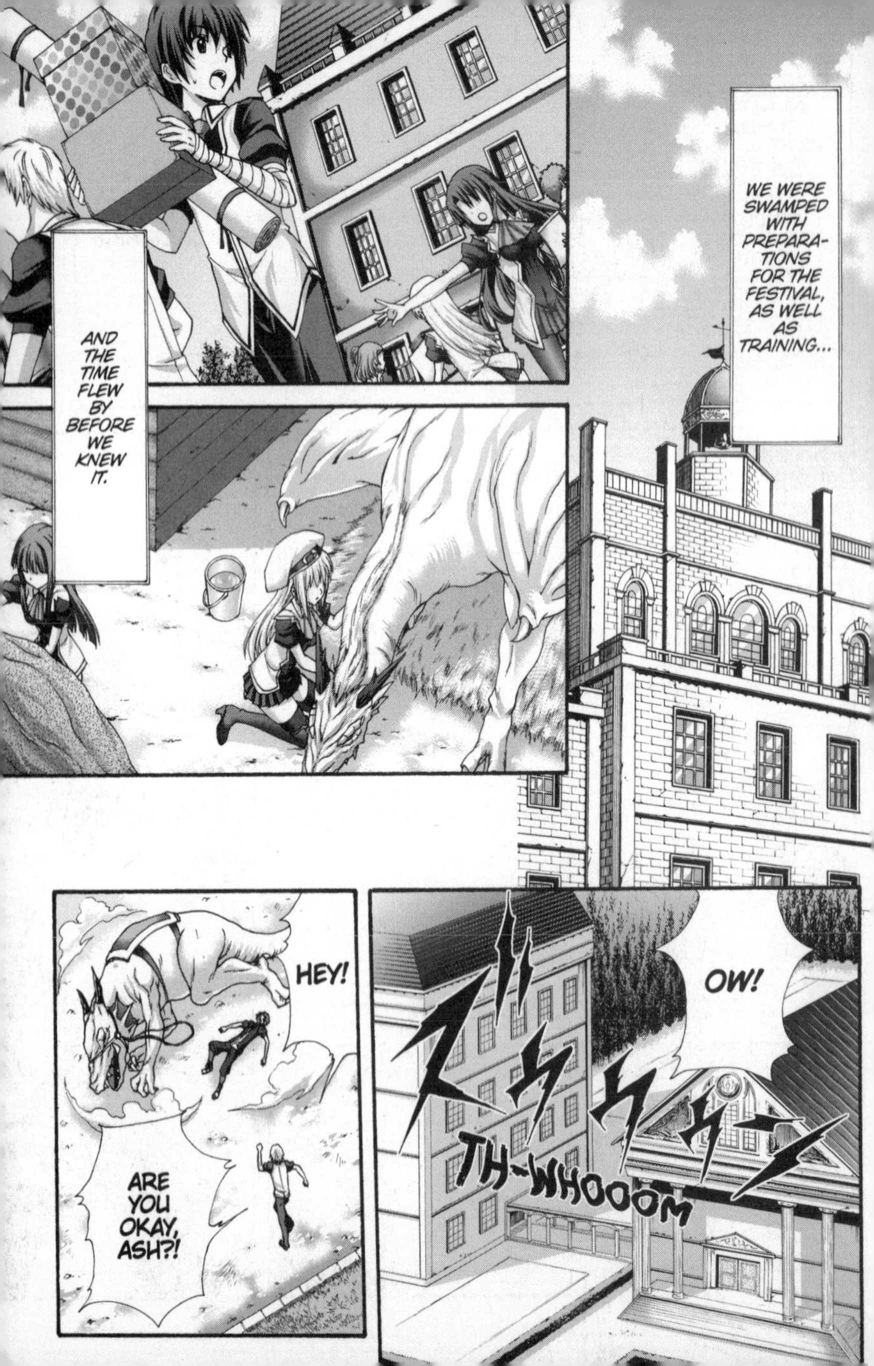
WE WERE SWAMPED WITH PREPARATIONS FOR THE FESTIVAL, AS WELL AS TRAINING...
AND THE TIME FLEW BY BEFORE WE KNEW IT.
OW!
TH-WHOOOM
HEY!
ARE YOU OKAY, ASH?!

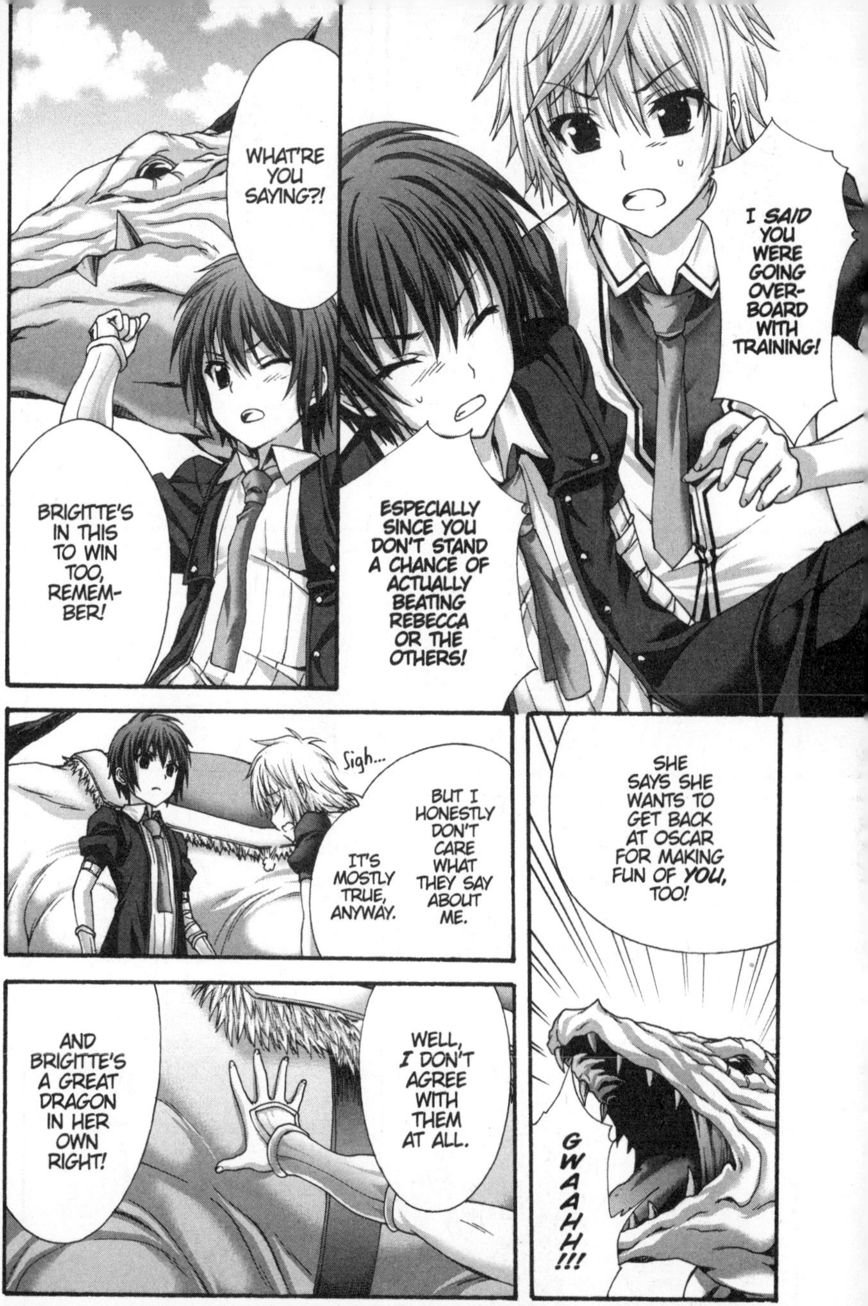
I *SAID* YOU WERE GOING OVER-BOARD WITH TRAINING!
ESPECIALLY SINCE YOU DON'T STAND A CHANCE OF ACTUALLY BEATING REBECCA OR THE OTHERS!
WHAT'RE YOU SAYING?!
BRIGITTE'S IN THIS TO WIN TOO, REMEM-BER!
SHE SAYS SHE WANTS TO GET BACK AT OSCAR FOR MAKING FUN OF ***YOU***, TOO!
GWAAHH!!!
Sigh...
BUT I HONESTLY DON'T CARE WHAT THEY SAY ABOUT ME.
IT'S MOSTLY TRUE, ANYWAY.
WELL, *I* DON'T AGREE WITH THEM AT ALL.
AND BRIGITTE'S A GREAT DRAGON IN HER OWN RIGHT!

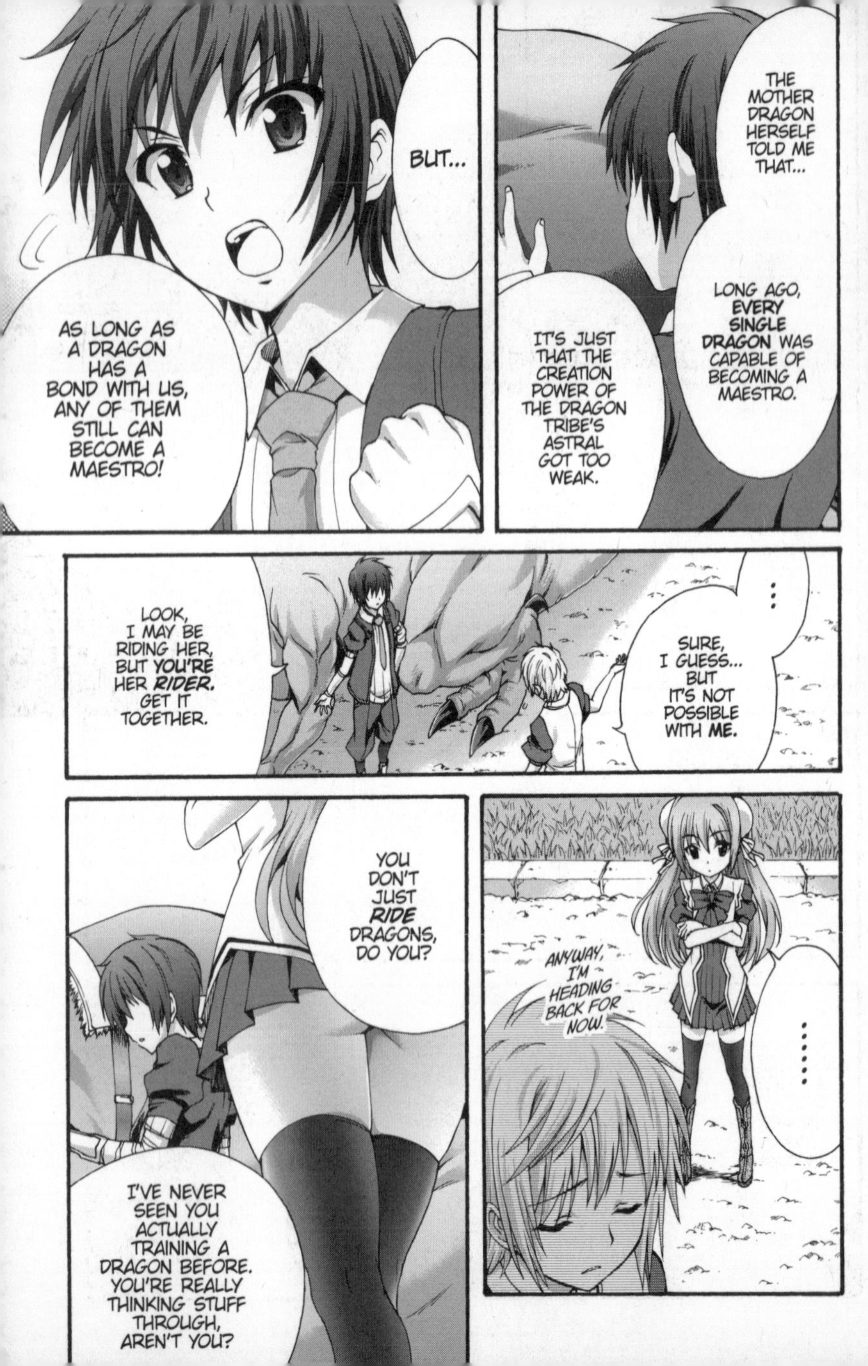
THE MOTHER DRAGON HERSELF TOLD ME THAT...
LONG AGO, EVERY SINGLE DRAGON WAS CAPABLE OF BECOMING A MAESTRO.
IT'S JUST THAT THE CREATION POWER OF THE DRAGON TRIBE'S ASTRAL GOT TOO WEAK.
BUT...
AS LONG AS A DRAGON HAS A BOND WITH US, ANY OF THEM STILL CAN BECOME A MAESTRO!
...
SURE, I GUESS... BUT IT'S NOT POSSIBLE WITH ME.
LOOK, I MAY BE RIDING HER, BUT YOU'RE HER RIDER. GET IT TOGETHER.
......
ANYWAY, I'M HEADING BACK FOR NOW.
YOU DON'T JUST RIDE DRAGONS, DO YOU?
I'VE NEVER SEEN YOU ACTUALLY TRAINING A DRAGON BEFORE. YOU'RE REALLY THINKING STUFF THROUGH, AREN'T YOU?

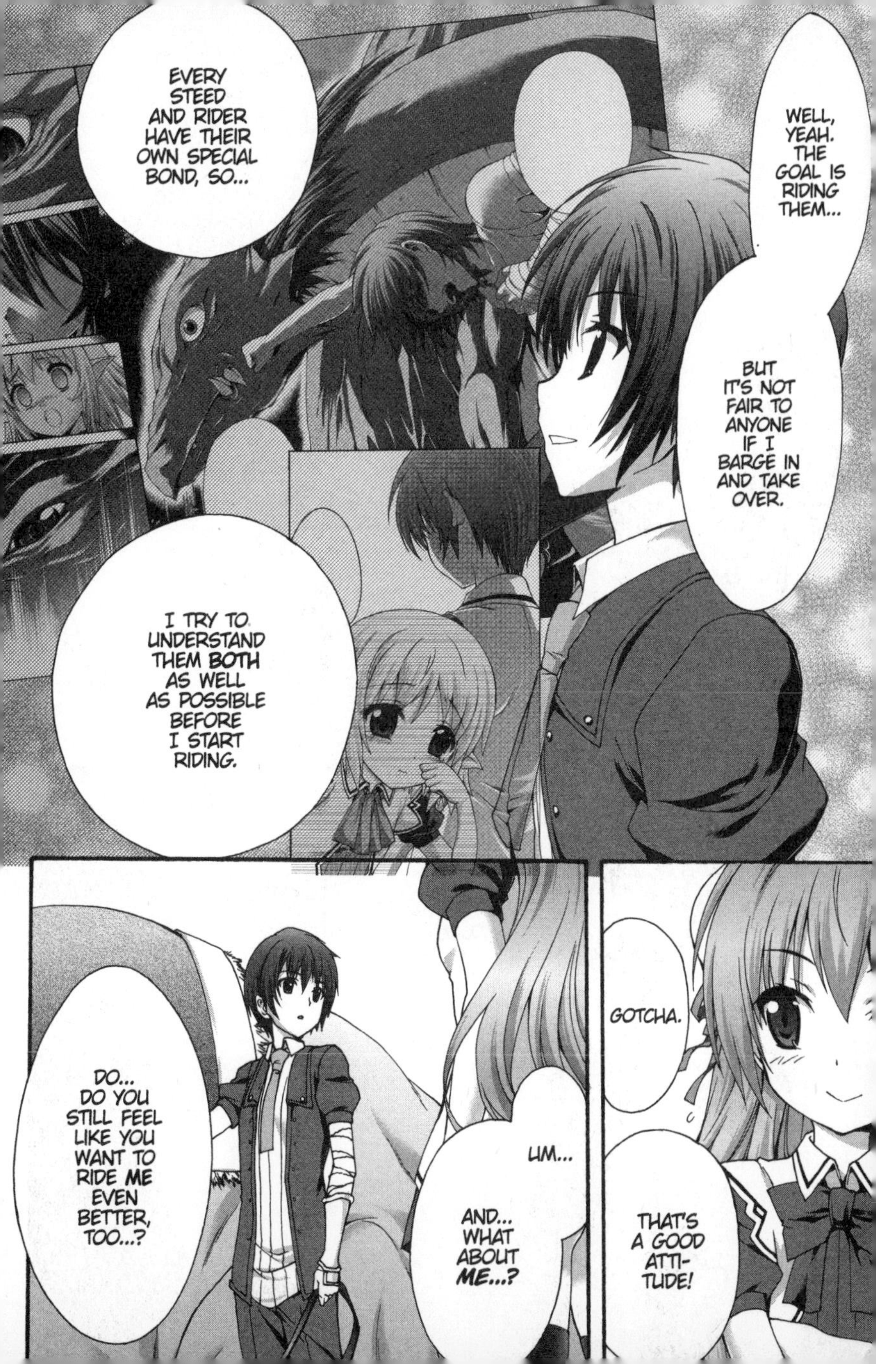
WELL, YEAH. THE GOAL IS RIDING THEM...
BUT IT'S NOT FAIR TO ANYONE IF I BARGE IN AND TAKE OVER.
EVERY STEED AND RIDER HAVE THEIR OWN SPECIAL BOND, SO...
I TRY TO UNDERSTAND THEM BOTH AS WELL AS POSSIBLE BEFORE I START RIDING.
GOTCHA.
THAT'S A GOOD ATTI-TUDE!
UM...
AND... WHAT ABOUT ME...?
DO... DO YOU STILL FEEL LIKE YOU WANT TO RIDE ME EVEN BETTER, TOO...?

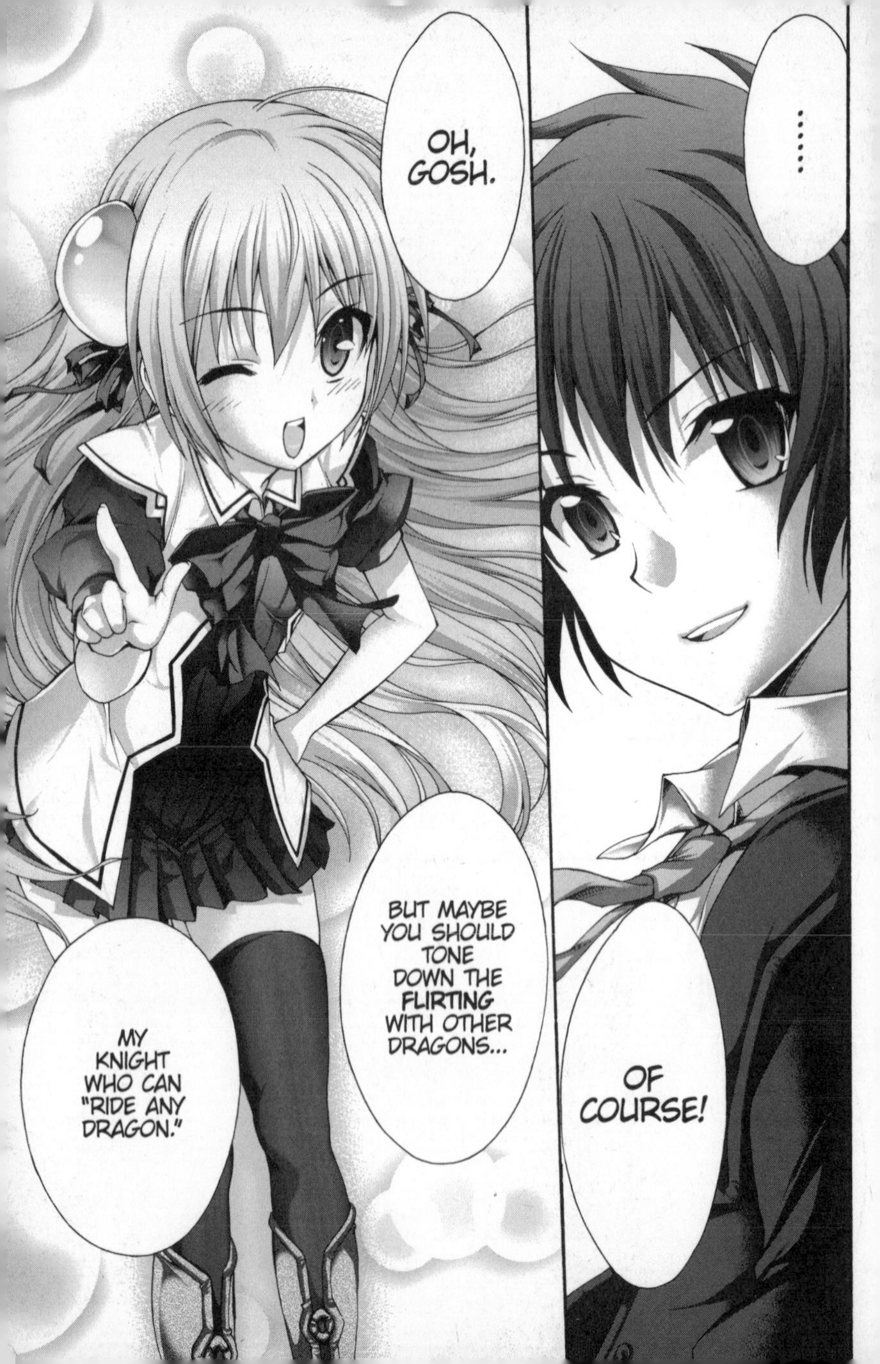
......
OF COURSE!
OH, GOSH.
BUT MAYBE YOU SHOULD TONE DOWN THE FLIRTING WITH OTHER DRAGONS...
MY KNIGHT WHO CAN "RIDE ANY DRAGON."

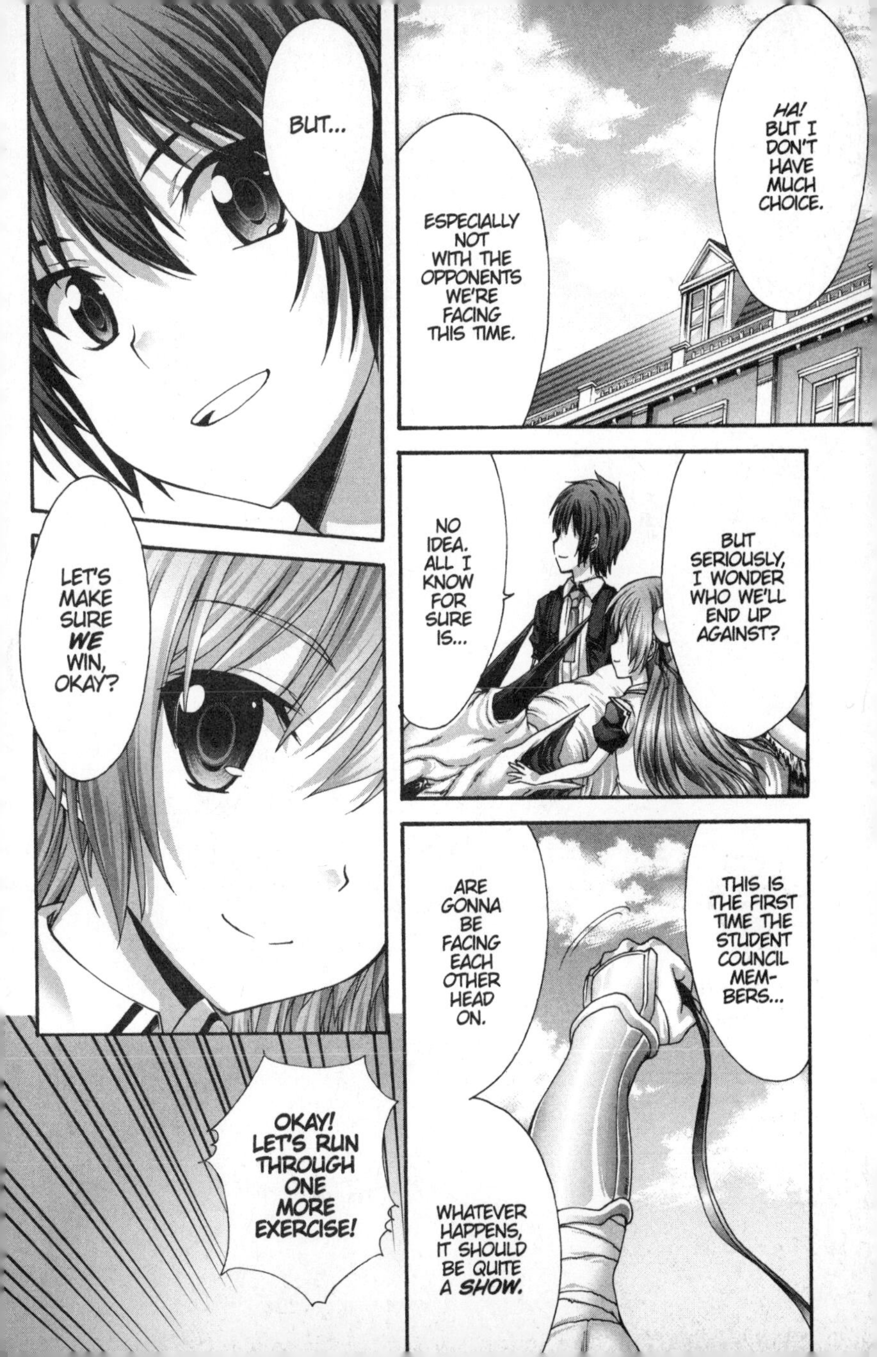
HA! BUT I DON'T HAVE MUCH CHOICE.
ESPECIALLY NOT WITH THE OPPONENTS WE'RE FACING THIS TIME.
BUT SERIOUSLY, I WONDER WHO WE'LL END UP AGAINST?
NO IDEA. ALL I KNOW FOR SURE IS...
THIS IS THE FIRST TIME THE STUDENT COUNCIL MEM-BERS...
ARE GONNA BE FACING EACH OTHER HEAD ON.
WHATEVER HAPPENS, IT SHOULD BE QUITE A *SHOW*.
BUT...
LET'S MAKE SURE *WE* WIN, OKAY?
OKAY! LET'S RUN THROUGH ONE MORE EXERCISE!

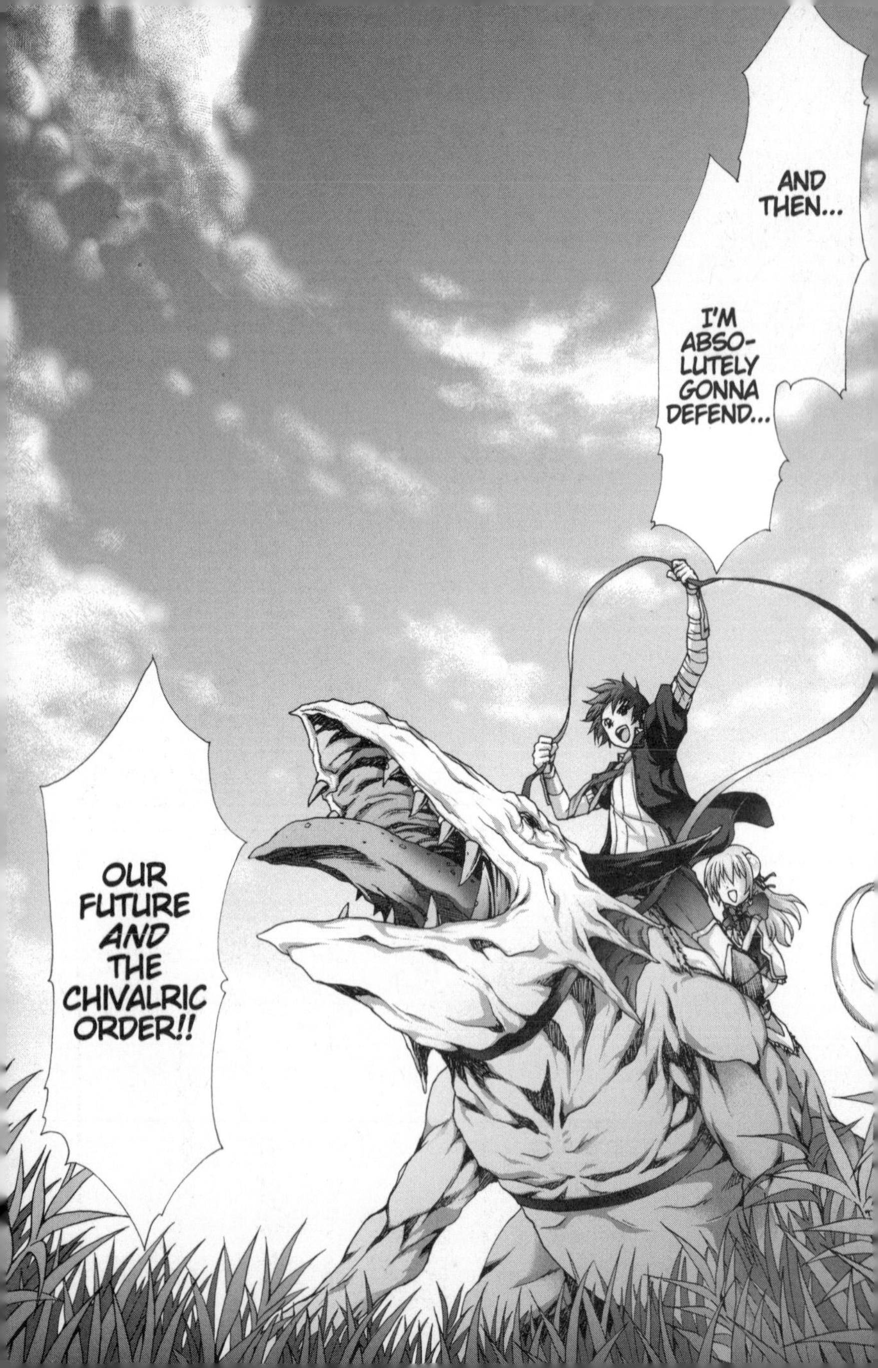
AND THEN...
I'M ABSO-LUTELY GONNA DEFEND...
OUR FUTURE AND THE CHIVALRIC ORDER!!

DRAGONAR
ACADEMY

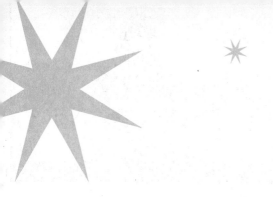

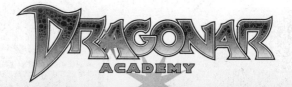

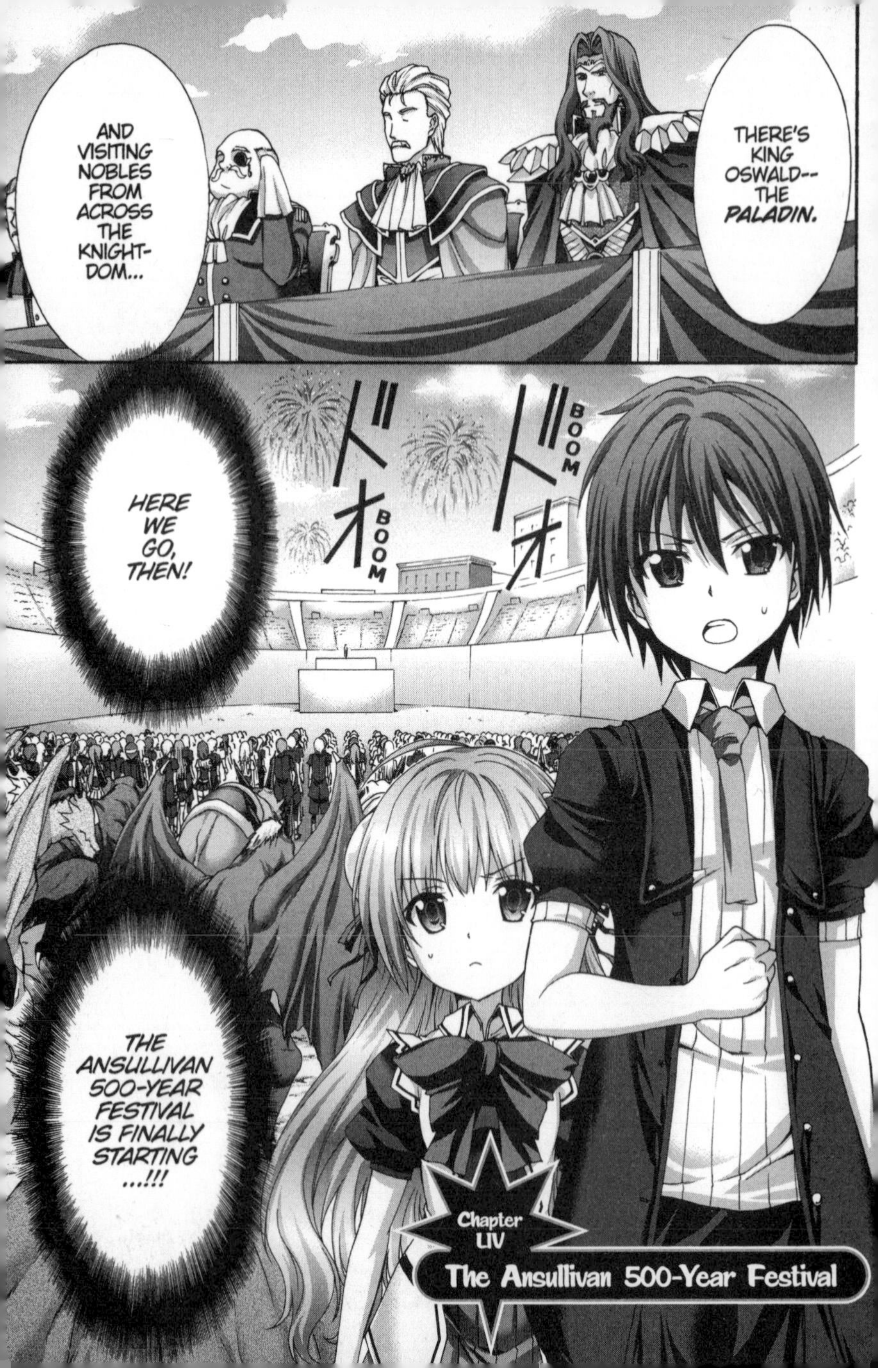
THERE'S KING OSWALD-- THE PALADIN.
AND VISITING NOBLES FROM ACROSS THE KNIGHT-DOM...
ドォ
BOOM
ドォ
BOOM
HERE WE GO, THEN!
THE ANSULLIVAN 500-YEAR FESTIVAL IS FINALLY STARTING ...!!!
Chapter LIV
The Ansullivan 500-Year Festival

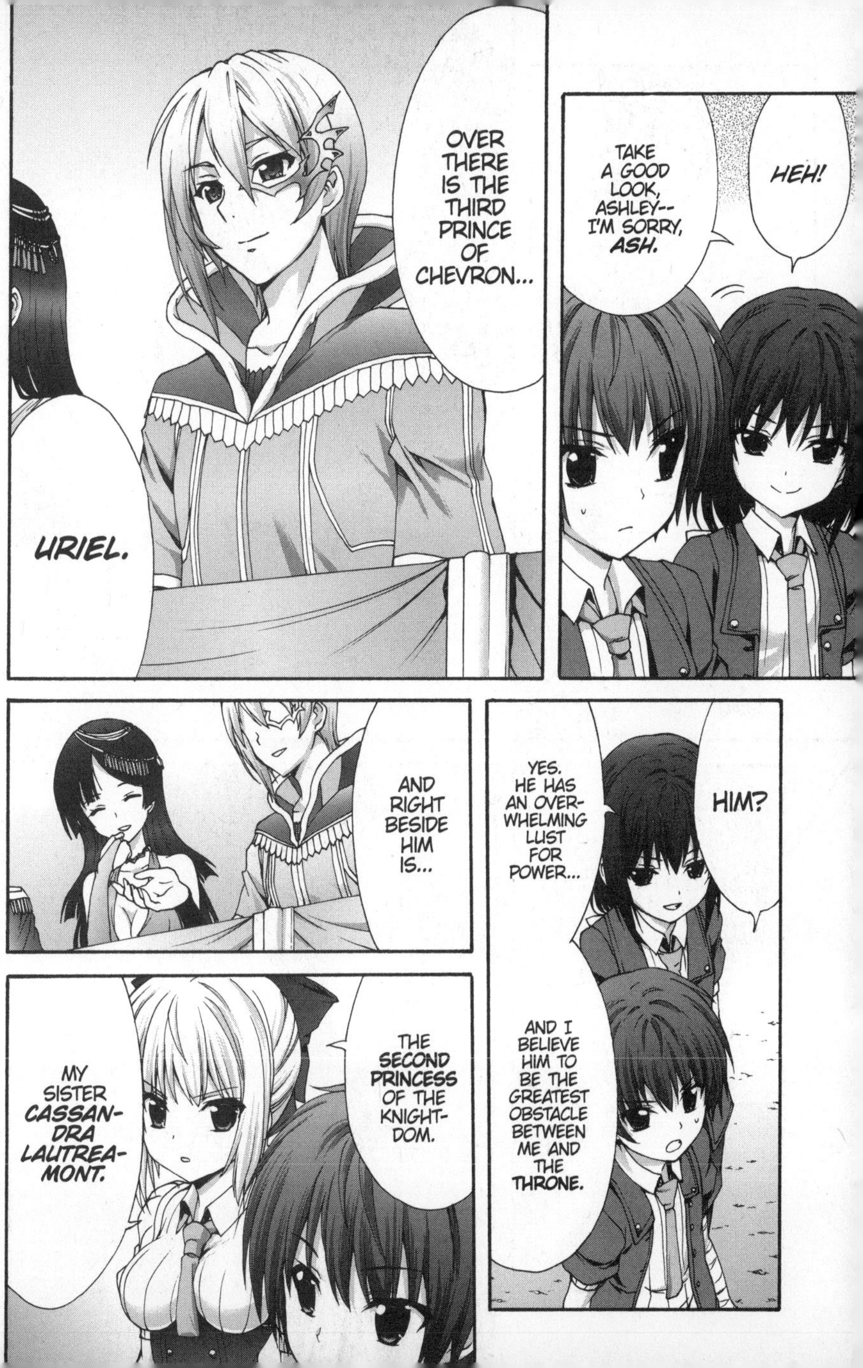
TAKE A GOOD LOOK, ASHLEY-- I'M SORRY, **ASH.**
HEH!
OVER THERE IS THE THIRD PRINCE OF CHEVRON...
URIEL.
HIM?
YES. HE HAS AN OVER-WHELMING LUST FOR POWER...
AND RIGHT BESIDE HIM IS...
AND I BELIEVE HIM TO BE THE GREATEST OBSTACLE BETWEEN ME AND THE **THRONE.**
THE **SECOND PRINCESS** OF THE KNIGHT-DOM.
MY SISTER ***CASSAN-DRA LAUTREA-MONT.***

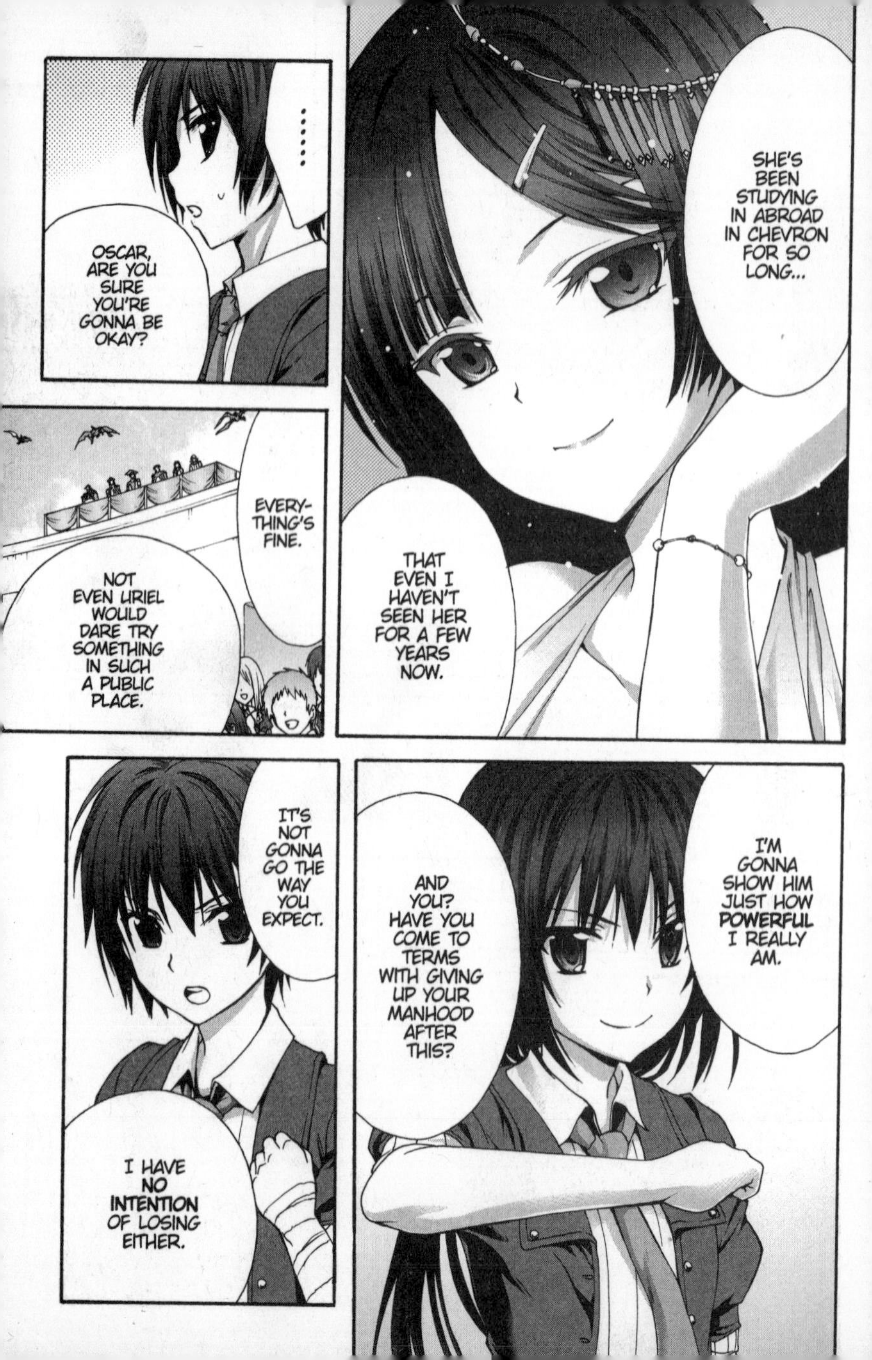
SHE'S BEEN STUDYING IN ABROAD IN CHEVRON FOR SO LONG...
THAT EVEN I HAVEN'T SEEN HER FOR A FEW YEARS NOW.
......
OSCAR, ARE YOU SURE YOU'RE GONNA BE OKAY?
EVERY-THING'S FINE.
NOT EVEN URIEL WOULD DARE TRY SOMETHING IN SUCH A PUBLIC PLACE.
I'M GONNA SHOW HIM JUST HOW **POWERFUL** I REALLY AM.
AND YOU? HAVE YOU COME TO TERMS WITH GIVING UP YOUR MANHOOD AFTER THIS?
IT'S NOT GONNA GO THE WAY YOU EXPECT.
I HAVE NO INTENTION OF LOSING EITHER.

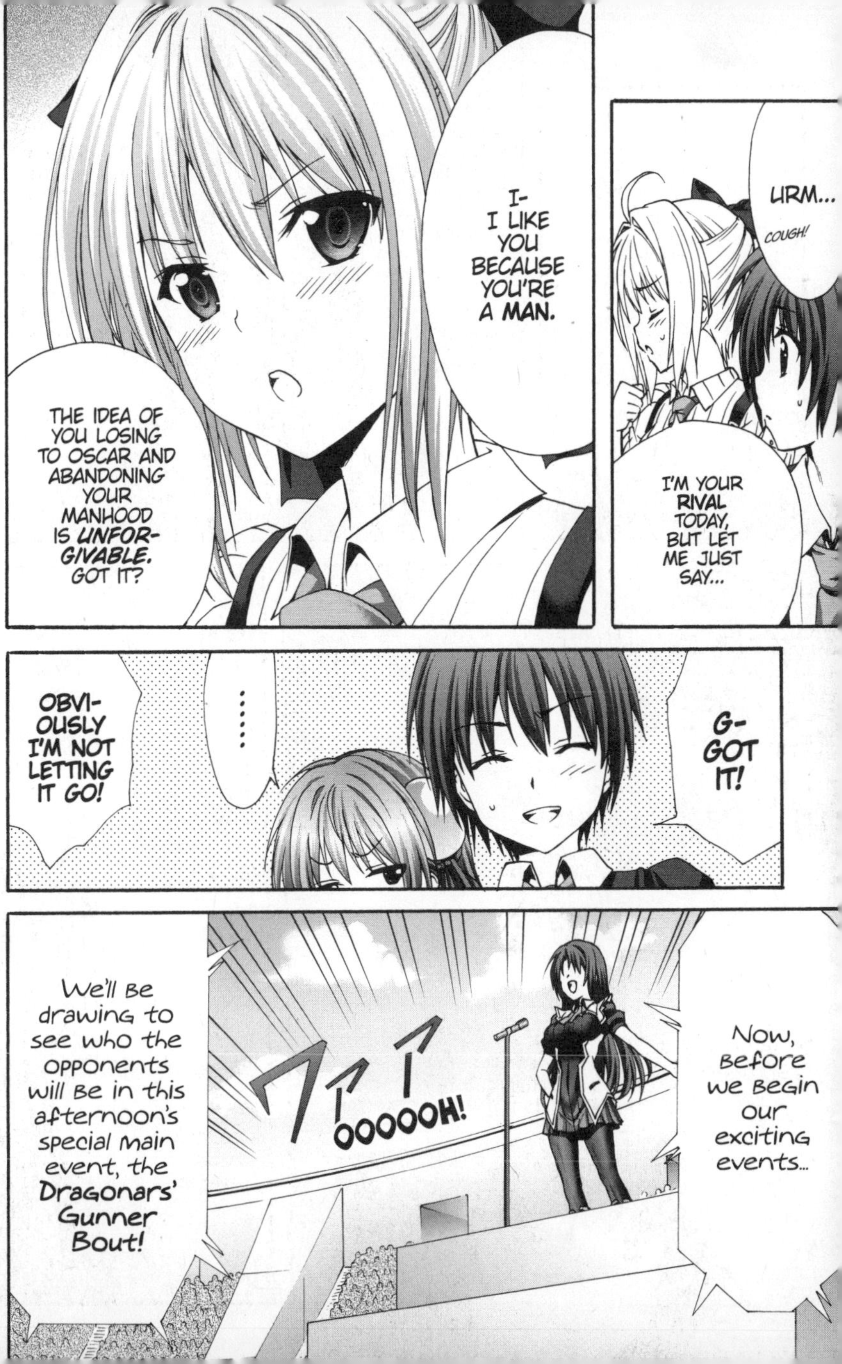
URM...
COUGH!
I'M YOUR RIVAL TODAY, BUT LET ME JUST SAY...
I- I LIKE YOU BECAUSE YOU'RE A MAN.
THE IDEA OF YOU LOSING TO OSCAR AND ABANDONING YOUR MANHOOD IS UNFORGIVABLE. GOT IT?
G- GOT IT!
......
OBVIOUSLY I'M NOT LETTING IT GO!
Now, before we begin our exciting events...
OOOOOH!
We'll be drawing to see who the opponents will be in this afternoon's special main event, the Dragonars' Gunner Bout!

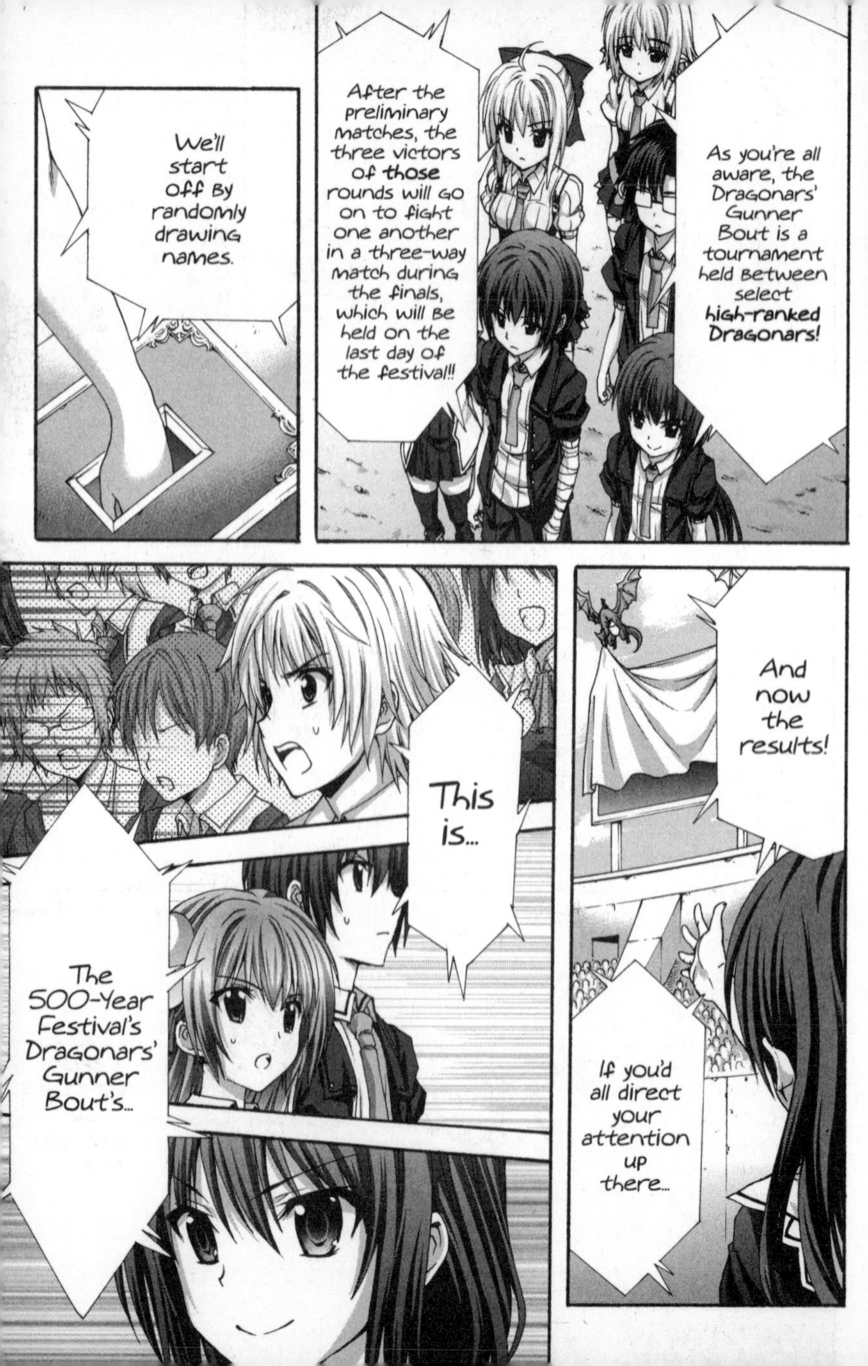
As you're all aware, the Dragonars' Gunner Bout is a tournament held between select **high-ranked Dragonars!**
After the preliminary matches, the three victors of **those** rounds will go on to fight one another in a three-way match during the finals, which will be held on the last day of the festival!!
We'll start off by randomly drawing names.
And now the results!
If you'd all direct your attention up there...
This is...
The 500-Year Festival's Dragonars' Gunner Bout's...

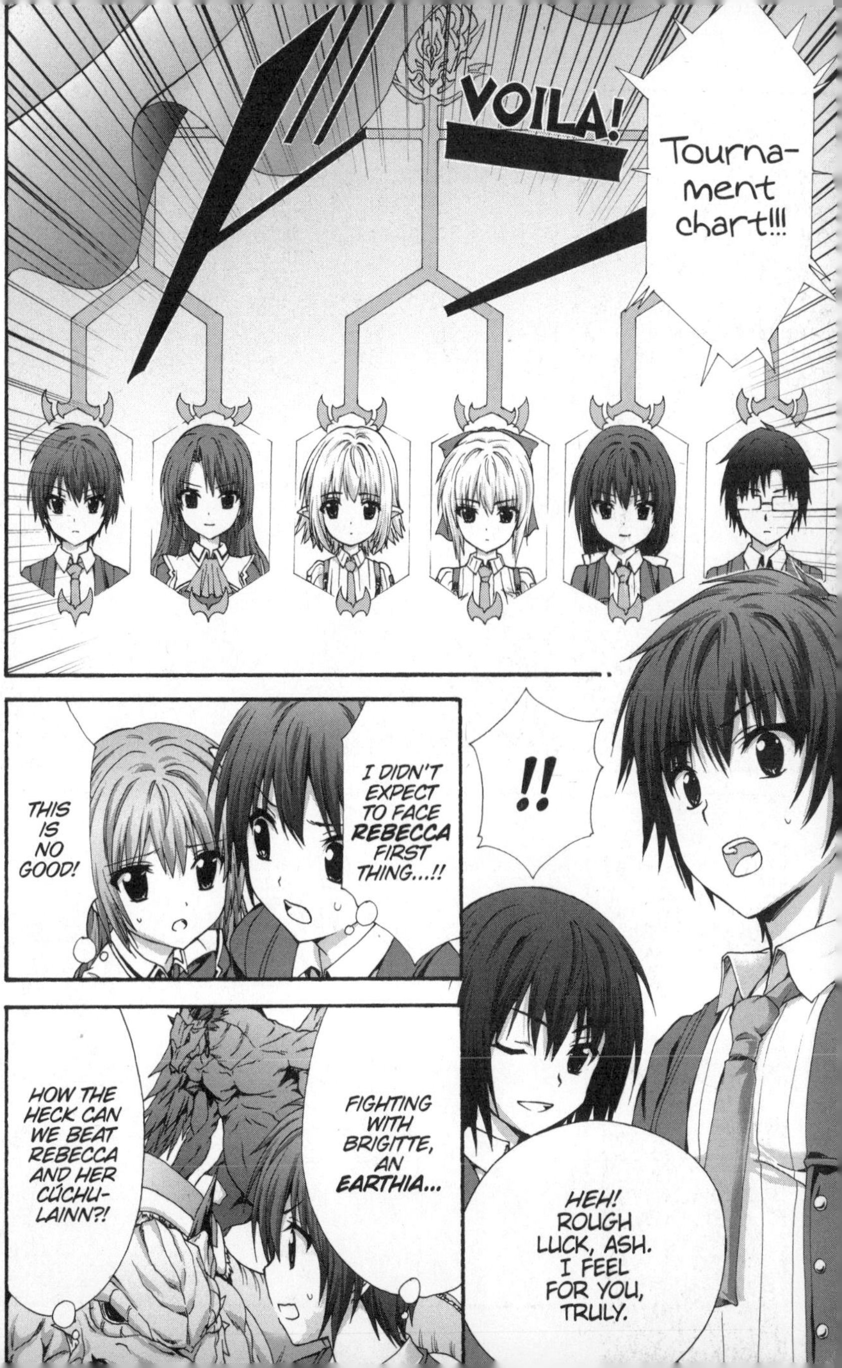
Tournament chart!!!
VOILA!
!!
HEH! ROUGH LUCK, ASH. I FEEL FOR YOU, TRULY.
I DIDN'T EXPECT TO FACE REBECCA FIRST THING...!!
THIS IS NO GOOD!
FIGHTING WITH BRIGITTE, AN EARTHIA...
HOW THE HECK CAN WE BEAT REBECCA AND HER CÚCHULAINN?!

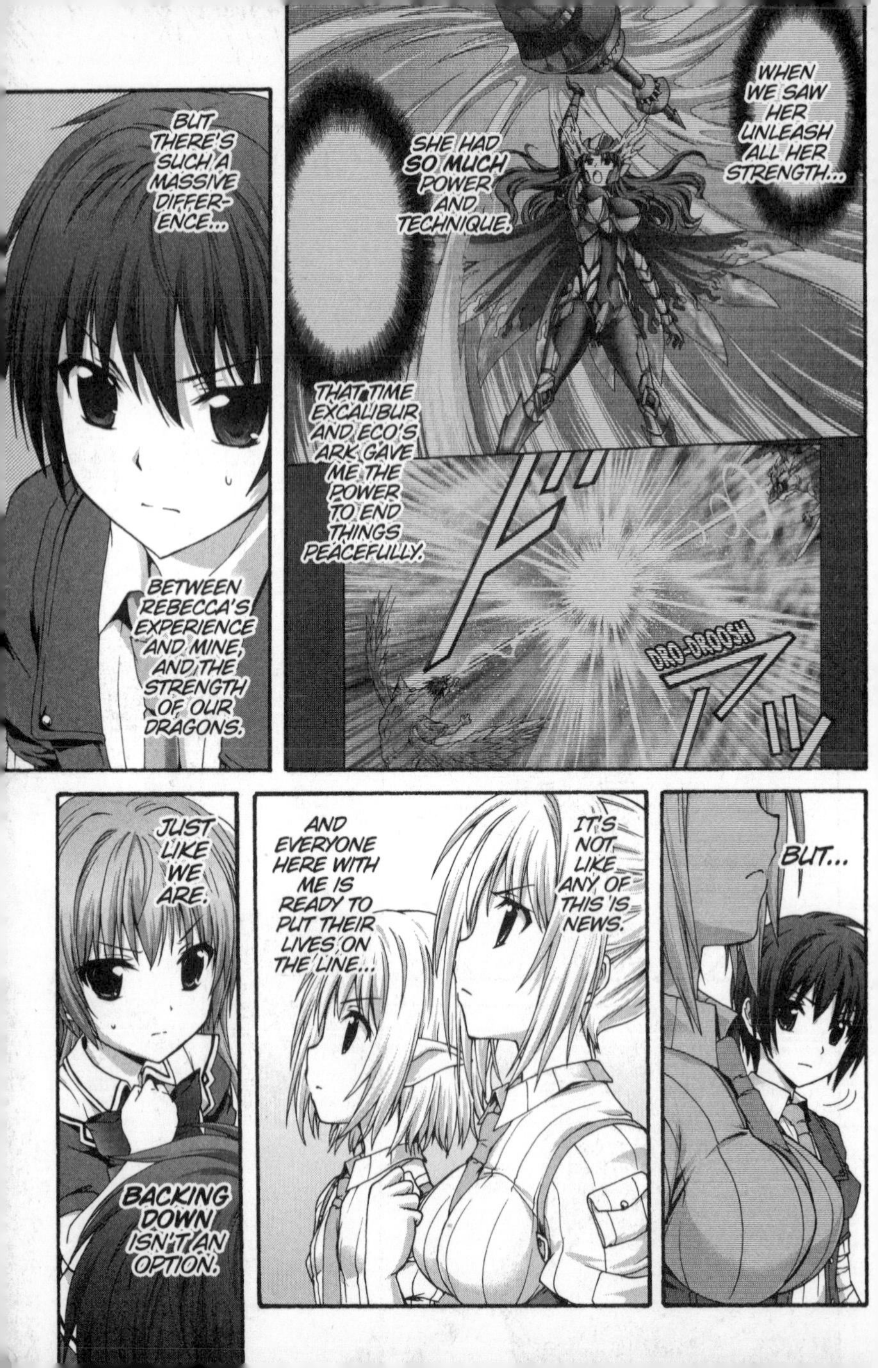
WHEN WE SAW HER UNLEASH ALL HER STRENGTH...
SHE HAD SO MUCH POWER AND TECHNIQUE.
THAT TIME EXCALIBUR AND ECO'S ARK GAVE ME THE POWER TO END THINGS PEACEFULLY.
DRO-DROOSH
BUT THERE'S SUCH A MASSIVE DIFFER-ENCE...
BETWEEN REBECCA'S EXPERIENCE AND MINE, AND THE STRENGTH OF OUR DRAGONS.
BUT...
IT'S NOT LIKE ANY OF THIS IS NEWS.
AND EVERYONE HERE WITH ME IS READY TO PUT THEIR LIVES ON THE LINE...
JUST LIKE WE ARE.
BACKING DOWN ISN'T AN OPTION.

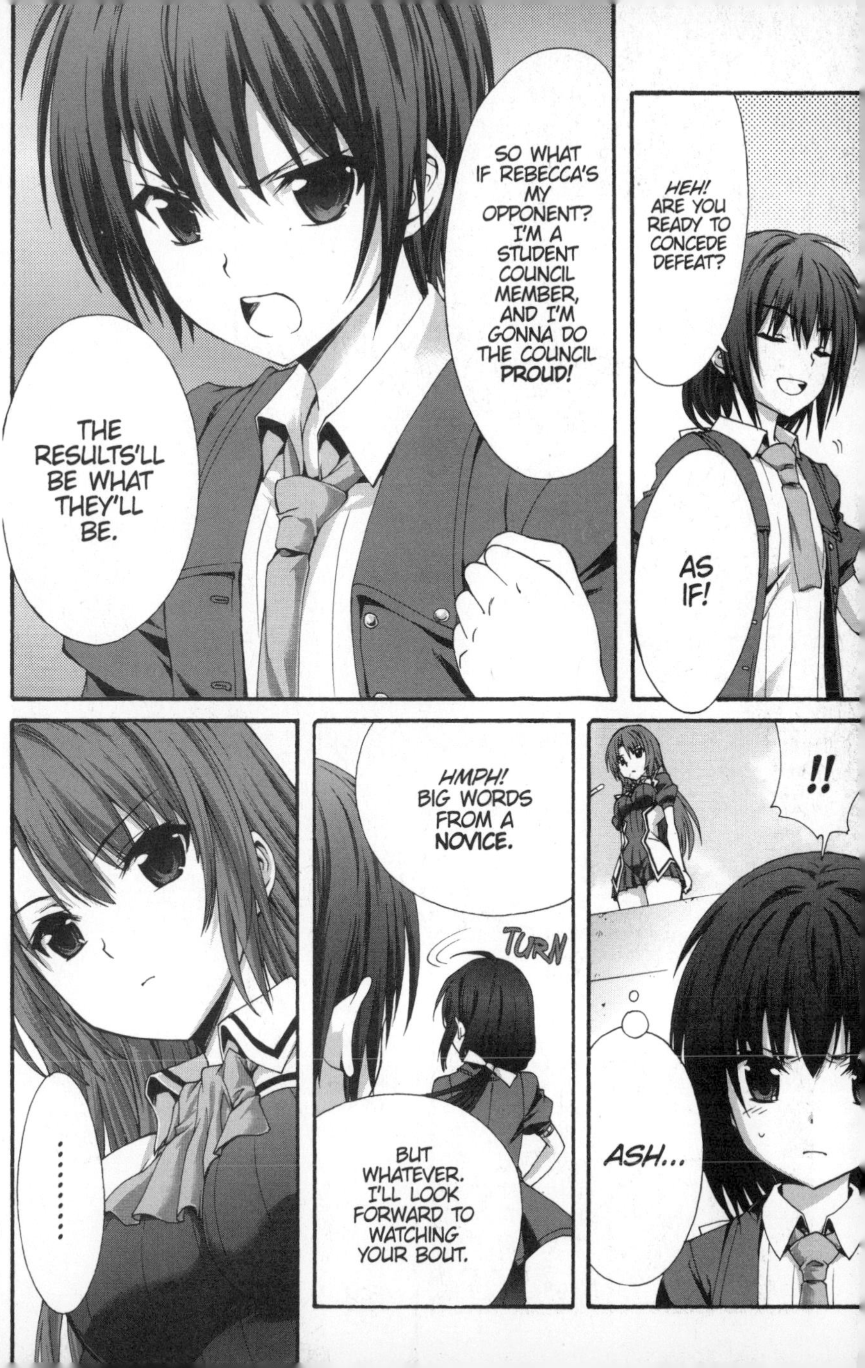
HEH! ARE YOU READY TO CONCEDE DEFEAT?
AS IF!
SO WHAT IF REBECCA'S MY OPPONENT? I'M A STUDENT COUNCIL MEMBER, AND I'M GONNA DO THE COUNCIL PROUD!
THE RESULTS'LL BE WHAT THEY'LL BE.
!!
ASH...
HMPH! BIG WORDS FROM A NOVICE.
TURN
BUT WHATEVER. I'LL LOOK FORWARD TO WATCHING YOUR BOUT.
....

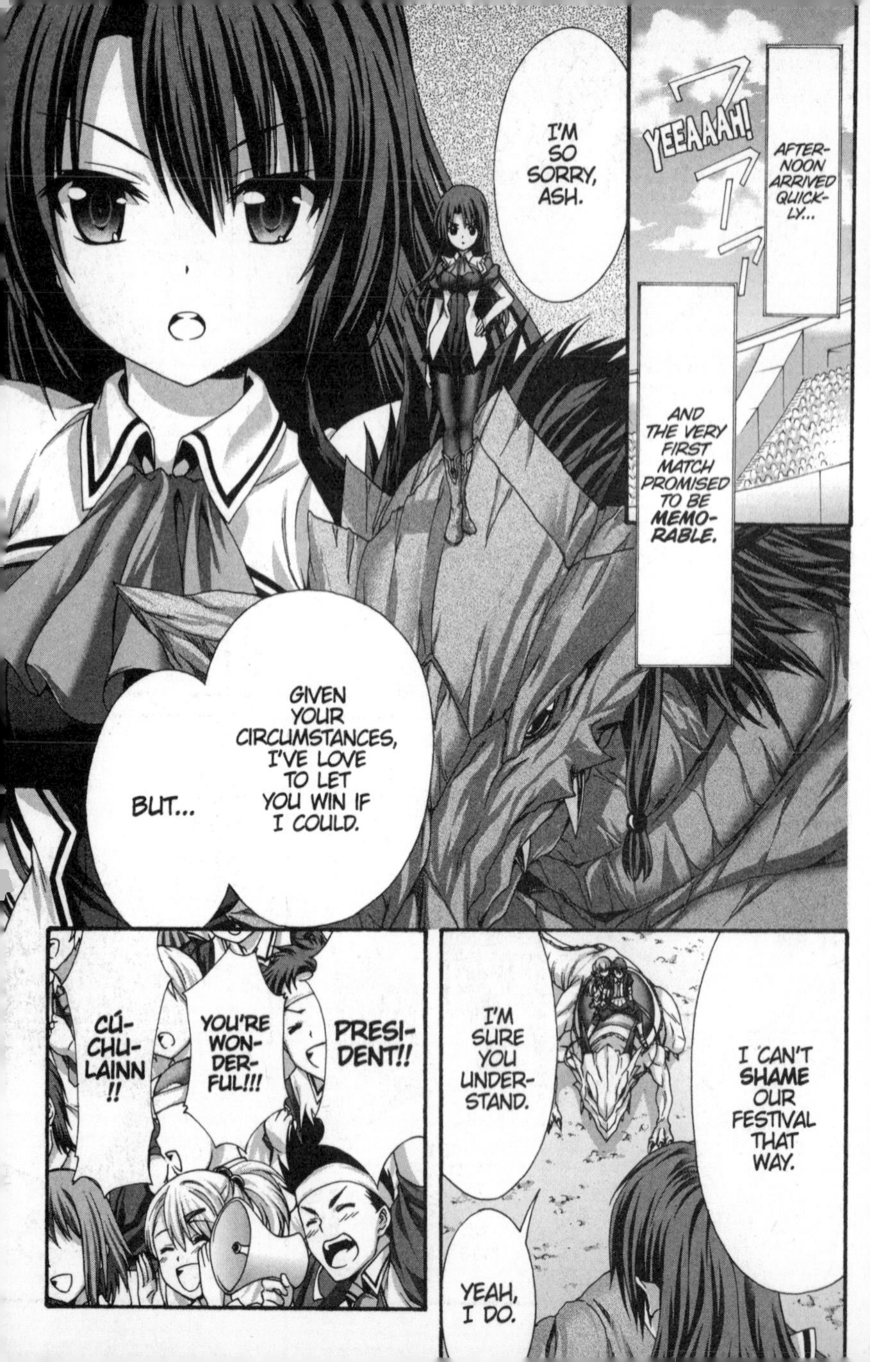
AFTER-NOON ARRIVED QUICK-LY...
YEEAAAH!
AND THE VERY FIRST MATCH PROMISED TO BE MEMO-RABLE.
I'M SO SORRY, ASH.
GIVEN YOUR CIRCUMSTANCES, I'VE LOVE TO LET YOU WIN IF I COULD.
BUT...
I CAN'T SHAME OUR FESTIVAL THAT WAY.
I'M SURE YOU UNDER-STAND.
YEAH, I DO.
PRESI-DENT!!
YOU'RE WON-DER-FUL!!!
CÚ-CHU-LAINN!!

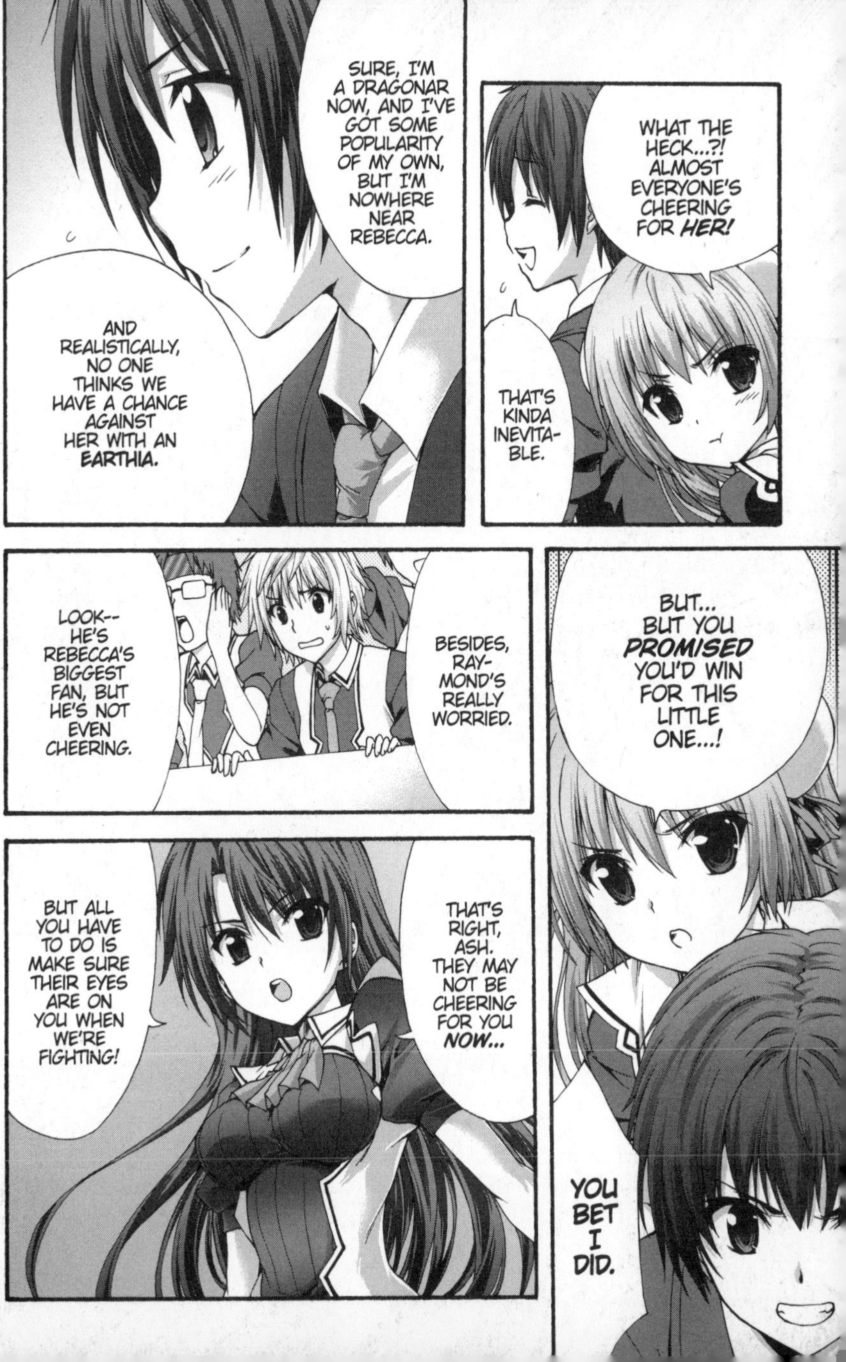
WHAT THE HECK...?! ALMOST EVERYONE'S CHEERING FOR *HER!*
THAT'S KINDA INEVITA-BLE.
SURE, I'M A DRAGONAR NOW, AND I'VE GOT SOME POPULARITY OF MY OWN, BUT I'M NOWHERE NEAR REBECCA.
AND REALISTICALLY, NO ONE THINKS WE HAVE A CHANCE AGAINST HER WITH AN **EARTHIA.**
BUT... BUT YOU ***PROMISED*** YOU'D WIN FOR THIS LITTLE ONE...!
YOU BET I DID.
BESIDES, RAY-MOND'S REALLY WORRIED.
LOOK-- HE'S REBECCA'S BIGGEST FAN, BUT HE'S NOT EVEN CHEERING.
THAT'S RIGHT, ASH. THEY MAY NOT BE CHEERING FOR YOU ***NOW...***
BUT ALL YOU HAVE TO DO IS MAKE SURE THEIR EYES ARE ON YOU WHEN WE'RE FIGHTING!

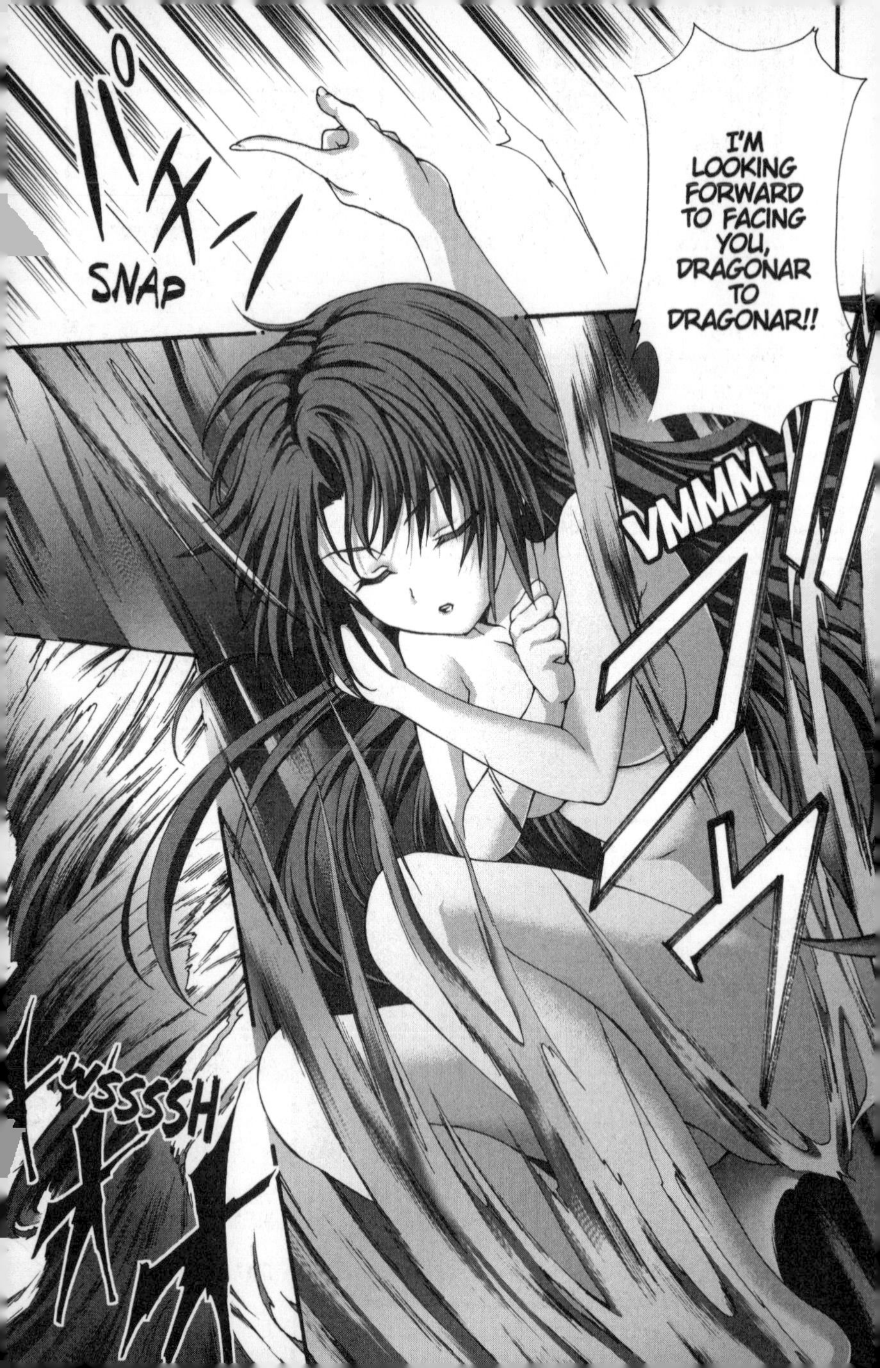
I'M LOOKING FORWARD TO FACING YOU, DRAGONAR TO DRAGONAR!!
SNAP
VMMM
WSSSSH

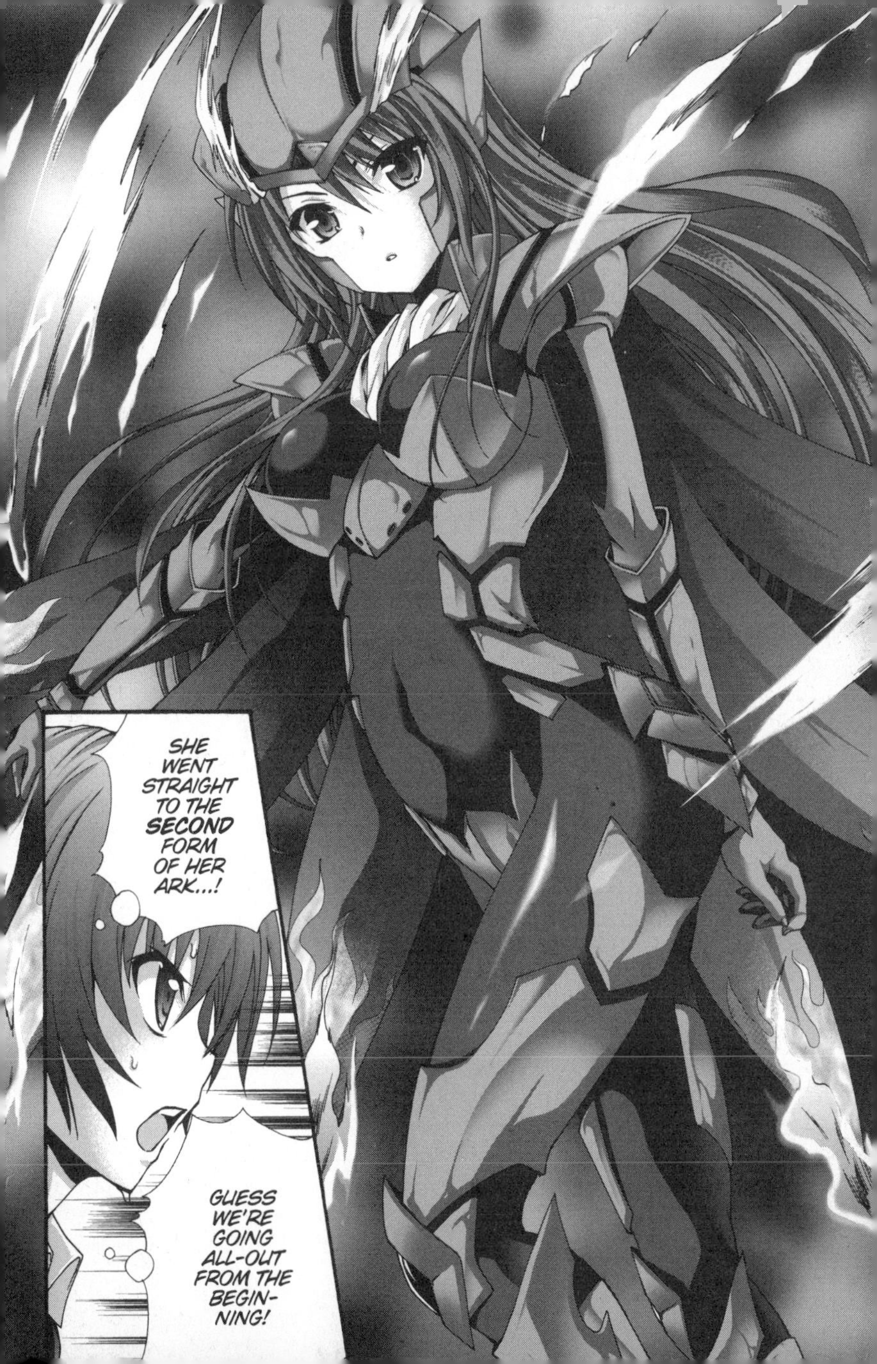
SHE WENT STRAIGHT TO THE **SECOND** FORM OF HER ARK...!
GUESS WE'RE GOING ALL-OUT FROM THE BEGIN-NING!

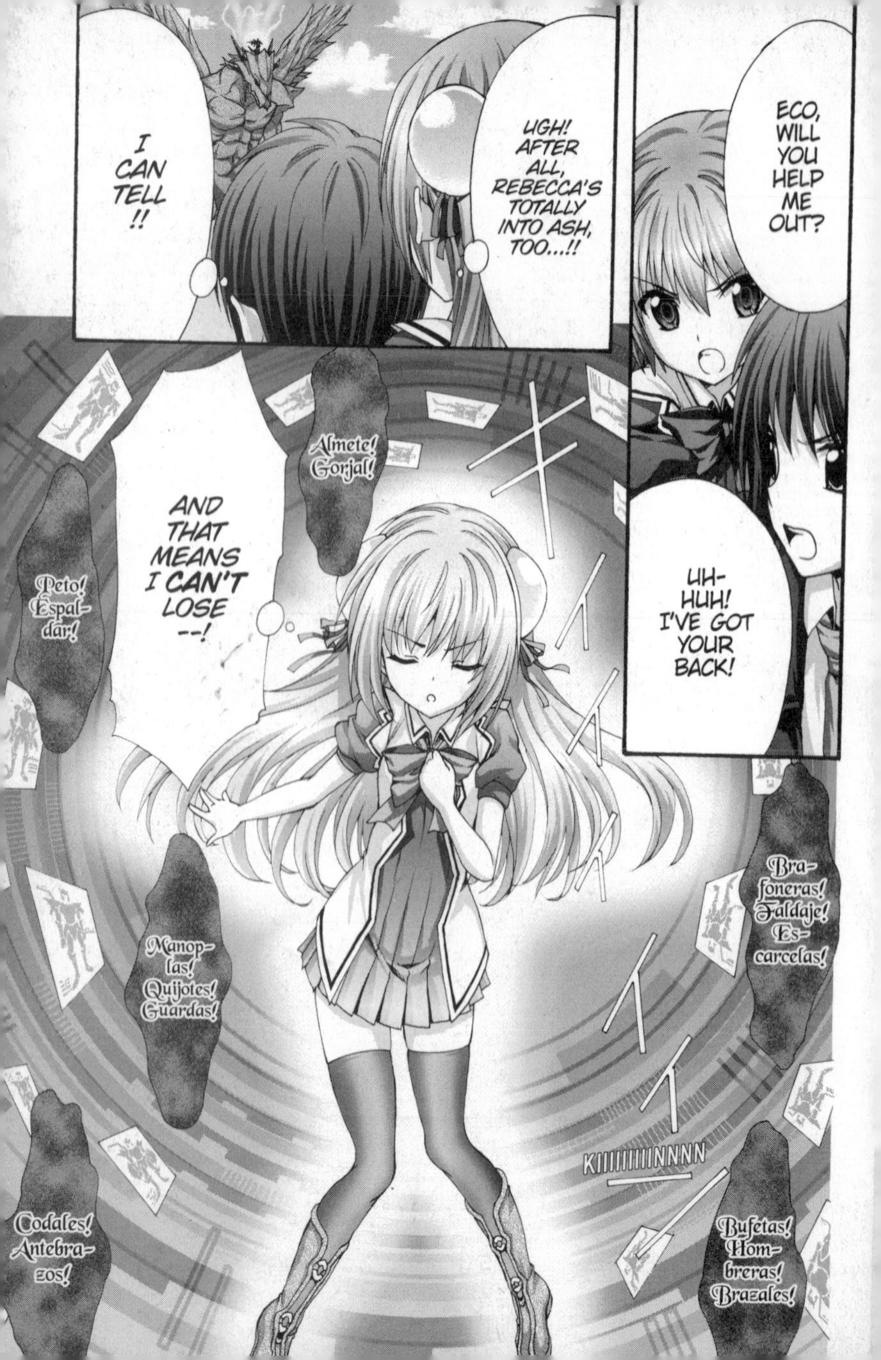
ECO, WILL YOU HELP ME OUT?
UH-HUH! I'VE GOT YOUR BACK!
UGH! AFTER ALL, REBECCA'S TOTALLY INTO ASH, TOO...!!
I CAN TELL!!
AND THAT MEANS I CAN'T LOSE--!
Almete! Gorjal!
Peto! Espal-dar!
Bra-foneras! Faldaje! Es-carcelas!
Manop-las! Quijotes! Guardas!
KIIIIIIIIIINNNN
Bufetas! Hom-breras! Brazales!
Codales! Antebra-zos!

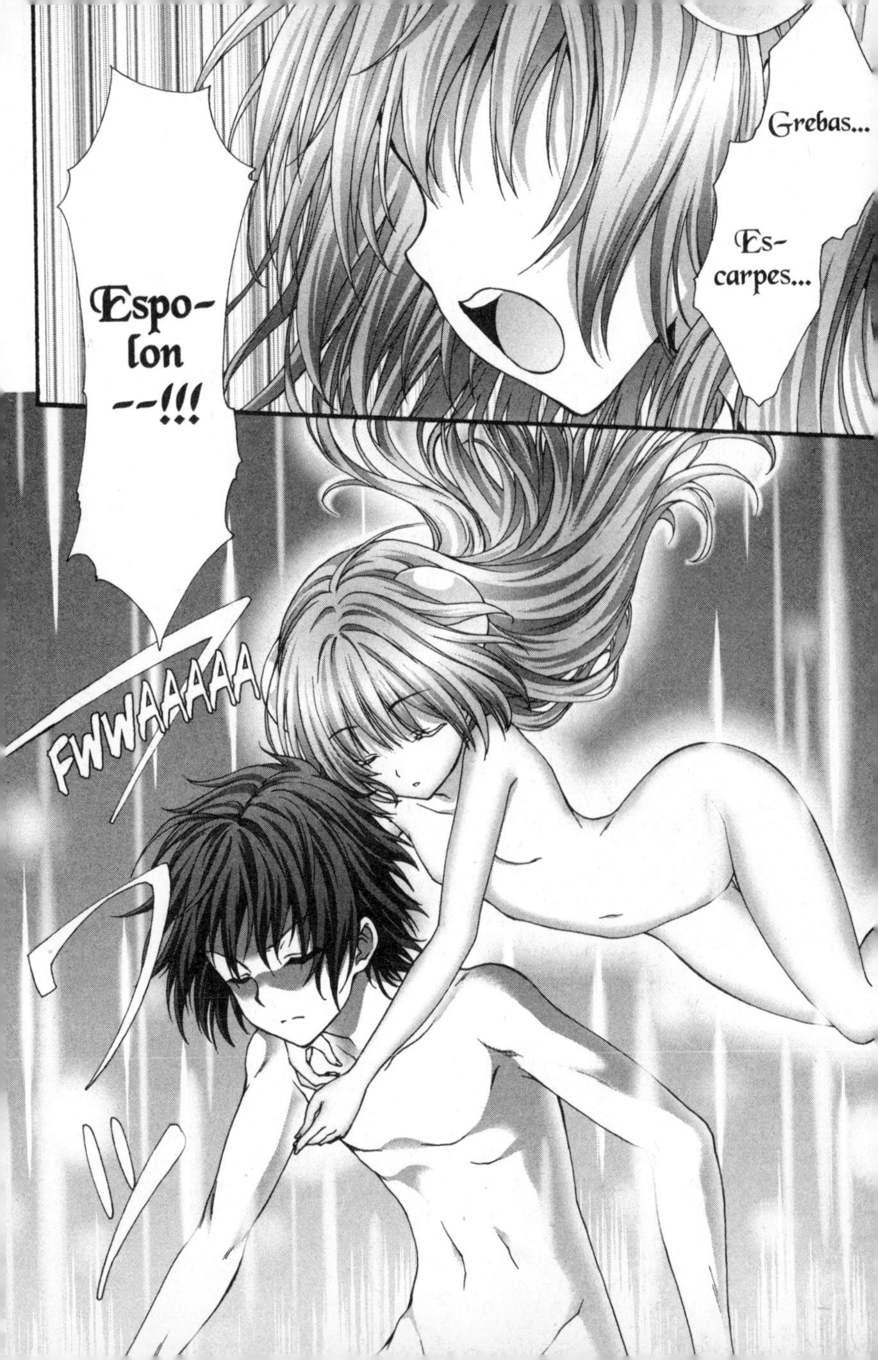
Grebas... Es-carpes...
Espo-lon --!!!
FWWAAAAA

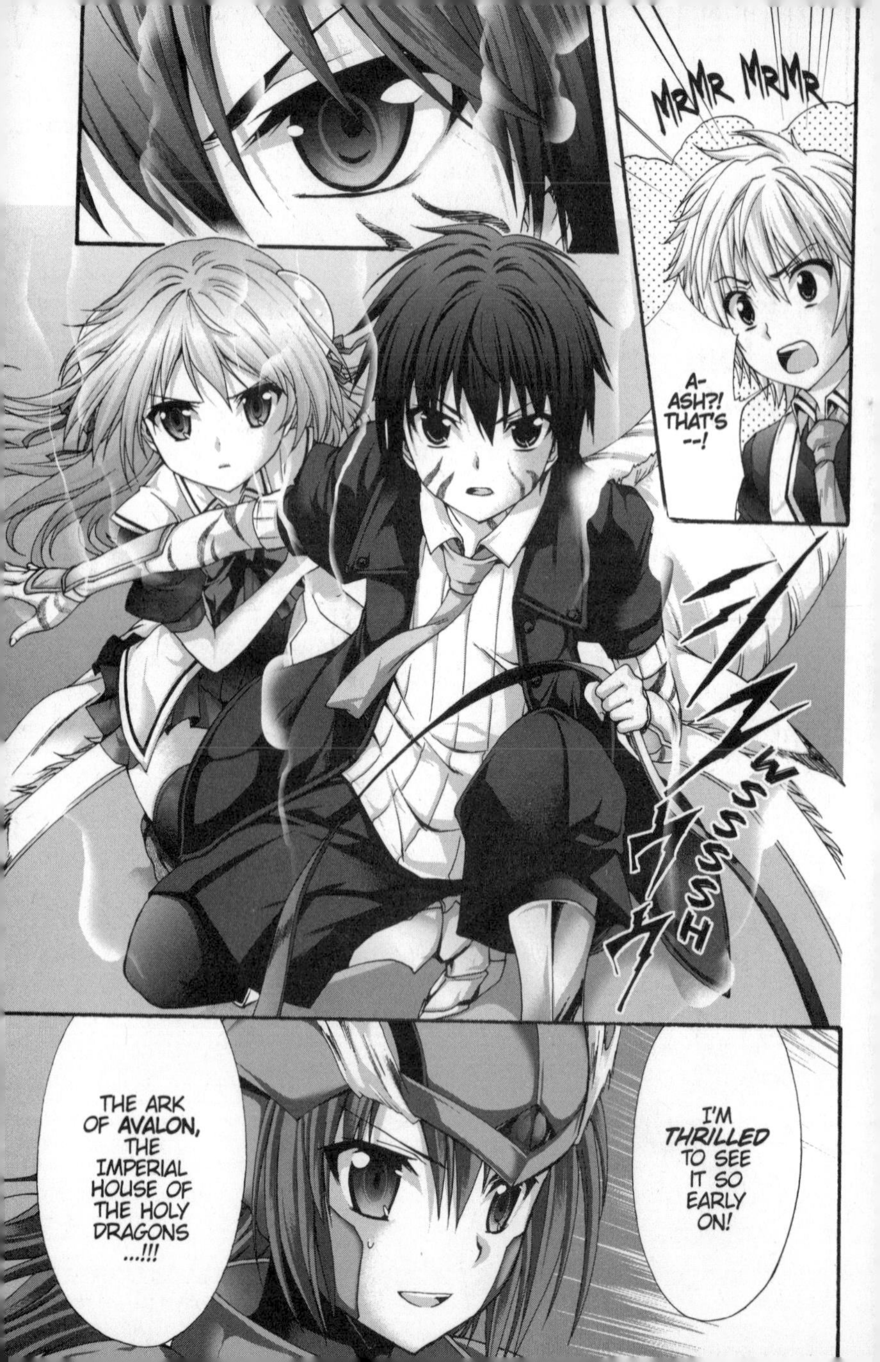
MRMR MRMR
A- ASH?! THAT'S --!
WSSSSSH
I'M **THRILLED** TO SEE IT SO EARLY ON!
THE ARK OF **AVALON,** THE IMPERIAL HOUSE OF THE HOLY DRAGONS ...!!!

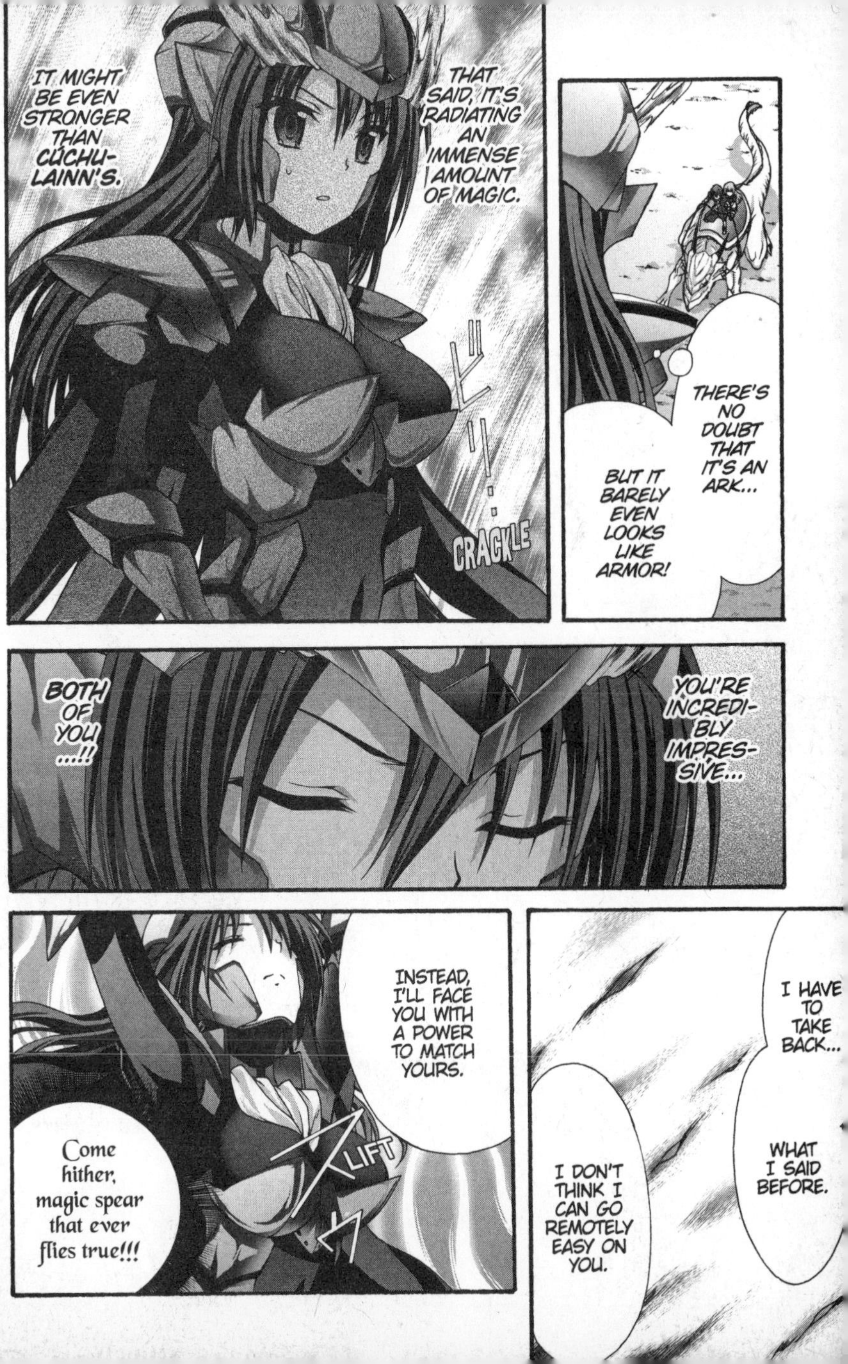
THERE'S NO DOUBT THAT IT'S AN ARK...
BUT IT BARELY EVEN LOOKS LIKE ARMOR!
THAT SAID, IT'S RADIATING AN IMMENSE AMOUNT OF MAGIC.
IT MIGHT BE EVEN STRONGER THAN CÚCHULAINN'S.
CRACKLE
YOU'RE INCREDIBLY IMPRESSIVE...
BOTH OF YOU...!!
I HAVE TO TAKE BACK...
WHAT I SAID BEFORE.
I DON'T THINK I CAN GO REMOTELY EASY ON YOU.
INSTEAD, I'LL FACE YOU WITH A POWER TO MATCH YOURS.
LIFT
Come hither, magic spear that ever flies true!!!

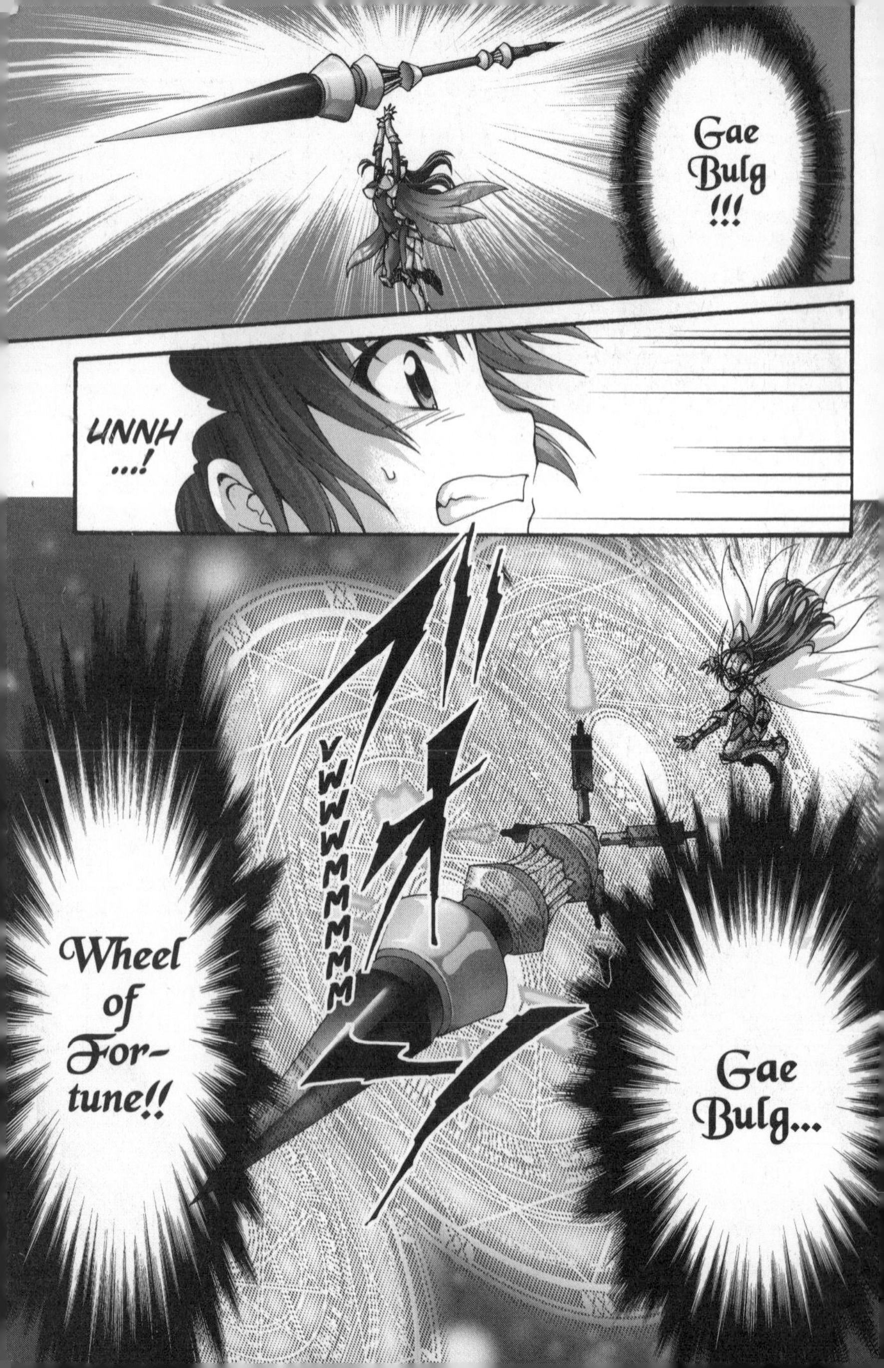
Gae Bulg !!!
UNNH ...!
Gae Bulg...
VWWWMMMMM
Wheel of For-tune!!

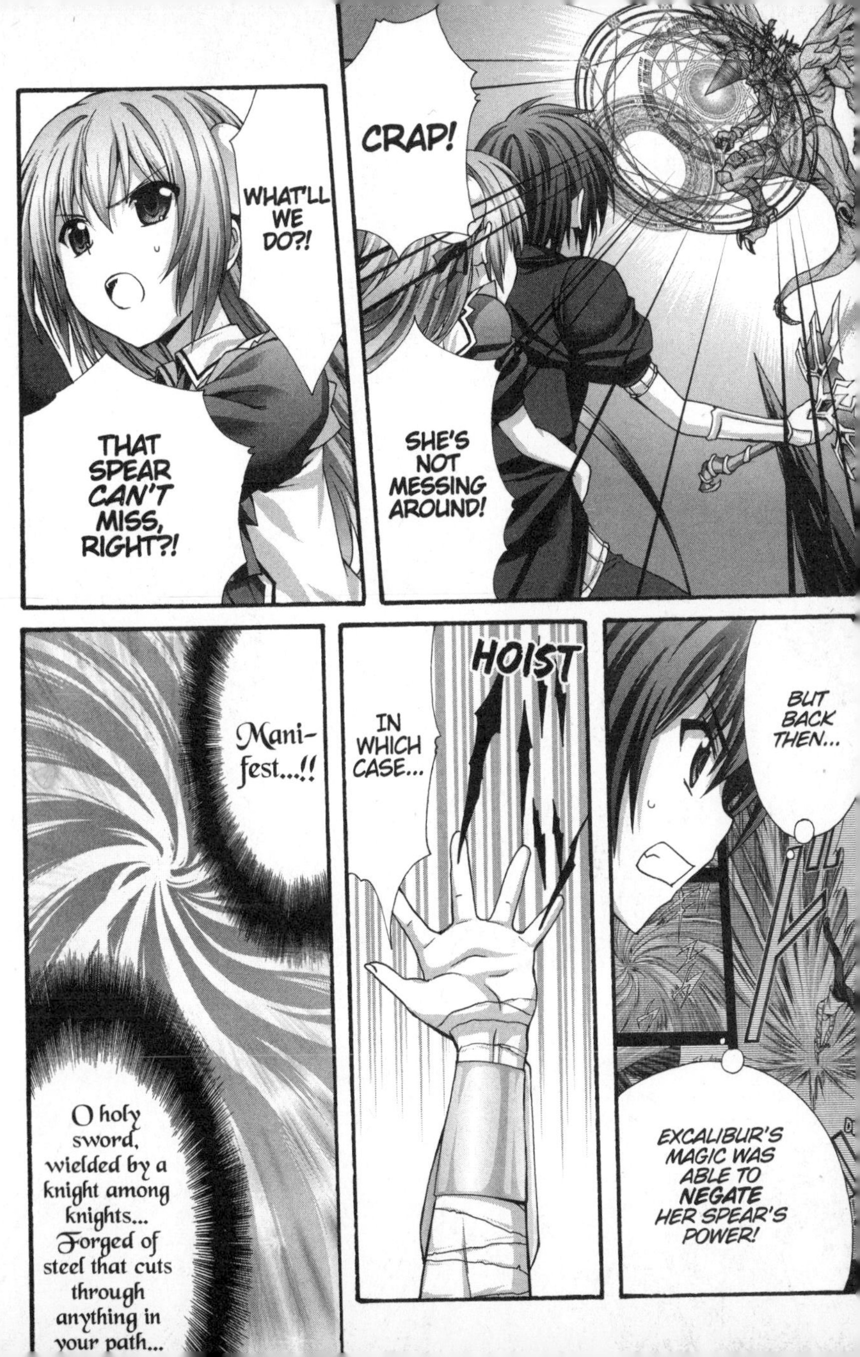
CRAP!
SHE'S NOT MESSING AROUND!
WHAT'LL WE DO?!
THAT SPEAR CAN'T MISS, RIGHT?!
BUT BACK THEN...
EXCALIBUR'S MAGIC WAS ABLE TO NEGATE HER SPEAR'S POWER!
HOIST
IN WHICH CASE...
Mani-fest...!!
O holy sword, wielded by a knight among knights... Forged of steel that cuts through anything in your path...

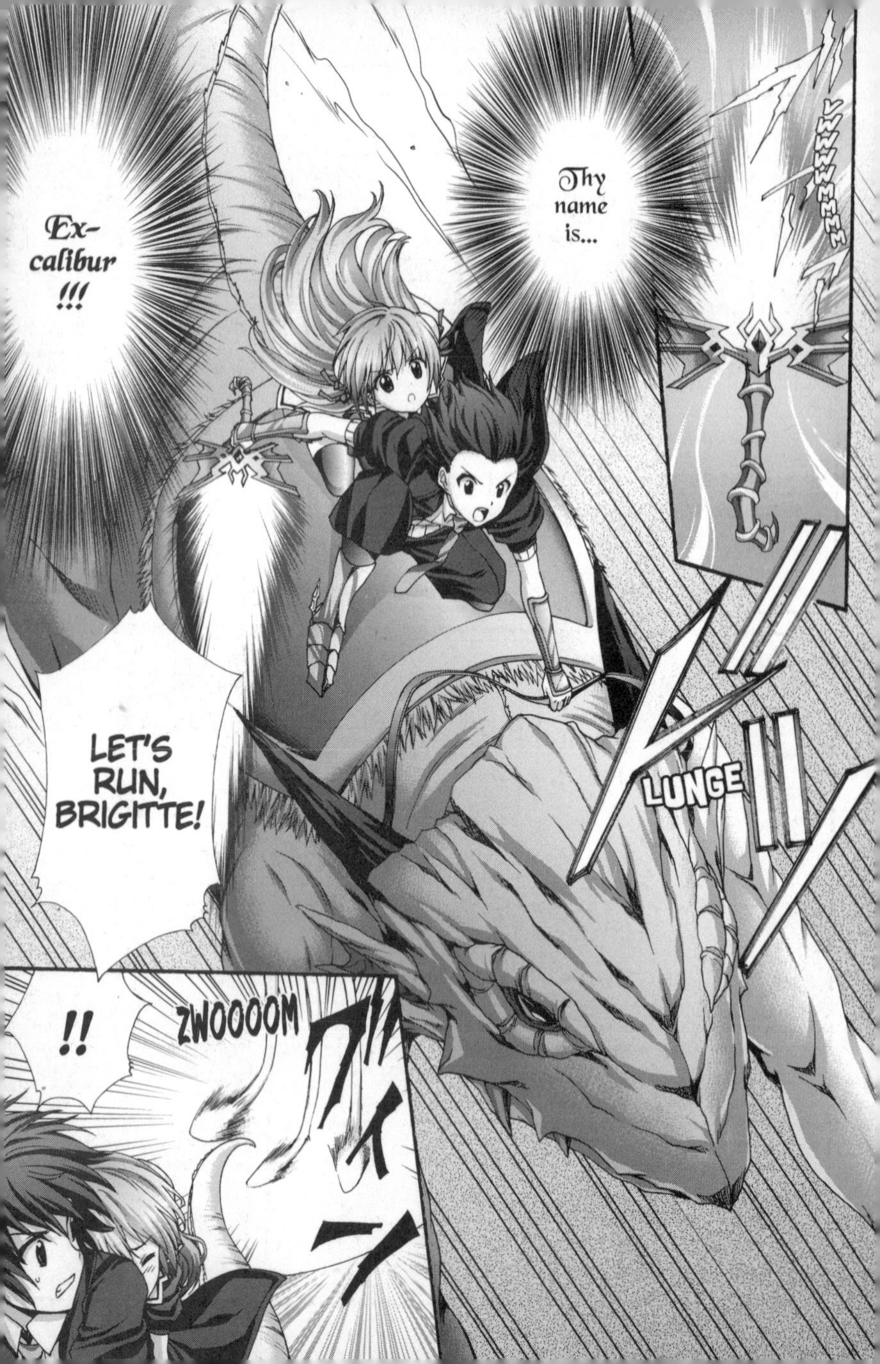
VWWWMMM
Thy name is...
Ex-calibur!!!
LUNGE
LET'S RUN, BRIGITTE!
ZWOOOOM
!!

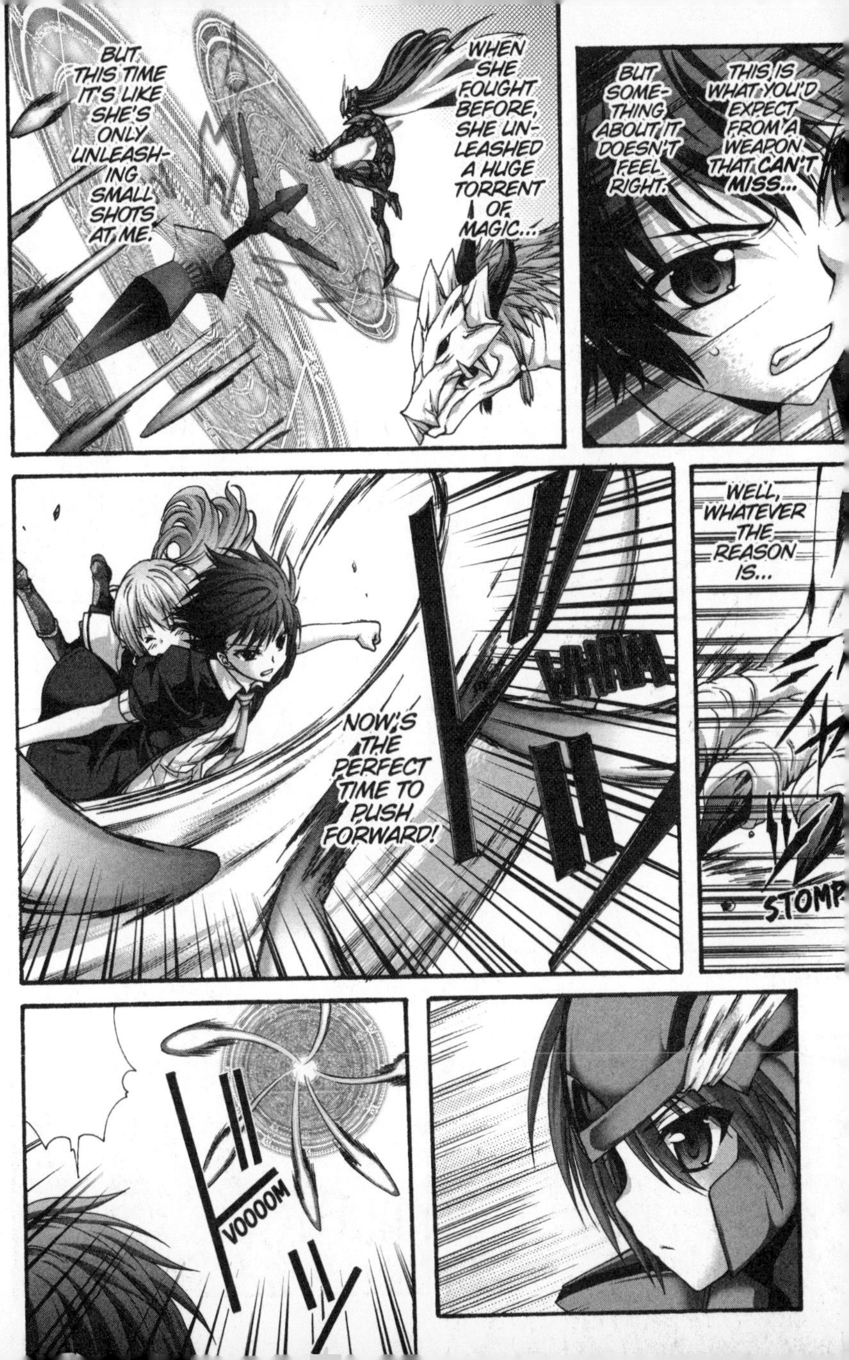
THIS IS WHAT YOU'D EXPECT FROM A WEAPON THAT CAN'T MISS...
BUT SOMETHING ABOUT IT DOESN'T FEEL RIGHT.
WHEN SHE FOUGHT BEFORE, SHE UNLEASHED A HUGE TORRENT OF MAGIC...
BUT THIS TIME IT'S LIKE SHE'S ONLY UNLEASHING SMALL SHOTS AT ME.
WELL, WHATEVER THE REASON IS...
STOMP
WHAM
NOW'S THE PERFECT TIME TO PUSH FORWARD!
VOOOOM

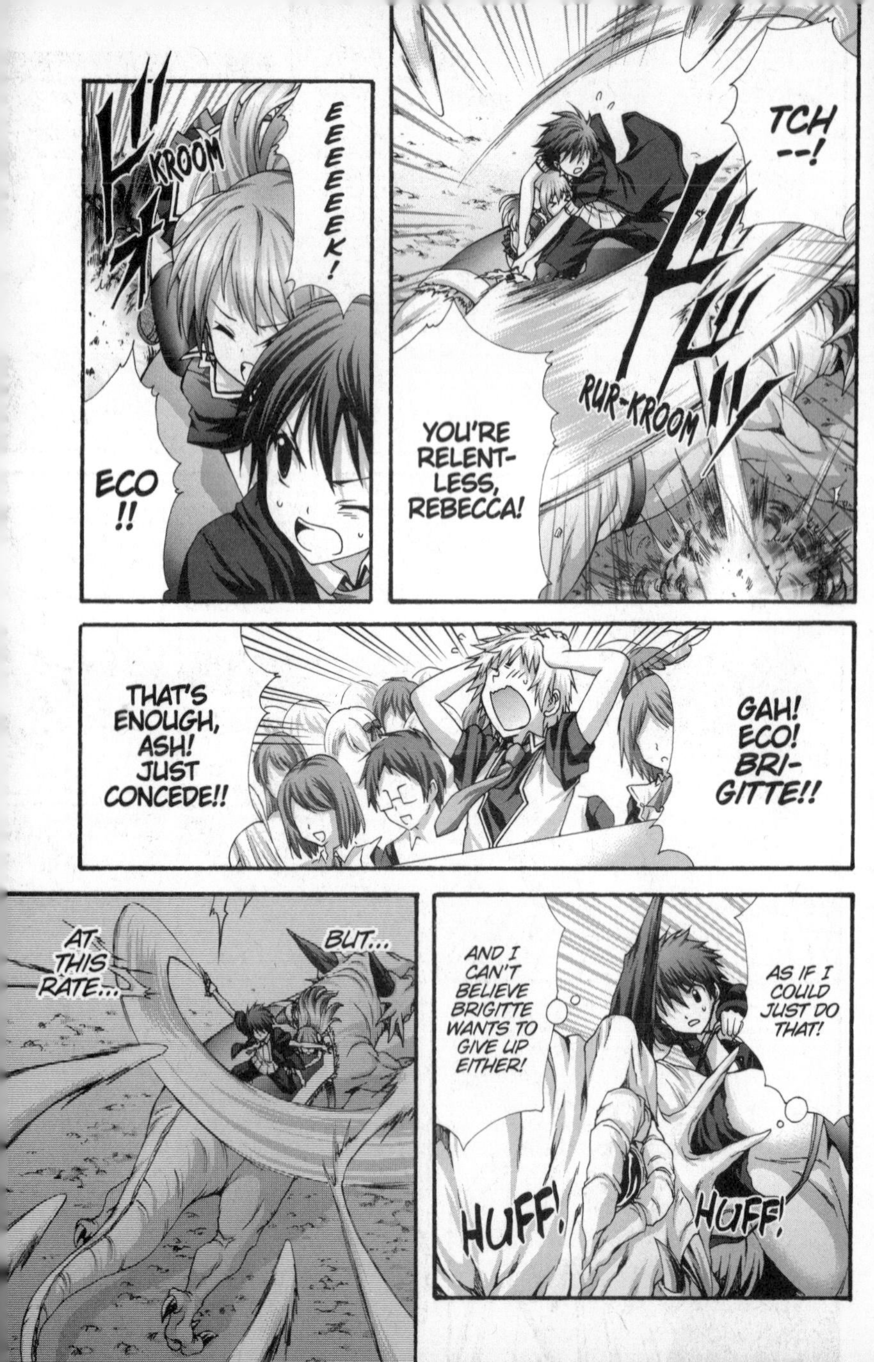
TCH--!
RUR-KROOM
YOU'RE RELENT-LESS, REBECCA!
KROOM
EEEEEEEK!
ECO!!
GAH! ECO! BRI-GITTE!!
THAT'S ENOUGH, ASH! JUST CONCEDE!!
AS IF I COULD JUST DO THAT!
AND I CAN'T BELIEVE BRIGITTE WANTS TO GIVE UP EITHER!
HUFF!
HUFF!
BUT...
AT THIS RATE...

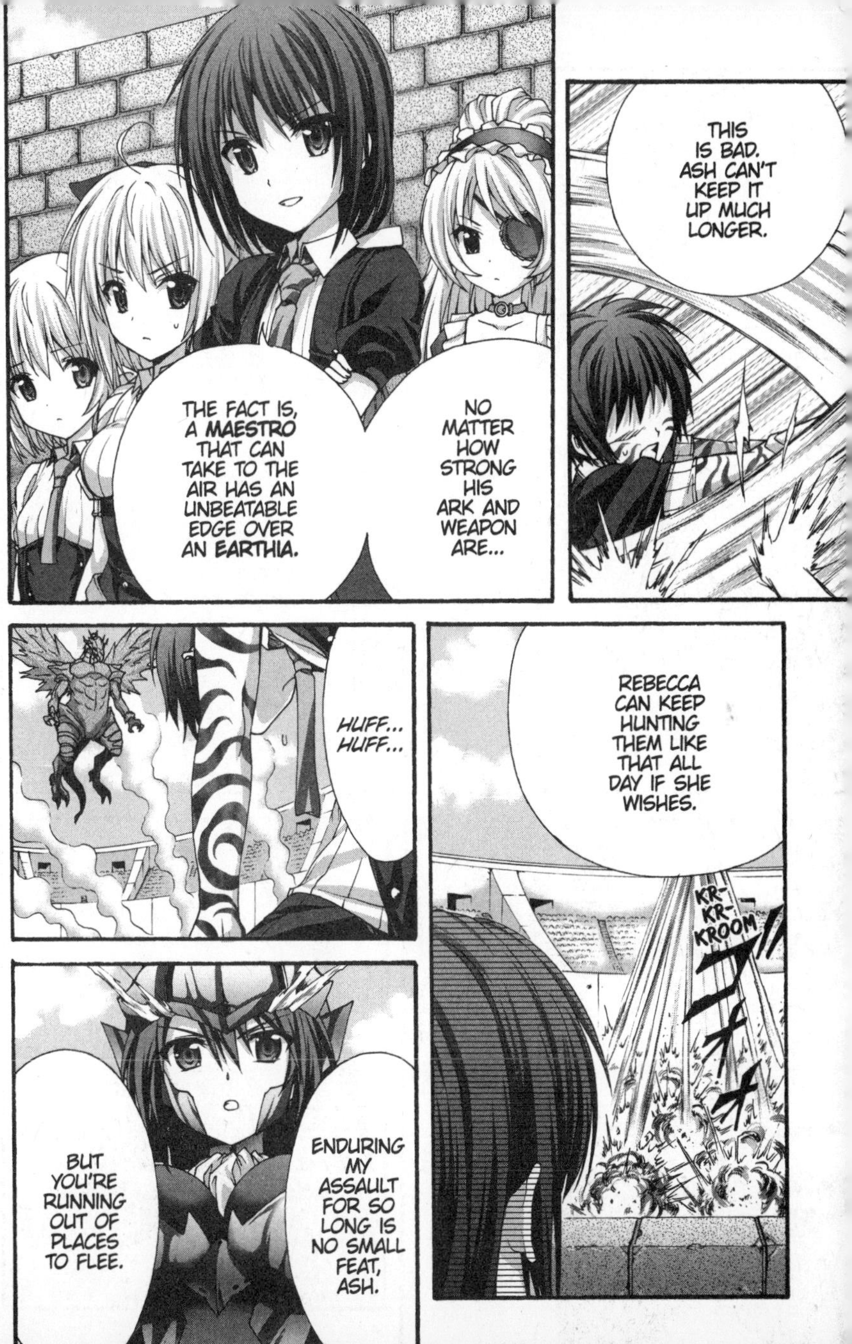
THIS IS BAD. ASH CAN'T KEEP IT UP MUCH LONGER.
NO MATTER HOW STRONG HIS ARK AND WEAPON ARE...
THE FACT IS, A **MAESTRO** THAT CAN TAKE TO THE AIR HAS AN UNBEATABLE EDGE OVER AN **EARTHIA.**
REBECCA CAN KEEP HUNTING THEM LIKE THAT ALL DAY IF SHE WISHES.
KR-KR-KROOM
HUFF... HUFF...
ENDURING MY ASSAULT FOR SO LONG IS NO SMALL FEAT, ASH.
BUT YOU'RE RUNNING OUT OF PLACES TO FLEE.

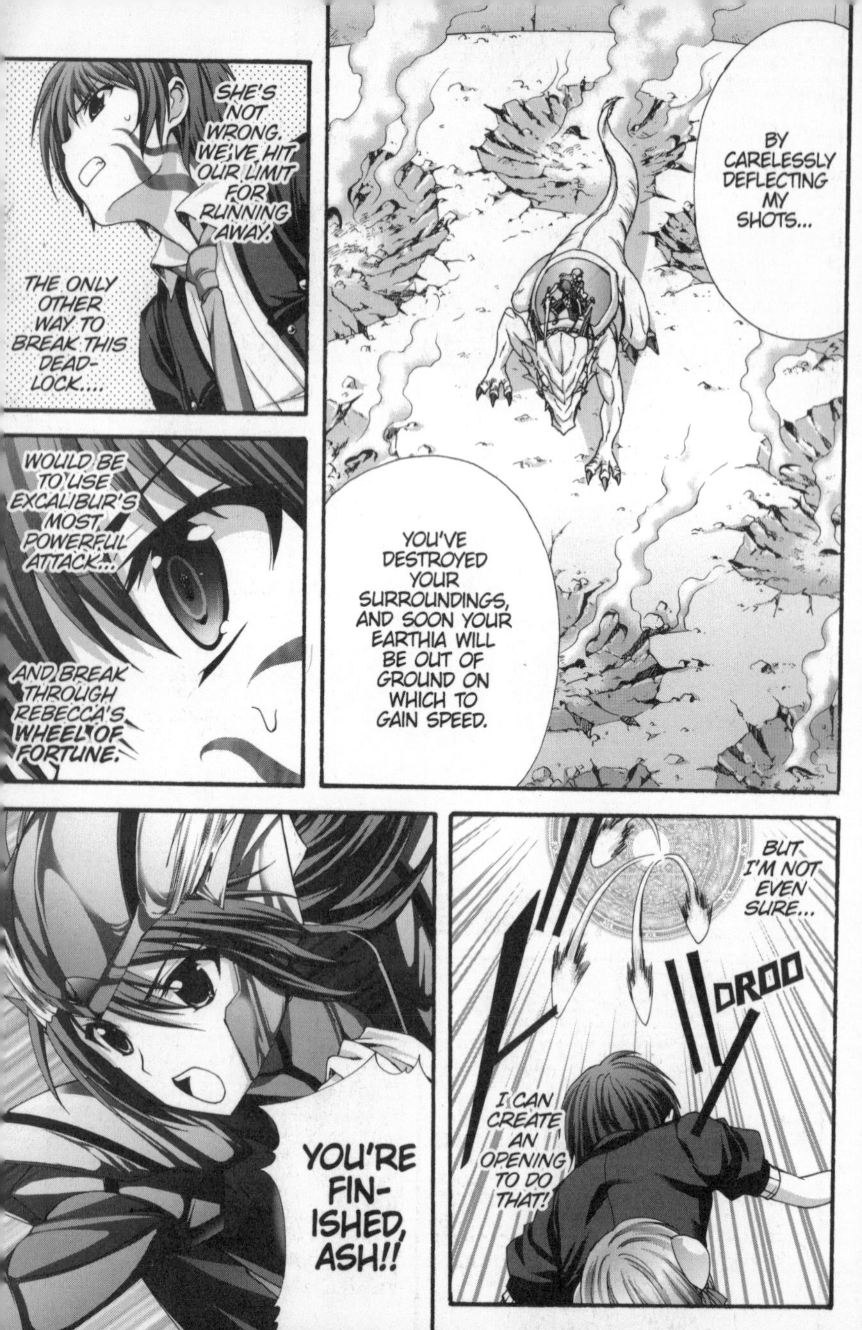
BY CARELESSLY DEFLECTING MY SHOTS...
YOU'VE DESTROYED YOUR SURROUNDINGS, AND SOON YOUR EARTHIA WILL BE OUT OF GROUND ON WHICH TO GAIN SPEED.
SHE'S NOT WRONG. WE'VE HIT OUR LIMIT FOR RUNNING AWAY.
THE ONLY OTHER WAY TO BREAK THIS DEAD-LOCK....
WOULD BE TO USE EXCALIBUR'S MOST POWERFUL ATTACK...
AND BREAK THROUGH REBECCA'S WHEEL OF FORTUNE.
BUT I'M NOT EVEN SURE...
DROO
I CAN CREATE AN OPENING TO DO THAT!
YOU'RE FIN-ISHED, ASH!!

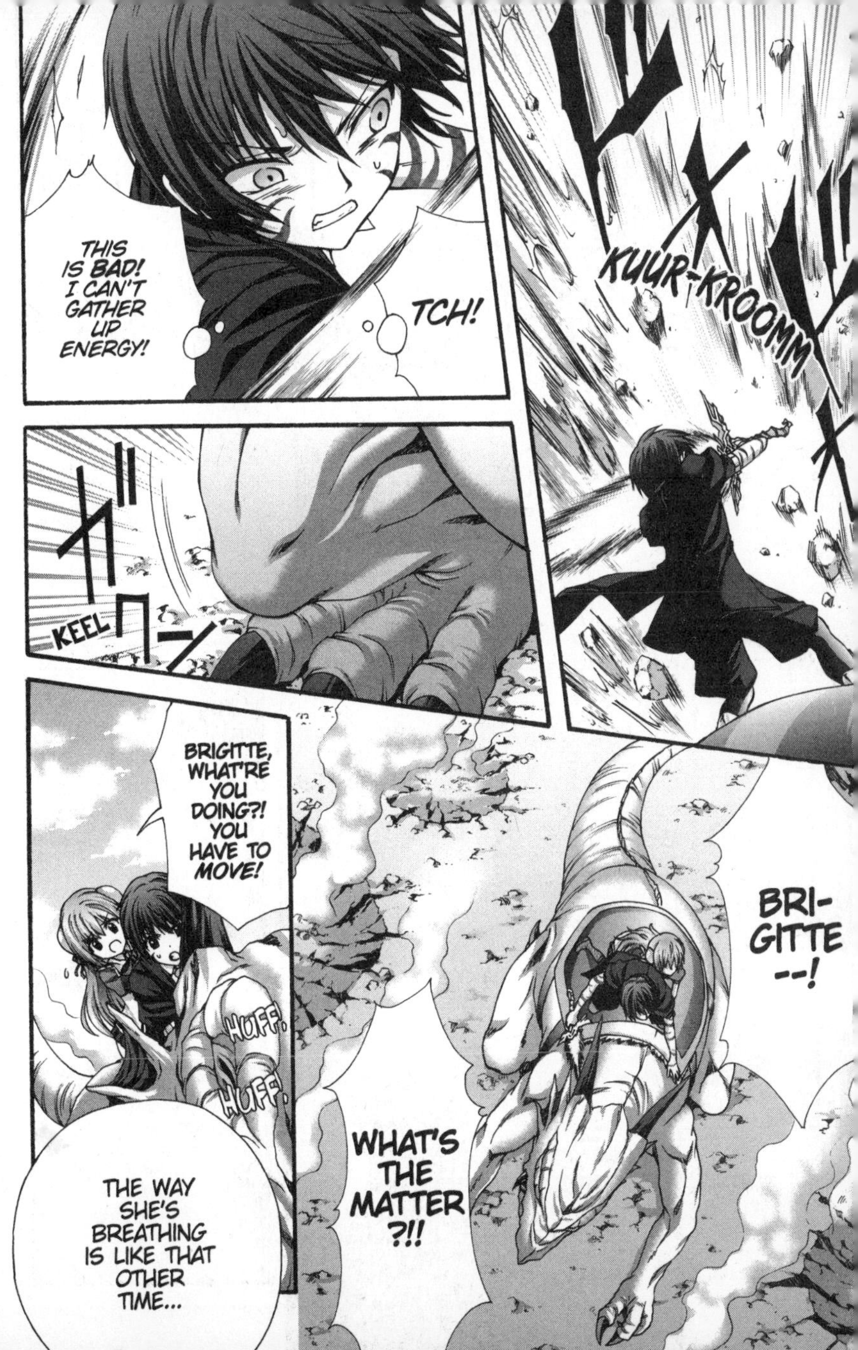
KUUR-KROOMM
TCH!
THIS IS BAD! I CAN'T GATHER UP ENERGY!
KEEL
BRI-GITTE--!
WHAT'S THE MATTER?!!
BRIGITTE, WHAT'RE YOU DOING?! YOU HAVE TO MOVE!
HUFF.
HUFF.
THE WAY SHE'S BREATHING IS LIKE THAT OTHER TIME...

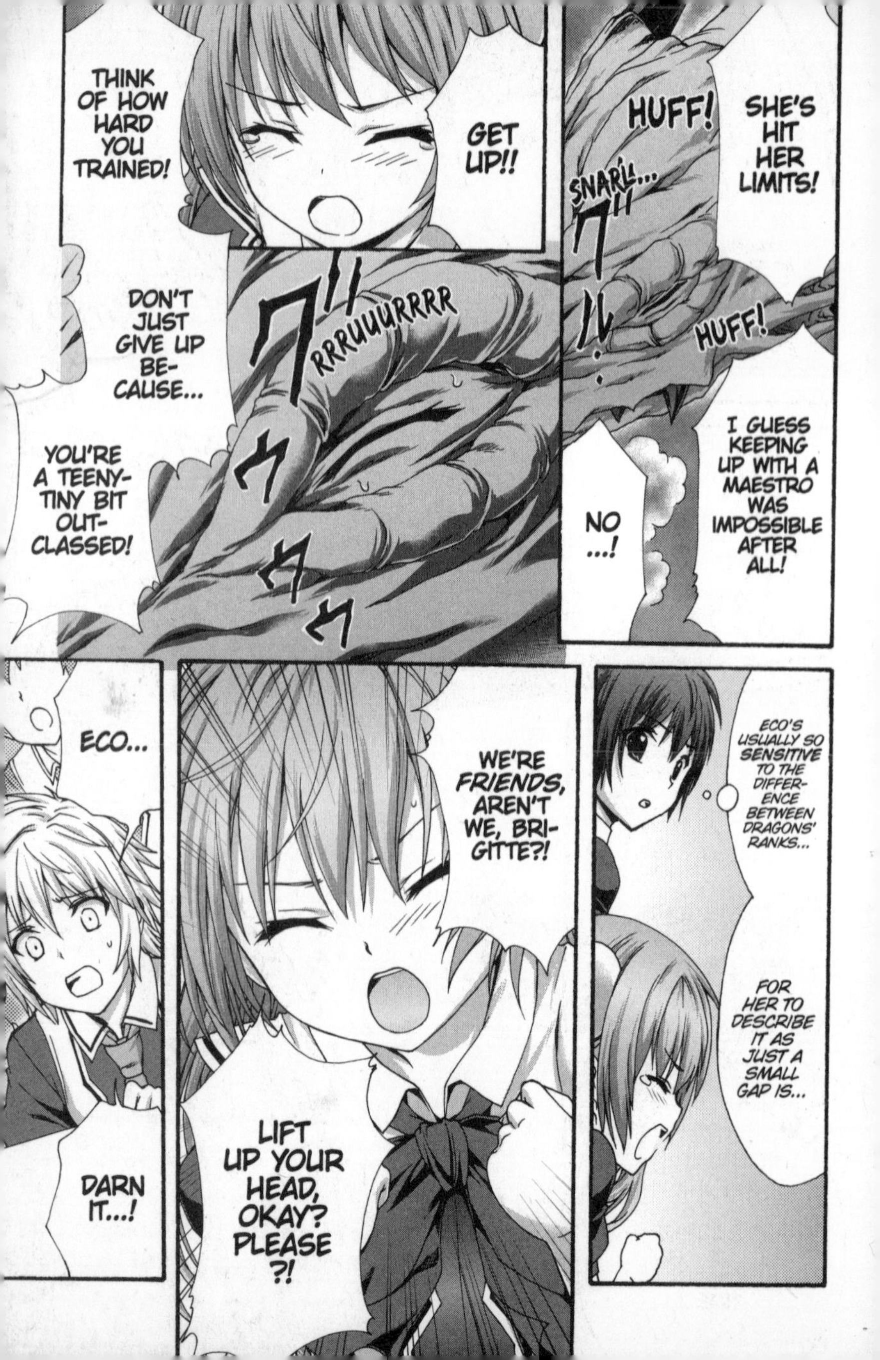

SHE'S HIT HER LIMITS!
HUFF!
SNARL...
HUFF!
I GUESS KEEPING UP WITH A MAESTRO WAS IMPOSSIBLE AFTER ALL!
NO ...!
GET UP!!
THINK OF HOW HARD YOU TRAINED!
RRRUUUURRRR
DON'T JUST GIVE UP BECAUSE...
YOU'RE A TEENY-TINY BIT OUTCLASSED!
ECO'S USUALLY SO SENSITIVE TO THE DIFFERENCE BETWEEN DRAGONS' RANKS...
FOR HER TO DESCRIBE IT AS JUST A SMALL GAP IS...
WE'RE FRIENDS, AREN'T WE, BRIGITTE?!
LIFT UP YOUR HEAD, OKAY? PLEASE ?!
ECO...
DARN IT...!

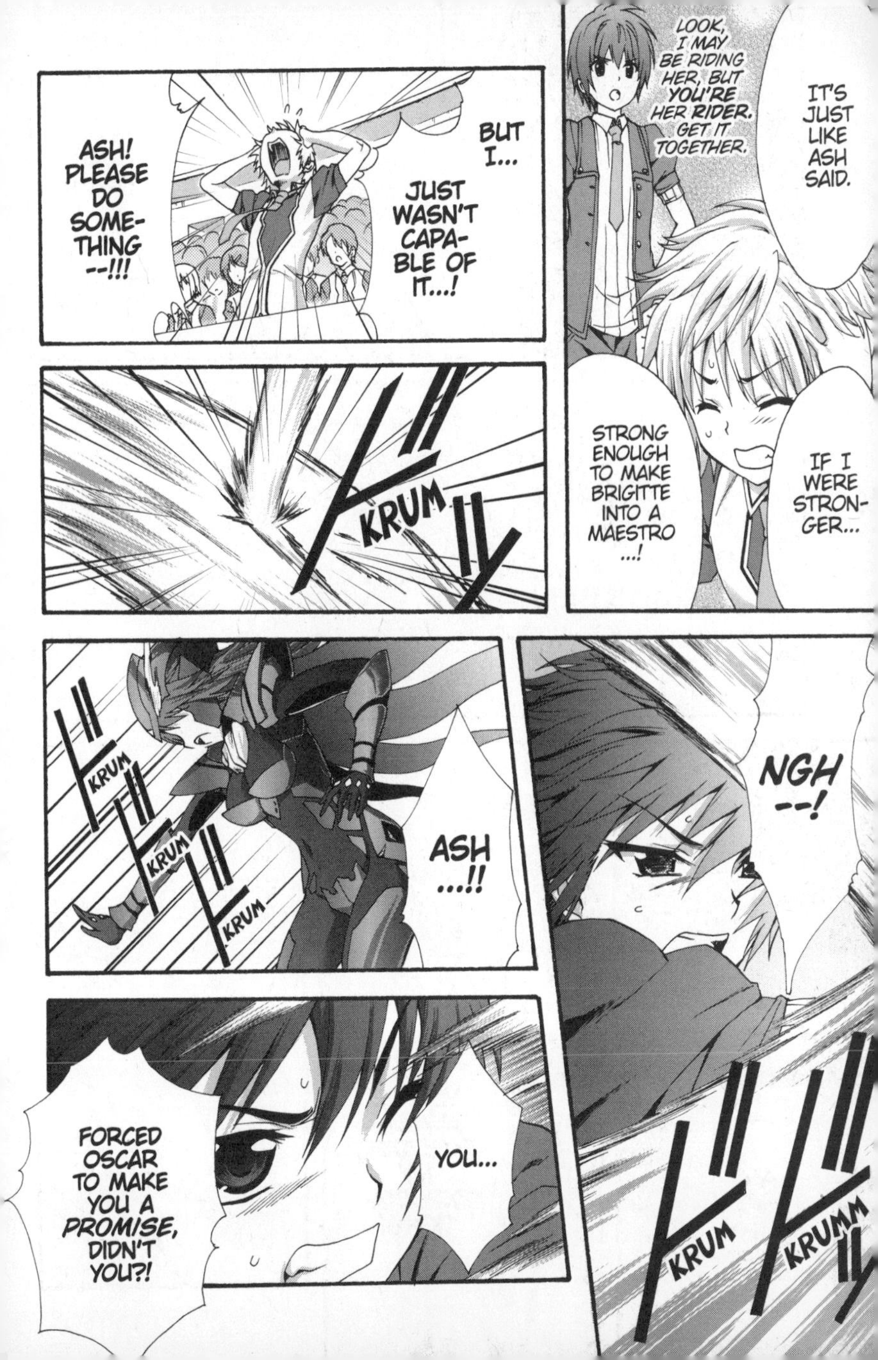
LOOK, I MAY BE RIDING HER, BUT YOU'RE HER RIDER. GET IT TOGETHER.
IT'S JUST LIKE ASH SAID.
IF I WERE STRONGER...
STRONG ENOUGH TO MAKE BRIGITTE INTO A MAESTRO ...!
BUT I...
JUST WASN'T CAPABLE OF IT...!
ASH! PLEASE DO SOME-THING --!!!
KRUM
NGH --!
KRUM
KRUMM
ASH ...!!
KRUM
KRUM
KRUM
YOU...
FORCED OSCAR TO MAKE YOU A PROMISE, DIDN'T YOU?!

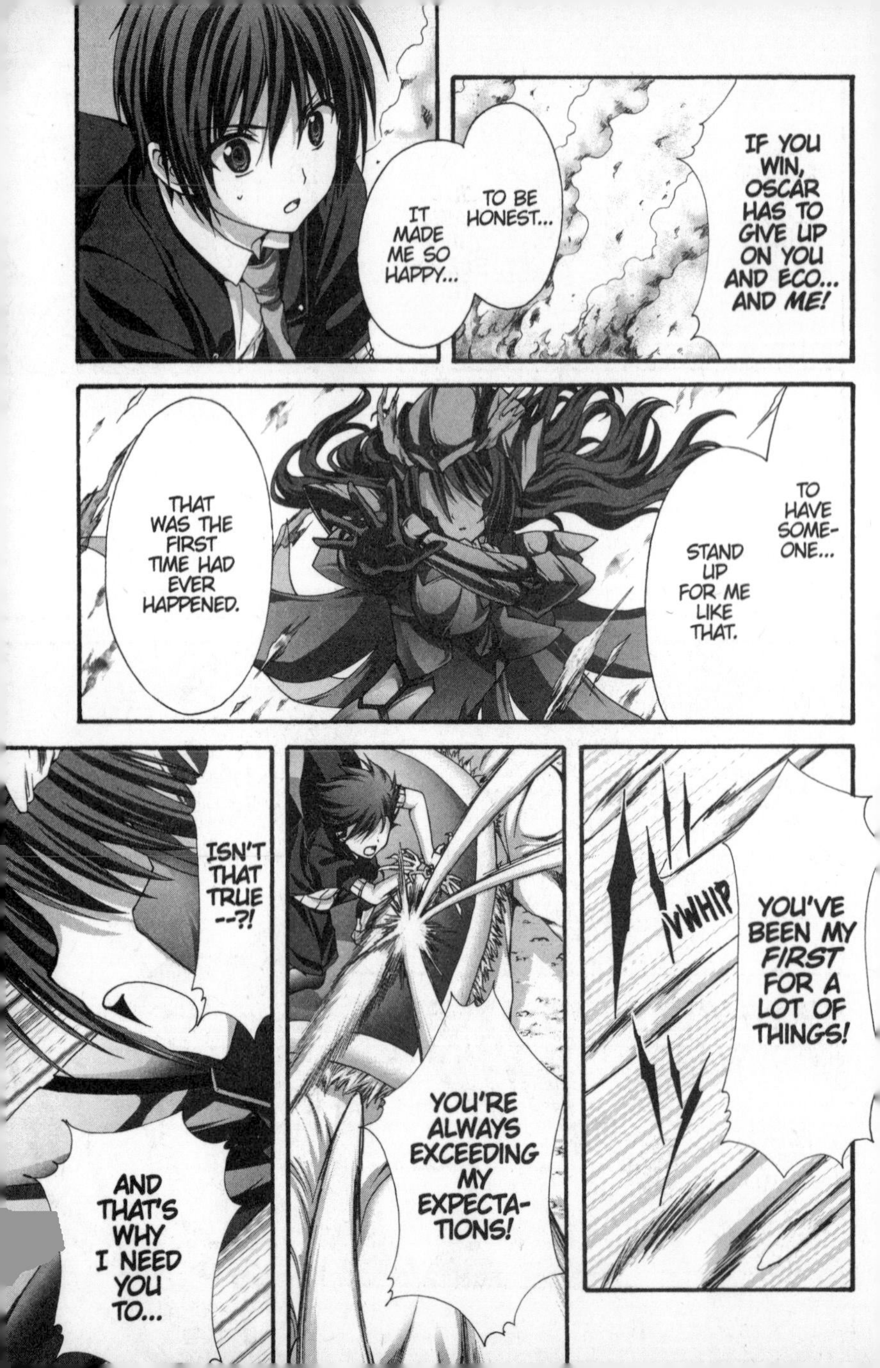
IF YOU WIN, OSCAR HAS TO GIVE UP ON YOU AND ECO... AND *ME!*
TO BE HONEST...
IT MADE ME SO HAPPY...
TO HAVE SOME-ONE...
STAND UP FOR ME LIKE THAT.
THAT WAS THE FIRST TIME HAD EVER HAPPENED.
VWHIP
YOU'VE BEEN MY *FIRST* FOR A LOT OF THINGS!
YOU'RE ALWAYS EXCEEDING MY EXPECTA-TIONS!
ISN'T THAT TRUE--?!
AND THAT'S WHY I NEED YOU TO...

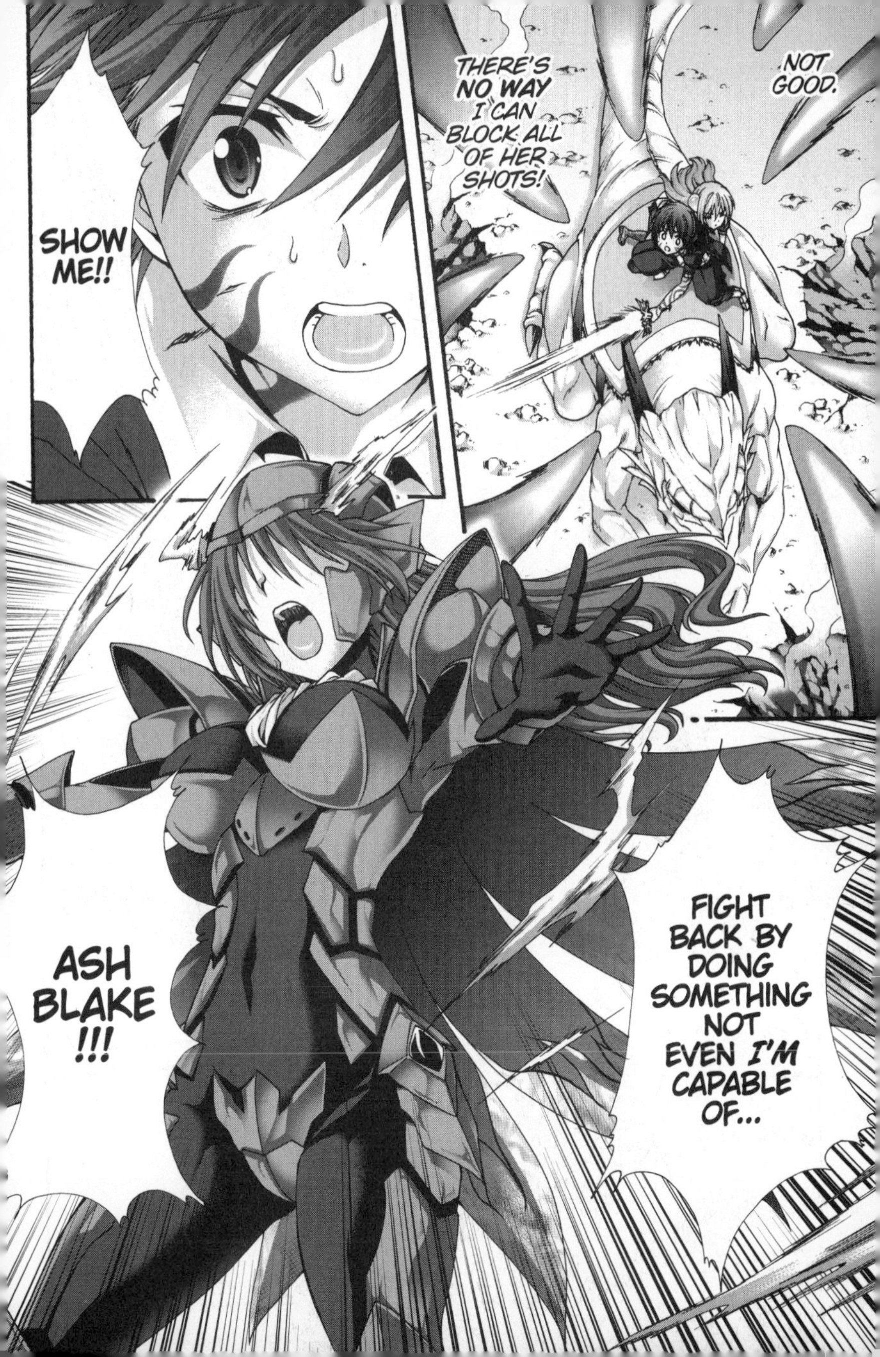
NOT GOOD.
THERE'S NO WAY I CAN BLOCK ALL OF HER SHOTS!
SHOW ME!!
FIGHT BACK BY DOING SOMETHING NOT EVEN *I'M* CAPABLE OF...
ASH BLAKE!!!

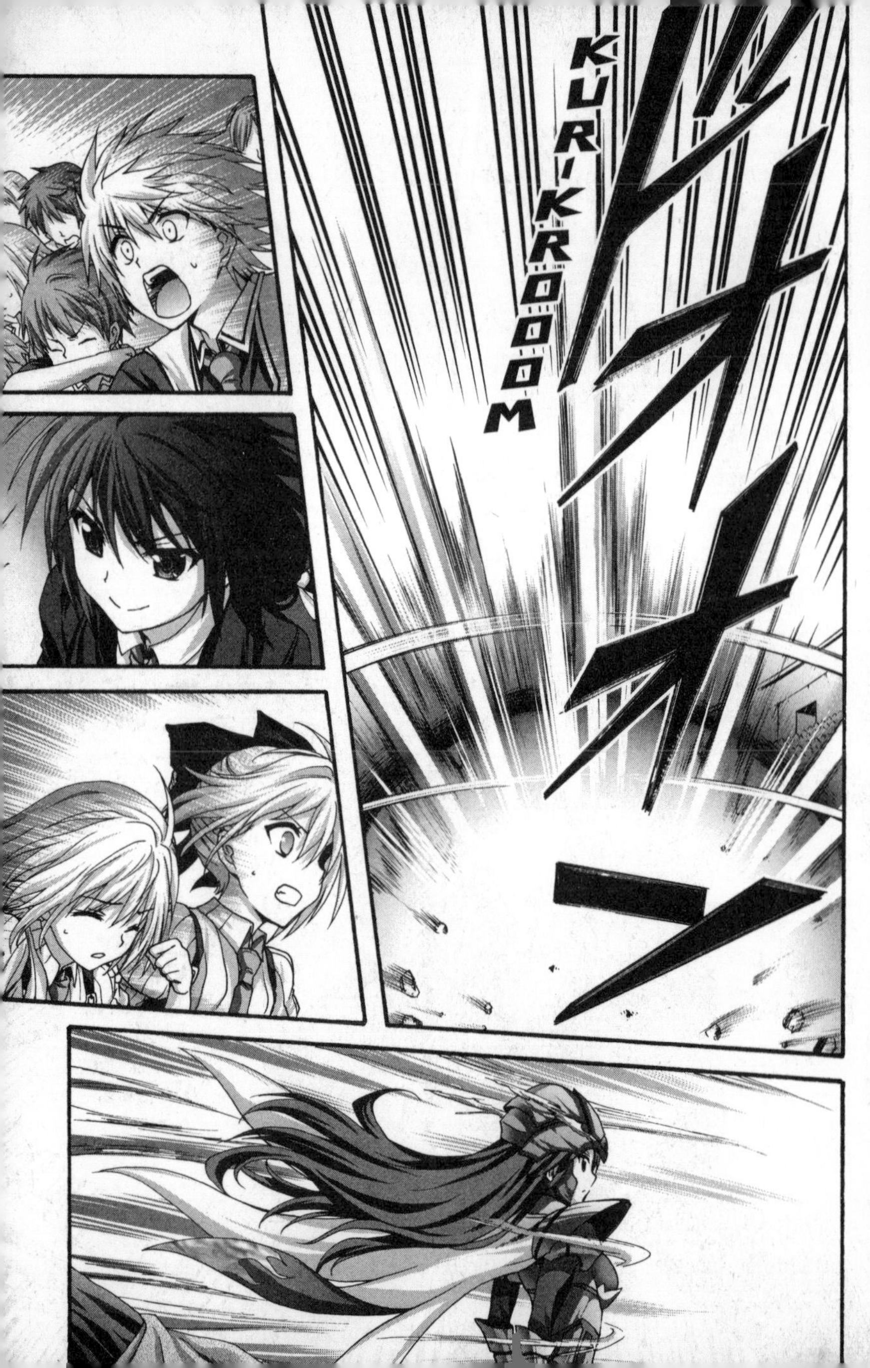
KURIKROOOOM

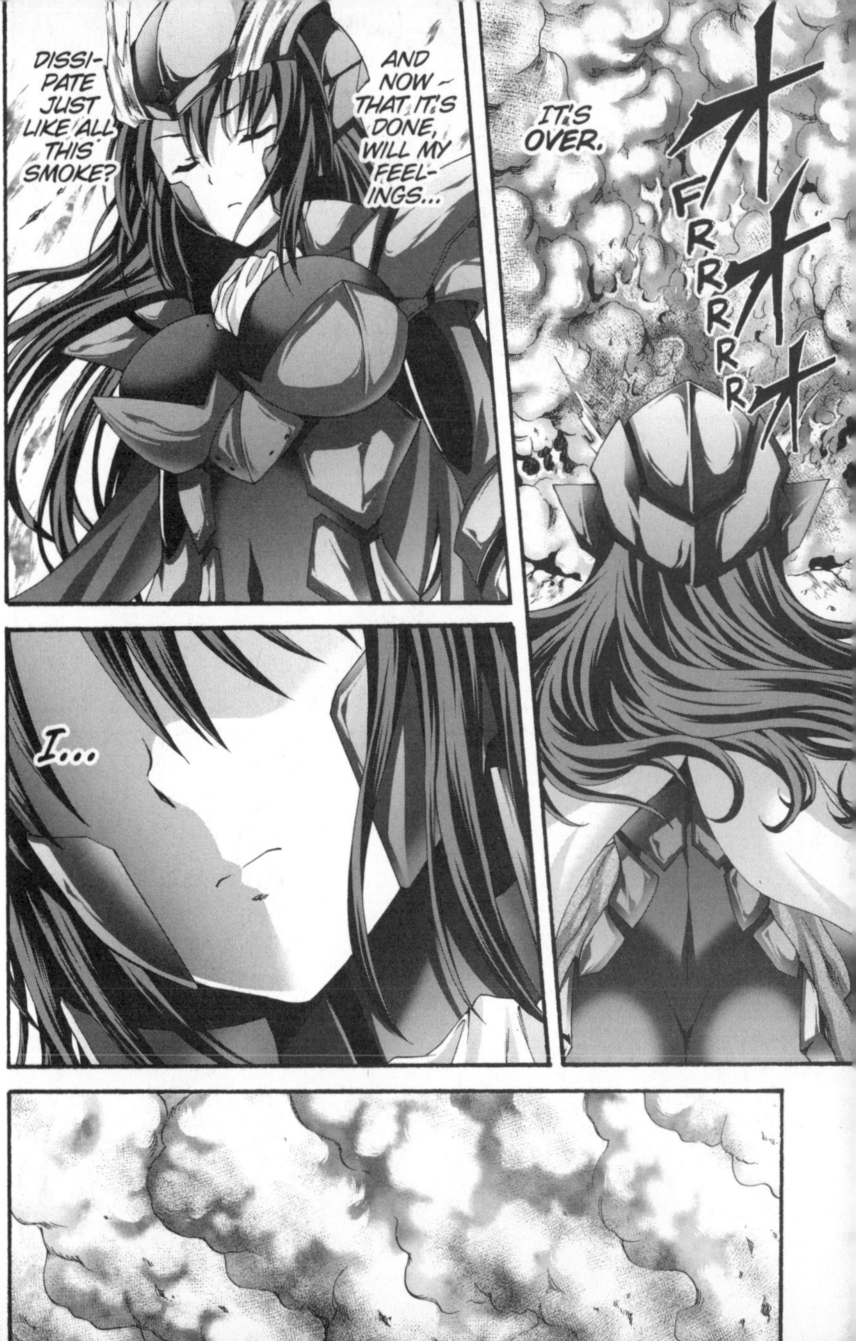
FRRRRRR
IT'S OVER.
AND NOW THAT IT'S DONE, WILL MY FEELINGS...
DISSIPATE JUST LIKE ALL THIS SMOKE?
I...

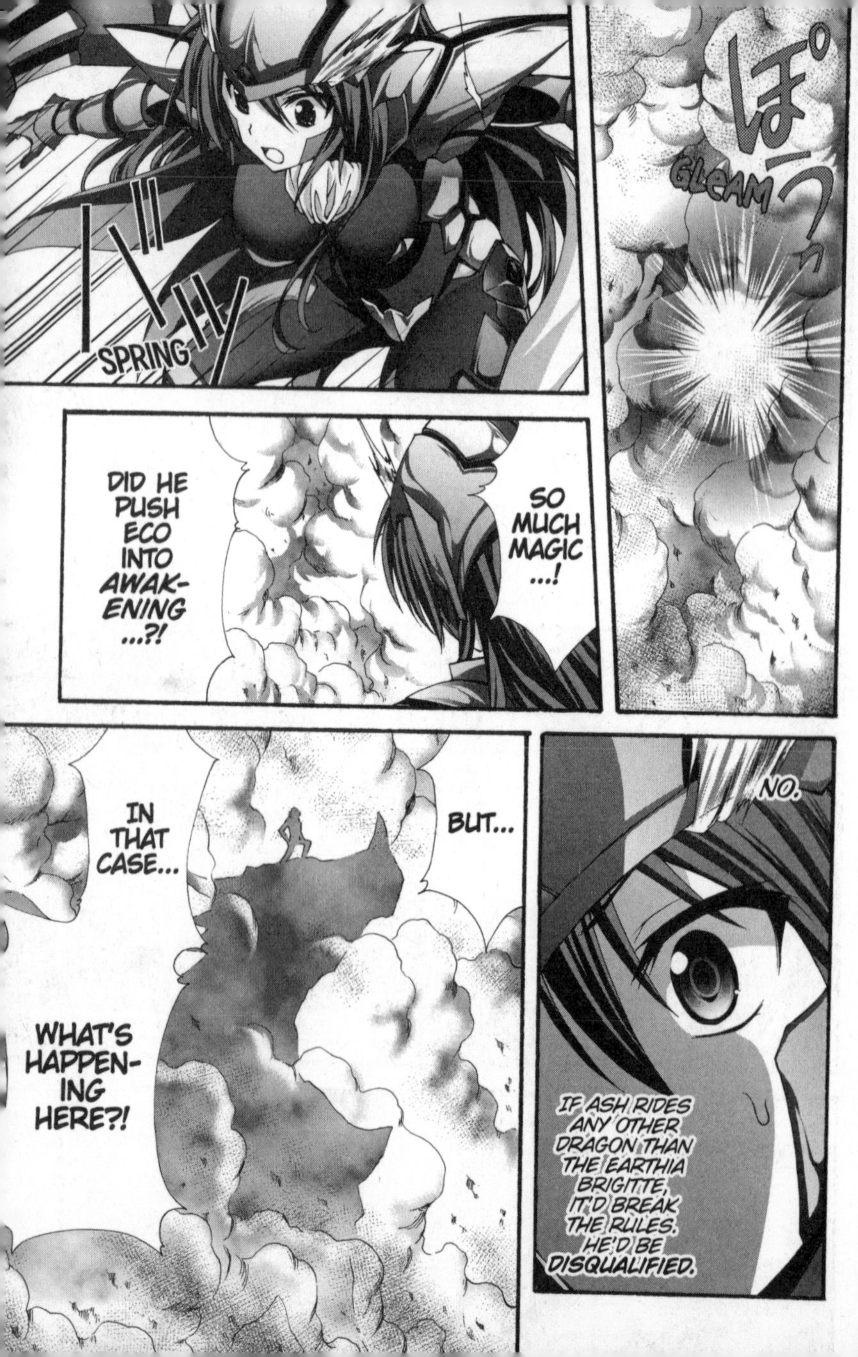
ぽっ
GLEAM
SPRING
SO MUCH MAGIC...!
DID HE PUSH ECO INTO AWAKENING...?!
NO.
IF ASH RIDES ANY OTHER DRAGON THAN THE EARTHIA BRIGITTE, IT'D BREAK THE RULES. HE'D BE DISQUALIFIED.
BUT...
IN THAT CASE...
WHAT'S HAPPENING HERE?!

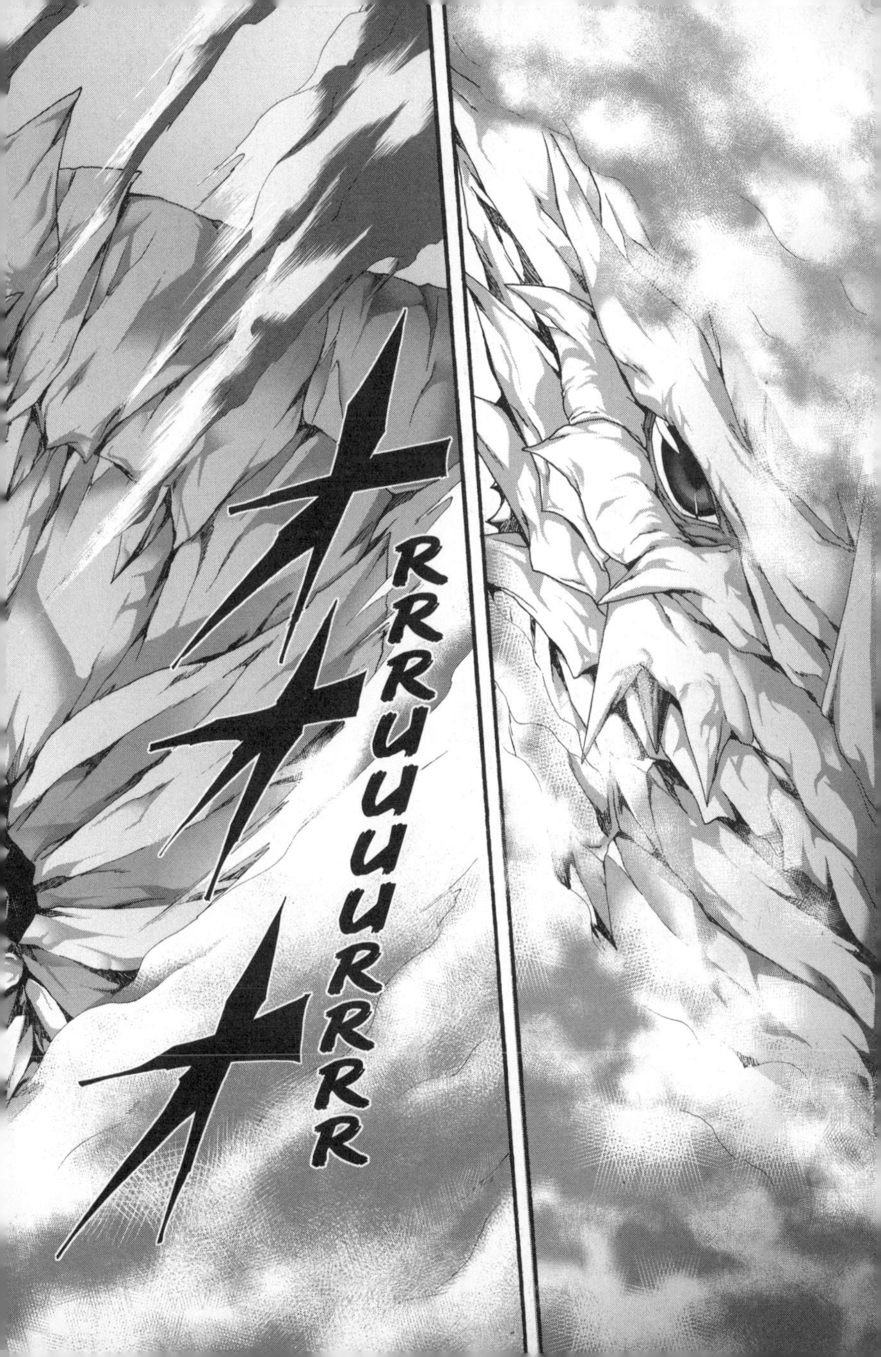
RRRUUURRRR

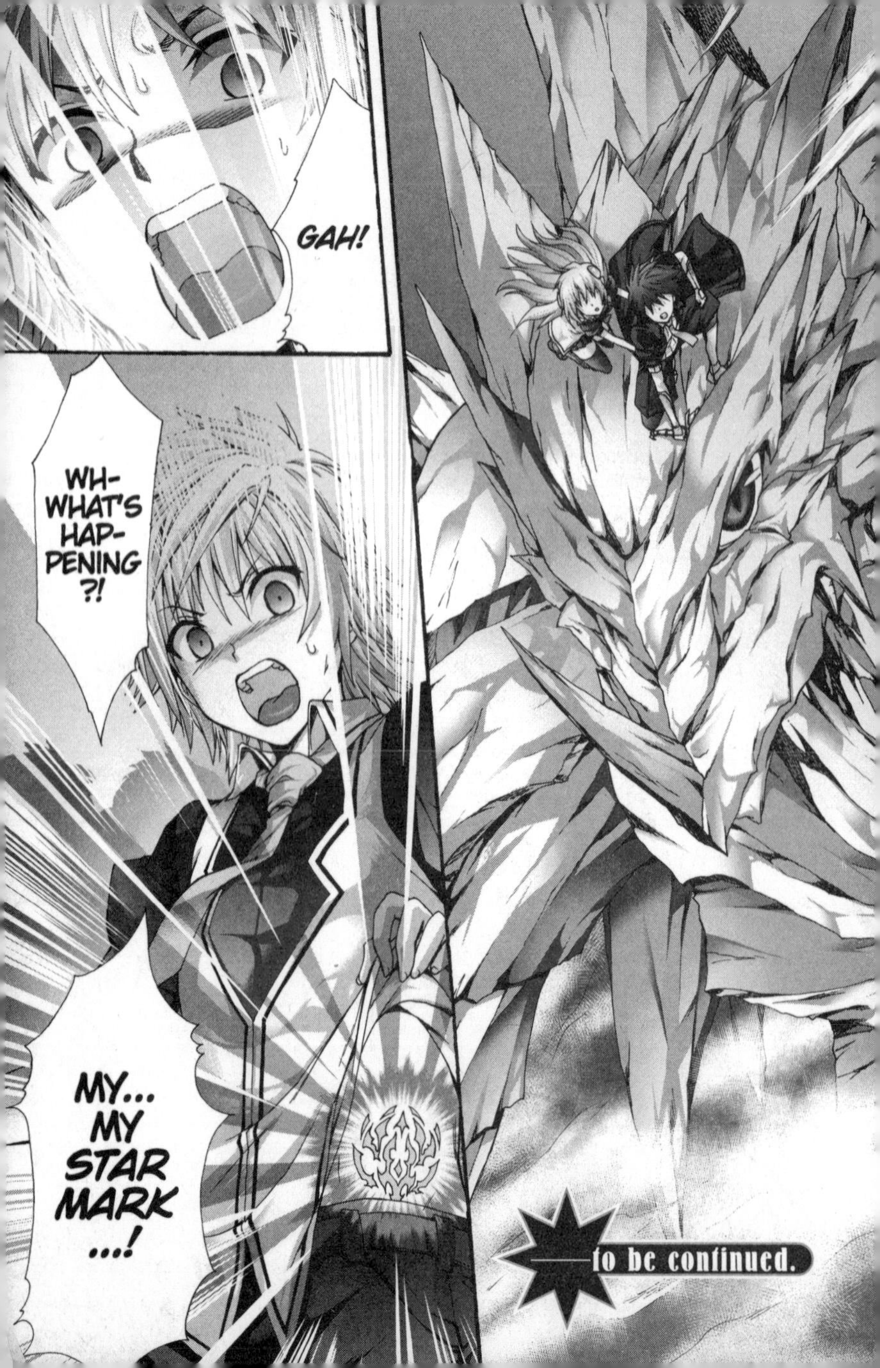
GAH!
WH-WHAT'S HAP-PENING?!
MY... MY STAR MARK...!
to be continued.

AFTERWORD

It's me, RAN.

Thanks so much to everyone who's picked up the manga version of Dragonar Academy!

We're now in the second part of the "Oscar Arc," so we're learning about her ambitions and about how Chevron works.

And now Ash is getting closer to Rebecca... and fighting her?!

We'll see what happens in the next volume! I hope you'll join me again then!

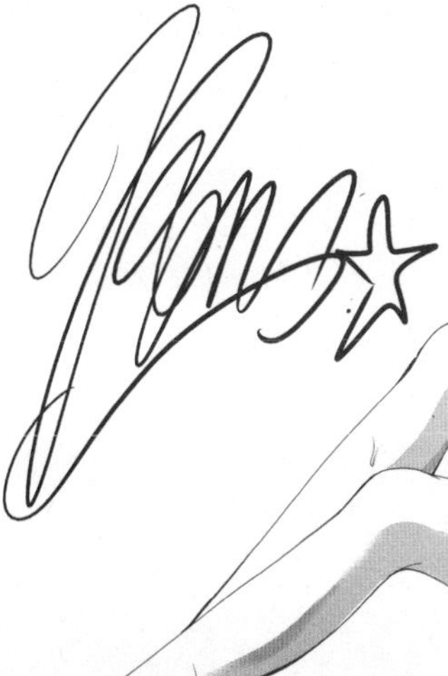

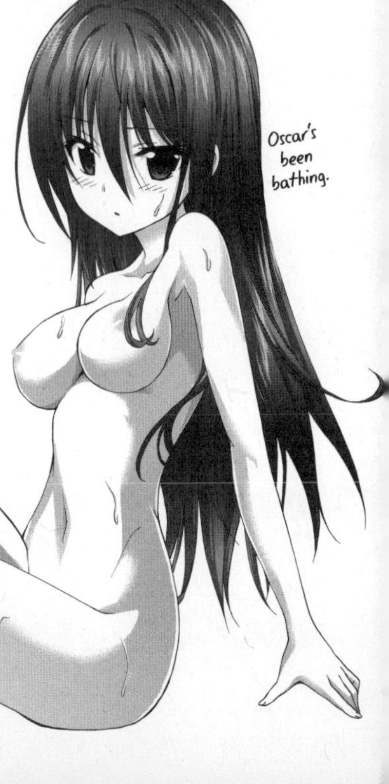
Oscar's
been
bathing.